ALSO BY EILEEN McNAMARA

The Parting Glass:
A Toast to the Traditional Pubs of Ireland (with Eric Roth)

Breakdown:
Sex, Suicide, and the Harvard Psychiatrist

EUNICE

THE KENNEDY WHO CHANGED THE WORLD

EILEEN McNAMARA

Simon & Schuster

New York   London   Toronto   Sydney   New Delhi

Simon & Schuster
1230 Avenue of the Americas
New York, NY 10020

First Simon & Schuster hardcover edition April 2018

SIMON & SCHUSTER and colophon are registered trademarks of Simon & Schuster, Inc.

For information about special discounts for bulk purchases, please contact Simon & Schuster Special Sales at 1-866-506-1949 or business@simonandschuster.com.

The Simon & Schuster Speakers Bureau can bring authors to your live event. For more information or to book an event, contact the Simon & Schuster Speakers Bureau at 1-866-248-3049 or visit our website at www.simonspeakers.com.

Interior design by Lewelin Polanco

Manufactured in the United States of America

1 3 5 7 9 10 8 6 4 2

Library of Congress Cataloging-in-Publication Data is available.

ISBN 978-1-4516-4226-1
ISBN 978-1-4516-4227-8 (ebook)

Insert 1: Photo, the Kennedy Family Collection: 1; Photo, circa August 1925, the Kennedy Family Collection: 2; Photo, circa 1931, the Kennedy Family Collection: 3; Photo, circa August 1933, the John F. Kennedy Presidential Library and Museum: 4; Photo, circa 1934, the Kennedy Family Collection: 5; Photo by the New York Times Co./Getty Images: 6; Photo by Bettmann Archive/Getty Images: 7; Photo by Hans Knopf/Pix Inc./The LIFE Picture Collection/Getty Images: 8; Photo, January 7, 1971, by Morgan Collection/Getty Images: 9; Photo by Fred Morgan/NY Daily News/Getty Images: 10; Photo by Hy Peskin/Getty Images: 11; AP Photo/Byron Rollins: 12; Photo by Lee Lockwood/The LIFE Images Collection/Getty Images: 13; Photo by Vic Casamento/The Washington Post/Getty Images: 14; Photo by Henry Clarke/Condé Nast/Getty Images: 15, 16; Photo courtesy of Anthony Shriver: 17; Photo by Lawrence Levin, courtesy of Special Olympics: 18; Photo by Stephan Savoia/AP Photo: 19, 20; Insert 2: AP Photo: 1, 13; Photo, John F. Kennedy Presidential Library and Museum: 3, 4, 5, 7; Photo by Rowland Scherman: 6; Photo by Bettman/Getty Images: 8; Photo by Anthony Camerano/AP Photo: 9; Photo by Charles Harrity/AP Photo: 10; Photo by Liaison/Hutton Archive/Getty Images: 11; Photo by Ed Kolenovsky/AP Photo: 12; Photo by Rich Pilling/Diamond Images/AP Photo: 14; Photo by Ron Galella/Getty Images: 15; Photo by John Dominis/The LIFE Images Collection/Getty Images: 16; Photo, courtesy of Special Olympics17, 19, 20; Photo by Ron Edmonds/AP Photo: 18

For Tim May and every unsung caregiver
who does the work that makes the difference

Don't call me a saint. I don't want to be dismissed so easily.

—DOROTHY DAY

CONTENTS

IN HER OWN RIGHT

AUTHOR'S NOTE

The language used to describe people with intellectual and developmental disabilities has changed over time. The use of the terms "mentally retarded" and "mental retardation" in the text reflects common usage in medicine and politics during the historical period described.

KENNEDY FAMILY TREE

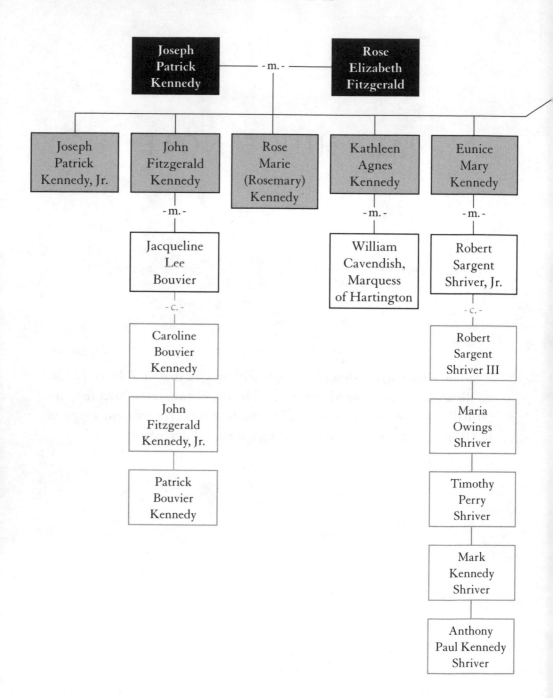

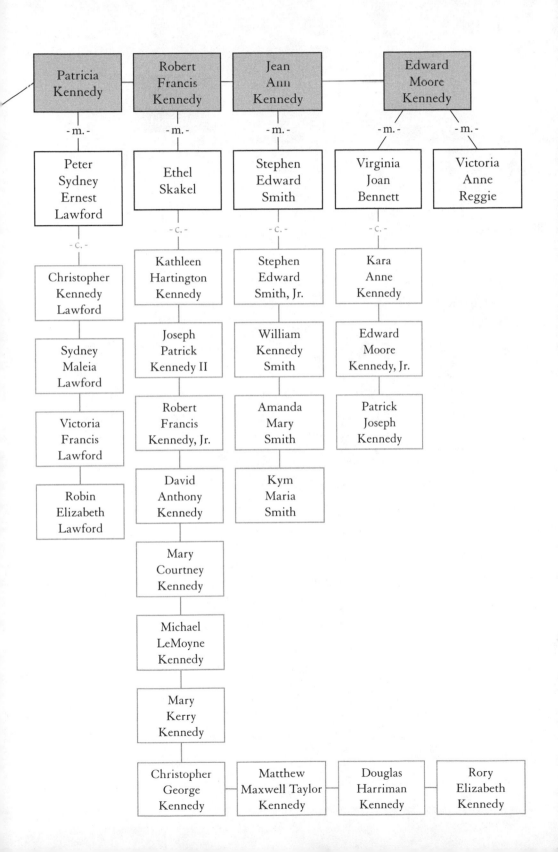

INTRODUCTION

[Y]ou are advising everyone else in that house on their careers, so why not me?

—EUNICE KENNEDY TO JOSEPH P. KENNEDY,
UNDATED LETTER

A correction in the *New York Times* on August 28, 2009, noted a number of errors in a photo caption that had accompanied the obituary of US Senator Edward M. Kennedy of Massachusetts the day before.

The caption, the nation's newspaper of record acknowledged, "misidentified two of his sisters and omitted a third in some editions. In some editions, Eunice's name was omitted, and in some editions, Rosemary and Kathleen were reversed."

Invisible or interchangeable. That was the lot of the daughters of Joseph P. and Rose Fitzgerald Kennedy, relegated to the role of decorative accessories to the outsized ambitions, first of their father and then their brothers. Charming London society when Joe was US ambassador to the Court of Saint James's in the late 1930s. Hosting ladies' teas during Jack's first congressional race a decade later. Accompanying one of their brothers during the continual campaign that defined the Kennedys' lives for more than a half century. From Jack's ascendancy as the first Catholic president, through Bobby's ill-fated run for the White House, to Ted's long career in the Senate, Eunice, Pat, and Jean—the three Kennedy sisters not lost young to tragedy—were a silent backdrop to the nation's storied political dynasty.

In the case of Eunice, that image was wildly out of focus. There was nothing silent or ornamental about the fifth of Joe and Rose Kennedy's nine children. Even as she hatched the idea for those tea parties, Eunice chafed at such a circumscribed role in what was fast becoming the family business. "Dear Daddy, I know you are very busy," she wrote to her father at Hyannis Port, probably in the late fifties. "I also know you are advising everyone else in that house on their careers, so why not me?"

The answer was simple: as much as Joe Kennedy loved all of his children, his sons, not his daughters, were his priority. Born in 1921, only a year after women in the United States secured the right to vote, Eunice came of age a generation before the second wave of feminism expanded expectations and professional opportunities for women. In many ways, her struggle to be seen—on the public stage and in her own family—mirrors the experience of so many ambitious women in mid-twentieth-century America who had to maneuver around the rigid gender roles that defined the era.

But nowhere were those roles more deeply ingrained than in the household of Joseph P. Kennedy. Bobby Kennedy surely was not thinking of his sisters when he wrote in praise of his father: "In how many families have the young been stultified? Again and again, young men with ability and talent have been kept from taking their places in the affairs of business or on the national stage because an older figure refused to make room and insisted on the glory and attention until the very end." When Joe Kennedy died in 1969, the subheadline above his obituary in the New York *Daily News* reflected the societal value accorded his five surviving children: "He Left One Son," it read.

Eunice accepted that hierarchy at an early age. "I am sure it's normal for girls to look up to their older brothers with some admiration and sense of dazzlement, but in our case it was fairly extreme," she said. "To us, they were marvelous creatures, practically godlike, and we yearned to please them and be acceptable."

Until the end of her life, Eunice would give fulsome credit to her brothers in the White House, the US Justice Department, and the US Senate for initiatives that had been her ideas. She would cede the spotlight to the boys, but she would use her wits, her famous name, her father's fortune, and her brothers' influence to make her own mark. In the process, she would advance one of the great civil rights movements, on behalf of millions of people across the world with intellectual disabilities. When she died, two weeks before her more celebrated kid brother, Ted, it was Eunice who left behind the Kennedy family's most profound and lasting legacy.

Her vision elevated a Chicago parks program into Special Olympics, which, on its fiftieth anniversary, served more than 4.9 million athletes in 172 countries with more than 1 million coaches and volunteers. Her fervor transformed her family's unfocused charitable foundation into an engine for scientific research at universities from Stanford, to Wisconsin, to Johns Hopkins. Her prescience led to the creation of a federal research institute devoted to maternal and child health. Her determination to empty Dickensian institutions for the mentally retarded sparked an unprecedented national commitment to community-based group homes, educational inclusion, and job training that changed the lives of millions who had been warehoused and forgotten.

Fueled by a religious conviction that every life, no matter how compromised, has value, she left her fingerprints on everything from the Mental Retardation Facilities and Community Mental Health Centers Construction Act of 1963; to the 1976 Hyde Amendment, restricting the use of federal funds for abortion; to the 1990 Americans with Disabilities Act, barring discrimination against the disabled in every area of public life.

And yet for all of her influence and impact, Eunice Kennedy Shriver lives in public perception at the fringe of her brothers' life stories rather than at the center of her own. Of the hundreds of books written about the Kennedys, none has focused on the member of the clan who made its most enduring mark.

This biography is an attempt to correct that record.

———————

I did not know Mrs. Shriver in life, although it was impossible as a reporter at the *Boston Globe* for almost thirty years not to have covered her and members of her family. As a congressional correspondent during the Reagan administration, I got to know her brother Ted, who represented Massachusetts in the Senate for forty-seven years, and from him I first heard the word most often used to describe his sister: *formidable*. The adjective echoed again and again in interviews with family and friends, with senators and congressmen, with the assistants she fired with numbing regularity and the professional staff she drove no harder than she drove herself—even with the five Shriver children, who carry on her work.

Today her name is synonymous with Special Olympics, but Eunice Kennedy Shriver's career in public service began decades before she opened the first games on a sunny July Saturday at Chicago's Soldier Field in 1968. She worked at the US State Department two years before Jack arrived on Capitol Hill in 1947. She administered a task force at the US Department of Justice on juvenile delinquency fourteen years before she talked Bobby into tackling that issue as attorney general in 1961. She denounced the long prison terms meted out to the nonviolent offenders she counseled at Alderson, the federal penitentiary for women in West Virginia, more than twenty-five years before Ted championed that same cause as chairman of the Senate Judiciary Committee in the late 1970s.

Eunice Kennedy took home only one paycheck in her life, from her first job, at the US State Department. She sent that check for $60 to her parents in Palm Beach, Florida, to spend "on something grand." Thereafter, she declined the proffered annual salary of $1,800 and became a "dollar-a-year-girl," the informal appellation for those wealthy enough to work without regular compensation. During and just after World War II, Washington was full of young women whose well-connected fathers found them interesting unpaid employment in what was expected to be a brief interval between college and marriage.

That interval lasted a decade in Eunice's case; the interesting work lasted a lifetime. When she married in 1953, it was to the man her father chose for her, the man who would become her devoted partner in parenthood, religious faith, and social justice, the passions that fueled their marriage and their lives. In the late fifties, while her father mapped out her brothers' political careers, he entrusted to Eunice and Robert Sargent Shriver the resources of the family's charitable foundation. Over the years, the letterhead would identify Jack or Bobby or Ted as president of the Joseph P. Kennedy Jr. Foundation, named for their oldest brother, killed in combat in World War II, but it was always Eunice who ran the show, turning a small family foundation into an engine of social change.

She exerted no less sway when Jack arrived in the Oval Office, goading her older brother into putting mental retardation on his agenda for the first time in his political career, pushing him to throw the weight of the US government behind efforts to combat juvenile delinquency, and prodding him to create the medical research institute devoted to women and children that today bears her name.

With the same persistence, she badgered lawmakers and eight US presidents after Jack, influencing public policy across four decades on issues that helped define the social upheaval of her times. In the 1960s, as the movement to decriminalize state abortion laws gained momentum, she partnered with the Harvard Divinity School to convene the first international conference on the issue. In the 1970s, even as she chastised the women's liberation movement for devaluing motherhood, she argued for both publicly funded child care and a welfare system that did not penalize mothers who stayed home to care for their children. In the 1980s, she lobbied for services for pregnant teenagers with the same vigor that she opposed the use of federal funds for fetal research. In the 1990s, she championed expanded educational, employment, and housing opportunities for those living with intellectual disabilities well into productive adulthoods because of medical advances spurred by her relentless advocacy on their behalf.

The ultimate family loyalist, Eunice was also in many ways the anti-Kennedy. Her work upended her father's dictum that only first-place finishers count. She idolized her father, but his competitive zeal had proven disastrous for Rose Marie, the older sister the family called Rosemary, who had been lobotomized in 1941, in a botched attempt to treat the mental illness that compounded her intellectual disabilities. The surgery, initiated by Joe without his wife's knowledge, left their twenty-three-year-old daughter incapacitated, exiled from her family by the patriarch's decree until Eunice brought her out of the shadows after her father's domineering voice had been silenced by a stroke in 1961.

In reclaiming her discarded sister, Eunice was redressing not just her father's choices but her own. How had it been so easy to acquiesce in the banishment of the sister she had taught to sail, with whom she had hiked the Alps and danced at debutante balls, to have put the inconvenient Rosie out of her mind as well as out of her sight?

Did she agree with her father, who wrote to one of the nuns caring for the institutionalized Rosemary in 1958 that "the solution of Rosemary's problem has been a major factor in the ability of all the Kennedys to go about their life's work and to try to do it as well as they can"? Had Rosemary been sacrificed so they could thrive?

There would be a mania in Eunice Kennedy Shriver's efforts to expiate that familial guilt for the rest of her life; a relentlessness that could intimidate subordinates who did not share her sense of urgency, congressional staffers who failed to do her bidding, and federal bureaucrats who obstructed her path.

————————

Tantalizing signs of Eunice in the public record—photographs at the House of the Good Shepherd in Chicago, memos over her signature at the US State Department, letters she dictated at the US Justice Department, her handwritten observations at Alderson prison—only hinted at the social activism in which she was engaged as a young woman.

The files of Special Olympics and the Joseph P. Kennedy Jr. Foundation and archives from Boston to London, from Palo Alto to Washington, DC, helped clarify the contours of her life, just as conversations with scores of her colleagues, family, and friends filled in its features. Unrestricted access provided by her children to her uncatalogued private papers—thirty-three boxes packed with everything from the well-ordered scrapbooks she kept as a schoolgirl in prewar London, to the poignant thoughts on motherhood she scrawled on a scrap of notepaper after a day of bodysurfing with twelve-year-old Maria at Hyannis Port—deepened the portrait.

What emerges is a complicated figure—a woman both ahead of her time and out of step with it. A devout Catholic in a secular age, she was a daily communicant likelier to be carrying rosaries in her purse than a wallet. An ambivalent feminist, she embraced the cause of gender equality but rejected the idea that access to abortion was necessary to achieve it. A champion of self-discipline, she enfolded without judgment those in her family who fell victim to depression or substance abuse or eating disorders, a private struggle she was loathe to confront in herself. A communitarian at heart, she elevated the welfare of the whole above the supremacy of the self, less as a political philosophy than a reflection of her Catholic belief that everyone is part of the body of Christ.

For all of that, Eunice Kennedy Shriver was not the saint her admirers hope the Vatican will one day declare her to be. She enjoyed the entitlements of wealth too much to emulate the selflessness of the women she revered most: Mother Teresa and Dorothy Day. Meekness did not become her. Patience was not one of her virtues. She resembled more the pioneer aviator whose pictures covered her walls as a teenager. She admired Amelia Earhart, the first woman to fly solo across the Atlantic Ocean, Eunice said, for her "courage and toughness in a male world and as an explorer of the unknown."

Eunice followed in her footsteps. She was part visionary and part master tinkerer, quick to recognize a good idea and quicker still to appropriate it in the service of her cause. She was "an intellectual mechanic," in the view of one of her mentors, Arthur J. Dyck, an ethicist who held a joint appointment at Harvard's Divinity School and its School of Public Health. "She wanted to fix things."

In Rockville, Maryland, she stunned the neighbors by operating a summer camp for retarded children on the grounds of Timberlawn, the 250-acre estate the Shrivers leased when they followed Jack to Washington in 1961. In Paris, she horrified the staff by turning the marble foyer of the ambassador's residence into play space for retarded children from nearby institutions when her husband was US ambassador to France. In China, she ignored protocol to elbow her way inside institutions for retarded children to see for herself the conditions in which they lived. In Washington, she went straight to the Oval Office to chide President Bill Clinton about changes to federal welfare regulations that took hard-won benefits from those she continued to call her "special friends" long after the phrase had fallen out of favor.

"If that girl had been born with balls, she would have been a hell of a politician," Joe Kennedy is reputed to have said of Eunice, an observation that reflected less on her talents than on the limits of his imagination. The self-made multimillionaire could envision either of his older sons the first Catholic president but could not picture his daughter in public office— not among the seven women serving in the House when Jack arrived there in 1947 or the three women in the Senate when he entered the upper chamber in 1953. Breaking barriers was for Kennedy men, not Kennedy women. Men play and women pray; that was Joe Kennedy's attitude toward his wife and daughters.

Perhaps the least introspective member of a clan scornful of self-reflection, Eunice wasted little energy ruminating about the second-tier status of women in her family, but it hardly escaped her notice that her father had vetoed Jean's plan to become a doctor or a nurse and Pat's ambition to pursue a career in business or the law. Of the sisters, only Eunice broke out of the box to which her gender consigned her, finding her way around their father to secure her place in the world and in history.

"Needless to say, after so many years of coming here to celebrate Jack and all the boys, it is nice to have an evening for one of the women," she told an audience gathered at the John F. Kennedy Presidential Library and Museum in Boston in 2007 to honor her. Her lips were parted in a smile, but her teeth were clenched.

Instead of stewing about the double standard, she had forged her own path, competing as a young woman with her brothers in athletics, the one arena where gender did not trump skill in the Kennedy family. She was the best sailor in a group of natural mariners, the best tennis player among siblings who had volleyed on the grass courts of Wimbledon and the clay at Cap d'Antibes. Trained by her father not to lose, she rarely did, despite a physical constitution so delicate her family called her "Puny Eunie."

In Eunice Kennedy Shriver's stubborn refusal to accept either her body's own limitations or her father's low expectations, the seeds of more than Special Olympics were sown. The same willful determination would chart her course on behalf of those denied a chair in the classroom, a place on the playing field, or a job in the workforce. She would provide them with the chance to thrive that had been denied to Rosemary, the sister whose fate, their mother wrote in her memoirs, was "the first of the tragedies that were to befall us."

It was "all so unnecessary" and so wasteful, Eunice wrote, remembering the long hours her mother had spent working with Rosemary and "taking her to psychologists and to dozens of doctors" only to be told her situation was hopeless. The disastrous lobotomy fulfilled that bleak prophecy, convincing Eunice that doctors knew no more about the causes and treatment of mental retardation than the eugenicists who, early in the twentieth century, had advocated forced sterilization as the most effective means of ridding society of those medicine variously labeled idiots, imbeciles, or morons.

To try to understand what the so-called experts did not about mental retardation became the purpose of Eunice Kennedy Shriver's life. It is impossible to make sense of that life without examining the cause that gave it meaning. Her story is that story, too.

Eunice was not the first to express outrage at the plight of those children. Her efforts built on a nascent movement led by parents struggling to keep their disabled children at home, by lawmakers fighting for funds to educate those children, by park workers developing recreational programs for them, by progressive superintendents at state institutions championing their right to be treated with dignity, and by civil rights lawyers seeking court orders to force reform on less enlightened asylum administrators.

Her genius was not in getting there first. It was in finding and promoting the best ideas and carrying them out on a grand scale. She used the Kennedy name to kick open doors all over the world, and for more than forty years, she barged through them, hectoring, demanding, and working harder than anyone in the room to get done what others said could not be done.

It turned out that Joe Kennedy had been wrong about his daughter. Her sex did not disqualify her from a career in politics. No one in Congress who tried to cut an appropriation she wanted, no one in a corporate boardroom who tried to dodge a sponsorship role in Special Olympics, no acquaintance who tried to avoid volunteering at the games doubted that Eunice Kennedy Shriver was as equipped as any man to work her will and get her way.

But a mercurial temperament, common enough in men but anathema in women, might well have proven an insurmountable bar to elective office. Impatient and insistent, she was the definition of impolitic. In her missionary zeal, she did not much care whom she offended in pursuit of her aims. She left it to others to smooth the feathers she invariably ruffled along the way. The same was said of her father and of her younger brother Bobby. But they were Kennedy men, not a Kennedy woman.

The qualities that might have inhibited a career as a politician enhanced Eunice's effectiveness as an advocate. Good intentions did not impress her; results did. She measured herself, and everyone around her, by what got done, not by what got promised. It is no wonder then that President Kennedy instructed his aides to "just give Eunice what she wants," not because she was an irritant, although she could be that, but because he trusted that, on issues that mattered to her, his sister had figured out what worked.

Her influence did not end that awful day in Dallas. For more than four decades, Republican and Democratic presidents alike took her calls, read her memos, and responded to her requests. Presidents from Lyndon B. Johnson to George W. Bush honored her. In 1984, Ronald Reagan awarded her the Presidential Medal of Freedom. In 1998, Bill and Hillary Clinton celebrated the thirtieth anniversary of Special Olympics with her at the White House.

Every award, whether from the Lasker Foundation for her contributions to medical research, or from the University of Notre Dame for her embodiment of Catholic principles, cited compassion as the engine that propelled her to fight for the forgotten. That she was moved by their plight is indisputable. But empathy alone did not fuel her activism. There was also rage. Rage at the impotence of a medical establishment that had no answers for her sister. Rage at the lack of respect for life in a society more focused on personal fulfillment than communal responsibility. Rage at the inability, or unwillingness, of government to deliver on America's promise of equality for all its citizens, no matter how diminished their capacities.

There is little doubt that at least some of that passion was private anger redirected to the public sphere. Anger at the adored but autocratic father who lobotomized a beloved sister. Anger at the pious but passive mother who submitted to Rosemary's long banishment from the family. Anger at herself and her siblings for allowing themselves to edit the inconvenient Rosemary out of their lives for so many years.

Ironically, it was from the father who had underestimated her that Eunice learned how best to advance her cause. "It is not what you are, it's what people think you are," counseled the man who, in one generation, recast the Kennedys from Irish American strivers into American royalty. Social acceptance, of a Catholic president or a retarded child, first required a change in public perception.

That is exactly what Eunice engineered in 1962, when she invited photographers from the *Saturday Evening Post* magazine to capture images of laughing children in pony carts, on rope swings, in the swimming pool of her backyard; and in 1968, when she recruited professional athletes as their coaches; and in 1972, when she convinced Roone Arledge to televise Special Olympics on *ABC's Wild World of Sports*.

"When she told me what she wanted, I thought, 'Nobody is going to watch this, a bunch of crippled kids running around,'" Frank Gifford, the former New York Giants running back and the program's host, recalled more than forty years later. "We captured it all on film, and it was one of the most moving things I have ever done. It took away the despair and the fear. They were just kids, having fun. After we put it on television, we picked up crowds all over the country. No one could tell her it wouldn't work."

In adopting Joe Kennedy's marketing methods, Eunice Kennedy Shriver had turned her father's idea of competition on its head. In the process, she proved herself more than the equal of any man in the Kennedy clan.

EUNICE

PROLOGUE

The mentally ill and the mentally retarded need no longer be alien to our affections or beyond the help of our communities.

—PRESIDENT JOHN F. KENNEDY, OCTOBER 31, 1963

I N HER COBALT-BLUE wool suit and white kidskin gloves, she could have been mistaken for a guest at a White House social reception instead of the architect of the pioneering legislation the president of the United States was about to sign.

As John F. Kennedy slid into his leather armchair at the center of the conference table in the Cabinet Room, the forty-two-year-old suburban mother of three receded behind a wall of dignitaries, including the Speaker of the House, the Senate majority leader, the secretary of labor, the chief of pediatrics at Johns Hopkins Hospital, and assorted senators and congressmen.

She does not appear in the formal group portraits from that day, having settled into a spot far behind the president against the east wall, nearly enfolded by the green brocade drapes bracketing the French doors that open onto the Rose Garden. President Kennedy does not mention her in his recorded remarks at the signing ceremony for the Mental Retardation Facilities and Community Mental Health Centers Construction Act of 1963, singling out instead Senator Lister Hill of Alabama, chairman of the Senate Committee on Labor and Public Welfare, and Representative Oren Harris of Arkansas, chairman of the House Committee on Interstate and Foreign Commerce, who shepherded S. 1576 to passage.

It was only after he had distributed all but one of the ceremonial fountain pens that the president turned to look for Eunice Kennedy Shriver and, rising from his seat, strode through the crowd toward the back wall to hand the last pen to his sister, the guiding force behind an unprecedented federal commitment to combating mental retardation.

"This bill will expand our knowledge, provide research facilities to determine the cause of retardation, establish university related diagnostic research clinics, and permit the construction of university centers for the care of the retarded," the president told those gathered. "For the first time, parents and children will have available comprehensive facilities to diagnose and either cure or treat mental retardation. For the first time, there will be research centers capable of putting together teams of experts working in many different fields. For the first time, state and federal governments and voluntary organizations will be able to coordinate their manpower and facilities in a single effort to cure and treat this condition."

There had been no reason to expect that Kennedy would make mental retardation a White House priority. Foreign policy was his primary focus in 1963, a year in which he declared to the people of the divided German city of Berlin that "in the world of freedom, the proudest boast is 'Ich bin ein Berliner,'" a year in which he would commit sixteen thousand US troops to South Vietnam and covert energy toward ousting Fidel Castro from Cuba. Civil rights was the most pressing item on his domestic agenda the year that Governor George C. Wallace of Alabama blocked the entrance of three black students into the University of Alabama, the year that a white supremacist murdered Mississippi NAACP field director Medgar Evers, and the year that the Reverend Dr. Martin Luther King Jr. delivered his "I Have a Dream" speech on the steps of the Lincoln Memorial during the March on Washington.

Kennedy's indifference to mental retardation had long frustrated advocates. The memory still stung of Kennedy, then a senator, brushing past Elizabeth M. Boggs, the president of the National Association for Retarded Children, in a Capitol Hill corridor where she was waiting to testify before the Senate Committee on Labor and Public Welfare on the educational needs of retarded children. Kennedy was a member of that committee, but he did not stick around for the hearing that April day in 1957 even though Boggs knew—as the nation as yet did not—that mental retardation had touched Kennedy's own family.

But Boggs and her cause would find an ally elsewhere in the Kennedy clan. Eunice Kennedy Shriver took the reins of the Joseph P. Kennedy Jr. Foundation around the time Jack blew past Boggs in that hallway, and she turned the attention of the previously unfocused family charity exclusively to the needs of the retarded. With her father's fortune and her husband's help, she traveled the country, consulting experts and educating herself about the scope of the problem and the dearth of resources devoted to addressing it. Her efforts culminated in millions of dollars in grants from the Kennedy Foundation to researchers at Harvard, Johns Hopkins, Georgetown, Chicago, Wisconsin, and Stanford universities.

It was only a beginning. She had learned enough by the time her oldest surviving brother was elected president on November 8, 1960, to know that the efforts of a small family foundation were no match for what the federal government could, and, in her view, should be doing for the 5.4 million children and adults in the United States with mental retardation. The few federal programs that did exist were scattered throughout the bureaucracy, intermingled with aid for the physically handicapped and geared toward adults. It was not nearly enough.

Her brother's election gave her an opportunity to do more. Before he had even taken the oath of office, Eunice secured from Jack a commitment to appoint a presidential panel to investigate the needs of the retarded and to propose federal legislation to meet them. The president gave her a free hand, and she seeded the twenty-seven-member President's Panel on Mental Retardation with the most knowledgeable people in the field, including Boggs, a chemist by training and herself the mother of a severely retarded son.

Eunice Kennedy Shriver was not a member of the President's Panel; she did not want charges of nepotism to overshadow the work. Officially, she was "a consultant" to the group that she had willed into existence and drove to produce a report for the president within one year and legislation for him to sign within two.

She had pulled it off.

At the edge of that gathering of luminaries in the Cabinet Room on the last day of October in 1963, how moved she must have been to hear the president pledge the nation's communal responsibility to those with mental retardation, a commitment that was unimaginable only a few years before.

"It was said, in an earlier age, that the mind of man is a far country which can be neither approached nor explored. But today, under present conditions of scientific achievement, it will be possible for a nation as rich in human and material resources as ours to make the most remote recesses of the mind accessible," the president vowed. "The mentally ill and the mentally retarded need no longer be alien to our affections or beyond the help of our communities."

It was the last bill John Fitzgerald Kennedy would ever sign. No one in the Cabinet Room on that sunny Thursday morning could have imagined that three weeks later in Dallas an assassin's bullet would end the life of the thirty-fifth president of the United States.

As much as John F. Kennedy's death would traumatize the nation he led, it would upend the dynamics in the family he left behind. There would be no more wall hugging for Eunice Kennedy Shriver. Without her brother in the White House, she would have to come out from behind the curtains to lead the movement she had just put on the national agenda.

PART ONE

IN HER PARENTS' IMAGE

ONE

THE MIDDLE CHILD

If my new granddaughter is like her mother, she's all right for me.

—JOHN "HONEY FITZ" FITZGERALD, JULY 10, 1921

ROSE FITZGERALD KENNEDY went to a dance the night before she gave birth to her fifth child in six years, on Sunday, July 10, 1921.

Her husband, the young financier Joseph P. Kennedy, had rented a summer cottage at Nantasket Beach, near the Victorian mansion owned by Rose's parents, Mary Josephine "Josie" and John F. "Honey Fitz" Fitzgerald, the colorful ex-congressman and former mayor of Boston. On Saturday night, Rose enjoyed the orchestra at the Hotel Pemberton, the forty-year-old Queen Anne confection of turrets and gables at the tip of a sandy peninsula just south of Boston on Massachusetts Bay.

The fashionable hotel on Windmill Point, with its wide wraparound porches, echoed the style both of her childhood home in the Boston neighborhood of Dorchester and the large white-trimmed wood-frame house in Brookline Joe had purchased for the then-extravagant price of $16,000 for his growing family the year before.

The dance in the elaborate ballroom and the fireworks that followed from the pier were a respite for the thirty-one-year-old expectant mother already managing a household of two schoolboys, two toddlers, and assorted cooks, maids, governesses, and a husband who was frequently away on business.

Joe had made an effort to be in town for the birth, declining an invitation to play golf in the White Mountains over the July 4th weekend. "Nothing I'd rather do than spend the three-day holiday on the 4th at Bretton Woods but on account of Mrs. Kennedy's condition, I do not feel I would want to be away from home at this time," he had written to Chris Dunphy, a friend who was then manager of the Mount Pleasant Hotel in the New Hampshire resort town. Rose insisted she would have understood had he gone: "The idea was [that childbirth] was something the woman had to do, and the less bother she gave to anybody else including her husband, the better it was, and the easier it was," Rose told Robert Coughlin, the ghostwriter of her memoirs, in 1974.

Labor pains had roused her from sleep before dawn that Sunday. After the twenty-mile drive from the summer house to Brookline, she arrived home at about six in the morning. The Kennedys' third daughter was born three hours later, in Rose's private bedroom in the twelve room house at the corner of Naples and Abbottsford Roads. "Mrs. Kennedy is an ardent follower of the Roosevelt doctrines, and she is dead set against race suicide," the *Boston Daily Globe* quipped in its account of the birth. "She is one of a family of six children, but Mrs. Kennedy is out to beat her mother's record."

Rose, who would eventually give birth to nine children, named this baby Eunice after her fragile youngest sister, living that summer in a sanitarium for patients with tuberculosis at Saranac Lake in New York's Adirondack Mountains. Eunice Fitzgerald had contracted the infectious respiratory disease while nursing veterans of World War I at a Red Cross station on Boston Common when she was nineteen. She would die of the disease at twenty-three, two years after her namesake's birth.

The baby would inherit her aunt's delicate constitution as well as her name. Eunice Mary Kennedy, the first of her children that Rose did not nurse, was colicky and slow to gain weight, an early sign of the medical problems that would plague her all her life. "Unfortunately when Eunice was born, she didn't get along very well because the bottle was not very well organized, and I couldn't nurse her at that time because I had breast abscess[es]," Rose recalled, conceding that she had never nursed the older children with much regularity either. It was "a little confining to be home every three hours to nurse the baby . . . [A] baby is usually fed at 10 or 10:30 [p.m.]. You're at the theater, so what do you do?"

The theater played an important part in the Kennedys' lives in 1921. Two years before, Joe had joined the Boston brokerage house of Hayden, Stone & Co. Among his clients were small and midsized film production and distribution companies. Negotiations to refinance or consolidate one overleveraged firm kept him shuttling between Boston and New York in the weeks before Eunice was born. During this period, he was also investing his own money in movie houses throughout New England and spending time in Boston's theater district, cultivating producers he hoped would recognize the potential he saw in the motion picture industry.

Joe had begun his business career far less glamorously, as a state bank examiner, after graduating from Harvard College in 1912. A year spent poring over the books of banks across eastern Massachusetts proved valuable in 1913 when the small East Boston bank founded by his father, Patrick J. Kennedy, and other Irish Americans was threatened with a takeover by a bigger downtown bank. P. J., as he was known throughout the neighborhood he had served as saloon keeper, state lawmaker, and Democratic Party ward boss, rewarded Joe with the presidency of the Columbia Trust Company when his son succeeded in keeping the bank in neighborhood hands.

Now, just a few years later, Joe's growing wealth from stock deals and burgeoning investments in the movie industry opened a new world to the Kennedys, one more exciting than Wall Street trades or the work he had done during World War I as assistant general manager of Bethlehem Steel's Fore River Shipyard in Quincy, Massachusetts.

The Kennedys' lives were changing in ways that reflected the social and political upheaval of the decade into which Eunice was born. The 1920s were not yet roaring in July 1921, but they soon would be, and fast. The nation's wealth would double during the decade as Americans moved from farms to well-paying jobs in the cities. Disposable income, in turn, paid for admission to amusement parks, dance halls, and movie palaces, and for the radios, phonographs, and vacuum cleaners in popular demand because two-thirds of American households now had electricity, up from only 16 percent a decade earlier.

Prosperity was not universally distributed. Two in five American families survived on subsistence wages, forgoing electric washing machines for basic necessities or buying big-ticket items on credit. But by the middle of the decade, Joe Kennedy had made his first million. He swapped his Model T Ford for a Rolls-Royce, and Rose exchanged her ready-to-wear wardrobe for the haute couture she displayed on their frequent forays to Boston's theater district.

"It was all a completely new and different environment, gay, exciting, and quite different and quite breathtaking to me, who was a convent-bred girl. I had heard that chorus girls were gay, but evil, and, worst of all, husband snatchers. But nothing shocking happened," Rose said. "One characteristic of my life with Joe was that we trusted one another implicitly. If he had occasion to go out with the theatrical people, he told me where he was going and he went. There was never any deceit on his part, and there was never any doubt in my mind about his motives."

Whether she was being discreet or disingenuous, Rose was certainly being less than candid. Her husband's serial philandering had prompted her to move home with her parents for several weeks in 1920 when she was pregnant with Kathleen. Since divorce was not an option for Catholics, her father sent Rose back to the man she had chosen—against his wish that she not marry the first man to propose—and with whom she would have five more children and live companionably, but largely independently, for the rest of their lives. She omitted their separation from her memoirs fifty years later, well schooled by then in the role of selective memory in the making of Kennedy mythology.

American women were at the center of cultural change in the 1920s. Flappers with short hair and shorter skirts had a freer attitude toward cigarettes, sex, and the bootlegged alcohol available in the speakeasies that sprang up during Prohibition. The Nineteenth Amendment to the Constitution, guaranteeing women the right to vote, had been ratified the year before Eunice was born. The year of her birth, Margaret Sanger founded the American Birth Control League, the precursor of the Planned Parenthood Federation of America, which would liberate women—including those with whom Joe Kennedy tarried—to have sex without fear of pregnancy.

Perhaps to compensate for how difficult it was to keep track of her husband, Rose kept meticulous track of her children's development. Her note-card system recorded their height and weight and each child's encounter with mumps, measles, or whooping cough. Eunice was worryingly thin, but Rose thought her precocious, noting in her diary that at eighteen months she was "walking alone and talking a lot. Best little talker of all. Also likes to take a bow and say, 'Little Partner, dance with me.'"

Reading her entries decades later, Rose thought "those jottings foretold something about the girl she became. Wonderfully well coordinated and with quick reflexes, one of the best athletes in our active family, a 'talker' with a special way of expressing herself in a pithy and witty manner that made her one of the livelier participants in our family conversations. But she was also a good listener, and marvelously generous in her interest in others, especially her brothers and sisters, but including waifs, strays, and anybody who needed her."

In her siblings, Eunice had a houseful of potential partners for dancing or conversation. When she was born, Joe Jr. was six; Jack was four; Rose Marie, whom the family called Rosemary or Rosie, was almost three; and Kathleen was a year and a half. Pat, Bobby, Jean, and Teddy were yet to come, born in 1924, 1925, 1928, and 1932, respectively.

Her detailed notes notwithstanding, Rose was neither a warm nor doting maternal presence. "I don't think she was quite the same role as most mothers," Eunice recalled. "Mother wasn't a nursemaid mother. We had a governess . . . I don't remember [Rose] sweeping the floor, quite frankly, or serving at table. I also don't remember her cooking. Her role was a little different." Still, a diary entry on January 7, 1923, hinted at how exhausting Rose found motherhood, even with a household staff to shoulder the routine tasks of diaper laundering and food preparation: "Took care of children. Miss Brooks, the governess, helped. Kathleen still has bronchitis and Joe sick in bed. Great life."

Rose was the enforcer of rules, the cultivator of manners, and the incubator of good taste and religious faith. She was not averse to using a ruler or a coat hanger to discipline a child or imposing a Spartan or fat-laden diet if a child came up too thin or too heavy at her weekly weigh-ins. Rose made St. Aidan's Church, a few blocks from home, a regular stop on neighborhood strolls with her children to teach them "that church isn't just something for Sundays and special times on the calendar but should be part of daily life."

No one absorbed those lessons more dutifully than Eunice, whom Rose described as "rather pale and of a nervous, highly conscientious demeanor." She craved her mother's attention but rarely got it because of Rose's extended absences. The first five months of 1923, when Eunice was not yet two, were typical of the long separations that marked the Kennedy marriage, ensuring that the children would seldom see both parents under the same roof at the same time. "Joe Sr. left on 5 o'clock for Palm Beach with Eddie Moore and a couple of other friends who joined them in New York," according to a January 14, 1923, entry in Rose's diary. He would work from Florida through the winter, enjoying the sun and the golf, returning in time for Rose to set off in April on her own six-week sojourn with her sister Mary Agnes to California.

To keep her household functioning smoothly during her frequent trips, Rose relied on Mary and Eddie Moore, an older, childless couple who served as surrogate parents for the Kennedy children. Eddie, for whom Ted would be named, had been the personal assistant to Rose's father when Honey Fitz was mayor of Boston. He now performed that role, and much more, for Joe. "Eddie Moore became his closest friend, someone he trusted implicitly in every way and in all circumstances," recalled Rose, who asked Mary to be Eunice's godmother because she had become "an equally great friend, confidante, and unfailing support for me."

The Moores made the Kennedys' lives work, especially after Joe led a group of investors in the purchase of the Film Booking Office of America, in 1926, and another deal, a year later, with Radio Corporation of America (RCA) that brought sound to what had been a silent picture studio. The acquisitions required him to spend more time in New York and Hollywood, leading to the decision in 1927 to move his family to Riverdale, a bucolic haven in the far reaches of the Bronx. The move, a practical response to his business ventures, was personal as well. Boston was a hidebound, parochial town, its Brahmin elites unreconciled to the growing influence of the Irish, even those, like Kennedy, who had graduated from Harvard and built a fortune that would soon eclipse their own. Joe's money was as good as anyone's on Wall Street, but in Boston, his bank statement could not gain him admission to the right clubs, to the inner circles of Protestant power and respectability.

Boston "is no place to bring up Irish Catholic children," Joe told a reporter, citing his conviction that his offspring would be denied their rightful places in society because of the city's intractable anti-Catholic and anti-Irish bigotry. Robert Francis was the last of the Kennedy children to be born at home in Brookline, in 1925. Two years later, Joe hired a private railway car to take Rose and their seven children, ranging in age from twelve-year-old Joe Jr. to two-year-old Bobby, to a rented three-story, twenty-room mansion on Independence Avenue at 252nd Street. Eunice spent the trip doubled over with stomach pains—whether from nerves or illness, the record does not make clear.

In Brookline, Eunice had attended the Edward Devotion neighborhood public school, but in September 1927, all of the Kennedys' school-age children—Joe Jr., Jack, Rosemary, Kathleen, and Eunice—were enrolled in the private Riverdale Country School, with its crisp uniforms, sweeping lawns, manicured playing fields, and stately academic buildings. The oldest of the girls, nine-year-old Rosemary, entered second grade with her seven-year-old sister, Kathleen, whom the family called Kick. Rosemary had repeated kindergarten and first grade in Brookline, where her teachers told her parents what they already knew: Rosemary was "slow" and her development "delayed."

Rosemary's struggles in school were not the first indication that the prettiest of the Kennedy girls was also the slowest. "Physically she was very healthy, and there were no signs I recognized that anything might be wrong," Rose recalled of her birth. "She crawled, stood, took her first steps, said her first words late, she had problems managing a baby spoon and porringer—and yet, as everyone knows, babies always have their own individual rates of growth and acquiring skills, so I was patient, concerned, beginning to be a little apprehensive, but not worried, partly, I suppose, because of wishful thinking."

By the time Rosemary reached school age, there was no denying her developmental delays. Her teachers in Brookline told Joe and Rose that Rosemary had scored lower than normal on the intelligence tests, just coming into use in the 1920s. How low is not clear from available records, but the news would have been devastating for any parent.

Rose "was puzzled by what all this could mean. I had never heard of a retarded child, and I did not know where to send her to school or how to cope with the situation." She consulted her family doctor, the head of the Psychology Department at Harvard, and a Catholic psychologist who ran a school in Washington. "Each of them told me she was retarded, but what to do about her, where to send her, how to help her seemed to be an unanswered question," Rose said.

There were no good choices, in Rose's view. If she had Rosemary tutored at home, her daughter would lack playmates. If she sent her to a school for retarded children, Rosemary might never overcome her deficits.

In lieu of an alternative plan, Rose hoped that, with persistence and the extra help their financial resources could provide, Rosemary might be able to hold her own in a regular classroom.

Those hopes collapsed after a year at Riverdale. Rosemary could not write in a straight line. She would sometimes write from right to left. She could not steer a sled or row a boat. She could not keep up on the playing fields, despite the hours Rose spent hitting tennis balls with her to develop her coordination.

Kennedy family biographers have speculated about the cause and extent of Rosemary's childhood disabilities, but available documents provide no definitive answers. Her letters to her family and examples of her schoolwork are open to researchers at the John F. Kennedy Presidential Library in Boston, but dozens of documents in the archives that could shed light on her condition—much of her parents' correspondence with her doctors, teachers, and tutors, for instance—remain closed or heavily redacted at the insistence of the family.

Conjecture has filled the vacuum. Could a nurse's decision to delay delivery until the doctor arrived have deprived Rosemary of oxygen in utero? Could the Spanish flu epidemic of 1918 have affected Rose's pregnancy? Could eighteen-month-old Rosemary's exposure to Jack when he nearly died of highly contagious scarlet fever in 1920 have compromised her intellectual development? Could the epileptic-like seizures she suffered as a child have caused brain damage? Did she suffer neurological damage from a bout of spinal meningitis?

That last explanation is what the family told Luella R. Hennessey, the nurse to two generations of Kennedy children from 1935 to 1963, and that is what Joe told a reporter for *Time* magazine in 1960. But the Kennedys were not always reliable reporters of their own story, and their narrative about Rosemary changed across the decades when it suited their political purposes.

Whatever their cause, Rosemary's limitations were not conspicuous to casual observers, who remembered her as quieter and less physically active than her siblings but not obviously disabled as a child. "I don't think that probably on the outside many people noticed that she was much different from the others, except that she was probably a little less quick on the up-take," Rose recalled.

She was able to do long division and to write simple letters to her parents and siblings. That her letters were full of misspellings made

Rosemary more similar to her siblings than not. That she printed in block letters rather than wrote in cursive script meant that her letters were more legible than those of her brothers and sisters, all of whom left their father "quite discouraged with the penmanship of the Kennedy children," as Joe wrote to Eunice in 1936.

But unlike her siblings, Rosemary's academic skills plateaued at about a fourth-grade level. Short of "curing" her, Rose focused on having Rosemary "pass" in polite society: "I always thought that if she had a veneer of information—such as the names of the presidents, the mayor, important cities, a little history and geography—and if she was attractive and well groomed and well mannered, she would be able to get by."

Rosemary's difficulties made it impossible for her to continue at Riverdale. Both her parents wanted to keep her at home, according to Eunice, who was only eight when Rosemary left day school. "When psychologists recommended that Rosemary be placed in an institution," she said decades later, her father resisted, asking, "What can they do in an institution that we can't do better for her at home—here with her family?" Rose, too, had been adamant. "Much as I had begun to realize how very difficult it might be to keep her at home, everything about me—and my feelings for her—rebelled against the idea, and I rejected it except as a last resort," she wrote in her memoirs.

That time came when the family moved in 1929 to the brick mansion high above the Hudson River that Joe purchased in nearby Bronxville for $250,000—or $3.57 million in 2017 dollars. Her parents decided to send Rosie, at age eleven, to the first of the many boarding schools for children with mental retardation she would call home for the next twelve years. All but her youngest siblings would head off to residential schools of their own in the next few years, perhaps making Rosemary's early separation from the family seem less unusual. But none of the other Kennedys went away from home so young.

Rosemary had a rocky adjustment to Devereux School, in Devon-Berwyn, Pennsylvania. While administrators reported that she demonstrated "excellent social poise" and could be "quite charming at times," her disappointing academic efforts were punctuated by "outbursts of impatience" and flashes of anger that would intensify as Rosemary grew into adolescence and young womanhood—symptoms perhaps of an underlying mental illness that went undiagnosed and untreated at a time when mental illness was even more stigmatized than mental retardation.

Joe's unrealistic expectation that Rosemary could learn by sheer force of will could only have exacerbated her anxiety. His letters to her over the years were alternately tender and tough-minded, praising her at any sign of progress but exhorting her always to try harder. Their father "was easily upset by Rosemary's lack of progress, her inabilities to use opportunities for self-development," Eunice acknowledged.

Rosemary's loneliness is palpable in her letters home. In one, to Eunice after an Easter visit to Bronxville in 1931, she reported having seen the "exciting" new movie *Rin Tin Tin*, but wrote plaintively of wanting everyone to write to her more often than they did. "Dear Eunice, I miss you very much. Didn't we have fun together when I was home? I was so sorry I had to leave all of you so soon. Tell the girls to write to me as much as they can . . . I will see you quite soon sweetheart. I'm dying to hear from Mother and Daddy. Tell Mother to send me my box of candy that she gave me Easter. I feel very upset when I don't hear from Mother tell her that. Write me a long long letter and make it as long as you can, darling. I know you will dear, love Rose."

Even without Rosemary at home, the Bronxville house was a noisy, chaotic place on which Rose imposed her own brand of discipline. She was, Eunice remembered, "quite stern. She knew there were certain ways to behave. We went to dancing classes once a week. We had our teeth straightened. I remember going five years with my sisters, five or six of us in a car. We'd go all the way into New York [instead] of going to the local dentist . . . We had to hop into the car once every three weeks. We'd drive for an hour to New York to go to the dentist and back we'd come. We'd wait our turn, and then we'd go to the chair. Then we'd go to dancing lessons, Arthur Murray. She bought the lessons, and then I would have to go with my sisters. We'd go once a week. We were really organized."

The Kennedy's Georgian mansion, known as Crownlands, sat on six acres on a hill above the Hudson River at 294 Pondfield Road, with a basement projection room for movie screenings and separate cottages for a chauffeur and a gardener. The third floor was the preserve of Joe, Jack, and Kick, with their bedrooms, a large playroom, and a room for the governess. Sickly, easily tired, and already her mother's reliable companion for a nightly recitation of the rosary, Eunice watched, at some remove, the spirited fun and social ease shared by Joe, Jack, and Kick, the latter of whom was just a year older than she. Her bedroom was on the second floor with those of Pat, Bobby, and Jean. Too young for the older set and too old for her younger siblings, Eunice made peace with her place in the middle, studying her more sophisticated brothers and sister, unnoticed, while honing her own athletic and intellectual skills.

Rose executed the morning ritual before school at Bronxville with military precision. "There was a downstairs bathroom in Bronxville, and after breakfast we'd file in and out one by one, then stand inspection for spots on our clothes and general neatness," Eunice remembered.

Playtime was no less regimented. Their mother "had us out no matter what the weather was. Today children stay indoors and watch television or you listen to the radio, but we were packed up with our clothes on, and out we'd go sled riding or go ice skating all the time," Eunice recalled. "I can remember going ice skating in Bronxville. Mother would take us, and I remember her skating . . . It wasn't a great emotional thing with her. She was more of a teacher or an inspirer. She was more interested in whether you were reading or whether, taking skating lessons, you just wouldn't go skating off into the blue yonder. She'd say, 'Use your right leg or use your left leg better.' There was quite a little pressure around, I think."

Appearances mattered to Rose, eager as she was to win the social acceptance that had eluded the family in Boston. Eunice learned that the hard way at age ten when she decided to raise some money for the Catholic missions in Africa. "We had a lot of apples in our apple tree. I had the apples in a big basket, and I was going down the street selling them in Bronxville; and then, suddenly, this low voice came up behind me and out pops my mama. She was absolutely outraged, told me to go right home. 'How dare I [sic] sell those apples? Never do that again! Go right to my [sic] room. See that you go; stay there till morning.' I thought it was one of the few times I saw her so angry. I guess she [thought], living in Bronxville at that time, it was unseemly. I was about ten years old"—too young to know that just a few miles south of her family's estate, men who had lost everything in the stock market crash of 1929 were selling apples and pencils on the streets.

The Kennedys were spared the fallout from the collapse of the then-unregulated stock market. With the help of insider information, not then illegal, Joe had become a successful Wall Street speculator. He saw the crash coming and sold off his holdings in time. He got richer still by shorting stocks as prices fell and by buying up real estate at discounted prices in the aftermath of the crash.

He had also been prescient about the movie industry. By the end of the decade, three-quarters of all Americans were going to the movies every week. Joe made certain his children enjoyed the perks of his Hollywood connections. He gave Joe Jr. and Jack chaps, like those worn by actor Tom Mix in Hollywood Westerns. He introduced Kathleen and Eunice to Gary Cooper at the tony restaurant 21, in New York. He even brought his mistress, the film siren Gloria Swanson and her daughter, "little Gloria," home to Bronxville for a Halloween party.

By then, Eunice had transferred from Riverdale to the lower school at Brantwood Hall, a private girls school in Bronxville. "Eunice [who] was not very strong went to a day school in Bronxville and came home for her meals, a necessity in her case on account of her weight," recalled Rose, whose extra servings of buttered bread and cream-covered oatmeal could not fill out her daughter's skeletal frame.

Health concerns prompted Eunice's change of schools that time, but maternal whim was just as often the precipitating factor behind a new school or a home tutor for the Kennedy children. Eunice would attend six different schools and be tutored at home for long stretches before she completed high school. Bobby attended three different boarding schools. Teddy went to ten schools by the time he was thirteen.

So many changes were not conducive to forming deep childhood friendships. The Kennedy children were never in any one school long enough. Such flux fostered, instead, the intense family loyalty for which the Kennedy siblings became so well known. "We liked each other more than we liked other people, but I guess that's natural," Eunice recalled.

Eunice's gastrointestinal ailments landed her in a Manhattan hospital when she was twelve, by which time Teddy had arrived to occupy the nursery, and Joe Jr. and Jack were away at school at Choate, in Walling-ford, Connecticut. Even so, Joe Jr. managed to visit her four days out of the seven Eunice was hospitalized, winning a $10 bet with her when she proved, as he predicted, unable to sit perfectly still for ten minutes.

That frenetic energy allowed her to report to her mother on October 1, 1934, that despite her frequent illnesses, lanky frame, and chronic fatigue she had been chosen as one of two team captains in gym class at Brantwood Hall. "I am getting along fine in school. I am being excused at 12:15, and then I can have time for a rest," she wrote.

Eunice took her illnesses in stride, having watched her even more sickly older brother, Jack, display the stoicism the family prized. She slept lightly, even with eye pads and earplugs, and adapted without complaint to the stomach cramps and insomnia that would follow her into adult-hood. Unlike Jack, who rode out his illnesses propped up on pillows de-vouring books, Eunice was too agitated to read quietly in bed. Instead, she propelled herself outside, willing her body to do what it should not have been strong enough to do. "I can remember thinking that the first time I stayed indoors in my life was after my thirties when I had a baby . . . I thought how odd, some people stay indoors and read all day," she said. "In our family, sickness was not a big deal. You just didn't pay attention to it."

It was not unusual for one or both parents to be away during those bouts of illness, to miss a holiday, a child's birthday, a school performance, a graduation ceremony. Rose went abroad seventeen times from 1929 to 1936, most often to Paris to shop. And, despite her emphasis on religious observance, she missed both Kick's First Communion and Joe Jr.'s Con-firmation.

Eunice's memory that Rose "was there all the time" is contradicted by dozens of letters in the family archives that make clear how often Rose traveled and how acutely Eunice felt her absence. "Dear Mother, I am sorry you are away," she wrote on February 13, 1929. "Tomorrow is Val-entine's . . ."

"Dear Mother, I am sorry that you are away," she wrote again five weeks later. "I hope that you will be home soon. I am getting along better at school. I am sorry that you will not be able to see the puppet show."

"Dear Mother, I miss you a[n] awful lot but hope you are having a nice time and hope you will be home soon," Eunice wrote on March 2, 1932, a month after Rose had returned to Boston for Teddy's birth. "I love you lots and lots"—a sentiment Eunice underlined four times.

Even when she was home, Rose was aloof. "Mrs. Kennedy didn't say she loved her children," recalled Luella R. Hennessey, the family nurse. "It just wasn't said. It was all about respect." When her father was home, Eunice remembered, "she let him sort of take over." When Joe bought a summer house on Cape Cod, in 1928, Rose had a garden shed installed at the edge of the water so she could escape her boisterous brood and read in peace. When a storm washed it away, she promptly installed another. "It's solitary confinement, not splendor, I need. Any mother will know what I mean," she said.

By the time she was thirteen, Eunice had adapted to her moth-er's detachment. She struck a breezy tone in her letters, updating Rose on the family news; it was a style Rose would emulate years later in the round-robin notes she wrote to keep her adult children apprised of one another's activities. "Dearest Mother, We all miss you but hope you are having a nice time," Eunice wrote on October 1, 1934. "I just talked to Kick and she is fine. I had a letter from Rose and she is having a nice time. Joe went to tea with her yesterday [Joe Jr. was at Harvard, and Rosemary was living in Brookline with a tutor], Kiko [the family governess] went to Boston today. Daddy left yesterday for Washington but expects to come home next Friday."

Like her mother, her father "was gone a lot," Eunice recalled. In 1934 Joe was living in Washington, serving what would become a fourteen-month stint as the first chairman of the Securities and Exchange Commission (SEC), the regulatory authority established by President Franklin D. Roosevelt to prevent the kind of stock manipulations that had shattered the economy in 1929 and made Joe Kennedy such a rich man. The post was Kennedy's reward for his support of FDR in the 1932 campaign. When the appointment provoked outrage from reformers who likened Kennedy regulating the stock market to a fox guarding the henhouse, Roosevelt countered that there was no one better to find the weaknesses in the financial system than someone who had exploited them so well.

In taking up his new post that July, Kennedy rented Marwood, an estate on the Potomac River, in Maryland, with fourteen bedrooms and as many baths, more than enough room to accommodate his wife and children. But Joe left Rose in Bronxville with the younger children and the older children at their various boarding schools. As if to underscore their separate lives, Rose sailed alone for Europe that summer, the trip a twentieth-anniversary gift from Joe.

Joe compensated for the distance with frequent affectionate letters to his wife and to his children, praising the younger ones for a race won or scolding them for a lapse in spelling. He was most focused on the education of his two oldest boys, seeing Joe Jr. settled into Harvard after a year in London studying with Harold Laski, the left-leaning economist and political theorist, and worrying about Jack, whose forays at the London School of Economics and Princeton University had both been cut short by chronic ill health. Her father, Eunice recalled, "was more concerned with the boys' future than the girls," sending her brothers to elite Protestant prep schools where they "would be more involved with people they would have to do business with later in life."

Rose, by contrast, steered the girls to convent boarding schools that replicated her own religious training and classical education with the nuns of the Sacred Heart order. She was preparing her daughters for lives as frugal wives of accomplished Catholic men. "[A]fter all, when girls grow up and marry, it is ordinarily they who actually spend most of the family income on food, clothing, and other necessities. They have to know how to budget, keep track of the dollars, how not to waste," she reasoned. "I have always felt sorry for a couple when the wife is heedless about money, piling up bills, forcing the husband into debt or to work harder and harder to provide the means. It must be very disappointing and discouraging if he has to follow her around pointing out unnecessary expenses."

The two places the Kennedy children could count on seeing their parents together were Hyannis Port, the resort village on Cape Cod where Joe had purchased the large, rambling house on Nantucket Sound that the family had rented for several summers, and Palm Beach, where in 1933 he bought a red-tiled villa on North Ocean Boulevard, with a pool and tennis court and direct access to the Atlantic Ocean.

While Palm Beach was a holiday respite from boarding school for the older children, the younger ones could find themselves enrolled for the winter in the local public school if it suited Rose to have them with her when she spent the cold weather months in Florida, as it did in 1935. In between both camps of siblings, thirteen-year-old Eunice was tutored at home in Palm Beach that winter by Alice Cahill, the family's governess. Other winters, the children returned to school up north after Christmas while Rose lingered for several more weeks enjoying the sun.

Eunice, whom Rose called "one of the most faithful correspondents in the family," began to add colorful details to her southbound letters: Bob had sold four of his rabbits for seventy-five cents apiece; there was a "terrible" blackout in New York one afternoon; Bob had gotten a bugle and was playing it in the house at a deafening volume; Teddy was shouting like a maniac because a big wad of gum was lodged in his hair and Kiko could not get it out.

But more than any place, Hyannis Port was the center of the Kennedys' family life. The white clapboard house with green shutters and two acres of lawn sweeping down to the sea had fourteen rooms, nine baths, wide ocean-facing porches, and a movie theater in the basement. Joe maintained a fleet of sailboats for his children to ply the waters of Nantucket Sound. Eunice was just three when she first dipped her toes into the chilly waters of Lewis Bay. No sensation would ever eclipse the feel of ocean water when she dove into the waves or the taste of salt sea air when she tacked into the wind. Hyannis Port was where Eunice would defy her Puny Eunie nickname, excelling at the sports and parlor games that dominated the siblings' interactions. In a sailboat or on a tennis court, at a game of charades or 20 Questions, she would challenge all comers, especially her brothers.

Here Joe Jr. would teach her to throw a football. Here she would learn to play golf at the Hyannisport Club, a short walk from what the Kennedys called the Big House. Here she would learn to swim at the West Beach Club, where her mother distributed matching bathing caps so she could identify her children in the water. Here she would pile into the blue Rolls-Royce touring car to be driven a short distance inland to Lake Wequaquet for a freshwater swim. Here the more motivated children would wake at dawn to accompany their mother to Mass at St. Francis Xavier Church on South Street or their father on his early morning rides on the Irish horses he stabled at a nearby farm in Osterville.

Eunice was more likely to choose church, but she was no less an acolyte of Joe's catechism of competition. Hyannis Port was where he instilled in his children the primacy of winning. "We don't want any losers around here," he told them. Eunice held her own against the "golden trio" of Joe Jr., Jack, and Kick, learning to race a sailboat as well as anyone and hoping that in so doing, she would command her father's respect. As a skipper, her voice could be heard echoing across the harbor before the start of each race, instructing her crew: "All right now! Everyone say a Hail Mary!"

Joe took less notice than her mother of Eunice's competitive spirit. "As a child, she was not outstanding in her scholastic abilities as her older brothers had been," said Rose. "But she was wonderful in athletics" and empathetic to the less fortunate.

Whether that empathy was the product of natural instinct or maternal mandate is not clear, but what is certain is that Rose fostered in Eunice the mentoring relationship she developed with Rosemary at Hyannis Port and that would follow them, with a long and significant interruption, to their graves. Eunice remembered that her mother "would say to me, 'Will you play with Rosemary?' She wasn't very good, Rosemary, but I played tennis with her. Or she would say, 'Would you take her sailing, racing?' I was quite good at racing in those days, so I handled a boat all right by myself, so I would take Rosemary. Then I'd tell my mother she did well on the boat, and she was pleased."

Eunice racked up more than her share of racing trophies in the 1930s at the Wianno Yacht Club, but she would say with some regret as she aged that she could have beaten Jack in more than a few of those contests had her mother not insisted she take Rosemary along as crew.

"I will admit now that I sometimes yelled at Rosie on the water," Eunice confessed seventy years later. "Many times, when we were headed for the mark, she would let the jib go and turn to me with a smile. 'Get the jib, Rosemary!' 'Rosemary, look, the jib is flapping. Pull it in!' 'For God's sake, Rosemary, pull in the *blasted jib*!!!' Usually Rosemary would then pull in the jib. Despite my tone, she would never lose her somewhat distant but happy smile."

Her father was harder to please. "After one race, Dad asked how I did with Rosie. 'We came in third, Dad.' 'For God's sake,' he thundered, 'can't you do better than that?' Off I went, never quite sure how to win but always sure that Rosie's smile somehow had a value of its own."

She was caught between her parents' dueling expectations, just as she was suspended between the "grown-ups' table" where Joe, Jack, and Kick held sway and the "kids' table" where she cut up Rosemary's meat and supervised her little brothers and sisters. "Pat had a special empathy with Bobby. Jean has always had a special relationship with Teddy," Rose recalled. That left Eunice hovering in that middle space, caring for Rosemary and developing a voice of her own. That voice could sound bossy to her younger siblings or grating to the older ones, but, in her struggle to reconcile her father's rigid notion of success with her mother's pious sense of duty, Eunice was figuring out an alternative way of being a Kennedy.

Luella Hennessey remembered her as fearless and determined to get some of the attention Joe lavished on her older brothers: "If anyone in the family wanted to do something but was afraid to ask, Eunice was the one who would jump up and say, 'I'll speak to Dad about that, don't worry.'"

Joe's prolonged absences in the nation's capital—Roosevelt appointed him chairman of the US Maritime Commission in 1937—increased his godlike status to Eunice, who wrote her father frequent, fawning letters telling him how impressed the nuns and her classmates at her convent school in Connecticut were by whatever he had done or said to merit a mention in the newspapers. It was a pattern she would repeat all her life.

She kept up with gossip about her father by reading Washington Merry Go Round, Drew Pearson's syndicated column, and In the Nation,

Arthur Krock's political column in the *New York Times*. "I have been hearing a number of stories about you in Washington, and I get more surprised every day, as everyone seems to know more about what you are doing than I do," she wrote to him on November 7, 1937, from boarding school. "Are you really going to be Treasury secretary?"

A few months later, she was expressing similar astonishment about the medical news she had just read about her mother. "Of all the surprising things that have occurred in the Kennedy family within the past few months, the greatest shock came when I heard that you had your appendix out," Eunice wrote to Rose.

So accustomed had Eunice become to rumors and a lack of definitive information that she would write to her parents on January 14, 1938: "Dearest Mother and Dad, Everyone that writes wants to know about Dad and are we going and, if so, how long. And I know none of the answers, which they think is quite strange."

Indeed, the Kennedys were going places. FDR would not satisfy Joe's ambition to be secretary of the Treasury, but the president would reward him for his generous campaign support with an appointment no Irish American had ever held—one laden with symbolism for a Bostonian whose Irish roots had rendered him a social pariah in that city's Brahmin preserves.

When the school term ended in April, sixteen-year-old Eunice and nineteen-year-old Rosemary boarded a luxury liner in New York to join the family, already ensconced in London, where Joseph P. Kennedy had presented his diplomatic credentials to King George VI as the new United States ambassador to the Court of Saint James's.

TWO

LONDON

It always seemed to me that if you worried less about your chances of getting into heaven and more about your chances of getting a man . . . it would take a great load off your brother's mind.

—JOHN F. KENNEDY IN A LETTER TO EUNICE, 1938

T FELL TO Joseph P. Kennedy and six-year-old Teddy to meet the *Manhattan* when it docked in Plymouth on April 27, 1938, carrying Eunice and Rosemary to England. The young women were escorted by Eddie Moore, who would serve as Joe's chief secretary in his new post. Even as war clouds gathered over Europe, the US ambassador had less pressing matters to attend to in London than did his wife, Rose, and their eighteen-year-old daughter, Kathleen.

The Kennedy women were caught up in the London "season."

The season, four months of parties, dinner dances, and country house balls that would culminate in the formal presentation of debutantes to King George VI and Queen Elizabeth in July, was to be the Kennedy family's formal introduction to British high society. Accompanying the festivities were fevered rounds of dress and hat shopping, curtsy practicing, and party planning preparatory to the imminent coming out of Kathleen and Rosemary.

As they always had, the Kennedys included Rosie in every rite of passage, but the public focus was squarely on Kick. In the seven weeks before Eunice and Rosemary arrived in London, Kick had already garnered the positive attention of the British press, primed no doubt by the public relations staff Joe was paying out of his own pocket to court just such coverage. Smitten with all the photogenic Kennedy children, London's newspapers touted Joe as "The Father of His Country" and "The U.S.A.'s Nine-Child Envoy."

Joe had just announced that because of the staggering number of requests, young women living in the United States would no longer be eligible to be presented at court. Excluding all but Americans living in England would ensure that his own daughters would rub shoulders with royalty and reap the lion's share of press attention.

Kick certainly did that. *Queen*, a British society magazine, dubbed her "America's Most Important Debutante." Nancy Astor, the American-born wife of Waldorf Astor, and the first woman to serve in the House of Commons, smoothed Kick's passage into the aristocratic world she would soon seduce with her American brand of high spirits. Edward Cavendish, the tenth Duke of Devonshire and Kick's future father-in-law, pronounced her on first meeting "very sharp, very witty, and so sweet in every way." He found her to be "no great beauty, but her smile and her chatty enthusiasm are her salvation," an opinion widely shared. "Of course everybody loved her," Deborah Mitford, a British debutante herself that season, said of the American girl who would one day become her sister-in-law. "It was the effervescent energy, all the things that go with, not beauty, but a kind of liveliness which is very rare."

Eunice was, once again, out of sync with the older siblings to whom she longed to be linked. A year too young to be a debutante in 1938, she would make her own debut the following spring, during the last fraught London season before a world war rendered slightly ridiculous the rituals of British elites. Now she watched with some bemusement as her mother and Kick prattled on about tiaras and tulle, townhouses and country manors, horse racing at Ascot and tennis at Wimbledon. Prettier than Kick, Rosemary had a far more circumscribed experience as a debutante, always chaperoned by a brother or a family retainer to ensure that her intellectual limitations did not expose her, or the family, to ridicule.

Joe and Rose had early fallen into the habit of pairing their older children by gender for competitive appraisal. In 1938 the sickly, bookish Jack could only suffer by comparison with the rugged, outgoing Joe Jr.; the gawky Eunice could only pale next to the vivacious Kathleen. It was an especially unfair contest for Eunice, premised as it was on the questionable proposition that perky and popular were more desirable qualities in a young woman than earnest and intelligent. In truth, the more compatible pairing would have been Eunice and Jack, who shared an intellectual curiosity that was as strong as their physical constitutions were weak.

Page Huidekoper, a young American press aide at the embassy during Joe's tenure in London, was one of many who became fast friends with Kathleen but was quick to acknowledge that the spirited Kick "did not have an intellectual bone in her body." Eunice did, Huidekoper recalled, "but she wasn't as much fun."

Their differences too often defined them as teenagers. Kathleen bantered, unhurried in her courtship of new British friends; Eunice rushed in headlong, peppering people with questions, impatient to get to know them. Kick was petite and graceful, sweeping into a drawing room with a quiet confidence that there could be no more charming girl there than she. At five foot ten, Eunice was tall and ungainly—as awkward in a social setting as she was impressive on a field hockey pitch. As a teenager, she thought her feet were too large, her teeth too prominent, her mouth too wide. But Eunice would grow into the prominent cheekbones and sharp, angular features that suited her strong personality, prompting later comparisons with the movie star Katharine Hepburn.

Come fall, as Kick threw herself into London society, seventeen-year-old Eunice headed to a cloistered world of cold water baths and blue serge uniforms. With her younger sisters Pat, fourteen, and Jean, ten, she was enrolled at the Convent of the Sacred Heart in Roehampton, in southwest London. It was a place of pastoral beauty, with rituals as arcane as any that Kick and Rosemary encountered at Buckingham Palace. Their deep curtsies to the British monarch mirrored the gestures of obeisance by Eunice, Pat, and Jean to Mother Superior at Roehampton.

Eunice had been initiated into the traditions of the Society of the Sacred Heart at Noroton, in Connecticut. The order of then-cloistered nuns, formed by Madeleine Sophie Barat in France in 1800 to educate Catholic girls, had expanded to the United States by 1818 and to England by 1842. To Kick, who attended Noroton before Eunice, the brick mansion at the tip of a narrow peninsula jutting into Long Island Sound had been a prison she could not wait to escape. To Eunice, it had been an inviting world in which smart women wielded power and authority. The nuns on the ten-acre estate on Long Neck Point were a self-sufficient lot, dependent on a man only when the boiler blew or the priest arrived to say daily Mass.

While Kick had balked at being "stuck behind convent walls" and yearned for the house parties and country club dances she enjoyed during vacations in Palm Beach, Eunice wrote to her parents after an initial bout of homesickness, "I really like Noroton quite a bit now."

Rose had sent Kick to the convent in 1933 at age thirteen when she found her spending more time on the telephone than on her studies. "She was quite pretty and was getting altogether too popular with boys," Rose recalled, adding that "Eunice never liked this story because, she said, by comparison it made her sound like a wallflower. At that age, Eunice was never distracted by boys, so I never had this problem."

That anecdote says less about Eunice than it does about Rose. The qualities she cultivated in her daughters—charm, virtue, style, and enough acquaintance with the world to hold one's own in superficial conversation with important men, preferably in French as well as English—were the skills she prized in herself. Most of those qualities held little interest for Eunice, who reported to her parents with some delight when Noroton eliminated the French requirement for third-year students.

A singular character among the Kennedy girls, she was indifferent to the surface markers of femininity, as careless in her appearance as a teenager as the adolescent Jack was in his. It would take marriage to a woman of style for her brother's wardrobe to reflect his public stature. The man Eunice would marry was as polished in his way as Jacqueline Bouvier Kennedy was in hers. But Robert Sargent Shriver's elegance and fastidiousness would never rub off on Eunice, who, well into adulthood, was still receiving churlish notes from her mother chiding her for wearing pants that were "too tight in the seat" or instructing her on "the way some people wear their beads on a blouse."

Eunice was attracted instead to ideas and to action, and she found an outlet for both with the Sacred Heart nuns. She sent newsy letters from Noroton about winning one field hockey game and losing another, snagging a role in a play, having snowball fights and sledding on toboggans, earning a prize in geometry one week and in English another, swimming in the frigid Sound, and learning the rhumba with her roommate. She wrote to her father about "a lecture up here last Thursday by a blind woman on conditions in Japan." The content was "interesting," she reported, but she was more impressed by the lecturer's seeming indifference to her own disability. "The woman herself was remarkable the way she talked and spoke to the girls even though she was completely blind," Eunice wrote.

In London, Roehampton offered Eunice the reassurance of familiar rituals in an unfamiliar setting. The nuns, like those at Noroton, wore floor-length black habits and crimped white bonnets under black veils. They carried book-size wooden signals they clapped to get their charges' attention. They presided over a campus dominated by a hilltop mansion known as Elm Grove, which the Society of the Sacred Heart had purchased in 1850 from a wealthy Protestant reluctantly parting with the estate he and his wife had owned for twenty years.

Four marble Corinthian columns supported a wide portico at the entrance, facing acres of rolling lawns and a small lake studded with rowboats and surrounded by willows and rhododendrons. A tunnel connected the main campus to a small farm on the west side of Roehampton Lane where the nuns grew vegetables and kept chickens, rabbits, and cows.

The nuns repurposed the rooms, turning the ballroom first into a chapel and then a reception room, where parents were welcomed for Sunday afternoon visits. Each room bore the name of a saint—no doubt a source of parental confusion when a daughter promised to meet them in Mary Magdalene rather than in the parlor.

Crowned with a statue of the Blessed Mother, the wing housing the dormitories and classrooms was the main school building when Eunice, Pat, and Jean arrived in 1938 at what was still an idyllic setting. That year, Mother Violet walked her rabbits across campus on leashes, a scene memorialized in a series of sketches by Mother Catherine, who had been an illustrator for *Punch*, the British satirical magazine, before taking her vows; girls boosted one another onto the boundary wall to watch polo matches at the posh Roehampton Club next door; and a thief made off with all the convent's chickens but left behind the cockerel wearing a black bow tie.

Despite the placidity of the surroundings, the Sacred Heart nuns stressed discipline and self-denial. Each day began with the Rising Bell at six thirty, followed by Mass and breakfast. Another bell summoned the girls to the large Study Room, where each was assigned a desk and a number to be inscribed on the inside of each book as insurance against loss or damage. The same number appeared on their uniforms and bed linens, guaranteeing order each week when they retrieved their fresh laundry from the Needlepoint Room.

A snap of the signal would send the girls scurrying to form a line for the silent walk to classes in Catholic doctrine, English, French, history, geography, classics, or mathematics. The sound of the large handbell would call them to the refectory for their midday meal at long wooden tables. An older student presided at each, saying grace and keeping order in the cavernous room dominated by a mural—showing the Blessed Virgin Mary ascending into heaven—and, incongruously, a stag's head "with magnificent antlers," a gift that year from an alumna.

Classes and games of netball and field hockey consumed their afternoons before the bell called the girls first to the evening meal and then to the Study Room for a silent review of the day's lessons, and, finally, to the large communal bathroom to wash up before nightly prayers and bed.

In the bathroom, installed a few years before the Kennedy girls arrived, "the washing basins were arranged on each side, [and] down the middle stood racks on which each child in the senior school had her own hand towel," recalled April O'Leary, who was at school with Eunice and later became a Sacred Heart nun and authored a history of Roehampton School. "It was a crime of the first order, frequently committed by the lazy or the absentminded, to wash one's hands and then move to the towel rail, which left splashes on the floor." No one "at school in the thirties [could] forget Sister Fenwick's "Towel to the basin, first, please, not wet hands to towels," Sister O'Leary wrote of the nun who always referred to the girls by their numbers rather than their names.

Each girl was assigned a curtained cubicle in the dormitory with a bed and a chair on which she laid out her uniform in the manner prescribed. Stockings could be draped over the back of the chair, but the more pious laid them out in the shape of a cross on top of their uniforms. Girls were to dress and undress behind their curtains and, to discourage "particular friendships," were prohibited from walking in twos or visiting one another's cubicles. A nun came with holy water for each student to bless herself before sleep.

The Sacred Heart convent was a closed world, with its own rites and language. Students were "new children"; alumnae were "old children" or "old ones." In a nod to the order's French origins, the midafternoon tea was the *goûter*, and a holiday from studies was a *congé*. Nuns who taught were "Mothers"; nuns who cooked and cleaned were "Sisters," a distinction, no longer made, that reflected the class divisions of the era. Sisters were often the maids of rich, young women who had brought them along when they joined the convent. Nuns interacted with the outside world rarely and always in the company of another nun when circumstances—a visit to a doctor or a dying parent, for instance—necessitated venturing beyond the convent's gates.

Every week, after a local Jesuit had heard their confessions, the girls assembled in the parlor, where the Mother Superior would read each name and hand out a pale-blue card for a "very good" overall performance that week, a dark-blue card for a "good" one, and a buff-colored card for work deemed "indifferent." Worst of all was not to have your name called, indicating effort or behavior so poor it merited no mention. A girl who accumulated enough blue cards might be awarded a blue or pink ribbon, which entitled her to a small treat or school privilege. The ribbon would be withheld, however, if the prospective recipient evinced any pride in her accomplishment. Vanity was a serious sin at convents of the Sacred Heart.

For all of its order and ritual, Roehampton was not immune from the rising tensions in the wider world. No sooner had the new US ambassador arrived in London than Germany occupied Austria, and Adolf Hitler's expansionist designs threatened to engulf the continent and Great Britain itself. Refugees from the Spanish Civil War were among Roehampton's boarders in 1938, as were princesses from the old royal families of Germany, Bavaria, and Luxembourg. The Mother Superior "lavished far more attention on these exiles than the 'commoners' of the school thought necessary," one student told Sister O'Leary.

The school's newspaper recorded preparations the convent was making in the event of war: "In September 1938 the school had an exciting start when the war scare brought gasmasks to be fitted and a wonderful rearrangement of the cellars, with electric lighting, matted floors, and accommodation for us all; rumors, too, there were of preparation for a general exodus, if necessary."

It wasn't quite yet. Eunice shared in the school's athletic victories that year as a member of the older girls' field hockey squad, playing with such vocal enthusiasm that her teammates had to caution her that shouting on the pitch was considered a breach of decorum at Roehampton. Reports in US newspapers that Eunice had been voted both the most popular girl at Roehampton and the girl who had contributed the most to the school were likely the invention of her father's public relations team. Seventy-five years later, a classmate laughed heartily at the idea of such awards. "No such thing," said Dorothy Bell, who sat beside Eunice in the last row of the Study Room. "That's an American thing, isn't it? Most popular? We certainly did not do that here!"

Equally suspect is the claim in *Parents'* magazine that at Roehampton Eunice had "made herself a suit—coat and skirt—which she can wear anywhere with pride." She had written to her parents only the year before from Noroton that "I have just finished trying to sew, but I am not so good at this point."

Joe did not record the girls' names in the official leather-bound school register, but their presence hardly went unnoticed. The Kennedy girls looked "like birds of paradise, bringing a glamour and worldliness that contrasted with the attitude of the dour daughters of displaced European aristocrats and English girls in tweeds," one classmate recalled.

In Dorothy Bell's memory, it was not Eunice's glamour that attracted notice; it was her piety. Eunice's devoutness marked her "as someone we all knew would become a nun," she said, citing Eunice's manifest devotion to the Virgin Mary as singular even in a convent school that encouraged daily recitation of the rosary. Dorothy became a Sacred Heart nun herself in 1947, after serving in China with the British Foreign Service during World War II, and the head of school at Roehampton in 1969. "I was more sure of her vocation in our school days than I was my own," she said.

It was not uncommon for Catholic schoolgirls—even wealthy heiresses—to wonder whether God meant for them to live out their faith by taking vows of poverty, chastity, and obedience. The Sacred Heart nuns certainly encouraged them to listen prayerfully for a call to the religious life. To hear that call was a mark of holiness; to spurn it was to turn one's back on God and the church. Eunice's prayerfulness went beyond the usual, according to Sister Bell. "She certainly spent a lot more time than the rest of us in chapel," where other classmates remembered her prostrate on the cold floor of Our Lady's Chapel, her arms outstretched in supplication.

Her brother Jack wrote teasingly from Harvard about her preoccupation with saying novenas and saving his soul after Eunice reminded him in a "charming letter" to remember to fulfill his First Friday obligation to attend Mass. "It always seemed to me that if you worried less about your chances of getting into heaven and more about your chances of getting a man . . . it would take a great load off your brother's mind," he wrote.

Her father, too, noted that Eunice was "going wild" with anticipation "as it becomes nearer to the time to receive her Child of Mary Medal" for special devotion to the Blessed Mother, on December 8, the Feast of the Immaculate Conception. The service, which Rose described as "the most mystic, most beautiful, most inspiring ceremony" of the Sacred Heart school year, culminated in a procession into the chapel by the select group of girls who were being inducted into the Child of Mary sodality, all dressed in white and carrying white lilies. From that day forward, for the rest of her life, Eunice would write "e. de. m," for *enfant de Marie*, next to her signature on all her personal correspondence.

Her father's diplomatic post provided an unexpected opportunity for her to serve the nuns she so admired as well as an early lesson in how to exert influence in her powerful family. More than two dozen nuns of the Society of the Sacred Heart were trapped that spring in Barcelona, enduring heavy bombardment during the Spanish Civil War. Six had died in an air raid. Alerting her father to the plight of the nuns, who were the subject of the students' daily prayers at Roehampton, Eunice spurred Joe to action. He met with Prime Minister Neville Chamberlain and Foreign Secretary Lord Halifax to plead their cause and, after months of negotiations with Spanish officials, prevailed upon the British to send a destroyer to evacuate the twenty-eight women. It was to Kennedy that the Roehampton School Association gave credit.

Perhaps to show their gratitude or simply to accommodate the circumstances that had brought the Kennedy girls to Roehampton, the nuns waived the usual requirement that boarders remain at school every weekend. This freed them to participate more fully in life at the US Embassy and at 14 Prince's Gate, the ambassador's thirty-six-room residence in London.

Joe made certain that his children maximized the opportunities afforded them by his appointment to the Court of Saint James's. For the older boys, that meant broadening their political education. He dispatched Joe Jr. on a tour of Europe before sending him to Paris to apprentice for US ambassador William Bullitt. He sent Jack back to Harvard for his junior year that fall but arranged for him to return to London at the end of term to travel as Joe Jr. had done and to research his senior thesis about Britain's unpreparedness for war. Joe would arrange in 1940 to have Jack's thesis published as a book, *Why England Slept*.

For the girls, opportunity meant entrée into the most rarefied social circles and travel designed to broaden their cultural appreciation more than their political perspective. Kick had been the immediate beneficiary in the spring of 1938. Her parents hosted a dinner for sixty at the US Embassy, followed by a coming-out party for Kick and Rosemary for more than three hundred guests. The celebration solidified Kick's place at the top of her debutante class, a status only reinforced as she moved from country house balls to garden parties at Buckingham Palace and the races at Ascot and Sussex Downs. Central to all those activities for Kick was Billy Cavendish, the eldest son of the Duke and Duchess of Devonshire, with whom she had quickly fallen in love. Billy was in line to preside one day over his family's eight homes, including an abbey in Scotland, a castle in Ireland, and a mansion in Derbyshire known as Chatsworth, where his family had been Anglican stalwarts for generations, a reality that could only have alarmed Kick's Catholic mother.

When the social bustle of the London season subsided, the Kennedys headed to the French Riviera to engage in the vigorous play they had perfected in Hyannis Port. Sailing. Golf. Tennis. Jumping from the cliffs above Cap d'Antibes into the clear-blue Mediterranean. Swimming at Eden Roc, the saltwater pool carved out of the cliff at the edge of the sea.

Joe had leased a villa adjacent to the Hôtel du Cap, where the Kennedys indulged their fascination with celebrities by dining with gossip columnist Elsa Maxwell and movie stars Beatrice Lillie and Marlene Dietrich, who began an affair with Joe that summer despite the presence of her husband, Rudolf Sieber, their thirteen-year-old daughter, Maria, and Marlene's lover Erich Maria Remarque, the author of *All Quiet on the Western Front*—to say nothing of Rose and the nine Kennedy children.

An only child, Maria was fascinated by the enormous Kennedy clan. "They looked and were so American," she recalled. "All had smiles that never ended, with such perfect teeth each of them could have advertised toothpaste." Lonely in the company of her mother's adult entourage, Maria was soon spending her days with the Kennedys, admiring "handsome" Joe Jr. and Jack, "the glamour boy," but wary of Eunice, whom she found to be "opinionated, not to be crossed, the sharp mind of an intellectual achiever." Rosemary, "the damaged child amidst these effervescent and quick-witted children, was my friend. Perhaps being two misfits, we felt comfortable in each other's company. We would sit in the shade, watching the calm sea, holding hands."

In September Joe sent his older children traveling. Kick and Jack went off to Austria; Eunice, Rosemary, Pat, and Bobby headed to Ireland and Scotland with the Moores and the governess, Elizabeth Dunn. Eunice reported to her father that on their first day in Ireland, they had kissed the Blarney Stone, "so we should be full of it when you see us next." From Scotland, she wrote to say that her camera was "working wonderfully and so is my diet."

Travel was one of the benefits Joe could offer his family in Europe, and Rose seized any opportunity to do so. That Christmas, when Joe was in Washington to consult with President Roosevelt and Jack was at Harvard, suffering from the stomach problems that would recur all his life, the rest of the family flew to Switzerland for skiing and ice skating in St. Moritz. "Joe has found no girl for himself yet, although he has gone to almost every hotel in St. Moritz," Eunice wrote to her father about his eldest son, assuring Joe Sr. "we still have some hope for him."

No outing impressed Eunice as much as the Kennedy family's trip to Rome for the installation of Pope Pius XII in March 1939. While students at Roehampton gathered in Mary Magdalene to listen to the live radio broadcast from the Vatican, the Kennedys were there—with the exception of Joe Jr., who was in Madrid monitoring the Spanish Civil War. The new pope, formerly Cardinal Eugenio Pacelli, was a Kennedy family acquaintance. He had come for tea in Bronxville three years before when he was secretary of state for the Vatican. Joe had arranged for him to visit President Franklin D. Roosevelt at his home in Hyde Park, New York, and the cardinal followed up with a house call. Rose kept the sofa on which he had sat cordoned off with a velvet rope.

Eunice, filled with adolescent religious ardor and contemplating life as a nun, was overcome by the family's private audience with the new pontiff, writing of the encounter in overwrought prose that bordered on the ecstatic, if not the hysterical: "On bended knee, I grasped his outstretched hand which combined the grace of a debutante, the strength of a ruler, and the gentleness of a child. Suddenly joy and peace radiating from this Man took possession of my being, and as I looked into the intelligent and sympathetic eyes which screened a floorless inner beauty, my thoughts turned to the Saviour. For if kneeling before the human man could give me such a feeling of sublime peace and Christian love, what then when I kneel before Christ? Yes! I want to die!"

Earlier that spring, Eunice had left Roehampton behind to prepare for her social debut, a prospect she faced with a mix of excitement and trepidation. When she visited Pat and Jean at the convent in May, "all the girls thought I was so lucky coming out, but don't I know it," she wrote in her diary. Decades later, Eunice would say that lucky was the last thing she had been feeling. "I hated those parties," she said. "They were terrible. I'd go into the ladies' room and wait for the dance to get over and talk to somebody. You'd go hide in there; anything to fill in the twenty minutes of the dance. Then you'd go back, and maybe your card was filled for the next dance. Then you're all right for a while, and then—bam—you'd go back into the ladies' room."

Almost everything she did that season prompted comparison with the more informal social life she preferred at Cape Cod, where summer dances at the Wianno Yacht Club were casual affairs and visits with friends were more spontaneous and relaxed. "Would it be funny if I took a maid with me when I went on a weekend in America," she scoffed in one diary entry after recording her discomfort with having a personal servant look after her clothes during country house weekends in England. "American dances are much gayer," she observed after attending a dance with Joe Jr. as her escort, on May 16. "Everyone at these dances behaves their best cool and formal."

At the horse races at Epsom Downs, too, she noted how reserved the English were after she placed a winning eight-shillings bet on Blue Peter and had to repress the urge to let out a whoop: "The Derby was terrifically exciting, although no one gets 'het up' during the race as we do in the U.S.A."

Her diary entries reveal Eunice to be, at turns, amused and annoyed by all the fuss related to the season. The dinner dances that lasted until the small hours of the morning. The frequent "deb" luncheons with girls so numerous and apparently so forgettable that she often left a blank in her diary where their names should have been. The cricket and polo matches in the rain. The endless fittings for evening gowns, at Paquin and Molyneux, for afternoon dresses, for tweeds, for hats, for an ermine wrap. "It takes about five times as long to buy clothes in this country as in America," she complained.

Her tone is wry and self-deprecating, that of a teenage girl swept up in the pageantry but not swept away by it as Kick had been. She is observer as much as participant, making notes on how other young women comport themselves to guide her own self-conscious steps. She took her "lovely mop" to Elizabeth Arden to be set in curlers. She "packed" for a weekend at yet another country estate and then admitted the maid actually had done the packing.

Eunice did get "dressed in great excitement," the night in May when the king and queen came to dine with the Kennedys. Deliveries of fresh strawberries and baby orchids had arrived from Paris early in the afternoon, and her father had set up the projector in a back room for an after-dinner screening of *Goodbye, Mr. Chips*, which had not yet been released. "It was a wonderful night," Eunice wrote in her diary, even though her mother had seated her at the children's table at the end of the dining room. Seventy-five Londoners, who had waited throughout the evening on the sidewalk, cheered the king and queen as they departed.

The equally anticipated four days of races at Ascot in mid-June were plagued with bad weather, but, Eunice noticed, "everyone dresses in their best clothes, a different dress each day, and parades them off at Ascot under the pretense of watching the horse races. Many, however, go for the horse races, as the races are excellent. Watched the 6 races and heard plenty of 'hot tips,' which were colder than ice."

The day she attended Ascot with her father and Clare Boothe Luce, the playwright and wife of Henry Luce, the founder and publisher of *Time* magazine, it was cold and rainy, but Eunice refused to wear a coat. "Not having all those fittings in vain to have my dress covered," she reasoned. In her diary, Eunice mangled Luce's name and showed no sign of seeing anything untoward in her father's relationship with "Mrs. Lucas, author of the 'The Women,' a very successful play at the present time in London and America." Rose was away, and Joe had been escorting Clare around London to the theater and to the races, as well as to bed.

As she had as a child, Eunice felt her mother's absence keenly. Rose had been a constant presence for the confident Kick during her debut the spring before, but just as the more reticent Eunice became consumed by debutante luncheons, country house weekends, and horse races, her mother returned to Hyannis Port for an extended stay. "Mother sailed for America today on the *Normandie*," Eunice wrote in her diary, "so life isn't as cheerful as usual."

Like all of the Kennedy children, Eunice had a complicated relationship with her parents. She admired them both beyond measure and without question. Her father was the smartest man she had ever met, and her mother the most glamorous woman. Any behavior on their part that might challenge that conviction went unnoticed or ignored. Any small act of kindness by Rose only confirmed her profound goodness in Eunice's eyes. When Eunice's bathtub overflowed and dampened a few of Rose's dresses and hats in a closet the floor below, Eunice braced for a reprimand that never came. "Mother wasn't a bit angry about last night. She was calmer than any of the others, but then Mother is amazing anyhow," she wrote in her diary not long before Rose left her to face most of the London season alone.

The pace of Eunice's social life left little time to brood about her mother's absence. She played tennis with Spencer Tracy when the actor visited London, finding him "terribly nice, a little older than I thought." She watched Bobby Riggs defeat Elwood Cooke at what the British press called the "American Wimbledon" because both finalists were US citizens. She accompanied her father to the BBC Symphony Orchestra to see Toscanini conduct and to the Royal Opera House to hear *Don Giovanni*. She went to see *Dracula*, a play she found "awful, awful spooky," especially after a woman in the audience fainted. "Still it was great fun."

She went to the ballet and to Parliament, where she observed Prime Minister's Questions, when the head of the government is required to field often-hostile volleys from the opposition. Sitting with other visitors in the Strangers' Gallery, Eunice was amused to watch members of the House of Commons all "start to speak at once," except for Lady Astor, who "spent most of the time opening her mail."

Rose returned to London in time to join Joe in greeting the king and queen at Waterloo Station, fresh from their own visit to the United States, where they had enjoyed an especially American lunch at Hyde Park when the president and Mrs. Roosevelt served hot dogs.

That night, the Kennedys hosted Eunice's coming-out party in the same mirrored ballroom at the US Embassy where Kick and Rosemary had debuted the spring before. She wore a peach gown by Paquin and a new diamond bracelet. The crowd was smaller than the year before, though, at 225, not truly small. The Bert Ambrose swing band entertained a no less raucous group of dancers, and Jack cut an impressive figure on the dance floor in white tie and tails. He stayed up with Eunice until five thirty, having breakfast and talking. "Wonderful party," she wrote in her diary. "Everyone says Best party of the year & I really think so. Danced the Big Apple about 10 times, everybody yelling and screaming from 1:00–4:00 running in snake lines through the halls. Mother had to stop it at 4:00."

At Berkeley Castle on July 2, Eunice explored with Joe Jr. and Jack the twelfth-century stronghold's two dungeons, rode horses, and played tennis. But no party was more extravagant than the coming-out ball for Sarah Spencer Churchill on July 7 at Blenheim Palace, the Oxfordshire estate of the Duke and Duchess of Marlborough. A thousand guests were in attendance, including the debutante's cousin Winston Churchill, the Duke and Duchess of Kent, Anthony Eden, and Jack and Eunice Kennedy. The grounds were illuminated by twenty-four floodlights, bathing in a soft glow the terrace beside the lake where the young people dined. The palace was so enormous that Eunice contented herself with a tour from Sarah of the stables and the chicken coops. "It would take hours to see the whole house," she concluded.

Massive stone palaces have their disadvantages, Eunice discovered in the middle of the night: "Last night I awoke about 6 times as I was so cold," she wrote, describing how she wore her overcoat on top of her nightgown "and yet remained freezing until 9:00 when I got up."

For her eighteenth birthday later that month, she had dinner with Joe Jr., Jack, and Kick at Café de Paris in London and saw the play *Alien Corn*, based on a short story by Somerset Maugham, whom the family had met the previous summer on the French Riviera.

Two days later, Eunice rode to Buckingham Palace with her mother and father to be presented at court, carrying a fan that Queen Mary, the mother of King George VI, had sent as a gift. She thought her dress by Paquin "really lovely, white with a big hoop and a number of white bows on the front . . . White dress, white flowers, gloves, and feathers in my hair. Also had a white train. Photographers took quite a number of pictures of Mother and I . . . One of greatest evenings in England."

In her ivory tulle and crinoline gown with its long satin train, she was not out to land a duke or a marquess. Marriage, on the minds of many of the English debutantes whose beaux would soon see war, was not on hers. Eunice could not imagine herself or her siblings married; they were having too much fun together. She knew that Kick was spending a lot of time with Billy Cavendish, but Eunice would laugh later that summer when a reporter for the *Boston Globe* called to ask whether they were engaged. "Certainly not true," she told her diary.

She attracted plenty of male attention herself during the season. Hugh Fraser, a future Conservative Party member of Parliament, found her funny and a little fresh. A soldier at Buckingham Palace invited her "to the barracks for lunch, but I had to refuse, for debs in this country go nowhere unchaperoned." She also "received an invitation from a navy boy to go on his ship for tea and to watch a navy drill." She spurned him, too.

When the debutante parties came to an exhausting end, the Kennedys went off again to the French Riviera. The pace hardly slackened. After a particularly energetic game of water polo, Eunice noted that "Jack almost drowned me." She visited a Trappist monastery and ran afoul of a local Catholic parishioner who "bawled me out for appearing in shorts at church."

Joe had leased a villa on the Côte d'Azur called the Domaine de Ranguin, but the approach of war cast a pall over the Kennedys' days of golf, tennis, sailing, and water skiing, a sport Eunice mastered that summer. Joe Jr. and Kick arrived with Hugh Fraser from Madrid, bringing stories of the fallout from the Nationalist victory in the Spanish Civil War. On August 21, Germany and the Soviet Union announced a nonaggression pact, sealing the fates of Poland and Britain, which had committed to intervene on Poland's behalf if Germany invaded. Joe returned to London to confer with Prime Minister Neville Chamberlain; Jack and his Harvard roommate set off on a brief fact-finding trip to Germany, where, Eunice noted, Jack found "85% of people for Hitler, 15% are not. Outside of Germany or Germans, everyone seems to hate him."

Summoned back to London, the Kennedys prepared to divide themselves among ships and planes to return to the United States. Joe would stay, as would Rosemary, who had been thriving since her convent school near the embassy had been evacuated to Belmont House, a pastoral estate in Hertfordshire, thirty miles outside of London, where she would be safe from German bombers.

"The whole issue rests with 1 man, Hitler," Eunice wrote in her diary, where she also noted the appearance of balloon barrages above London to thwart German dive bombers, the silence in the streets—the children having been evacuated to the countryside—the car fenders painted white so they could be seen in a blackout, the trenches dug in Hyde Park, and the instructions for air raids posted in the Underground.

Both the weighty and the mundane occupied her thoughts during those last days of peace. She nearly fell from her horse in Rotten Row when the horse stepped into a rabbit hole. Eunice did fall from her bicycle, opening up a cut on her arm that took three stitches to close. She went to the tailors to pick out a tweed. "Don't know if it is to be for Scotland or New York," she wrote. "Depends on Mr. Hitler. War or not."

It would not be for Scotland. On September 3, two days after German troops crossed into Poland, Britain declared war. While Joe met with Chamberlain in advance of his speech, Rose, Joe Jr., Jack, and Kathleen went to Parliament to hear the prime minister tell the nation and the world, "Everything that I have worked for, everything that I have hoped for, everything I have believed in during my public life has crashed into ruins." Though her diary is filled with her thoughts on the deepening European crisis, Eunice did not accompany her siblings. She was not with them when a photographer snapped a celebrated photograph of the glamorous trio of Kick, Jack, and Joe Jr. striding through the London streets on their way to witness the most historic moment of their young lives. Eighteen-year-old Eunice had been left at home with the younger children.

In the next few days, Joe scrambled to get his family passage back to New York. Jack flew home on the *Yankee Clipper*. Pat, Jean, and Teddy went with Luella Hennessey on the *Manhattan*. Joe Jr. boarded the British ship *Mauretania*. Rose, Eunice, Kick, and Bobby sailed from Southampton on the *Washington*.

The Kennedys' extraordinary sojourn in London was at an end.

"Kick doesn't want to go at all and neither do I," a despondent Eunice wrote in her diary, calling her sister "heartbroken" and their situation "so sad." Kick wanted to stay to be near the man she loved. Eunice wanted to stay to help the war effort. But neither would think of defying her parents. "I want to be a nurse or driver, but family says no," Eunice wrote. "They want Kick and I to go to college. What a puzzle. God help us."

THREE

FROM THE SACRED HEART TO
STANFORD UNIVERSITY

Give me the Cape and a boat, man or no man, I don't care.

—EUNICE KENNEDY, LETTER TO HER FATHER, 1939

T CAPACITY, THE *Washington* usually carried 1,040 passengers, but as the transatlantic liner pulled away from the Southampton docks on September 12, 1939, there were 1,746 people on board, sleeping seven to a cabin. The swimming pool had been emptied and outfitted with cots, as had the lounge, the gym, the ballroom, and the post office.

British submarines formed a protective corridor in the English Channel to shield the departing ship, the sides of which had been painted with enormous American flags to identify it as the vessel of a noncombatant. There was good reason for caution. On September 3, only hours after war was declared, a German U-boat had torpedoed the *Athenia*, an unarmed British passenger liner. As the ship sank off the coast of Ireland, 1,306 people were rescued, but 112, including 30 Americans, died. Five survivors of the *Athenia* sinking were on board the *Washington*.

Spying torpedo netting in the channel as she strolled the deck with Rose, Kick, and Bobby, Eunice understood the danger, but she was cheered when several passengers stopped them to say "they felt safe, as the American ambassador's wife is on board."

Eunice might well have imagined that the parents she idealized possessed magical protective powers. In letters to her mother and father throughout her adolescence, she heaped praise on them, conveying the admiration she heard from, or projected onto, unidentified nuns, classmates, and strangers. This trip would be no exception. On their fifth night at sea, she wrote to her father: "Everyone we have met on the boat, even the young people, think you have done and are doing a marvelous job."

There was something surreal about this return trip across the Atlantic. Their hasty evacuation from London and the congested conditions on board did not keep Eunice or her siblings from finding it all "great fun." They attended daily Mass and played games of deck tennis, shuffleboard, and ping pong. She and Bobby played catch with "a big medicine ball" so vigorously she reported she "almost got my chest crushed." They resumed the celebrity stalking that had been a favorite pastime in Cap d'Antibes, spotting the novelist Thomas Mann, the impresario Sol Hurok, the violinist Fritz Kreisler, and the movie star Robert Montgomery, who had been assigned a cot in the drained swimming pool.

One hundred forty Mormon missionaries, returning home from a year of proselytizing abroad, were on board, as was Democratic senator Robert R. Reynolds of North Carolina, a staunch isolationist, who had just been in Paris and seen soldiers boarding trains for the front. The passengers had to ration their bath water and eat in shifts, but it was not all privation on the *Washington*. The *Ocean Press* was distributed every day with the latest baseball scores and war news from the United Press wire. The dinner menu for the last night of the voyage included iced beluga caviar, clear turtle soup, and tenderloin steak with béarnaise sauce.

The day before they docked in New York, Eunice spent time circulating a letter for signature among the passengers thanking Captain Giles C. Stedman, his officers, and the crew for making them as comfortable during the six-day crossing as circumstances allowed. "Some refused," she noted. "Said they thought trip hadn't been well managed." More than a thousand did sign the letter, which was presented to the captain as they steamed into New York Harbor.

It was destined to be a difficult reentry. How could it be otherwise? The boys Eunice and Kick had danced with just weeks before at debutante balls had already been called up for military service. Many of the debs had signed up to work in munitions factories or as nurses or ambulance drivers. There was an unnerving disconnect for the returning

Kennedys between the danger in London and the relative tranquility in New York. At home, the war was happening three thousand miles away, to somebody else.

"It can't be eighteen months since we were on this boat going in the other direction," Kick wrote to her father from the ship the day they docked. "It all seems like a beautiful dream."

That prewar dream would turn to wartime nightmare for the American ambassador. Joe's support of Conservative prime minister Neville Chamberlain's policy of appeasement toward Hitler had associated him with the failed Munich Pact that, a year before, had ceded German-speaking regions of Czechoslovakia to the dictator in the vain hope it would stop more annexations. Joe's voluble defeatism now that war had arrived further undermined his standing in England, but it underscored the Kennedy patriarch's overarching goal: to keep America, and his sons, out of war.

In 1939 most Americans shared Joe's opposition to US entry into the war. Still in the grip of the Great Depression, the people of the United States, more than 17 percent of whom were unemployed, were focused on domestic economic recovery, not international affairs. The cost, in blood and treasure, of World War I had soured the public on the "entangling alliances" George Washington had warned against in 1796 in his farewell address. In 1935, Congress had passed the first Neutrality Act, barring the United States from selling arms to belligerent nations. Strong public support for the measure had overcome President Franklin D. Roosevelt's opposition to the bill. But two years later, when Congress revisited the topic, the president lobbied successfully for a temporary provision to permit the sale of goods, other than armaments, to a country at war if the buyer paid cash and transported the material on non-American ships. The so-called "cash-and-carry" clause permitted Great Britain to buy oil and other raw materials from the United States, providing indirect US support for the war effort against Hitler.

Or rather the cash-and-carry provision *would have* had it not expired by 1939; that March Congress had spurned Roosevelt's pleas to restore cash-and-carry after Hitler occupied Czechoslovakia. Come autumn, however, after the invasion of Poland, Roosevelt found more receptive ears. Two days after returning home to Bronxville, Eunice tuned in to a live radio broadcast of President Roosevelt's address to a joint session of Congress to hear his appeal to reinstate and expand cash-and-carry by lifting the embargo on arms sales. While pledging to keep the nation out of war, Roosevelt argued that the United States could not stand by and do nothing. "Destiny first made us, with our sister nations in this hemisphere, joint heirs of European culture," he said. "Fate seems now to compel us to assume the task of helping to maintain in the Western World a citadel wherein that civilization may be kept alive." On November 2, after a long and acrimonious debate, the House voted 243 to 181 to give the president what he wanted.

That same month, the fact that the Kennedys' oldest daughter had remained in England attracted the attention of the *Boston Globe*, which requested an interview with Rosemary, then living contentedly in a convent of Assumption nuns in Hertfordshire, thirty miles northwest of London. Joe handled the inquiry by manufacturing a story line for Rosemary that would go unchallenged for more than two decades. "When my mother and the rest of the children left England, I thought it was my duty to remain behind with my father," she informed the newspaper in a letter actually written by Eddie Moore. "I have always had serious tastes and understand that life is not given us just for enjoyment."

She had earned her teaching degree the previous year, the letter claimed falsely and had remained in England to keep house for her father and to teach children at the convent school. In fact, she, too, was in the care of the nuns, who encouraged Rosemary to read to the children as a way of bolstering her limited skills and her even lower self-esteem. She saw her father on occasional weekends and the Moores more regularly.

Eunice had begun her first semester at Manhattanville College of the Sacred Heart in New York City that fall. Founded in 1847 as a boarding school in West Harlem for the daughters of socially prominent Catholic families, Manhattanville was accredited in 1917 to grant undergraduate and graduate degrees. Rose had graduated in 1910, when Manhattanville was still an academy. It was the logical next stop on Eunice's educational path.

In a letter on November 5, Eunice told her father it was good to be home, "although we all miss you, Rosie, and dear old England. Everyone thinks I have a decided English accent, and the priest asked me in confession if I were an English girl. As you know, I am at Manhattanville boarding and I am really crazy about it. Every time I turn the corner at that place a nun grabs me by the arm and tells me how wonderful you are and are doing in England and how marvelous it was that you got the nuns out of Spain. I hope they remember that when they are looking at my exam papers."

She had had a shaky start of term, sick with what she, Rose, and family nurse Luella Hennessey referred to as "her difficulty." Eunice was hospitalized often throughout her life, sometimes for "operations," the nature of which are not disclosed in her diary entries or in the family's correspondence. After one undated operation, her blood pressure dropped dangerously low, and, Hennessey said, "She was diagnosed the same as with Jack: Addison's disease."

It is not clear who determined Eunice had the disease or when, but Jack was diagnosed in 1947 with the life-threatening autoimmune disorder. It occurs when the adrenal glands fail to produce enough cortisol, a hormone that helps regulate metabolism, blood sugar levels, and the balance of salt and water in the body, which controls blood pressure. Eunice exhibited many symptoms, including fatigue, weight loss, and mood swings. Like Jack, she took corticosteroids to compensate for her malfunctioning adrenal glands. The drugs enhance energy and physical stamina but can also thin bones and weaken the body's immune system. That left Eunice vulnerable to the broken bones and infections that plagued her later in life.

By mid-November 1939, mother and daughter reported that Eunice was much improved. She had even gained a few pounds. "Everyone at College loves Eunice, as everyone did at the launching and every place else," Rose wrote to Joe. "She certainly has the nuns gaga . . . She likes college very much but is incredibly busy."

She had been elected captain of the freshman swim team, had earned her driver's license, and, after three weeks of tryouts, won a spot on the tennis team in the spring. Before the fall term ended, she was no longer living on campus, however. Rose had hauled her out of the small single room she had occupied near the chapel and taken her home to Bronxville. "Mother heard a rumor there were a few mice running around there, and she took me out so fast that I couldn't even explain, although she said no explanations needed," Eunice told her father. The chauffeur drove Eunice to and from school thereafter.

She filled her letters to her lonely, embattled father in London with news of her brothers' and sisters' romances. "As for myself, there is little to report," she said. A young man named Basil Harris had taken her to a dance at Georgetown University but she assured Joe that "my heart still belongs to Daddy" and that "all the boys down there think you should run for president." Her classmates were excited about an upcoming dance at Manhattanville, an eagerness she did not share. "Give me the Cape and a boat, man or no man, I don't care," she wrote.

She was too busy for romance. At Manhattanville, Eunice participated for the first time in the direct social action that would inform her Catholicism and transform her life. It was not the radical activism of Dorothy Day, a leader of the Catholic Worker Movement who embraced the poverty of those she served, but it was Eunice's first contact with people in need. Beyond its classical curriculum, the Manhattanville that Eunice entered in the fall of 1939 bore little resemblance to the conservative finishing school Rose had attended thirty years before. Social work had displaced needlework as a serious emphasis.

In May 1933, the two-hundred-plus students at the college had adopted the "Manhattanville Resolutions," denouncing prejudice and pledging to work for racial justice. Five years later, Mother Grace Dammann, the president of the college, admitted the first black student to Manhattanville, a move that garnered the support of 80 percent of the student body but the vociferous objections of a small group of prominent alumnae.

Mother Dammann was not deterred. In "Principles vs. Prejudices," a Class Day address to alumnae on May 31, 1938, she said the opposition of so many alumnae to the admission of a single black girl would have been "a humiliation to us as educators" had their letters not been outnumbered by so many notes of support. "The day has gone by when we can blithely live as compartmentalized Catholics, with our political, business, social activities in airtight compartments functioning separately like parts of a well-oiled machine. Catholicism is nothing if it is not a *life*, unified, coordinated to its end, building up the entire personality into a likeness of Christ."

That life had to be part of the world beyond the convent gates, and that is where Mother Dammann sent her charges, who, in 1939, included a receptive eighteen-year-old Eunice Kennedy, ready to experience this more active expression of her faith than the contemplative Catholicism she had explored at Roehampton. The Barat Settlement House on the Lower East Side was celebrating its thirty-fifth anniversary during Eunice's freshman year. Sixty-eight students from Manhattanville, including Eunice, spent time every week working in the medical clinic and nursery school or teaching classes in religion, athletics, knitting, crocheting, dressmaking, embroidery, art, and music.

Eunice volunteered as well at Casita Maria, a five-year-old settlement house in East Harlem. It had been founded by Catholic Charities and was run largely by volunteers coordinated by Elizabeth Sullivan, a young, single Manhattanville graduate who was a fifth-grade public school teacher. The four-story house was only twelve feet wide, but, within its walls, there was a nursery school and classes in sewing, cooking, music, and English for the six hundred Puerto Rican adults and children who visited each week for everything from Boy Scout troop meetings to painting courses taught by eight artists paid by the Work Projects Administration.

Doing good works interested Eunice more than some of her required courses that first year at Manhattanville. In Eunice's memory, Rose had been a tough taskmaster who brooked no excuse for academic sloth. But the evidence is otherwise. Rose paid a visit to Manhattanville during Eunice's freshman year to ask that she be excused from Latin and mathematics, the two courses she least enjoyed. The written response from Mother Mary Patterson was unambiguous. "It means something to graduate from Manhattanville," her lengthy reply to Rose began. Were she to waive requirements on request, "we should forfeit our standing and more or less rank with Junior Colleges."

Praising Eunice for showing "character and intelligence in her rapid and peaceful adjustment to strenuous college life," Mother Patterson did not yield. Rather than reduce her workload, Mother Patterson suggested Eunice join the freshman debate club for "the training in speaking, rapid and clear thinking 'on your feet,' seeing the point or the weakness of an argument, and framing good questions and answers to them."

When not intervening with the nuns on Eunice's behalf, Rose was monitoring her daughter's weight, telling Joe on March 28, 1940, that she intended to stop Eunice from "playing tennis in the tournaments" if she lost another ounce. Eunice must have gained sufficient weight to appease her mother because, with her partner, Sonia E. Wise from York, Pennsylvania, she won a doubles championship at Manhattanville that spring and then traveled to Cleveland to play in the Lake Erie College Championships in June.

"The chief topic of conversation during the trip was your brains and what a wonderful job you were doing. Also how young looking Mother was," she wrote to her father, her role as parental cheerleader in chief by now well established. "You can imagine how upset Mother was when I told her this. She almost jumped over the table in her excitement." Eunice was not immune to flattery herself. She came home to Hyannis Port clutching a newspaper article that described her as "rivaling the beauty of Hedy Lamarr," the movie star. "We all nearly collapsed, and Eunice hasn't heard anything but 'Miss Lamarr' since," Pat wrote to their father.

Across the Atlantic, the Nazis' relentless advance through Western Europe left Joe no choice but to get Rosemary out of harm's way. He did so reluctantly, knowing this was the first placement that had yielded some genuine happiness for his daughter. Rosemary had embraced the loving care of Mother Eugenie Isabel and Dorothy Gibbs, the young woman the Kennedys hired to be both her tutor and companion. She responded positively to the less-structured Montessori teaching methods used at the convent. Encouraging children of different ages and abilities to learn alongside one another in an open classroom, the nuns nurtured each child to learn at her own pace. It was a far cry from the pressure Rosemary had been under to conform to the Kennedys' high standards of achievement.

In this setting, the much-older Rosemary behaved toward the younger children just as Dr. Maria Montessori, the Italian physician and educational innovator, might have predicted: she mentored them, supervising their play, serving them at lunch, and reading to them the simple storybooks she was able to understand herself. Acting as an informal teacher's aide, Rosemary grew in confidence and self-control, although Mother Isabel told Joe she still had to be cautioned to be less "fierce" with the children.

Convinced though he was that Rosemary could thrive only if she lived a quieter life, away from her driven siblings, Joe sent her home with the Moores, hopeful that she would be able to return one day to Mother Isabel's care. It had been a year since Rosemary had lived with her family, and her adjustment in that summer of 1940 to life in the chaotic Cape Cod household was difficult from the start. The competitive sailing was especially tough that year at Hyannis Port, and Rosemary found herself back in her familiar role: responding to Eunice's shouted directives as they plied the waters of Nantucket Sound. But Rosemary and Eunice were no longer children. Once sweet and compliant, Rosemary had trouble readapting to the pace of activity among her high-spirited siblings. She "had begun to get sort of emotional," Eunice recalled. "She was high strung and had quite a lot of tantrums all the time." Rose, too, noted "disquieting symptoms began to develop. Not only was there noticeable regression in the mental skills she had worked so hard to attain, but her customary good nature gave way increasingly to tension and irritability. She was upset easily and unpredictably. Some of these upsets became tantrums, or rages, during which she broke things or hit out at people. Since she was quite strong, her blows were hard."

For the first time, Rose wrote decades later, she recognized that Rosemary's problems included mental illness as well as mental retardation. "Manifestly, there were other factors at work besides retardation. A neurological disturbance or disease of some sort had seemingly overtaken her, and it was becoming progressively worse," she wrote.

Still, Rosemary was part of the celebration in September when she, Jack, Eunice, Pat, Bobby, Jean, and Teddy won twelve sailing trophies at the awards ceremony to mark the end of summer. Jack had also won a more competitive race at Edgartown, Massachusetts, which, Eunice informed her father, "spruced him up a good deal." Joe Jr. made a splash of his own that summer, casting his ballot for Postmaster General James Farley as a delegate to the Democratic National Convention in Chicago that would draft Franklin Delano Roosevelt for an unprecedented third term.

Days after the Kennedy siblings walked away from the Wianno Yacht Club clutching their silver cups and pen sets, the first German bombers appeared in the skies over London on September 7. For the next two months, night raids rained destruction on the city. The Luftwaffe unleashed thirty thousand bombs in the first thirty days in raids that would continue sporadically until May 1941. The places Eunice had come to know and love would not be spared.

Students at the Convent of the Sacred Heart at Roehampton had been evacuated on the eve of war and relocated to the Hotel Marina in Newquay, a fishing port in Cornwall. Dorothy Bell recalled the fleet of coaches lined up on the terrace to take them to safety, buses that Joe Kennedy had sent. "The coaches turned out of the gates—nuns and children, one of the latter clutching a teddy bear, sat side by side," she remembered.

There were still some nuns in residence at Roehampton a year later, by which time the Nazis had overrun Denmark and Norway and occupied Belgium and Holland. France had fallen in June. Britain had a new prime minister in Winston Churchill, who was contemptuous of those who underestimated Britain's resolve. "You ask: What is our aim? I can answer in one word: it is victory, victory at all costs, victory in spite of all terror, victory however hard and long the road may be, for without victory there is no survival," Churchill told Parliament on May 13, 1940, in the speech that predicted an immediate future of "blood, toil, tears, and sweat."

All four were visited upon London in the night bombings that fall. In October the Elm Grove mansion at Roehampton and the main building where the Kennedy girls had slept, studied, and played were hit. Our Lady's Chapel, where Eunice had lain prostrate on the floor in prayer, lay in ruins. The small Chapel of the Sacred Heart, with its painted statutes of the founder of the Sacred Heart order kneeling before Christ, survived the Blitz.

The Sacred Heart students would never return to Roehampton. After the war, the school would be relocated to Surrey, in southeast England, and renamed the Woldingham School, after the village in which it is located. In the decades since the war, the University of Roehampton has grown up on the site of the Kennedy girls' former convent school, its squat academic buildings and parking lots replacing the Georgian mansion and lush playing fields where Eunice once had to be asked to temper her vocal enthusiasm during field hockey games.

Joe was summoned home that October to confer with President Roosevelt, who had exhausted his patience with his ambassador's defeatist talk but who still needed his political support. A delicate dance ensued during a White House dinner at which Roosevelt feigned great affection for his ambassador in order to court the endorsement he needed to hold on to Catholic voters for whom Joseph P. Kennedy embodied the ultimate success story. By then, Joe was most interested in coming home to focus on the future of his sons, who were fast entering adulthood.

He agreed to endorse the president in a nationally broadcast radio address, assuring listeners that Roosevelt would keep them out of the war. "In my years of service for the government, both at home and abroad, I have sought to have honest judgment as my goal," he said. "After all, I have a great stake in this country. My wife and I have given nine hostages to fortune. Our children and your children are more important than anything in the world."

After the president's reelection that November, Joe resigned his ambassadorship. He then sealed his own political fate in a less than diplomatic interview with the *Boston Globe*. "Democracy is finished in England; it may be here, too," he told the reporter, Louis Lyons, in what Joe later claimed had been an off-the-record conversation.

As her father's public career was coming to an unceremonious end, Eunice had returned as a boarder to Manhattanville for her sophomore year. "I really have much more free time this year, and it's so much nicer, and best of all no Saturday classes," she wrote to Rose in the fall. She went to a friend's twenty-first birthday party at the St. Regis hotel and to Yale for a football game and house dance. She also saw a Broadway revival of Eugene O'Neill's *Ah, Wilderness!* at the Guild Theatre, pronouncing the dramatist's uncharacteristically lighthearted play from 1933 "very good."

She stayed in touch with her parents and siblings by telephone and letter. Joe Jr. was at Harvard Law School. Rosemary was in Washington, DC, enrolled at St. Gertrude's School of Arts and Crafts, a Benedictine convent school for mentally retarded girls ages seven to twelve; the Kennedys hoped that there the twenty-two-year-old Rosie could reprise the teacher's aide role she had carved out so successfully in England. Kathleen was taking courses in interior design in New York, and Jack was at Stanford, auditing courses at the business school and basking in the success of *Why England Slept*, his Harvard thesis, which had been published as a book.

It was one of six titles on the list of required reading for a modern history course Eunice was taking. "Please tell Johnny," she wrote to her mother, and "Please tell Dad that some books he gave to the Sacred Heart nuns just arrived safely over the ocean. The hysterical nuns, which is just what they are at this point, want to know what to put on the plaque underneath the books. Please let me know as soon as possible; e.g., do you want Gift of J. P. Kennedy or Gift of Mr. and Mrs. Kennedy or what. They insist on something. No wonder life runs so smoothly for me at the Sacred Heart!"

That smooth run was about to end. There had been no respite from medical ills that fall. In December a hospitalization prompted Eunice's formal withdrawal from Manhattanville before final exams, and revived an idea, first floated by Jack, that she transfer to Stanford. His few months auditing courses there had convinced him that the weather agreed with him more than the business school, and that the regular sunshine and intellectual rigor would suit his sister.

At Christmas, Jack raised the topic of Stanford again. "He was quite enthusiastic about it, in fact, so much so that he talked me into going there," Eunice said. "I remember very distinctly him talking to me in the living room at Palm Beach, saying, 'You ought to go to Stanford. It's a very good college. You could really learn a lot. It's also healthy. You swim out there. You can exercise, you can do all those things, Eunice. You really feel well. You might as well do that. It's a terrific place to go.'" Rose, too, attributed the move to Eunice's health. "We sent her out there because we thought that the mild climate would be better for her during the winter, as she was not very strong during those college years," she said.

Even for a Kennedy, it was not simply a matter of showing up with a check to enroll in a degree-granting program at Stanford. The coeducational university thirty miles south of San Francisco was on its way to establishing its reputation as "the Harvard of the West." In her three semesters at Manhattanville, Eunice had not completed enough courses to transfer.

It would take the intervention of former President Herbert Hoover, a member of both the board of trustees and Stanford's first graduating class, to get Eunice in. Joe was a friend and admirer of the former Republican president. Both men kept suites at the Waldorf Astoria in New York and socialized regularly. But even Hoover could not engineer a spot overnight. Eunice would need another semester of course work before she could enroll, in January 1942. "There was a little question about the transfer," Rose recalled, "but anyway, Mr. Hoover made it very easy and facilitated all the arrangements."

Her health fragile and her education temporarily on hold, Eunice remained in Palm Beach throughout the winter of 1941, swimming, boating, horseback riding, playing tennis and golf at the Seminole Country Club, dining and dancing at the Everglades Club, and attending fund-raisers for Bundles for Britain, a private charity that shipped clothes and medical supplies to the besieged island throughout the war. Surrounded by such luxury, it was sometimes hard for her to remember that the country was still in an economic depression or that war was raging elsewhere in the world.

She spent many evenings at a nightclub called the Patio with the dissolute socialite set. "I and they look the worst for it, too, so tired and worn," she wrote, recalling a night there with friends from Yale. "Only 1 sandwich ordered yet bill about $30. Where's the Depression?"

She recognized that disconnect in her own life, too. On March 28, Eunice noted in her diary, she "bought a new set of golf clubs due to Dad's generosity," but a few days later, she wrote that "we are even economizing now, as I almost broke my legs trying to search for a place where we could get cheaper fish . . . This house sure spends a lot of money in one month."

In her diary, she recorded without challenge her father's ever more pessimistic outlook for England—it would all be over in ninety days, he told her in March—and made respectful note of his casual assertion that "more people killed in auto accidents in two months than in the entire bombing of England during the war."

Rose invited Eunice to join her for a six-week sojourn to South America come May if she gained thirteen pounds. She was so skeletal, she had refused to model an evening dress at a charity benefit "as I look rather thin and this other girl looked rather well." Her father, she told her diary, "won't touch my arms or legs 'cause he is afraid he will cut himself. Also told me doctors said I would die if I got any sickness and that he and Jack didn't have a black suit and he doesn't feel like going into mourning. He is so funny today. Ha, ha, ha!!!"

In truth, her health issues were serious. Her inability, all her life, to sustain a healthy weight was exacerbated by parents so fixated on whether their children were too fat or too slim that Eunice was almost always on a special diet. Her lack of body fat caused her thyroid levels to drop and those of the stress hormone cortisol to rise, triggering a reduction in the hormones that regulate menstruation.

She was as preoccupied with the war in Europe as she was with her weight in the spring of 1941. In the "war diary" she kept, Eunice recorded developments at home and abroad, noting everything from the signing of the Lend-Lease Act on March 11, to the Axis occupation of Greece in April. She recorded her father's plans to write his memoirs when the war ended and the lectures she attended by the Reverend James Keller, whose message of individual responsibility for improving the lives of the less fortunate reinforced the lesson Eunice had learned at Casita Maria and the Barat Settlement House: that religion without action was a hollow faith.

Eunice had first met the young Maryknoll priest as a teenager when he spoke at Noroton. In the years since, Keller had visited the family at Hyannis Port and in Palm Beach, winning the admiration of her parents and siblings as well. After the war, he would found the Christophers, a movement that called on young people to do volunteer work with the poor and others in need. In the 1950s, Eunice's youngest sister, Jean, would work on Father Keller's radio and television programs.

By May 9, Eunice had gained enough weight to share a stateroom with Rose on the *Brazil*, which sailed from New York that midnight. The first few days of the trip involved sore arms and low-grade fevers from the inoculations against typhoid they had received on board. When well enough to stroll on deck, Eunice was unimpressed with her traveling companions.

"People all foreigners and quite unattractive, all older, mostly men with fat stomachs who stare at you with long faces," she noted.

The talk on board was all about the capture of Rudolf Hess, a senior deputy to Hitler who had flown to Britain on a quixotic and unauthorized peace mission. He had been arrested after parachuting from a German fighter plane onto the field of a Scottish farmer. "Quite a catch for England," Eunice wrote in her diary.

Cousin Eve, a society writer for the *Chicago Daily Tribune*, filed dispatches from aboard ship about traveling notables, including Eunice, whom she described as "the tallest, slimmest miss" among the two hundred first-class passengers. Also aboard was Salvatore Baccaloni, a basso buffo at the Metropolitan Opera in New York, whom Eunice pronounced "the fattest man I ever saw."

A Dominican priest returning to his native Brazil after nine years in the United States said Mass on Sunday at an improvised altar. "Father also told the interesting fact that the president of the Argentine must be thirty-four years old, must have been born in the Argentine, and must be a Catholic," Rose noted. "This bit of news was a great surprise and interesting piece of news because in New York I had heard so many times the fact that a Catholic could not become president here. In London I heard that a Catholic could not become king and probably not prime minister. But here was an immense, important country which evened things up by decreeing in their Constitution that only a Catholic could become president." She might have shared this point with Jack, who joined his mother and sister briefly in Rio de Janeiro during his own sojourn in Latin America.

For all of her travels, Rose lived a cosseted life largely in the company of rich white people; her exposure to other classes and non–Western European cultures was superficial at best.

As mother and daughter traveled through Brazil, Argentina, Chile, Peru, Ecuador, and Panama, Rose complained if hotel clerks and shop girls spoke imperfect English, or if the food was not "to the American taste." A tourist rather than a traveler, she concluded that there was "not anything of special historical interest in South America compared with all the multitude of things in Europe and those monuments which there are mean little to us, since we are unacquainted with the history, while in England or Italy we are familiar with most of the landmarks through study and experience of our friends."

When the *Brazil* anchored off Barbados, the passengers were greeted by what Rose described as "half a dozen rowboats riding at anchor which had brought out dusky swimmers who were swimming around, waiting for the passengers to flip them coins . . . It must be quite a feat to swim, duck, dive, with your mouth full of coins. I must have Bobby and Ted try it out next summer, as Teddy cannot even hold his breath now."

Eunice was annoyed when officials barred her from bringing her camera ashore. The island, a British possession, was technically at war, and photographs were deemed a potential security risk. She made note of the racial makeup of the island as "3/4ths Negro, 1/4th white. Negro and whites mix very well. No hard feeling." At a Catholic school they visited, "the black and white [children] sat side by side. Children so clean and neat . . . So polite people in the shops, polite and all seem contented."

At that juncture, her mother was "plenty mad, and I don't blame her one bit," Eunice noted, after Rose weighed her one night and the scale registered only 105 pounds—alarmingly thin for a young woman who stood five foot ten. "Have eaten pretty well, but it's pretty hot to gain," Eunice complained.

Rose and Eunice returned to Hyannis Port in late June. While mother and daughter were away, Joe Jr. had enlisted in the US Naval Air Corps. Jack would follow suit in the fall, enlisting in a naval officers' training course after barely passing the physical on his second try. After his father's intervention, he would be assigned to the Office of Naval Intelligence, in Washington, DC.

Jack's arrival meant that three of the Kennedy children were living in the nation's capital that fall. Rosemary had returned to St. Gertrude's, and Kick had joined the staff of the *Washington Times-Herald* as an assistant to the editor, Frank Waldrop. The job reunited her with Page Huidekoper, who had worked for Joe as a press assistant at the embassy in London and was now a reporter. Kick introduced Jack to her colleague Inga Arvad, a popular gossip columnist and a former Danish beauty queen, a meeting that would trigger one of the future president's more problematic love affairs. Jack and Kick were unaware that Inga, married and four years his senior, had been under FBI surveillance since a photograph surfaced of her in Hitler's private box during the 1936 Olympics in Berlin. Soon after columnist Walter Winchell published an item about Jack's and Inga's affair, Jack found himself transferred to Charleston, South Carolina, a move widely attributed to his father, who was determined to end Jack's relationship with a suspected foreign agent.

It was an unhappy fall for Rosemary as well. She had developed a habit of wandering away from St. Gertrude's at night. "Many nights the school would call to say she was missing, only to find her out walking the streets at two in the morning," her cousin Ann Gargan said. "Can you imagine what it must have been like to know your daughter was walking the streets in the darkness of the night, the perfect prey for an unsuspecting male?"

How aware Eunice was of Rosemary's troubles is unknown. She was winding up her time at Manhattanville that fall, preparing to transfer to Stanford in January. In a letter to Joe on November 12, 1941, Herbert Hoover had inquired whether Eunice had "completed all the entrance requirements, as that needs to be done very promptly. If I can be of any help, I will be very glad to do so in any way that I can." Three days later, Hoover wrote to the Stanford University registrar on Eunice's behalf. "She is a wonderful girl, and would be an acquisition," he said. Some historians have linked Eunice's move to California to her distress about what happened to Rosemary that November, but the record is clear that her plans to attend Stanford had begun a full year before.

What the record does not make clear is when Eunice learned that Rosemary underwent a prefrontal lobotomy that November, leaving her almost fully incapacitated, no longer able to walk or speak. As was their habit, the Kennedys have offered conflicting versions of who knew what when about Joe's decision to treat Rosemary's increasingly combative behavior and mood swings with experimental psychosurgery—and to prohibit the family from visiting her once he realized how disastrously the operation had failed.

In her memoirs, in 1974, Rose wrote that she and Joe had agreed to the surgery, but thirteen years later, she told historian Doris Kearns Goodwin that Joe had acted on his own, and she learned about the operation and its consequences only when she saw Rosemary sometime after Joe suffered a stroke in 1961.

Joe himself did not explain his decision to have Rosemary undergo an operation that had been the subject of two high-profile and contradictory reports in the six months before he authorized the lobotomy. The procedure involved drilling two holes in the skull and inserting a surgical tool to cut the tissue that connects the frontal lobes to the rest of the brain in hopes of reducing a patient's mental distress. But because the frontal lobes control key cognitive functions such as language, judgment, memory, problem solving, and emotional expression, patients were often left nearly catatonic, their personalities erased. In May 1941 the *Saturday Evening Post* praised the "sensational procedure" for alleviating the suffering of the mentally ill, while an August report in the *Journal of the American Medical Association* warned that the surgery had not been studied sufficiently and should be suspended pending further research, because "there is ample evidence of the serious defects produced."

Jean and Teddy, ages thirteen and nine when Rosemary disappeared from the family, accepted their father's explanation that their sister was teaching in a school for mentally retarded children in the Midwest and that doctors had deemed it in her best interest to live apart from her family.

In three separate letters he wrote between 1942 and 1944, Joe assured Joe Jr., Jack, and Kick that Rosemary was doing well, after which her name vanished from his correspondence. Had he confided in his older children? What, then, of Eunice, the sister paired with Rosemary from childhood— the sister who swam and sailed with her, who played endless sets of tennis with her in Hyannis Port, who toured Notre-Dame Cathedral with her in Paris and hiked the Swiss Alps with her as the two teenagers made their first grand tour in 1936? Was she kept in the dark about what had happened? Had she, once again, been relegated to the kids' table?

Eunice said she had no idea where her sister was "for a decade" after the surgery, when Rosemary was being cared for at Craig House, a private psychiatric facility north of New York City that was ill-equipped to provide the rehabilitative services she needed if she was ever to relearn how to walk and talk. Joe Kennedy's authority over his children was such that Eunice might have known better than to ask.

Correspondence that is open to researchers at the JFK Library suggests Joe might have revealed Rosemary's condition to Eunice in 1949, when, on the advice of Boston archbishop Richard Cushing, he transferred his oldest daughter to the care of the Sisters of St. Francis of Assisi at St. Coletta School for Exceptional Children, in Jefferson, Wisconsin. In 1971, the administrator of St. Coletta wrote to Rose to ask for her recommendation for a new doctor for Rosemary after the sudden death of Dr. Harry Waisman, Rosemary's personal physician and a leading University of Wisconsin researcher on mental retardation. Rose told St. Coletta she would forward the letter to Eunice, "since I believe she talked over the idea of a physician with her father when Rosemary first went to St. Coletta. I am sure she will be able to advise you."

In a lighthearted round robin letter to her children on December 5, 1941, two days before the Japanese surprise attack on Pearl Harbor and only a few weeks after the surgery, Rose said she had closed up the Bronxville house for the last time. Addressing the letter to "my darlings," she said she and Joe had decided to sell the house. They would divide their time from now on between Palm Beach and Hyannis Port. Rose recalled the children growing up in Bronxville "very happily, romping over the lawns in the spring and fall and coasting down the sloping hill in the winter." She was nostalgic but "quite relieved and very free with nothing on my mind except the shades of blue for my Palm Beach trousseau."

Rose made no mention of Rosemary in this letter, which chronicled the comings and goings of everyone else in the clan. "Eunice is still at Manhattanville, but is very optimistic about entering Stanford in early January," she wrote.

Whatever Eunice did or did not know about Rosemary, early on the morning of December 29, she took a "smooth as glass" plane ride to Chicago and boarded the *City of San Francisco*, the Union Pacific's premier passenger train, to California, where she was met by Arthur Poole, a former business associate of her father's.

She arrived at a campus on high alert. On December 10, three days after Pearl Harbor, 3,500 students had crammed into Memorial Auditorium to hear Stanford president Ray Lyman Wilbur warn, "We're right up against the guns." He urged students to accelerate their studies to be free to contribute to the war effort and issued a plea for generosity toward Japanese American students. "They are just as good Stanford people as we are," he said. A month later, President Roosevelt would sign an executive order authorizing the internment of Japanese Americans for the duration of the war.

Stanford was unlike any academic institution Eunice had seen. "Mrs. Poole has taken me sightseeing most of the afternoon. This Stanford is certainly a great place. If the people are as nice as the University, then Dad you and Johnny underestimated it rather than overestimated it. I wish the nuns had a college like this. When I think of Manhattanville's five acres!" she wrote to her parents of the more than eight thousand acres of foothills and plains surrounding a central campus dotted with palm trees, grassy quads, arched walkways, and bicycle paths.

She moved into Lagunita Court, a new dormitory arranged around a central courtyard and refectory. From the dining commons the hundred or so students in residence could see the "little lake" from which the dorm took its name. "The room I am in has about 50 huge banners in it saying such things as—'Does your lappa have a kappa—if not you are a sappa.' What kind of a house am I in?" she wrote to her parents.

The cost of room and board was $157.50 per quarter. Rooms were equipped with a bed, mattress, chest of drawers, desk, chair, bookcase, wicker armchair, and curtains. Eunice asked her mother to send extra blankets. Room 275 in Lagunita had plenty of heat, she reported, but she was still freezing and also sleepless because of the noise in the dorm. "I just invested in a pair of earplugs, and they are simply marvelous," she told her mother. "I am going to start charging admission, since so many girls want to come in and see me decked up in my complicated sleeping attire i.e. sleep shade, bed socks, pad & plugs, but God helps those who help themselves."

She decorated her room with illustrations from Walt Disney movies and photographs of her brothers and sisters. "Nothing like showing off one's family, I always say. If Jack or Joe ever go into politics, they will get 200 votes from Lagunita women," she said.

As different as Stanford looked, its mission statement could have been written by Mother Dammann, the Manhattanville president who sent her students into the settlement houses of New York City. The goal of a Stanford education, according to its founding grant, was to "qualify its students for personal success, and direct usefulness in life."

A new academic program was introduced soon after Eunice arrived on campus. A brochure for the War Time Program for Stanford Women described "a preprofessional social services course intended to train for assistantships and positions in social services and leading to an AB [bachelor of arts] degree in Social Sciences." The courses Eunice took in psychology and sociology to earn that degree explored issues confronting the family and society, including the needs of retarded children and the mentally ill. The program also included training in casework and social data collection, skills Eunice would later put to use.

Even from three thousand miles away, her parents kept obsessive watch over her weight. Her mother urged her to give up gum chewing because "it looks badly" and "will also prevent you from gaining weight, which of course you don't want to do." In February, Joe wrote to urge

Eunice to focus on her diet more than her schoolwork, advice it is hard to imagine him giving to rail-thin Jack. "We received a letter from the doctor yesterday in which he thought you were cooperating but that you only weighed 107 1/2 pounds, and that, of course, discouraged mother no end, because you really aren't gaining anything out there, and that gives her a great deal of worry," he wrote, suggesting her behavior was as much to blame for her condition as any physical cause. "Now, I hope you are doing all the things that you should do that will add to your weight, because your mother considers your health more important than your studies, and I don't want to have her upset by the fact that you are out there and not gaining—so for goodness sake, sit yourself down and eat."

Before she even registered for classes, Eunice made appointments to see Dr. Helen B. Pryor, the medical advisor for women and head of the School of Health at Stanford, and Dr. Ludwig Emge, a gynecologist in San Francisco. Following a physical exam, Dr. Pryor had pronounced her "in good shape" and Eunice wrote to her mother: "So don't let that head of yours think about your fifth born any more, at least not until Easter." For his part, Dr. Emge impressed on Eunice that her menstrual periods would not resume unless she gained weight. So rare were her periods that Virginia Carpenter, one of her friends at Stanford, thought Eunice wouldn't be able to have children.

Rose urged Eunice to ease slowly into her new surroundings. "I am not recommending that Eunice see too many people, as I think that is her great difficulty in life," she told Kick. "It would be much better for her to stay more quiet and not go rushing around."

But rush she did, joining the ski club for an excursion of a hundred Stanford students to Sun Valley, Idaho. She shared a chalet with ten other girls, including Ann Clare Brokaw, the only child of one of her father's paramours, Clare Boothe Luce, the playwright who had accompanied them to the Ascot races during Eunice's debutante spring. Ann and Eunice become fast friends. The skiing was "simply wonderful, although much harder than in Switzerland," she reported. They went ice skating every night and swam in an outdoor heated pool. "Tomorrow night we are going on a sleigh ride, so you see we don't lack a thing. Ann sends you her love. I really better close now, as there is so much shrieking in this room I can't write another word."

Her letters home were full of enthusiastic reports about her academic and social life. She took a class in religions of the Far East to better understand the Japanese. She went regularly to the symphony on Friday nights with a group of friends. She went skiing in Yosemite National Park. She went out "a couple of times" with a friend of Jack's named Henry James, whom she described as "really great fun." She became an air-raid warden in her dorm, a post that worried her because "I am supposed to account for about 60 girls, and I only know about 20 names," which is why she had taken to shouting "Hi, Girl!" whenever she passed anyone she vaguely recognized on campus. She bought a black convertible, which was stolen but quickly recovered undamaged in a parking garage in San Francisco. "They didn't even use my gas coupons, so that shows you what prayers will do," she wrote her mother. She went to one engagement party after another. "They come and they go, but the Kennedy girls go on, forever single," she wrote.

Eunice made a big impression in her course on public speaking when she was assigned to make an "entertaining speech" and told a story about "Ted feeding Ex-Lax to his girlfriend." She needled her mother about a study she read in her psychology course that found learning Latin only marginally improved one's command of the English language. "You can say I am right again," she wrote. She defended her father against a professor's assertion that he had been forced out of his diplomatic post because of disagreements with President Roosevelt. She sent home a picture of herself in her fencing outfit but said the class was not winning her any friends. "I had my first 'engagement' today," she wrote to her father about her first match, "and although I scored 1 point, I also scored 2 fouls on my opponent's 'unprotected area,' so I am quite unpopular with her tonight."

She kept her eye out for celebrities, reporting back to her mother when she saw the actor Jimmy Stewart in a restaurant. "He certainly isn't attractive, for he has great bags under his eyes & his hair is turning gray & he looks worn to a frazzle." She saw the radio broadcaster Lowell Thomas and the movie stars Ray Milland and Claudette Colbert on the ski slopes, and Loretta Young, Lana Turner, and William Powell on an Easter trip to Palm Springs with a group of Stanford girls. Ann was on that trip, talking about dropping out to help her mother campaign for the congressional seat from Connecticut that Clare Boothe Luce would win that fall. "We'll see what her mother says about that," the ever-obedient Eunice wrote her own mother.

Thirty years later, she said of her time at Stanford: "I loved it. I skied. It's lovely country. I thought it was a beautiful part of the world. I liked the weather. It wasn't like it is today. It was wartime. There weren't men there with the war."

Her memory was correct that there were few civilian men on campus. In the wake of Pearl Harbor, students and faculty alike were enlisting in the war effort. By August 1944, 141 professors would be on leave for war service. But the campus was hardly bereft of men. In the three semesters Eunice spent at Stanford, the campus housed thousands of soldiers enrolled in the Army Specialized Training Program, the Civil Affairs Training School, and the Quartermaster Corps. "These soldiers—3,000 strong—have virtually taken over the Stanford University, where they are being rushed through intensive courses in the languages, customs, climates, resources, and geographies of far-off lands," United Press reported in 1943. "The Stanford Quadrangle resounds with young soldiers going to class in formation, books and slide rules under their arms, shouting the 'Hut-two-three-four!' cadence instead of the 'Rah-Rah' of former college days."

Eunice participated in all the campus drives to support the war effort. There was the "Clean Your Plate" campaign to prevent wasted food, "Car-less Wednesdays" to save gasoline, "Stamp Day" Thursdays to promote the sale of twenty-five-cent defense stamps, and "Dimes for Diplomas" to help Stanford men in uniform complete their educations when they returned after the war.

At Eunice's invitation, Rose came west in April to share the Stanford experience. She stayed at the President Hotel near campus, attended classes with Eunice and took her on weekend excursions to Palm Springs and Pebble Beach. She audited a political science course about Latin America that Eunice was taking with Graham Stuart, who would soon be serving as a consultant to the Department of State. She took Eunice to lunch at the home of President Hoover and his wife, Lou Henry Hoover.

When the term ended, Eunice checked into the Beverly Hills Hotel for a week where she was feted at luncheons and teas by her old tennis partner Spencer Tracy and two of his fellow movie stars, Mary Pickford and Norma Shearer. "She is probably the envy of every deb," Rose wrote to Joe in June. "The list sounds almost fantastic, but of course we saw all these people abroad."

Rose wrote Joe when Eunice got home at the end of June that "Eunice even said she had hesitated about coming home, so dearly does she love California. Of course, she is all primed to go back again." After her parents vetoed a trip she wanted to take to Mexico, Eunice spent the summer enjoying Cape Cod, ignoring the advice of an editorial in the *Stanford Daily*: "Swimming, boating, and all kinds of summer sports would have been fine last summer and the summer before, but now that we are in this war up to our necks, we have a far more important job to do than getting a beautiful sun tan."

When Eunice returned to her room in Lagunita in the fall, Rose fretted that she had made a mistake by not joining a sorority. "Jack gave me a point of view about the Sororities which I did not understand, and I am sorry we did not know about it sooner, but I suppose it is too late now to do anything about it. His point is that you should have joined a sorority and known a few of the most desirable girls well, including their beaus, who evidently hover around the sorority houses. If you still cannot join a sorority, then I advocate that you cultivate some of those girls rather than make friends among the masses, none of whom mean anything in particular to you."

It was more likely that Eunice was indifferent to, rather than ignorant of, sorority culture at Stanford; Ann Clare Brokaw, one of her closest friends, was a member of Kappa Kappa Gamma. She liked living in Lagunita, telling Pat, who would spend one quarter studying at Stanford the next year at her mother's insistence, there was a consensus on campus that it was the best place to live.

Rose came to visit again that November, telling the other children in a letter that she was accompanying Eunice to another political science class, where she enjoyed hearing the students criticize FDR, the president her isolationist husband had been unable to keep out of the war: "It is often very exciting as several of them hate the president, and Eleanor's trip abroad has evoked violent discussion, so I hope they start something tomorrow." The previous month, First Lady Eleanor Roosevelt had visited Great Britain at the invitation of Queen Elizabeth, to see what English women were doing to aid the war effort and to visit US servicemen stationed there.

Eunice remained in California over the Christmas holidays, vacationing with Ann and other Stanford friends in Palm Springs, but her plans to do so again the following year were not to be. After she completed another term at Stanford in June 1943 without resolving her weight issue, Rose insisted Eunice return to Massachusetts and finish her course work at Radcliffe College in Cambridge. Joe had purchased the farm in Osterville, where he had long boarded the family's horses and, in retirement, had started using the land to grow vegetables and raise beef cattle—which Rose intended to feed to her emaciated daughter.

It would be a time of change and not only for Eunice. That June, Kathleen crossed the Atlantic, bound for England as a volunteer with the Red Cross. She was going back to Billy Cavendish at last. Joe Jr. was also headed to England, assigned to an airbase in Cornwall. Jack was in the South Pacific, the captain of a patrol torpedo boat, PT-109.

That fall, Eunice enrolled at Radcliffe, living at first with her old Noroton roommate, Evelyn Ford, at her family's home in Brookline, and later on Avon Street, in Cambridge, near the Radcliffe quadrangle. "I am very happy about it, as I dreaded sending her out there where she would eat nothing but that slimming food again, with no chance to ever get a square meal," Rose wrote in one of her round-robin letters of having Eunice close to home.

Eunice, too, seemed glad to be back. That winter, she went skiing with friends in New Hampshire and dancing at the Copley Plaza Hotel in Boston with Bobby, then a senior boarding at Milton Academy, and with Joseph F. Timilty, the former Boston police commissioner and a friend of her father. She introduced the Catholic Club at Radcliffe to Father Keller and organized a British booth at a college benefit to aid the war effort. "I think the Kennedys are becoming more British than the British themselves," she wrote to her mother in Palm Beach, boasting that she had gained another pound and a half and weighed 111 pounds. She was "practically the only girl in college who hasn't had the grip in some form or other," Eunice said of the flu-like symptoms that had sent many of her classmates to bed with aches and fevers.

She had begun studying classical music at Radcliffe. "I am no Chopin," she acknowledged. "But I think I know him better than he ever knew himself." Aside from the approach of exams, for which she solicited "a few prayers" from her mother, Eunice reported in January 1944 that "life goes on as merry as ever."

Then came word from California that Ann Clare Brokaw had been killed in a two-car crash not far from the Stanford campus. Ann died at the scene, her death a portentous beginning to what would be a tragic year for the Kennedy family.

FOUR

DOLLAR-A-YEAR GIRL

What with working in the State Dept. and having JP Kennedy as a Papa, people think I know almost as much as [Secretary of State Edward R.] Stettinius.

—EUNICE KENNEDY, LETTER TO HER MOTHER, 1945

THE SUDDEN, VIOLENT death of Ann Clare Brokaw came at the start of the third year of American combat in World War II. As shocking as was the loss of Ann just months before her Stanford graduation, in small towns and big cities across the United States, official telegrams were daily delivering stunned parents fatal news from far-off battlefields.

"What a crowding and jostling and a milling of young people there is at the gates of Paradise these days," a grieving Clare Boothe Luce wrote to Eleanor Roosevelt about Ann and those in uniform, no older than her daughter. The battles of Monte Cassino and Anzio were raging on the Italian peninsula, producing fresh graves as Luce, a member of the US House Committee on Military Affairs, laid her only child to rest.

"I thought I had become hardened to losing people I liked, but when I heard the news today, I could not have been sadder," Lieutenant John Fitzgerald Kennedy wrote to Luce. He was just back in the States, suffering from malaria, a duodenal ulcer, and debilitating back pain five months after surviving the ramming of PT-109 and watching two of his crew die, one of whom, like Ann, was only nineteen.

War and death were distorting young people's sense of time, heightening every precious moment because every moment brought painful reminders that life was finite. Back in England, Kick had found her prewar crowd deeply changed, the debs at work and the boys in uniform. She had begun serving, as soon as she arrived in June 1943, as a Red Cross volunteer at the Hans Crescent Club in the center of bomb-ravaged London, dancing and playing cards with soldiers and sailors on leave or soon to be off to the front. Billy Cavendish came to London from his post in Scotland with the Coldstream Guards as soon as he heard Kick was back. They had not seen each other in four years, not since the last London season before the war. It was immediately clear that their feelings had not changed.

Neither had the religious complications. Marriage between an Anglican aristocrat and an Irish American Catholic heiress was no more acceptable to either side in 1943 than it had been in 1939. "It really is funny to see people put their heads together the minute we arrive any place," Kick wrote to her parents. "There's heavy betting when we are going to announce it. Some people have gotten the idea I'm going to give in. Little do they know."

By January, when Billy was granted a leave from his regiment to stand for Parliament in Derbyshire, the seat of the Cavendish family for more than two centuries, Kick's resolve was weakening. She campaigned with Billy for Parliament with the same enthusiasm that Rose had once stumped for Honey Fitz in Boston in his bids for mayor and a seat in Congress. But the politically unseasoned Billy lost the by-election and returned to the Coldstream Guards just as the Allies were finalizing plans for the invasion of Normandy, France. If Billy and Kick were to be together, it had to be now, and one of them had to bend. Kick did.

In April, when Rose learned that Kathleen had agreed to Billy's condition that they raise their children in the Church of England, she was "heartbroken and horrified." She checked herself into New England Baptist Hospital in Boston to avoid the press, her spiritual suffering more acute than any physical ailment. "Everyone pointed to our family with pride as well behaved, level-headed and deeply religious. What a blow to the family prestige," she wrote in her diary.

Had Joe's gift for public relations convinced even Rose that the fawning press coverage of her family reflected reality? She might have been unaware that in England, Joe Jr. had taken up with Pat Wilson, a twice-married mother of three, while her husband was under combat fire in Italy, or that Jack's affair with a suspected German spy had prompted Joe to engineer his son's transfer from Washington to Charleston, South Carolina, in 1942. But she was certainly not blind to her husband's serial infidelities. If Kick, as Rose believed, was sacrificing her immortal soul for the fleeting pleasure of a happy marriage on earth, what were the reckless Kennedy men risking? Rose's paralyzing grief at Kick's decision to marry a non-Catholic made one wonder what she imagined became of the souls of philandering spouses and skirt-chasing sons.

Joe Jr. was the only member of the bride's family in attendance at the Chelsea Registry Office on Saturday morning, May 6, when Kathleen Agnes Kennedy married William John Robert Cavendish, the marquess of Hartington. His parents, the Duke and Duchess of Devonshire, were there, as were his sisters, Anne and Elizabeth. "The power of silence is great," Joe Jr. cabled his father, who responded with a cable of his own to Kick: "With your faith in God, you can't make a mistake. Remember you are still and always will be tops with me."

After a weeklong honeymoon at a Cavendish estate in Eastbourne, a seaside resort on the south coast of England, the newlyweds took up residence in the Swan Hotel, near Billy's regiment in Alton, fifty miles southwest of London. "Don't let anybody say I am not going up in the world. Now I'm living in a pub, just above the bar. Isn't it wonderful?" Kick wrote to Lady Astor, who had attended the wedding with Marie Bruce, an old friend of Rose's who had enraged the Kennedy matriarch by urging her to be happy for Kick.

The ice had already begun to thaw with her mother, Kick reported to Lady Astor a few weeks later. Her siblings, too, were being supportive. "Mother, Jack, and that religious old soul, Eunice, have written the nicest letters," Kick wrote. "Mother said that she was in the hospital and just didn't want to discuss the wedding with the papers, so everyone guessed that she was too upset. I am not saying that she was pleased about the whole thing, but she has adopted a very rational point of view. As Jack said, there were a few 'begorras from Boston, but all anyone wants is that you should be happy.' My goodness, it was a nice letter. It really makes the whole difference."

Eunice's letter to Kick has not survived, but in her nonjudgmental embrace of her sister's decision, once it was made, she displayed the pragmatism that would guide her adult life in matters of faith, morals, and politics: argue passionately, make your case, and, if you lose, move on, if only to fight another day. Jack wrote of her reaction to the marriage in a letter to LeMoyne Billings, his friend from Choate. "[A]s sister Eunice from the depth of her righteous Catholic wrath so truly said: 'It's a horrible thing—but it will be nice visiting her after the war, so we might as well face it.'"

It was a quieter summer than usual in Hyannis Port, with Kick in England and Joe Jr. finishing up his tour as an aviator there. Nineteen-year-old Bobby was in the navy's V-12 training program at Harvard. Jack was home after being hospitalized for eight weeks. A winter in the sun in Arizona had not restored him to health after his discharge from the navy. He had back surgery at New England Baptist Hospital and further treatment at the nearby Chelsea Naval Hospital, but he was still in fragile health. That "religious old soul, Eunice," spent part of her summer organizing the display and sale of religious pamphlets and magazines in the vestibule of the local church, St. Francis Xavier. She was perplexed by the anemic sales, she wrote to Father Bertram Conway, a Paulist priest in Manhattan she consulted at her father's urging, because the parishioners were "of quite a devout nature" and "of fairly substantial means."

Most of the family were on the large sun porch on August 13, listening to a new Bing Crosby record, when twelve-year-old Teddy saw two naval chaplains emerge from a black car in the circular gravel driveway. "Mother looked up from the Sunday paper she'd been reading in a tiny rocking chair that only she could fit into," Teddy recalled more than sixty years later. "As she received the clerics, we could hear a few words: 'missing,' 'lost.' All of us froze."

Joe Jr. had volunteered for one last mission the day before, flying a plane packed with twenty-two thousand pounds of explosives toward a site on the Belgian coast where Germany had been launching "doodlebug" bombs, so named because of the terrifying buzzing sound the V-1 flying bombs made as they fell on London. The plan was for Joe and his copilot to activate the guidance system, aim the flying bomb toward its target, and bail out. Instead, the plane exploded before either man could parachute to safety.

The youngest son remembered a "sunroom awash in tears" for his eldest brother until Jack took charge. "Joe wouldn't want us sitting here crying," he told his siblings and his cousin Joe Gargan. "He would want us to go sailing." So that is what they did, demonstrating the emotional resilience, or repression, that would become the Kennedy family's default response to tragic news.

Kick came home from London to be with her family. She found her father shattered by the loss not just of his son but also of the dreams he had invested in him. Joe Jr. was to have finished what Joe Sr. began and one day claim the White House as the first Irish Catholic president of the United States. Kick tried to comfort her father, helping him answer the hundreds of condolence letters pouring into Hyannis Port. Rose, the more contemplative of the pair, walked alone along the shore, finding her solace there and at daily Mass.

That Labor Day weekend, Jack invited some navy buddies and their wives, including Jim and Jewel Reed and Lennie and Kate Thom, to Hyannis Port. Though the house was in mourning, the usual pace of activities prevailed. Jewel Reed remembered that "we were organized from the moment we arrived. The Kennedys organized everybody. I hated playing tennis, so Eunice invited me to play golf. The next day, we played touch football, which was hideous."

Eunice recruited Kate Thom to crew for her in a sailing race. "I'd never been in a boat in my life, and I was made her crew," she recalled. "They were in everything to win. Not just to participate. I remember how cruel I thought she was because she kept barking orders at me, and if I did something wrong, she'd scream. But she knew what she was doing, and what she had to do to win. And we won the race."

It had been weeks since Kick had heard from Billy. After Labor Day, she distracted herself from her grief for her brother and her fears for her husband by accompanying the family to New York, where, as was their habit, Joe went to the Waldorf Astoria and Rose checked herself into the Plaza Hotel. Kick was shopping at Bonwit Teller on Fifth Avenue on September 16 when Joe sent Eunice to bring her to his hotel suite. He had just learned that Billy had been killed by a sniper in Belgium a week before as his company advanced on the small town of Heppen, then in German hands. "So ends the story of Billy and Kick," the twenty-four-year-old widow wrote in her diary on September 20.

She returned to England, and the Kennedys returned to form, dulling the pain with manic activity. Eunice and her mother took a golf-and-foliage trip to the White Mountains in October, accompanied by former Boston police commissioner Joseph F. Timilty, the family retainer they called "the Commish." She kept her letters to her grief-stricken father, already in Palm Beach, light and cheery: "I just checked the items that the Commish put away for breakfast and dinner. I really think it is inhuman. This afternoon he wonders why he can't button his jacket on the golf course." Rose, she reported, could not walk through the lobby or the dining room without eliciting "a heigh-ho" from the other guests: "Mother should wear a pink wig and wear a stuffed pillow if she would like to go someplace where nobody knows her."

With her Radcliffe credits, Eunice had earned her Stanford degree the previous spring and was eager to find work in Washington, where Kick assured her the social life was as interesting as the political scene. With her father's connections, she was confident enough to move to the Federal City in January 1945 without having secured a job. She arrived in time for the inauguration of Franklin D. Roosevelt, on January 20, for an unprecedented fourth term. The scaled-back wartime ceremony took place on the South Portico of the White House, followed by a luncheon for invited guests. Eunice attended both, wearing a mink coat Rose had sent from storage. "We really shouldn't let that coat waste away at Bergdorfs' when it looks so divine on me," she wrote her parents. The day had been "great fun, and I saw all your buddies, Dad. Even if you don't like them, they are all asking for you."

Sidelined by the president whose policies he blamed for the death of his son, Joe had no fond feelings for either Roosevelt or his advisors. "We have an incompetent secretary of state. We have a worse than incompetent secretary of the Treasury, and yet, the two most important problems of the salvation of the world will be foreign policy and financial policy," he wrote to Kick that January. "Of course, Roosevelt will be his own secretary of state and his own secretary of the Treasury, but his course of action would be much more intelligently guided if the men in those two offices knew anything."

Eunice lived first with the family of Max Truitt, who had served as general counsel to the US Maritime Commission when Joe was its chairman, and later in an apartment on Connecticut Avenue near Dupont Circle she sublet for $62.50 a month. When Rose and her youngest daughter, Jean, came to visit soon after Eunice arrived, the Truitts hosted a dinner party with Supreme Court Justices Frank Murphy and Stanley Reed, and Senator Millard Tydings of Maryland and his wife, Eleanor, among the guests. Justice Murphy, whom Eunice had found "a little overdignified and stuffy" a few days earlier when he had entertained her, Rose, and Jean at the court for tea, proved himself quite "hilarious" and was the last to leave the party.

Within days, Eunice had job offers from the Office of Special Investigations in the US Department of Justice and the Office of Strategic Services, the World War II–era intelligence agency, but, she told her father, she was holding out for a position in the State Department. An offer from the department's Special War Problems Division arrived soon, no doubt after Joe put a well-timed word in a well-placed ear. "The important thing is to have interesting work," her father told her, encouraging her to quit and find something else if she became bored.

Eunice would have preferred a post in the European section, but "they say it is impossible to get into that section without experience, so I have decided to work in the special area. I like the people over there, and it is a very convenient place to work." She was self-deprecating about what it had taken to land the job. "I am not sure whether they want my name or my personality," she quipped. She was offered a salary of $1,800 a year, so there would be "no more Hattie Carnegie," she told her father, a reference to an expensive fashion boutique in Manhattan. "There's opportunity for a raise but don't retire until you hear *I have* the raise." Her salary was, in fact, $300 a year more than what full-time female civilian workers earned on average in 1945, according to the US Census Bureau.

In what her father described to Kick as a "grand gesture," Eunice sent her parents her "first hard-earned" paycheck in March. "Uncle Sam took twelve dollars, but I want you both to have the rest. Do spend it on something grand, preferably a party at Bradley's," she wrote, referring to a private social club that also operated a popular illegal casino in Palm Beach. At Joe's insistence, she from then on declined the proffered salary and worked without compensation, her financial needs met by her father.

Joe had made certain that money would never be a worry for his children, the profits of his stock market and real estate deals freeing them for political careers or other forms of public service. He had established separate trusts for each of the children and for Rose in 1926 and again in 1936. The children could make withdrawals from the 1926 trusts once they turned twenty-five. The sons were allowed to tap into the 1936 trusts at age thirty-one, but the daughters could not make withdrawals until they turned forty-one, ensuring that there would be inheritance enough for future grandchildren. The sum total of the trusts by the end of 1946 has been estimated at about $8 million, the equivalent of $91 million in 2017 dollars.

Still, the entire family was tight-fisted, and Eunice in particular had alarmed her mother a few years earlier when she was at Stanford and had vowed to find the cheapest available accommodations when she and Ann Brokaw went skiing in Sun Valley. "This whole family is quite disturbed about your talking economy so frequently, and I really wish you would adopt a more sane view of the situation," Rose had written to her then. "You must realize that you have money enough to do things comfortably, and I do not think there is any danger of your doing them extravagantly, so please adopt a level-headed attitude, as everyone thinks you are carrying this economy idea to the extent of being parsimonious."

Eunice first exhibited her respect for a dollar in elementary school, writing to her parents that they really should reconsider spending $50 up front for "a season of dancing school. All the other children bring $1.25 for 1 lesson. It is so much cheaper and if your [sic] absent you don't pay anything."

With her financial arrangements in Washington settled, Eunice eased into her new job. "I am the assistant to a Mr. McCahon [William H. McCahon], who is in charge of Prisoners of War Camps in Germany and in the United States. We write reports on the camps and handle all the complaints of the prisoners or the belligerent powers," she wrote her father. "I even have a secretary to do my typing, which I am sure will please you after reading this letter."

Eunice liked McCahon and his wife, Louise. They invited her to their home for dinner even though they knew "I was a very busy woman socially." She was glad she made the time. Louise, a native of Pittsfield, Massachusetts, had been a social worker in New York before the couple moved to Washington. Her work with the Westchester County Department of Child Welfare echoed Eunice's own experiences volunteering in the city's settlement houses in the Bowery and East Harlem during her Manhattanville days.

She wrote to Mother Mary Tenney, her history professor at Manhattanville, to describe her new job and to ask which books she should read to better familiarize herself with modern European history. Mother Tenney recommended the textbook she was using in her course that spring on twentieth-century Europe, *Europe Since 1914*, by F. Lee Benns. "I chose Benns this year for what may seem a queer reason—because it is colorless.

I don't want some people's views on Spain, etc. I think you will know what I mean," she wrote, no doubt a reference to the Catholic Church's support of the Nationalist rebels led by General Francisco Franco who ousted the elected left-wing Republican coalition government during the Spanish Civil War. The anti-Communism of the Catholic Church, and the Kennedy family, had been forged in that conflict.

The Special War Problems Division was responsible for the more than four hundred thousand Axis prisoners of war in more than five hundred camps across the United States in 1945. Most were housed in barracks built on fairgrounds, ball fields, and race tracks in rural areas, mostly in the South and West to reduce the cost of heat in winter, although dozens of camps were also opened in the Northeast, Midwest, and Middle Atlantic states. Camps that had housed the public work relief program, the Civilian Conservation Corps, a decade earlier were converted to accommodate the mostly German and Italian detainees who began arriving in the United States in 1943 from overcrowded facilities in Allied countries.

Living conditions for the prisoners of war, as mandated by the 1929 Geneva Convention, were comparable to those of the US soldiers guarding them. Inmates could not be forced to work in jobs that aided the Allied war effort, but tens of thousands of detainees did other work, hired out as laborers, farmhands, and mill and factory workers at a time when the usual local workforce was abroad serving in uniform. Employers paid the US government 45 cents per worker per hour, helping to defray the costs of housing and feeding the prisoners. The POWs earned 80 cents a day to spend at the camp canteen on small indulgences such as candy and cigarettes. Escapes were rare, and POWs often became friendly with their employers, with farmhands taking their midday meals with the families they toiled alongside. Many returned to the United States to live after the war.

The camps were not without problems, and those problems often landed on Eunice's desk. Anthony Wegner, for instance, was being held as a German POW at Camp Carson in Colorado despite the fact that he was a Polish national forced into the German army after spending almost four years in the Auschwitz concentration camp for trying to leave occupied Poland with his American-born wife, Mary Wolski Wegner.

His wife, from Holyoke, Massachusetts, appealed to First Lady Eleanor Roosevelt to secure Wegner's release. Eunice reviewed Wegner's case with the War Department for her supervisor, who replied to both Mrs. Roosevelt and Mrs. Wegner that "the term 'German prisoners of war' includes all persons who were serving in the German armed forces at the time of their capture, irrespective of their nationality.'" Wegner would, however, be moved as soon as possible from Camp Carson "to a camp in North Carolina for Polish nationals" and then be repatriated to Poland. His ability to reenter the United States "will depend upon the immigration laws in effect at the time when he seeks admission."

Mostly, Eunice dealt with family members worried about the welfare of relatives being held in German POW camps, where conditions deteriorated as the Allied victory neared. She could be flippant when writing to her parents about her job—"Must get back & answer some mad woman who wants to know why we don't fly food supplies to Am. POWS in Germany instead of letting them starve"—but she was reassuring in her letters to anxious correspondents.

Typical was an exchange with Virginia Lee Wilson of Norfolk, Virginia, whose grandson was being held in Stalag Luft I on the Baltic Sea, near Barth, Germany. Swiss authorities had last visited the camp in December 1944 and found sufficient food and medical supplies from the Red Cross on hand and reported that the "morale of the prisoners of war was said to be good." But Mrs. Wilson worried that the chaos in Europe as the end of the war neared would cut off those supplies. Eunice, writing to Mrs. Wilson only weeks before the Allied victory in Europe, on behalf of the acting assistant chief of the Special War Problems Division, reassured her that supply depots in Moosburg, Bavaria, and in Lubeck in northern Germany were still being maintained by the International Red Cross Committee and the American Red Cross.

Work was not the only focus of Eunice's life. She socialized with new acquaintances and friends of Kick from Washington and from London, some of whom were now living in DC. The Kennedy siblings shared friends throughout their lives, in much the way they shared boats and tennis rackets in Hyannis Port. At Kick's urging, Eunice looked up Dinah Brand, Nancy Astor's niece, and Patsy Field, the sister of John White, Kick's sometime suitor and colleague when she worked at the *Washington Times-Herald*.

Eunice was also being courted by James Cross, the son of a prominent New York architect, and by Richard Wood, the son of Lord Halifax, the British ambassador to the United States, who, as British foreign secretary at the outbreak of the war, had shared her father's preference for the appeasement of Hitler. After Kick had a visit in England from Cross, whose father designed the Tiffany Building on Fifth Avenue and the Barclay Hotel in Midtown, she wrote her parents, "Please tell Eunice she has an ardent admirer there."

But it was Wood who pursued Eunice, even as newspapers on both sides of the Atlantic linked him to her widowed sister. Kick was not interested in him romantically but thought Eunice should be. "I lunched with Richard's sister today," Kick wrote from London, coaxing her sister along. "Have you been seeing any more of him? He liked you so much."

In 1942, Richard's older brother, Peter, had been killed in combat, and two months later, Richard was seriously injured himself at the Battle of El Alamein in North Africa. A German bomb had shattered both of his legs, but he had adapted with grace to the prosthetics he now used with crutches. Richard spent time in the United States, accompanying his parents to veterans hospitals, reassuring injured soldiers that there was life after amputation. In a letter to "Darling Eunice" from New Orleans on one such trip, Richard reported "the best news in the world. I was yesterday referred to in the papers as 'tall, slim, and handsome.' So there."

When Richard wrote to tell Kick he had been seeing Eunice but that she had stood him up for dinner, she wrote to her sister right away. "He gave the great news that you had finally come into his life," Kick wrote. "Also you had been asked to come to dinner but somehow the message had gone wrong and you never appeared. It sounds like more of one of your 'usuals' to me."

Eunice's "usual" was avoiding romantic entanglements in favor of casual dates, often in groups, and weekend ski trips to New England with Radcliffe friends who had not yet graduated. Wood would not be the only young man in the next several years to write Eunice ardent love letters, begging her to respond. She saved many of her suitors' letters, but none of her replies, if there were any, have survived.

That she took none of her suitors too seriously is certain. "We were all having a marvelous time, not interested in getting married. None of us were," she said of herself and her siblings. "No pressure to get married. We all had a good time around. I don't know why people would want to get married at twenty-one."

At twenty-four, Eunice was serious about her work. Although years later she would characterize herself as "a rather lowly functionary" at the State Department whose "job was mostly to receive telegrams, review them, summarize them, and catalog them," she liked being in a position to watch history unfold. She had finished work for the day on Thursday, April 12, when word came that President Roosevelt had died suddenly in Warm Springs, Georgia, a month before the war in Europe came to a close. More than ever, she appealed to her father to share his perspective on world events with her as he had once done with Joe Jr., and as he did still with Jack and Kick.

Conscious of the gaps in her knowledge, she wrote to him often, soliciting his views on "any important developments," including the Potsdam Conference that summer in Germany, where the leaders of the United States, the Soviet Union, and Great Britain negotiated territorial terms for the end of the war. For Eunice, Joe Kennedy was still the source of all wisdom. "What with working in the State Dept. and having JP Kennedy as a Papa, people think I know almost as much as [Secretary of State Edward R.] Stettinius," she wrote to Rose. Eunice was determined to give them no reason to doubt it.

Her father answered her policy questions at length but cautioned her that no one would take her seriously until she learned how to spell, to punctuate, and to write legibly, skills that would elude Eunice all her life. Thanking her for a Father's Day card she sent him that June, he noted that, in her haste, "you spelled Joseph 'Joesph.' If Stettinius or Grew ever saw that, you'd have no problems in the State Department—you'd be out on your ear!"

Because gossip was valued currency in the Kennedy household, Eunice wanted the inside story on the men who ran the State Department. Early on, she had asked her father's opinion of "Grewsy-Woosie," Joseph Clark Grew, an undersecretary of state who had served as US ambassador to Japan until Pearl Harbor. "Is he not in part responsible for our unprepared state when Japan attacked us? Would not our foreign policy toward the Japanese have been firmer if Grew had been less of a pacifist, e.g. he didn't want us to stop selling scrap iron, etc.," she asked Joe. "I am trying at the moment to stick up for the Department here at home, so if you could give me any ideas on the above, please transmit such information to me."

Joe did not hold back: "Now to Grew. [Former president Herbert] Hoover told me the other day that he appointed him undersecretary while he was there, and Grew was so stupid that after ninety days they had to find a place to send him in order to get him out of the Department, and they hit on Japan. I would think the consensus of opinion from fellows like Welles [Sumner Welles, an undersecretary of State under FDR] and Hoover, confidentially, of course, is that he's just of very ordinary intellect."

One of the cases that crossed Eunice's desk that spring concerned the son of the man President Roosevelt had appointed to replace her father as US ambassador to the Court of Saint James's, John Gilbert Winant. A liberal reformer who supported FDR's domestic initiatives as well as his foreign policy, Winant was a tall, handsome former Republican governor of New Hampshire. Kick had met him in January at a dinner party in London and found him "the soul of shyness." He confided that he had torn up two hateful postcards that had arrived at the US Embassy addressed to her after her marriage to Billy. "I read them, didn't like them, and tore them up," he told Kick. "I've been waiting to tell you this. Hope you didn't mind."

A complicated and lonely man, Winant had secrets of which Kick apparently was unaware. He had come to London without his wife or three children, the oldest of whom was already married, when he became ambassador in 1941. In contrast to Joe Kennedy, Winant forged an immediate bond with Winston Churchill, often spending weekends at Chequers, the family's country estate. Winant had won the hearts of the British as soon as he stepped onto the tarmac at an airfield in Bristol on March 1, 1941, when he declared: "There is no place I would rather be at this time than in England." It was a far different tone from that struck by Joe Kennedy, who had decamped for the countryside in the fall of 1940 when the first bombs began falling on London and who, early and often, predicted that England could not withstand the punishing assault from the Nazis and would soon surrender.

Winant was at the dining table at Chequers on December 7, 1941, when news came of the Japanese attack on Pearl Harbor, ensuring that the United States would enter the war. It was also at Chequers that the fifty-one-year-old American ambassador began an affair with Sarah Churchill, the prime minister's married twenty-seven-year-old daughter, that would last throughout the war but end unhappily for him when she refused to consider marriage.

Winant's older son, John Jr., had dropped out of Princeton to join the US Army Air Forces after Pearl Harbor and was attached to the Eighth Air Force in England. In the summer and fall of 1943, the ambassador's son took part in bombing raids in Germany known as Operation Pointblank. The combined British and US forces aimed to destroy German aircraft production by bombing their factories. The goal was to decimate the Luftwaffe, but the opposite happened. Flying without escorts, many of the Allied bombers were shot down before they reached their targets. That October, John Winant Jr.'s B-17 Flying Fortress was shot from the sky as he was returning to Britain from a bombing run.

It was five weeks before Winant learned that his son was alive and a prisoner of war. John Jr. was held with other well-connected Allied prisoners, whom the Germans called "the Prominente," including Giles Romilly, a nephew of Winston Churchill. Heinrich Himmler, the head of the SS, the Nazi paramilitary force, considered the prisoners his personal hostages and detained them with other POWs in Colditz Castle, a Renaissance fortress near Leipzig, to use as bargaining chips if need be. When American soldiers liberated the prison days before the end of the war in Europe, the Prominente were not there. As Germany fell, Himmler had ordered his subordinates to take the hostages to the Black Forest and shoot them. Fearing Allied retribution for the execution of well-connected POWs, prison officials turned the detainees over to the Swiss instead.

"I am rather busy at the moment with John Winant," Eunice wrote to her father on May 25, by which time the ambassador's son was at an American command post in Austria. "We have been receiving daily telegrams as to his whereabouts, his health, his morale, even the color of his hair . . . He is as safe as a baby with his bottle, which I wired to Papa Winant (in slightly different words)."

By October, the work of the Special War Problems Division was winding down. Within a year, all of the POWs in American camps would be repatriated to their home countries. "I guess I shall stay on at least for a while. Four of our staff are leaving this week, but the section won't close for at least six months," Eunice wrote to Joe. "Our chief told us not to worry about what happens after that, as most of the sections are expanding and we would be given first preference. I'll let you know."

Always restless, she had been toying with other options. Kick had written gossip items and reviewed plays at the *Washington Times-Herald* before joining the Red Cross in London. Jack, a published author at twenty-three, had covered the charter conference of the United Nations, in San Francisco, in April, for Joe's friend, the newspaper publisher William Randolph Hearst; in June Hearst had dispatched him to England to cover the British elections that turned Conservative prime minister Winston Churchill out of office. Given her admiration for Kick and near veneration of Jack, it is hardly surprising that Eunice would consider a career in journalism.

She wrote two short essays on topics of public interest, neither of which survives in her personal papers, and sent them to Sister Mary Cleophas Costello, the president of Mount Saint Agnes College, in Baltimore, for a candid critique. She got one. Describing one of Eunice's essays as "dull and repetitious," the Sister of Mercy was blunt but not unkind, concluding that "on the superficial knowledge which I have, I would say you are not especially gifted in the art of writing; but, on the other hand, intelligent study and determination can produce wonders."

Eunice was nothing if not determined. She undertook her "intelligent study" by writing again to Mother Mary Tenney, her professor at Manhattanville, for reading suggestions. Mother Tenney recommended Virginia Moore's *Distinguished Women Writers*, which included seventeen portraits of literary women, including Sappho and George Eliot, and *Living Biographies of Famous Women*, by Henry Thomas and Dana Lee Thomas, which profiled social and political activists as well as literary figures, from Cleopatra and Joan of Arc, to Jane Addams and Madame Chiang Kai-shek. For good measure, and perhaps mindful of Eunice's attraction to the religious life, Mother Tenney suggested she also read the profiles of fifteen Catholic saints in *Heroines of Christ*, by Joseph Husslein, a Jesuit priest who taught at Fordham University and also wrote about workers' rights and social justice issues for the Jesuit magazine *America*.

But Joe had something else in mind: a family project that would bring Eunice back to Massachusetts. For months, her father had been reemerging on the public stage. He accepted an appointment from Governor Maurice J. Tobin to serve as chairman of a commission studying the state's economic future, a position that allowed him to scout opportunities for Jack as he reacquainted himself with the political players across Massachusetts. He spent $13 million to buy the Merchandise Mart in Chicago, the largest commercial building in the world in 1945, committing a quarter of its profits to the establishment of the Joseph P. Kennedy Jr. Foundation in memory of his fallen son. That July, nineteen-year-old Jean Kennedy christened a navy destroyer at the Quincy shipyard for Joe Jr., who had been her godfather, and the Kennedy Foundation made its first big grant, of $600,000, to the Archdiocese of Boston to build a hospital for children with disabilities. Putting philanthropy in the service of politics, Joe made sure that the local newspapers ran photographs of Jack handing the check for the Joseph P. Kennedy Jr. Memorial Hospital to Archbishop Richard Cushing.

His father was laying the groundwork for a political future that Jack was not entirely sure he wanted or was physically able to pursue. The still-sickly war hero spent that autumn making tentative dinner speeches and appearing at charity events arranged by Joe, who had also convinced *Reader's Digest* to publish a condensed version of John Hersey's account in the *New Yorker* of Jack's heroism on PT-109, ensuring the widest possible audience for the story of Jack's courage under fire.

To veterans groups, Kiwanis clubs, and communion breakfasts in Massachusetts, Jack told the tale of his Solomon Islands encounter with the enemy, emphasizing the valor of his crew above his own personal bravery. On September 15, 1945, Eunice wrote her father to say she had bought all of the Boston papers at her Washington newsstand "to see how Jack's speech went over, and all I could find was 'Kennedy Stresses Work for Vets,'" a front-page report in the *Boston Globe* three days before about a speech that *Joe* had delivered urging businesses to invest in human capital to promote a postwar economic revival in Massachusetts. The emphasis on the potential of veterans to lead that charge underscored the leadership promise of the generation just out of uniform, Jack included. A much smaller account of Jack's speech about the state of postwar Europe to an American Legion post appeared in the same edition, buried on page nine.

The indifference of newsmen to Jack's maiden speeches was a small matter next to a political development that would have major consequences for his career. Perhaps not so coincidentally, a congressional seat had just opened up. James Michael Curley, the colorful incumbent congressman from Massachusetts's Eleventh District, announced he would resign his seat in Washington if elected mayor of Boston in November, an office Maurice Tobin had vacated after being elected governor in 1944. If Curley defeated the acting mayor, John E. Kerrigan, it would be his fourth term as Boston's mayor since 1914. The fact that he was under federal indictment for mail fraud was not a particular handicap to his mayoral bid, but money was. No definitive paper trail has surfaced, but historians have long suspected that Joe Kennedy cleared the path for Jack's congressional run by paying off Curley's debts and legal bills and financing the saturation radio advertisements that helped him win nineteen of the city's twenty-two wards that fall. Curley would spend five months of his mayoral term in Danbury federal prison after his fraud conviction, but he would later win a full pardon from President Harry S. Truman—to say nothing of the gratitude of the Kennedy clan for his timely preference for municipal over national office.

It was true that Jack had lived in the Eleventh Congressional District only during his college years at Harvard, but his Fitzgerald roots ran deep in the North End, an Irish stronghold until a later wave of Italian immigrants recast the neighborhood. His mother, Rose, had been born there and was as well known as the daughter of Boston's affable former mayor, John F. "Honey Fitz" Fitzgerald, as she was the wife of the former ambassador to Great Britain. Jack's Kennedy roots in East Boston, another working-class neighborhood in the district, traced to his paternal grandfather, P. J. Kennedy, who had been a state lawmaker and ward boss there.

Money was not an issue. To win the race for Jack, Joe spent more than $300,000—six times what a state lawmaker and future speaker of the House named Thomas P. "Tip" O'Neill Jr. would spend six years later to secure the same seat. Joe Kane, a well-known local political operative and Joe Kennedy's cousin, provided entrée to the district, which included Cambridge, Somerville, and Charlestown, the latter one of Boston's biggest Irish neighborhoods, as well as East Boston and the North End. Honey Fitz supplied the connective tissue, having intermittently represented most of the district across more than five decades either on the city council, in the state senate, in the US House, or as mayor of Boston. He campaigned enthusiastically for Jack.

Jack was an ambivalent candidate, uncertain of his ability to play a part that had been written for Joe Jr. In an interview in 1957, his father acknowledged that Jack had been more conscript than volunteer in that first run for elective office. "I got Jack into politics. I was the one," Joe Kennedy told a reporter. "I told him Joe was dead and that it was therefore his responsibility to run for Congress."

Looking back thirty years later, Eunice rejected the idea that her father had forced a political career on her unwilling brother. Jack had flirted with journalism and had considered a career in academia, but he was drifting, in her view. "It wasn't like he was headed to be a doctor and had to change his course. Nothing like that," she said. "He was very interested in politics. It was just a natural culmination of his interests."

There were so few Republicans in the Eleventh Congressional District that the race would be decided in the Democratic primary, on June 18, 1946. Jack would need to defeat nine other Democrats vying for the seat. He did not have much time to win over voters, who needed no introduction to the top tier of his competitors, including Cambridge mayor Michael J. Neville, Charlestown native John Cotter, and Boston City Councilor Joe Russo.

His opponents derided Jack as a rich carpetbagger—to establish residency in the district, he took rooms in the Hotel Bellevue on Beacon Hill—who did not understand the needs of the largely working-class district. The *East Boston Leader* mocked his candidacy: "Congress Seat for Sale—No Experience Necessary—Applicant Must Live in New York or Florida—Only Millionaires Need Apply." One of his opponents pinned a $10 bill to his lapel and called it a Kennedy button. If Jack was to win, it would take more than money and marketing; it would require the energy of the entire clan.

Joe summoned Eunice from Washington. She moved into the Ritz-Carlton in Boston's Back Bay with twenty-two-year-old Pat and eighteen-year-old Jean and got to work. "I used to go around and ring doorbells up and down housing projects, telling them—it was like a song—'Here's a piece of literature on his record,'" she recalled. "I remember there was a number of house parties."

One was especially memorable. There were close to a hundred people in Mary McNeely's parlor in Charlestown when Jack rose to speak. He was twenty-nine years old, a naval hero of the world war just ended. But peering out from under a shock of unruly russet hair, he looked more like a teenager pressed by his parents into reciting a party piece for the laborers, longshoremen, secretaries, and salesclerks crammed that night into McNeely's modest apartment.

He began haltingly. Writing came more naturally than speech making to the gaunt young man with the ashen pallor who wanted to be a journalist, not a politician. Months of appearances before the Veterans of Foreign Wars and the Rotarians and the Knights of Columbus had done little to enliven his wooden delivery. Many nights, after making the rounds of four or five house parties like this one, he would sit up late at night with his father, dissecting his performance. "I can still see the two of them sitting together, analyzing the entire speech and talking about the pace of delivery to see where it worked and where it had gone wrong," Eunice remembered.

She stood directly in front of her brother as he began his speech to the working men and women from Precinct 7. She had memorized it.

Eunice "was saying every word along with him, and it was very noticeable," Mary McNeely recalled eighteen year later. "When he finished his
speech, he called her out to our kitchen and said, 'Eunice, you made me
very, very nervous. Don't ever do that to me again.' She said, 'Jack, I
thought you were going to forget your speech.'"

As annoyed as he was, Jack valued Eunice's political instincts, asking
her to campaign in the blue-collar neighborhoods of Cambridge, where
he faced his strongest opponent in Mike Neville, the city's popular mayor.
The house parties had been such a success in Charlestown and East Boston that Eunice and Joe DeGuglielmo, a Cambridge city councilman everyone called DeGug, wondered whether a larger, formal event wouldn't
attract even more women voters.

"The Irish are social climbers. I thought if we got a hotel, a ballroom,
sent out engraved invitations to the women voters in the name of the ambassador and Rose, we'd be sure to draw a crowd," the councilman recalled. "I mentioned it to Eunice, and she said, 'We'll do it.' Just like that.
I said it would cost a lot of money. She asked how much. I said, 'Plenty.'
We had to invite every registered Democratic woman on the voting list. If
you left anybody off, they'd be furious and you'd risk losing that vote and
maybe others besides. There was some opposition. John Droney [a navy
veteran and recent law school graduate who later became district attorney
of Middlesex County] was against it—too effeminate. They argued that
the people who'd come were people who had probably already made up
their mind to vote for you, so you wouldn't be making any converts, and
you'd be wasting time and effort. And the old pols would rather have
spent the money on beer busts. But Eunice said, 'Let's go!' And she got
twenty-five volunteer secretaries and had the invitations engraved, and
they started addressing them."

The formal tea party, at the Hotel Commander in Harvard Square
on Saturday, June 15, attracted 1,500 women, many in rented ball gowns,
who sipped tea from china cups and nibbled finger sandwiches. The reception line to meet the candidate and his family snaked around the block.
"I was dead wrong," Droney said when he saw the front-page coverage in
the Sunday newspapers.

It rained on June 18, keeping turnout down on primary day to 30 percent of registered voters, but the Kennedy campaign was well prepared.
Joe had rented taxi cabs and hired private cars to get Jack's voters to the
polls. He won 40.5 percent of the vote, almost twice as much as Neville. In

November he would win 72 percent of the vote in a year when Massachusetts Republicans took a US Senate seat from the Democratic incumbent,
won nine of the state's fourteen House seats, and ousted the Democratic
governor, Maurice Tobin, who had inadvertently set the table for Jack by
leaving the mayor's office open for James Michael Curley.

Had Eunice ever resented giving up her State Department job to
launch her brother's career? "I don't think I would have risen to Secretary,"
she scoffed decades later. "I don't think I made any great sacrifice."

PART TWO

IN HER BROTHERS' SHADOWS

FIVE

JUVENILE DELINQUENCY

The unhappy squalor these children exist in was a shock to me.

—EUNICE KENNEDY, 1947

T HE THREE-STORY BRICK row house in Georgetown was equal parts political salon, teen drop-in center, and boutique hotel after Eunice and Jack Kennedy set up housekeeping on Thirty-First Street in 1947. On any given day, a juvenile delinquent from the National Training School for Boys—a federal juvenile detention center in Washington administered by the Justice Department—might be eating a peanut butter sandwich opposite the freshman congressman reading a briefing book beside the US Justice Department bureaucrat gathering her papers to head for the office. On any given evening, the Irish cook might be putting the finishing touches on her signature chocolate cake in the kitchen while a high-volume game of charades in the parlor pitted Eunice and writers Joseph Alsop and Charles Bartlett against Jack and his Republican freshmen colleagues Senator Joseph McCarthy of Wisconsin and Congressman Richard Nixon of California.

In a historic neighborhood that was home to foreign ambassadors, senators, and university professors, the house at 1528 Thirty-First Street had the feel of a Hollywood hotel, with movie stars, Kennedy siblings, and prep school and college pals passing through at unpredictable intervals.

Billy Sutton, a campaign aide from Charlestown, Massachusetts, who had joined the Capitol Hill staff of the freshly minted congressman, recalled: "You never knew who the hell was going to be there, but you got used to it."

Sometimes guests would appear for dinner and find no sign of their host or hostess, to be greeted instead by Margaret Ambrose, a longtime Kennedy family cook sent to Washington to keep the scrawny siblings well nourished, or by George Thomas, Jack's black valet. Alsop, the syndicated columnist and consummate Georgetown host, recalled with horror his first visit to "a small and very, very, very disorderly house. I still remember how surprised I was when I arrived on time and found no one at all, living room in complete disorder; some kind of athletic contest had been going on. I think there was a half-eaten hamburger—at any rate, there was some kind of unfinished sandwich on the mantelpiece, and, as I say, no one in sight. Gradually, one by one, everyone appeared, and finally we had dinner."

As promising as their futures looked and as great as their potential appeared, Eunice and Jack Kennedy in 1947 were rich, spoiled, and heedless of the social conventions that governed the lives of the less entitled. Jack showed up on the floor of the US House of Representatives in sneakers and khaki pants. Eunice walked out the front door with runs in her stockings and stains on her blouse. Both always ran late. Neither carried cash, leaving it to staffers to pick up the tab for lunch, a newspaper, or a taxi ride. Their father had raised them not to worry about money, and they didn't, knowing that the accountants in Joe's New York office would sort out their bills.

As Jack began work that January on Capitol Hill, Eunice, at age twenty-five, began her own new job as a special assistant to US Attorney General Tom C. Clark on the problem of juvenile delinquency. "I was lucky," she said of landing the unpaid position with the unwieldy title of executive secretary of the Continuing Committee of the National Conference on Prevention and Control of Juvenile Delinquency. "Financially, I had private means, and I could take on that kind of a job and devote all my time and energy to it."

Joe Kennedy had secured Eunice's job the same way he had engineered a US House seat for Jack: with good connections and cold cash. Congress had appropriated no funds for Clark to carry out the recommendations of his National Advisory Committee, which, the year before, had documented a postwar spike in juvenile crime. Without resources, Clark was stymied in his goal of making juvenile justice part of the "permanent work of the attorney general's office." Timothy A. McInerny, who handled public relations for Clark, knew Joe Kennedy from his time as chief editorial writer for the *Boston Post*. McInerny "went to Mr. Kennedy and told him of the problem and asked him if he'd put up the money," according to James V. Bennett, then the director of the Federal Bureau of Prisons in the Justice Department. "He said yes, provided Mr. Clark accepted as a member of the staff his daughter Eunice."

Clark's correspondence with Joe is more ambiguous about the quid pro quo, but, in a letter on Christmas Eve 1946, the attorney general noted, "Tim told me of your call, and we have this to suggest . . . Would your daughter Eunice care to take over this work as the executive secretary?"

Clark touted the experience she would gain and the contributions she could make toward solving a serious national problem. "She would be in close contact with other government agencies such as the Children's Bureau, and would immediately be in touch with all of the big, national organizations who are members of the panel. I think that somebody with her training and background would do wonders in keeping this worthwhile work going," Clark wrote. "At present, she could work with Tim and other members of my staff who are familiar with what has gone on in the past. Planning for the future is needed. While the job is not clearly defined in the pattern right now, I think that with her background, Eunice could very well make something very worthwhile out of it."

The job's lack of definition and limited resources would prove problematic for both Eunice and the Children's Bureau, the federal child welfare agency, which was wary of having what it saw as a pressing social issue co-opted by the office of the chief law enforcement official in the country. But there was no hint of potential problems in the news coverage that greeted Eunice's return to the capital city. *Newsweek* ran her picture with the announcement. The *New York Times* carried word of her new job. Kathleen's old beau John White, at the *Washington Times-Herald*, wrote a profile of Kick's kid sister, noting that Eunice was "energetic and ambitious, with a lot of her old man's ability." Her headlines eclipsed those that heralded Jack's arrival on Capitol Hill. "Eunice Kennedy Helps U.S. Fight Juvenile Crime," read one. "Eunice Kennedy Not Interested in Pay—She Wants to See Young America Play," read another.

Juvenile delinquency was a major public preoccupation during and after the war, with politicians, police, and social scientists variously assigning blame to the disruptions of wartime, absent fathers, working mothers, negligent parenting, and popular culture. Comic books and pinball machines came in for especially harsh criticism for their purported corrosive influence on American youth. J. Edgar Hoover, the director of the Federal Bureau of Investigation, attributed the rise in youthful offenders to a moral breakdown "in the fundamentals of common decency."

The federal government had been focused on the welfare of children since 1909, when, under pressure from such Progressive Era reformers as Jane Addams of Hull House in Chicago, President Theodore Roosevelt convened the first White House Conference on Children and Youth. The creation of the Children's Bureau, in 1912, was designed to address the immediate need for child labor protections, but reformers also aimed to shift policy away from incarcerating juveniles to preventing delinquency through education and recreation. Settlement houses, including those where Eunice had volunteered in New York City, had already incorporated organized sports into their programs toward just that end.

With the support of President Harry S. Truman, in 1946 Attorney General Clark made combating juvenile delinquency an unprecedented priority for the US Justice Department. "There are extremely interesting and potentially powerful personalities entering into the limelight as the first year of the Truman administration nears its close," the *Boston Post* wrote on February 17, 1946. "One of those is Attorney General Tom Clark, who has embarked on one of the most unusual crusades ever taken by a Cabinet officer—that of trying to solve our very serious juvenile delinquency problem in America from the top level of government."

Clark framed the federal government's interest in eradicating juvenile delinquency as a moral imperative, his language anticipating that which the Johnson administration would use in the 1960s to advocate a partnership between Washington and community action groups in the War on Poverty. "If every community in America strengthened and united its resources for all of its children, it would save many of them from taking the first stumbling steps toward delinquency," Clark said in a speech a few weeks before Eunice came on board. "Delay in community action to mobilize resources to lead children into rich and purposeful living until some are already in trouble is more costly, more difficult, and often too late."

Just how much juvenile crime was increasing was itself a matter of dispute, with the FBI touting higher numbers of arrests and the Children's

Bureau focusing on the smaller number of cases that made their way through the courts. In one of her first speeches on the topic, Eunice told a gathering of Jewish War Veterans of the United States that 51 percent of all criminals in the country were under the age of twenty-one. Whatever the actual numbers, the perception was that young people were running wild across the country, and something needed to be done.

Eunice's immediate mandate was to circulate the eighteen separate reports produced by the conference the previous year—on everything from juvenile courts to school truancy—to state and municipal officials, encouraging them to hold local meetings on the issues. As the department's point person on juvenile delinquency, she was inundated with inquiries and suggestions from fraternal organizations, charitable groups, and churches, as well as mayors, governors, and state lawmakers. But when she arrived at the Justice Department, she had neither a desk nor a secretary. There was no money beyond a few grants from foundations and private citizens such as her father.

In her first report to the attorney general, written one month after she began work, Eunice did not mince words about the need for more help and a larger work space. A good start would be two permanent secretaries, two assistants, a part-time press aide, and a designated suite of offices with desks, filing cabinets, and adequate shelf space, she wrote: "Shortages of personnel and facilities have prevented the office from achieving more than the minimum. It has been impossible to take the initiative. Save in rare instances, the job has been to maintain position, not to get ahead."

Stasis was not a natural condition for Eunice Kennedy, and she displayed none of the reticence one might expect of a young woman in a new job in the nation's capital. In her first week, she had already surreptitiously sent her father the outline of Clark's "plan for scholarship aid for delinquent youth," soliciting his suggestions for promoting the idea with the moneyed class. She was eager to get out of the office and into the field to work with delinquents directly and to put the conference recommendations into action. When the Justice Department finally did assign her a desk, the last thing she wanted was to sit behind it.

Joe advised her to test the scholarship plan in one community. A pilot program in Boston or another city in Massachusetts—presumably one in Jack's Eleventh Congressional District—could help her "find out all the bugs in the program and how much it would cost," he suggested, stressing that "the accent should be on who is going to see that the boy is in the right

environment while he is getting his schooling." There was no provision
for delinquent girls in the plan.

Girls got short shrift for reasons that had more to do with gender
stereotypes than their actual needs. Visiting a mentoring program at the
Washington Boys Club, sponsored by the police department, Eunice took
notes on her conversation with a Lieutenant Murphy. "Lt. Murphy talked
about need for kids yelling and screaming. It's natural for them. Let 'em
do it. Don't plan a program for the rough, tough kids. Just give 'em a place
to play. Otherwise they won't bother with you," he said. In her notes, Eunice starred the lieutenant's observations about girls: "Girls don't commit
crime as much as boys. They have objectives they are searching for. They
have purpose in life. Boys haven't real objectives. They haven't got the
same sense of responsibility girls do. Just watch men shifting along the
streets. Girls don't do that."

The foundation that Joe had established in memory of Joe Jr. "would
be glad to defray any expenses up to a reasonable amount in Boston" for
a scholarship program, he told Eunice, underscoring the random nature
and mixed motives of the Kennedy Foundation's early philanthropy. Solving social problems did not preclude advancing his children's careers.

Recognizing that with so few resources, Eunice would be unable to
accomplish much in her new job, Joe decided to send her an assistant he
would pay himself. He had just the man. Robert Sargent Shriver was already working for him in Chicago, scouting new tenants for the Merchandise Mart, which Joe had bought two years before. Shriver had been in the
job only a few months, trying to fill the twenty-five-story behemoth that
spanned two city blocks on the north bank of the Chicago River, when Joe
abruptly redirected him to Washington. Shriver packed enough clothes
for a week; he stayed for eighteen months.

Sarge and Eunice had already met. Kick introduced them a year before at a party in New York when she was visiting from London. Eunice's
older sister had first met Shriver when he was a student at Canterbury, a
Catholic prep school in Connecticut that Jack had attended briefly during
the same period. Sarge had dated one of Kick's closest friends at nearby
Noroton. A navy veteran and a graduate of Yale College and Yale Law
School, Sarge in 1946 was a junior editor at *Newsweek*, the handsome
scion of a distinguished, although cash-strapped, family with deep roots
in Maryland and the Catholic Church. James Cardinal Gibbons, the archbishop of Baltimore, had baptized him and served as his spiritual mentor.

The Kennedys had more money, but the Shrivers' Catholic pedigree was without peer.

Eunice had accepted Sarge's invitation to tea at the Plaza Hotel a few days after their first meeting, extending the evening through dinner and dancing. "Never had I met a woman so intelligent, so sure of herself, so well versed on so wide a range of topics. We ranged from domestic politics, to world affairs, to religion, to her experiences abroad, to interest in the problems of juvenile delinquency," he remembered. "I was dazzled by her intellect and seriousness."

She was not so besotted. In a letter to Eunice long after that first date, Sarge recalled the moment he kissed her at the end of that evening, "only to find you picking morning glories out of the window box behind me." She had been impressed enough with him, though, to recommend him to her father as an editor who could judge whether Joe Jr.'s letters and diaries about his prewar travels through Europe and during the Spanish Civil War were publishable.

When Sarge answered his phone at *Newsweek*, he was surprised to find Joe Kennedy on the line, inviting him to breakfast at his suite in the Waldorf Astoria. Would Shriver read Joe Jr.'s writings to determine whether his son's observations merited a wider audience? Shriver agreed to take a look and concluded that the letters—full of a teenager's awe at German military might and enthusiasm for such practices as forced sterilization "to do away with many of the disgusting specimens of men which inhabit this earth"—would not be well received in postwar America. Kennedy rewarded his candor with a job offer. Shriver could not turn down the chance to apprentice himself to a famous financier and perhaps to court the boss's daughter as well.

That Eunice exhibited less interest in him than her father failed to discourage the ever-optimistic Shriver. He chose to conclude that her mind was elsewhere, preoccupied with Jack's congressional ambitions and her own myriad interests—the most pressing of which was trying to decide whether she had a religious vocation, an idea she had toyed with since childhood.

In the fall, with Jack's election assured, Eunice had visited Kick in London for six weeks. ("Arrived safely. Great trip. Kick very well. House terrific. Send two thousand dollars travelers cheques if possible," she wired her father on September 28, 1946.) In Kennedy lore, Kick and Eunice are often reduced to caricature, portrayed as polar opposites: the defiant free spirit and the pious prig. But the sisters were far more complicated than that. They were, in fact, as alike as they were different.

Both took their Catholicism seriously. Kick once described a solemn High Mass at Notre-Dame Cathedral in Paris as "the most impressive thing that I have ever seen." She had agonized over her decision to marry a Protestant, meeting with Catholic clerics in England and praying for divine guidance.

A year after Billy's death, trying to find a spiritual path forward, Kick reached out to Eunice to ask the nuns she had known at Roehampton if she could join them for a religious retreat. The older, retired nuns were living in a convent in remote Westmorland. "I could go up there as long as I liked," Kick reported back. "It being in the most northern part of England, I had to give the matter another thought. However, I decided to go (ain't you glad?), not knowing what I was going to be in for. I was the only member present without 'the habit,' and I must say it felt mighty queer after residing these many months with so many Prots. There was a chaplain in residence, but, as he had one foot in the grave and the other not far behind, he wasn't giving me much advice about faith and morals."

She took her meals alone in a small room heated only by a wood fire and went on brisk walks with Mother Poett, "a terrific walker [who] walked me off my little legs every day." The nuns "were all so kind and tearful about Billy. It seems so funny because when he was alive, he might have been the devil . . . I bet there isn't another Protestant who has had so many prayers said for his black soul in one way or another than darling Billy." It is hard to imagine Kick sharing such sentiments with a sister she thought more censorious than sympathetic.

The retreat, Kick wrote to Eunice, was "a good chance to get a perspective on things," not least of all on her sister. In her four days at the convent "with your fans, the Mothers of the Sacred Heart," Kick told Eunice, "they all seemed to know you, and each one had some little tale about your saintly character, the shining star. The Sisters all seemed to know you too."

Did Eunice confide in Kick about her own internal struggle over whether she was called to the convent? The subject does not appear in their correspondence, but it is hard to believe it never came up in their private talks. They had a lot of time alone together during that visit, despite a social whirl that began with a feast of oysters and grouse and champagne at a ball at London's Dorchester Hotel hosted by the former Deborah

Mitford, their debutante friend who had married Billy's younger brother, Andrew, to become the "other" Lady Hartington, the one now destined to become the Duchess of Devonshire.

Kick had also become an accomplished hostess, holding a reception every evening between six and eight o'clock on Smith Square, turning her three-story white Georgian house near Parliament into a political salon for the young smart set. "Kick's house is really very cute and very nicely furnished," Eunice wrote home. "It's a typical Georgetown house with a cute little garden and lots of atmosphere. She adores furnishing it and I must say has done far better than I would have expected."

On a ten-day driving tour of Ireland in November, Kick took Eunice to visit Lismore Castle, in County Waterford, the estate Billy would have inherited had he lived to become the Duke of Devonshire. It would go to Andrew and Debo now. Kick also took her sister to Coolattin House, in County Wicklow, the 120-room estate owned by Peter Wentworth-Fitzwilliam, the married Protestant peer nine years her senior with whom she had become infatuated. Biographers have suggested that Kick would not have confided in her purportedly prim younger sister about her new paramour, but their correspondence intimates otherwise.

In December, after Eunice had returned to the States, Kick wrote to her about Peter: "I have seen Peter Fitz several times since Ireland! He has given me the most lovely Xmas present!!!" All those exclamation points suggest Kick shared more with Eunice than previously thought. Their letters also indicate that they spoke regularly, and at length, on the telephone, so it was perhaps during those transatlantic calls that they shared their deeper confidences. A year later, after her flirtation with Peter had bloomed into a full-blown affair, Kick would ask Eunice to tamp down rumors in the States that she was in love with a married man. However, having confided in several of her friends Stateside about Fitzwilliam, it was Kick herself who was the unwitting source of the gossip.

Eunice was not without her own admirers in England and at home, and her indifference to her suitors only increased their ardor. In a letter to the family, Kick told her parents that Hugh Fraser had more than a passing romantic interest in Eunice. Fraser was a Catholic aristocrat who had been in their social set before the war, attending their debutante parties and visiting the Kennedys during their summer holidays on the Côte d'Azur. He had distinguished himself as a soldier and intelligence officer in World War II, awarded the 1940 Belgian Croix de Guerre and appointed a member of the Order of the British Empire. He was elected a Conservative member of Parliament in 1945. "He asks a lot about her and hopes and prays that she is not taking herself into a nunnery," Kick wrote.

A few days after Eunice arrived in London to see Kick, their mother addressed that question directly. Rose had joined her daughters at Kick's house on Smith Square for a brief visit before one of her regular shopping trips to Paris. At a small party in her honor, the Kennedy matriarch announced to a room full of dinner guests that Eunice intended to become a nun.

If that was her intention, it was a long-term goal rather than an immediate plan. In a letter home from England, Eunice asked her father to be on the lookout for a job for her. Joe had a good reason to help. The political strategist in him had to have been wary of how a Kennedy sister in a floor-length black habit and veil would play in West Virginia. For just that reason, Joe had instructed Jack to limit the number of photographs he took with nuns and priests, common fare for Catholic politicians of lesser ambition.

Joe had mixed motives, too, for bringing Sargent Shriver to Washington the following year, encouraging his aide's courtship of his daughter along with his professional assistance. Years later, he would intervene more urgently on Sarge's behalf with Eunice. In 1947 he might well have hoped that proximity alone would produce a spark.

But Eunice did not have marriage on her mind. Like Kick before her, and Pat and Jean after her, Eunice had developed into an accomplished flirt. She had not discouraged Hugh Fraser's romantic interest or Kick's lobbying on his behalf. But she had not encouraged it, either. Eunice wrote to the much more marriage-minded Kick that she was also continuing to ignore Sargent Shriver's persistent marriage proposals. "Please marry Sargent," Kick wrote. "It's an excellent plan!"

Whatever his amorous prospects with Eunice, Sarge realized that Washington was a longer-term assignment than he had anticipated. He checked out of the Statler Hotel and moved into a cramped apartment not far from Eunice's and Jack's townhouse with his college friends Merle Thorpe and Walter Ridder. Both roommates would be awakened regularly in the next eighteen months by late-night telephone calls to Sarge from Eunice, an insomniac who knew her admirer would be only too happy to keep her company in her chronic wakefulness.

The medical problems that had made Eunice a frequent visitor to doctors in college had not abated. Cramps and stomach distress woke her during the night, and the lack of sleep left her exhausted during the day. Between 1946 and 1949, she consulted a half dozen specialists in Washington, Baltimore, New York, and Boston, filling prescriptions for sleeping pills, antispasm medication, iron pills for anemia, and estrogen and thyroid supplements, as well as such over-the-counter remedies as Ceravim, a vitamin-enriched cereal usually given to infants and convalescents, and Vitules, a vitamin supplement. She was still woefully underweight—whether from her medical issues, an eating disorder, or a combination of the two is unclear.

"I am sorry the pep is slow in coming back, but I really believe it is just the aftermath of the years of malnutrition, and I think it will be recovered as you go along in better condition," Dr. Sara M. Jordan, a prominent gastroenterologist at the Lahey Clinic, in Boston, who also treated Jack, reassured Eunice after her patient wrote from Mont Tremblant Lodge that she was too tired to enjoy skiing at the Quebec resort.

Before Eunice's visit to Kick in London, Dr. Emil Novak, a Baltimore gynecologist who had coauthored a textbook on his specialty, had urged her to adopt a slower pace. "I hope that on your projected trip to England you will not be obliged to do a lot of running around, because I have an idea that you are not ideally designed for a highly active life of this sort with the burning up of a lot of nervous energy," he wrote. "See if you can't manage to get a certain amount of rest and relaxation out of your trip."

But Eunice was constitutionally incapable of slowing her pace. She ignored medical advice to rise by eight o'clock each morning and retire by ten each evening, and refused to follow the regimented high-calorie diets her doctors prescribed. By 1949, at least one of her doctors was exasperated by her lack of compliance. Dr. John W. Norcross, an internist at the Lahey Clinic, wrote to acknowledge receipt of a recent letter from Eunice: "[A]nd since you seem to be so upset about the whole situation, I am going to suggest another program for you. I hope that you will continue to carry out the general suggestions that I have made in the past with regard to going to bed on time and not trying to do more than your physical and nervous systems will allow . . . You must keep your general speed of nervous expenditure below the speed limit, which in your case is much less than you would like to have it."

Norcross prescribed Mebaral, a barbiturate derivative, to be taken before bed and after breakfast. Eunice needed to take the medication as directed to regulate her nightly sleep pattern and to relieve her daily anxiety. "I cannot evaluate the problem nor this particular system if you do not do these things," he told her.

These would be reasonable requests to make of most patients, but her doctors were asking the impossible of Eunice; if she slowed down, how would she ever measure up?

Charles Bartlett, a journalist who would one day introduce Jack Kennedy to Jacqueline Bouvier, recalled the nervous energy that propelled Eunice through her work days: "Sarge was in love with Eunice. Eunice was not so sure that she was romantically interested in Sarge, but she was not fickle in her demands. She worked with him all day, calling out his name again and again—'Sarge, Sarge, Sarge'—in an overwrought voice that was less a request than a command."

Mary Pitcairn, who became a close friend to Eunice in Washington, first met her and Jack when Merle Thorpe brought her to the Kennedy townhouse for dinner. Eunice made a strong and immediate impression: "She was highly nervous, highly geared, and worshipped Jack," Pitcairn said. "I always thought she should have been a boy."

Had she been, George Smathers was certain that Eunice, not Jack, would have occupied Room 322 in the Old House Office Building, down the hall from his own congressional warren. "Of all the kids in the family, Eunice was far and away the strongest minded. Sort of the leader of the clan. Very tough when she wanted to be," said Smathers, who was a freshman congressman from Florida in 1947 and a regular at the young Kennedys' dinner table. "Eunice would have loved to be the one the father picked to run in the Eleventh Congressional District in 1946. If she'd been a little older, and if it had been like today, when a lot of women are running for office, I suspect the history of the Kennedy clan would have been quite different. You might have seen Eunice as the first woman congressman from that district."

The times and the dynamics of her family might have locked her out of a political career, but Eunice's own determination to get into the room where interesting conversations were held and important decisions were made ensured that she would never be excluded entirely. Richard Nixon, who was a frequent guest at Jack's and Eunice's table in Georgetown, remembered that, when the men adjourned for cigars and political talk after dinner, Eunice went with them, lighting her own stogie, refusing to be relegated to the drawing room to gossip with the women.

She also refused to confine to office hours her efforts toward eradicating juvenile delinquency. She brought troubled girls and boys home to the Georgetown row house for supper, telling them, "We want you to be happy children. Happy children become happy men and women." The shallow understanding of childhood poverty and juvenile crime she had gleaned from college textbooks and volunteer work in well-managed Catholic settlement houses in the Bowery and East Harlem would soon deepen.

In March, a matron at the DC Receiving Home for Children was assaulted by a gang of girls, twelve of whom escaped. Eunice visited the facility in the aftermath and was thunderstruck by what she saw in the government-run juvenile detention center in Northeast Washington. A residential center designed to accommodate 65 children was housing 125 from three years old to fifteen. Children slept on the floor for lack of beds. No effort had been made to separate children charged with violent crimes or diagnosed with psychiatric disorders from those who had been surrendered by indigent parents because they could not afford to feed them.

Regulations stipulating that no child be held at the center for longer than three days before being settled into a foster home were being flouted; some children told Eunice they had been there for months. There was no heat in the building and no doctor or nurse on staff. None of the children attended school, and there were no classrooms on site. There was one matron for every fifty children. The "recreation room" was barren, with boys and girls sitting on the floor because there were no chairs that were not broken. "They had nothing with which to amuse themselves except one Chinese checkers game and a crossword puzzle," Eunice noted, describing the building as a "firetrap" and the pervasive stench of urine, mold, and filth as "nauseating."

It was an eye-opening experience for Eunice, accustomed to order and cleanliness in the settlement houses where she had worked. "The unhappy squalor these children exist in was a shock to me," she told the *Washington Times-Herald*. "While I was shivering from the cold, I saw little shavers crying, huddled in cramped rooms bare of furniture." The conditions were "a disgrace to the community and to the nation." There was as much fury as sympathy in Eunice's response to the plight of those children. Alleviating their suffering for her was less about charity than about justice, less about benevolence than about basic human rights.

One can only imagine the conversation that night at 1528 Thirty-First

Street. Her brother sat on the House Education and Labor Committee and the District of Columbia Committee. Couldn't either panel hold hearings? Demand an investigation? Insist on a supplemental appropriation? If Eunice appealed to Jack for help, it is unlikely he was of much use. He was already bored in the House, impatient with the glacial pace of lawmaking and often absent because of the back and stomach ills that continued to immobilize him. He would be diagnosed with Addison's disease later that year while on a congressional trip to London and prescribed a course of corticosteroids that would ease his pain and help fill out his frame. In the meantime, he cut a distinctly unimpressive figure on Capitol Hill.

"Eunice was really more interested in what she was doing than Jack was interested in what he was doing. He was never fascinated by the House of Representatives. And she was working very hard," George Smathers remembered.

"It's fair to say that I was more concerned with social problems than Jack," Eunice acknowledged. "He was challenged mentally and emotionally by it, but he wasn't running around concerned with things such as housing for the poor. [In] his early years, he was more of a searcher. He wasn't totally engrossed in what he was doing." It was a lackluster start to a political career on which Joe Kennedy had staked so much. "He sort of drifted along. He wasn't making any effort to be the speaker of the House. He did an ordinary probably performance," in Eunice's assessment.

She, on the other hand, was on fire, determined to speak for the children languishing in the DC Receiving Home and institutions like it all across the country. She went to Nashville to speak to a local conference on juvenile delinquency and consulted with similar groups from Philadelphia to Kansas City. She made a speech to one women's group after another about young people that she called "Tomorrow's America." She stole secretaries from various divisions of the Justice Department to help her distribute thousands of pamphlets outlining the recommendations of the advisory group. With the *Washington Post*, she organized an annual celebrity golf tournament that in 1948 included Bing Crosby, Bob Hope, Arthur Godfrey, and Sam Snead, with the $34,000 in proceeds benefitting projects for youthful offenders in Washington. She worked with a national organization of sportswriters and broadcasters to encourage its members across the country to write about the issue and to coach local delinquents in any sport they had mastered themselves.

Athletics was the arena in which Eunice had distinguished herself in her own crowded and competitive household. All her instincts told her that playing fields, riding paddocks, swimming pools, golf courses, and basketball and tennis courts were life-changing venues. If she had found her confidence there, these kids could, too.

But even with Sarge's help, the administrative tasks at Justice were daunting, the resources scarce, and the progress slow. What she was accomplishing would be no more than window dressing, she told the attorney general, unless the federal government earmarked more money and personnel for the cause.

"The government of the United States is now publically committed, by presidential and other statements, to an active role in the campaign against juvenile delinquency," Eunice wrote in a memo to Clark. "Those statements by the president and others have not implied that our government is content with conditions as they are. Nor was the National Conference on Prevention and Control of Juvenile Delinquency called into being by the Department of Justice merely to deliberate, utter pious hopes, and disband," she wrote with characteristic bluntness. "The recommendations of that Conference are mandates directed to not only participants in the Conference but, in some cases, to the Department of Justice, other departments of the Federal Government, and to the people of the United States. Many of those directives require action on a national scale . . . To those tasks, I am eager to apply my time and my thoughts. But let no one be deceived. Neither the position of the Government on matters of juvenile delinquency nor the effectiveness of the National Conference's Continuing Committee can be maintained by one person working in one room with one stenographer."

Action, not words. That would be her mantra for the next half century, whether the issue was juvenile delinquency, mental retardation, or teen pregnancy. At twenty-five, for the first but not the last time, Eunice was discovering just how maddening government bureaucracy could be. Nothing would exasperate her more than to reach consensus on how to solve a problem only to have it undermined by a lack of resources or interagency squabbling. She encountered the latter with the Children's Bureau, which saw the Justice Department's efforts on juvenile delinquency as amateurish and duplicative of its own work.

Eunice no doubt thought she was being respectful to Katharine F. Lenroot, the director of the Children's Bureau, in a letter expressing her gratitude for "the interest you are taking in our juvenile delinquency program," and offering her services "if we can be of assistance to you." But Lenroot was the same age as Eunice's father and had been doing government work on behalf of women and children for more than thirty years by the time Eunice turned up in the Justice Department. It was Lenroot who could have been of assistance to her.

Lenroot had spent her career in Washington at the bureau, which was established only two years before she arrived as a social worker and investigator from Wisconsin in 1914. At the child welfare bureau, she studied juvenile courts and administered provisions of the Social Security Act of 1935 that provided limited federal aid for maternal and child health and for dependent and disabled children. In 1947 Lenroot was also serving as US representative on the executive board of a new international aid organization for children, setting the direction of what would become the United Nations International Children's Emergency Fund, or UNICEF.

A mentoring relationship between Lenroot and Eunice apparently was neither offered nor sought, a loss for both women. Only in retrospect is it clear how closely their interests aligned. In her official correspondence with Eunice, Lenroot could be subtly dismissive of the attorney general's young aide. When Eunice asked if Lenroot could recommend someone to be her assistant, for instance, the older woman made an indirect point about Eunice's own thin credentials by submitting the names of candidates far more qualified than Eunice herself. "It is difficult to make such suggestions, as there are not many people with experience as broad or as desirable for such a position," Lenroot wrote before recommending the chief probation officer in an Ohio juvenile court who also taught social work at the university level, and a deputy commissioner for the New York State Department of Social Welfare who supervised state institutions for juvenile delinquents. It is hard to imagine either man taking orders from a boss whose social-work experience consisted of some volunteer work in college.

Eunice's direct contact with juvenile offenders helped blunt her office frustrations. She took every opportunity to connect with them on her visits to local institutions. She formed a bond with two brothers confined to the National Training School for Boys. She exchanged letters with Henry and Alonzo who lived in Cottage 4, urging them to participate in the sports programs she was busy planning, often with a stunning lack of awareness about the realities of their lives. Only someone reared in the rarefied world of the Hyannisport Club and the Seminole Country Club could have encouraged juvenile delinquents locked up in Washington, DC, to consider taking up golf and tennis.

She was equally obtuse about the opportunities awaiting the brothers upon their release. "I am sure that Alonzo would like to go to college, and I think it would do him a lot more good than harm, and the same goes for me as well," Henry wrote to her. But a poem he enclosed with his letter to Eunice indicates he did not find the prospect very realistic:

> *Maybe you need some knowledge*
> *but know no professors or deans.*
> *Just go right on to college*
> *but only in your dreams.*

Busy as she was, Eunice did not neglect her correspondence with her globe-trotting mother, whom she pronounced "harder to keep in touch with than my juvenile delinquents" as Rose flitted between Europe and the spa at Hot Springs, Arkansas. "Jack has just been chosen as 1 of the 12 handsomest men in Washington," Eunice informed Rose. "I suppose you would rather have had him the most devout Catholic young man."

There was not much chance of that. Jack might have said his prayers every night and attended Mass on Sunday, but he exhibited none of the religiosity that distinguished the faith of his mother, Eunice, and Bobby. His was a reflexive Catholicism, ingrained as much by habit as conviction. If he learned the tenets of the religion from his mother, he learned how to skirt them from his father, especially in relation to the women he enjoyed primarily for the passing pleasure they provided.

Friends of the Kennedy siblings who visited Hyannis Port were always taken aback by Joe's open display of his affairs and Rose's apparent acquiescence. "Spending the amount of time I did in the house with the old man, with his mistresses at the house, and being there for lunch and supper, no small town kid from Philadelphia, P.A., could possibly ever understand. It was unheard of," said Elizabeth Coxe Spalding, who spent her childhood summers in Hyannis Port in the 1930s with her family, roomed with Kick in Washington in 1942, and returned to the Kennedy orbit when she married Jack's friend Chuck Spalding in 1945.

Eunice's friends were well aware of Joe's reputation. Jack even warned Mary Pitcairn, when she was visiting Hyannis Port, that the ambassador had a tendency to roam at night. "One night I was visiting Eunice on the Cape, and he came into my bedroom to kiss me good night! I was in my nightgown, ready for bed," Pitcairn recalled. "Eunice was in her bedroom. We had an adjoining bath. The doors were open. He said, 'I've come to say good night,' and kissed me. Really kissed me. It was so silly. I remember thinking, 'How embarrassing for Eunice.'"

Eunice probably was not embarrassed. All her life, she dismissed reports of her father's affairs with Gloria Swanson, Marlene Dietrich, Clare Boothe Luce, and various secretaries as unfounded gossip circulated by those who did not recognize the fine art of flirting, encouraged of men and women alike in the Kennedy family. Teasing one another and flirting with strangers was a skill to be cultivated as assiduously as any other, with the tacit understanding that one did not cross the line into immoral behavior. Eunice chose to believe that her father never did.

Decades later, Mary Pitcairn would say that Joe's behavior was "confusing for Jack. He was a sensitive man, and I think it confused him, as to what kind of an object is a woman to be treated as his father treated them." How much more confusing must it have been for Eunice and her sisters?

Eunice herself had been toying with Sargent Shriver while they worked together at the Justice Department and socialized outside of the office. She let him steal a kiss now and then but refused to take seriously his declarations of love. "Remember how you would let me chase you around the Justice Department office, letting me kiss all the lipstick off your face just before you were to see the attorney general," Sarge asked her in a letter a year after their work in Washington was through and he was no closer to winning her hand. He could have found his answer in an offhand remark she made to a newspaper reporter in that era: "I'm sure all my sisters will be married long before I am," Eunice said.

Jack's attitude toward women would prove to be no different from his father's. A parade of young women—airline stewardesses and secretaries, mostly—came through the house he shared with Eunice. Rip Horton, a friend from Choate, recalled an evening after dinner at the Georgetown house: "A lovely-looking blond from West Palm Beach joined us to go to a movie. After the movie, we went back to the house, and I remember Jack saying something like, 'Well, I want to shake this one. She has ideas.'

Shortly thereafter, another girl walked in. Ted Reardon [Jack's married administrative assistant] was there, so he went home, and I went to bed figuring this was the girl for the night. The next morning, a completely different girl came wandering down for breakfast. They were a dime a dozen."

In Kick's view, that was just the way men behaved, so women needed to adapt. Eunice turned a blind eye to her brother's dalliances. He was single, after all, and a man. It was hard to imagine what Jack could do that would tarnish him in Eunice's view. "They are all blocked, totally blocked emotionally," Betty Coxe Spalding said of the Kennedy siblings. "Eunice is the one I think who survived the best. I don't know how or why or what. But she thought she was part of Jack, in a way."

It wasn't just their voices, which even family members could not distinguish if Jack and Eunice were within earshot but not in sight. For years, the always-anxious Eunice had been studying her friends and family, especially Jack, taking notes during or after dinner parties and weekends at Hyannis Port, trying to weave a more confident identity for herself by borrowing the best stratagems she observed in them. In seven brown spiral notebooks, beginning in 1947, she copied down the rules for party games, the jokes—some of them off-color—told at their Georgetown dinner table, opening gambits that her sister Pat employed when entering a room, and conversation starters Mary Pitcairn used when talking to a man she did not know.

"Mary Pitcairn is very interested in men. Expresses her own feelings about a thing—I love double features—then maybe a statement and a question. She manages to steer the conversation onto a point or an angle or subject she knows about," Eunice wrote.

It was as though the social cues so obvious to others sailed right past her, leaving Eunice either tongue-tied or too talkative. "Secret of Kick's success: She gives & always has funny little stories to tell, talk about. She always afterwards asks the news—who was there, what were they doing and acts very, very interested." Eunice underlined "acts very, very interested," a reminder to herself, perhaps, that listeners have an obligation to be actively engaged in a conversation, too.

When she was not taking notes on clever aphorisms she could recycle— "Saying: You're the kind of girl that puts a psy[chiatrist] on the couch"— she was recording the political views of the guests she and Jack invited to parties. "Joe McCarthy came to dinner," she wrote in an undated post

that mentioned several Washington notables whom the Republican senator from Wisconsin accused of being Communists or homosexuals in the
State Department, the White House, the FBI, and at the *Washington Post*.
If McCarthy's hosts offered any objection to their guest's allegations, Eunice did not record it. On one evening, she did note when an unidentified
guest "says McCarthy ought to be burned at the stake." Eunice recorded
her brother's response as well: "Jack says Baloney. He's been very reliable.
Everyone he has said a commie has proved to be a commie."

McCarthy squired Eunice and Pat around Washington to embassy
parties and other social events, a casual escort of sisters who made a practice of sharing the men they dated. "If he likes one of us, he might as well
like all of us," Kick once said about men to a reporter who had observed
the sisters trading dance partners. "It really doesn't matter which one he's
with. He's bound to be with all of us sooner or later."

Being comfortable in social settings would never come as naturally
to Eunice, but she was an attentive student. She watched and learned. If
she could not share the ease with which Jack and Kick moved through
the world, she would try to mimic it, in much the way Rose had trained
Rosemary to "pass" in society by having her memorize the name of the
president, a smattering of current events, and proper table manners so no
one would detect that she was different.

In the winter of 1948, as Eunice entered her second year at the Justice
Department, Kick was back in the States with her sister-in-law Elizabeth
Cavendish for a two-month visit. They spent time in Palm Beach with
Joe and Rose and in Washington with Jack and Eunice, but it was not
until the end of her trip, at the grand reopening of the Greenbrier Hotel
in West Virginia, where Joe and Rose had honeymooned thirty-four years
before, that Kick announced her intention to marry Peter Fitzwilliam as
soon as he secured a divorce from his wife of fifteen years.

Rose's reaction was as fierce as it was predictable. Fitzwilliam, whose
infidelities were legion and well known in England, was not merely a
Protestant; he would be a divorced man, the father of a twelve-year-old
girl. Kick was courting banishment from her family, Rose warned, as well
as her church. Eunice's attempt to intervene, by arranging for Kick to see
Bishop Fulton Sheen in New York before she sailed for England, back-
fired. Kick cancelled the appointment. She went back to London more
determined to marry one of the richest men in Great Britain, despite her
family's objections and his reputation as a cad. Rose's decision to follow

her to England to try to dissuade her only reinforced Kick's resolve to marry Fitzwilliam.

As painful as the rupture in the family over the prospective marriage must have been, it was eclipsed only a month later by Kick's sudden, violent death. She had convinced her father, who was visiting Paris, to at least meet Fitzwilliam. The couple planned a two-day holiday on the French Riviera before joining Joe for lunch at the Ritz Hotel on Saturday, May 15. On Thursday, having stopped at Le Bourget airfield near Paris to refuel their chartered twin-engine plane, the couple made an impulsive trip into Paris to meet some of Fitzwilliam's friends for lunch on the Champs-Élysées.

By the time they returned to the airfield, the weather had turned ominous. The pilot and copilot warned they would be flying directly into a thunderstorm over the Rhône Valley en route to Cannes. Fitzwilliam insisted they chance it, even after learning that all commercial flights had been cancelled.

It was Eunice who took the call at midnight in Georgetown from a *Washington Post* reporter asking about a wire service dispatch that "Lady Hartington" had been killed with three others in a plane crash in France. Any chance that it was the "other Lady Hartington"—Kick's sister-in-law Debo—was dashed when Jack's assistant Ted Reardon confirmed that the passport found near the wreckage on the mountainside above the tiny village of Privas was Kathleen's. Jack had been lying on the couch, listening to a recording of *Finian's Rainbow*, a popular musical comedy that had opened on Broadway and in London's West End the year before. Ella Logan was singing "How Are Things in Glocca Morra" as Eunice hung up the telephone.

SIX

WOMEN IN PRISON

You are free and I am free to do what we want with ourselves and our lives.

**—EUNICE KENNEDY, TO THE INMATES OF
THE FEDERAL PENITENTIARY FOR WOMEN,
ALDERSON, WEST VIRGINIA, 1950**

EUNICE RESIGNED FROM the US Justice Department a month after Kick's death. Her work there, underfunded and understaffed, had run its course. Her father had told her years before not to stay in an unsatisfying job, and Eunice always heeded her father's advice.

She left unsure what might come next, beyond a long trip to Europe in the fall with her sister Pat and a pause in her still-undefined relationship with Sargent Shriver. She had declined his marriage proposals repeatedly in the last year, but now she asked him not to contact her for at least three months and to start seeing other women.

Devastated but undeterred, Sarge tried to respect her wishes. Physical distance helped. He was back in Chicago, working for her father at the Merchandise Mart. When she was not traveling, Eunice divided her time among Washington, New York, and Hyannis Port. He did not see her, but he could not stop himself from writing to her.

"I wish that today you had enough confidence in me to tell me all the reasons you have for putting things off," he wrote from her father's suite in Chicago's Ambassador East Hotel, where he was again living, "but I've enough confidence in our Lord and in myself and in you to let you search the world for a better man and to look myself for a better girl. That I shall do as I believe you, too, will, with no preconceptions or inhibitions; but I believe that one day your glorious person and sparkling eyes will be mine and mine yours—for such people are not to be found everywhere or everyday!"

Eunice launched herself into a wider world in August, embarking on a three-month European tour with Pat to England, France, Belgium, Spain, and Italy, after attending the 1948 Republican and Democratic national political conventions, both held that year in Philadelphia. "Lloyd Bowers asked for you today," Sarge wrote of an old friend from elementary school with whom he had reconnected in Chicago. "Following your instructions, I begged him to help me locate some girls, and he protested you were the best thing he'd ever seen and why didn't I marry you. When informed bluntly 'you'd have nothing of me,' he protested again, claimed it was all my fault for not asking you, & swore he'd close the deal with you for me in one hour's conversation . . . I wish I could joke with you about my situation. I even wish I could write you how much I love you. But the latter means nothing to you—that's obvious, and you refuse to believe me—and I'm not full of jokes, I assure you."

Dorothy Kilgallen could not have gotten it more wrong on August 9, 1948, when her syndicated Voice of Broadway column reported that "Eunice Kennedy, daughter of the former ambassador Joe Kennedy, is on the verge of announcing her betrothal." Sandwiched between news of an Andrews Sisters performance at the London Palladium and Jane Russell's latest diet, the item did not identify the prospective bridegroom.

Sargent Shriver would not have been the only candidate. Hugh Fraser, the Catholic Tory member of Parliament Eunice had met a decade earlier in London, was still in her thrall. She saved Hugh's love letters all her life, but she was cavalier about his affection in 1948. "Saw a good bit of Hugh in London," she wrote to her father from the Hotel George V in Paris. "He is coming over to Paris today. He says he has the Kennedy disease. He claims to love us all. However, I really wish he would have himself treated in England, as I'm quite busy with a French foreign lover."

In truth, the Kennedy sisters were as often ducking male companionship as they were enjoying it during their time in Europe. "We are off to

Brussels tomorrow for 4 days," Eunice wrote to her father during the trip. "Pat has George & I'll probably have that mental midget of a friend of his again for the duration. I always said, 'No greater love hath a man than to love his friends.'" George was George L. Niels, who had won an Olympic silver medal in bobsled for Belgium that year. He entertained the sisters during their visit to Brussels, claiming in a plaintive letter to Eunice that he had fallen madly in love with Pat. "Pat reacted in her giggling, nervous, nail-biting, hysterical way," Eunice told her father.

Eunice did not say in her letters home whether she visited Kick's grave while she was in England that fall, but it is hard to imagine that she did not. Fraser had attended the High Mass for Kick at the Farm Street Church in Berkeley Square in London the previous spring and, with two hundred others, had taken the private train to her burial in the church-yard at Chatsworth. Joe had been the only Kennedy at the graveside on May 20 as Kathleen's coffin was lowered into the earth of her adopted country on the expansive estate of the Duke and Duchess of Devonshire.

Whether wracked by personal grief or paralyzed by political con-siderations, Joe had left arrangements for the funeral of his beloved but rebellious daughter to her British in-laws. Even her epitaph—"Joy She Gave, Joy She Has Found"—was chosen by the family into which she had married rather than the one into which she had been born. Neither her mother nor any of her siblings flew to England to lay Kathleen to rest. They attended a private Mass in Hyannis Port instead.

Kick just disappeared, as Rosemary had before her, with no chari-table foundation, endowed scholarship, or memorial building to remind the world that she had lived. Joe's efforts turned instead to sanitizing the circumstances of her death. She had bumped into Peter Fitzwilliam in Paris, his story went. A casual acquaintance, the earl had offered her a seat on his plane when he learned that she, too, was going to Cannes. All just a terrible coincidence.

But Eunice did not want Kathleen to be forgotten. Their parents' plan to name a gymnasium after Kathleen at the Manhattanville College of the Sacred Heart, a school Kick had never even attended, did not strike Eunice as sufficient. She proposed a living memorial to her sister, a schol-arship program for women in prison.

Eunice had visited the Massachusetts Reformatory for Women, in Framingham, during her tenure at the Justice Department and had come to believe that a predisposition to crime was less responsible for the incarceration of women than poverty, domestic abuse, and lack of education. That was also the view of Miriam Van Waters, the progressive warden at Framingham who had earned national acclaim for policies that emphasized education and training above isolation and punishment. Like Eunice, Van Waters had begun her career working with juvenile delinquents and concluded, as Eunice had, that punishing youthful offenders without addressing their educational and emotional needs only perpetuated their criminal behavior. Van Waters, the daughter of a Protestant minister, had placed a chapel at the center of Framingham life, a move that surely would have impressed the devout Eunice.

She had written to Van Waters before Kick's death about establishing a scholarship fund for women paroled from Framingham. Now she hoped to endow it in Kick's name. Eunice likely found a receptive ear, but the far less reform-minded state corrections commissioner fired Van Waters in January 1949, accusing her of undermining the administration of the prison by, among other things, tolerating sexual contact among the inmates, whom Van Waters called "students." Van Waters, herself a closeted lesbian, appealed her removal and, with the support of former First Lady Eleanor Roosevelt and other prison-reform advocates, won reinstatement after months of headline-grabbing public hearings.

By then, developing a plan for prison scholarships was competing with Eunice's many other preoccupations. She was orchestrating the move from the Georgetown house on Thirty-First Street to one on Thirty-Fourth with Jack, who had just won reelection. She was busy hiring painters and upholsterers to brighten the dark decor. She was visiting county jails and prisons to survey conditions in which women were confined. She was auditing courses at Catholic University of America and seriously contemplating the religious life.

That year was also when her father decided to move Rosemary from Craig House, the psychiatric hospital in Beacon, New York, where she had been living since the lobotomy, receiving little in the way of rehabilitative care. After consulting with Boston Archbishop Richard Cushing, Joe ruled out transferring Rosemary to St. Coletta by the Sea, the new residential school for mentally disabled children that Cushing had built in Hanover, Massachusetts, and staffed with nuns from the Sisters of Saint Francis of Assisi. Joe had donated more than $100,000 to the school's building fund through the Joseph P. Kennedy Jr. Foundation, but Cushing convinced him that "it would be impossible to avoid public attention" if he placed Rosemary, now thirty-one, so close to home.

Cushing suggested instead that Joe send his daughter to the St. Coletta School for Exceptional Children in Jefferson, Wisconsin. Since 1904, the same order of nuns had been operating that facility for adults and children with mental retardation. "There, and not Hanover, will solve your personal problems," Cushing told the Kennedy patriarch.

Except for a 1971 letter from Rose to the administrator of St. Coletta, asserting that Eunice "talked over the idea of a physician with her father when Rosemary first went to Saint Coletta," available documents do not indicate how much Eunice knew about the transfer of her sister to Wisconsin. Mary Moore, the wife of Joe's long-serving aide Eddie Moore, had spent more time with Rosie in England and at Craig House than anyone. She was also Eunice's godmother. Mary or Joe might well have turned to Eunice for help the summer Rosemary went to St. Coletta. It is impossible to know.

Eunice's first stop when she returned from Europe in November 1948 had been the Deaconess Hospital in Boston. The nature of her ailment is not clear, though it is certain that she had not followed medical advice to slow down while she was traveling. Sarge was rightly skeptical of her claim that she was only having X-rays taken. "I can't understand why you have to stay in the hospital for a whole week just for X-rays," he wrote to her at the Deaconess. "Please write and tell me what is really going on & I mean I want a full explanation!"

She had agreed to visit him in Chicago with Pat, and his letter was full of plans. Dinner at the fashionable Pump Room, where Sarge had a regular table. A day in the country with William McCormack Blair Jr., a new friend with whom Sarge shared a passion for tennis and politics. A top aide to Democratic governor-elect Adlai Stevenson of Illinois, Bill Blair had recruited Sarge that fall to write campaign speeches, but Joe Kennedy vetoed the idea—the first of many times he would nix political activities by Sarge if they did not directly advance Jack's career.

Sarge, who called Eunice "Cookie" in letters that he signed "Spookie," suggested several books for her to read while she was hospitalized and expressed some surprise when she said she was not interested in *The Seven Storey Mountain* by Thomas Merton, the Trappist monk and mystic whose writings on peace and nonviolence would become a touchstone for

Catholics in the US civil rights and antiwar movements in the 1960s. "I think it's a fine book, one that reveals a lot about the problems both intellectual & spiritual of many fellows my age, and it certainly is well written & full of insight into human nature," he wrote, before recommending instead a less-weighty sea story set in nineteenth-century Massachusetts.

Her impending visit had raised Sarge's hopes, but Hugh Fraser had not given up, either. Sarge might well have been aware of the competition, telling Eunice in one letter that if she feared being overwhelmed by his ardor, she might want to "latch onto a cool, dispassionate Englishman." But there was nothing cool about the letters Hugh had been writing to Eunice since she left England. "This is a boring letter, and I should have written it better, and I should have written more often, but please love me back a little because I love you," he confessed. "I've never written this to anyone before—except my family—so it does mean a little. Please write."

If Eunice did reply, she did so without any urgency, prompting Hugh to write again and again, begging for a letter. "I wonder how much you are thinking about me. I guess just about 0, right? I have begun to think about you again, tho, a hell of a lot. Maybe it's the spring," he wrote in May. "When I first got back [from rendezvousing with Eunice the previous autumn in Venice, Italy] I thought I was going to die for love . . . But I haven't. Not yet, God love you. Come back now here to me quick. If you don't, I'll have to make one of those god awful trips to America. Write!"

All her adult life, Eunice relied more on the telephone than the pen. The pace at which her mind raced kept her moving too fast to linger long over a letter. That could be frustrating for her suitors, who poured their hearts into their correspondence. Sarge saved copies of all the love letters he wrote to Eunice during their long courtship and bound them in a commemorative book on their fiftieth wedding anniversary. All that survives of her reaction to those letters are three scribbled jottings on the backs of the envelopes in which they came. "Very cute," she wrote of his letter to her at the Deaconess. "Best of all love letters Sarge writes. Reveals himself completely," she wrote three months later on another envelope that was waiting for her at the reception desk at the Challenger Inn, in Sun Valley, Idaho, where she had gone skiing with Pat. "Very, very sweet," she scribbled on yet another.

Hugh Fraser waited in vain for even that much of a response. "I am still waiting for that letter you promised me after that ridiculous telephone conversation when you told me that my speeches stunk and then asked me to marry you—which I still intend—in front of a dinner party of six or seven quite amazingly boring people. It struck me as exhibitionism straight from the snake-pit. However, you're now almost forgiven," he wrote. "But to make up send me a letter."

Ethel Skakel, Jean Kennedy's roommate at Manhattanville College, who would marry Bobby Kennedy in June 1950, remembered how earnestly Fraser pursued Eunice, courting her in the summer of 1949 when Eunice again toured Europe, this time with Jean. "He was so crazy about her, and so much fun, and in politics—perfect in every way," Ethel recalled. "She clearly liked him but, no," marriage was not on Eunice's mind. In 1956, Fraser would marry Lady Antonia Pakenham, daughter of the Earl and Countess of Longford. They would divorce in 1977, after Antonia, by then a best-selling author, left Fraser for the playwright Harold Pinter.

At twenty-eight, Eunice was in no hurry to choose between her suitors or to take a husband at all. No doubt she was flattered by the attention, especially after an adolescence of hearing her mother compare her looks and social graces unfavorably to Kathleen's. But Eunice's focus was firm. It was on doing good works, not on making a good match.

The convent retained a powerful grip on her imagination. "That's pretty accurate, that she was thinking it over," Ethel said of Eunice's interest in the religious life. "She was very spiritual. Eunice's [devotion to the Blessed Mother] was very overt and obvious. She talked about it."

As the decade turned, Eunice found herself in a cloister of another sort: the Federal Reformatory for Women, in Alderson, West Virginia. Eunice had been corresponding for months with Helen Hironimus, the warden at Alderson, about identifying inmates who would benefit from further education or employment she could arrange with her socialite friends or her father's business contacts. The warden wrote to her on June 10, 1949, for instance, that her cook, whom she described as "a colored girl from a good family, who is an excellent cook and housekeeper," was about to be paroled and would be a "good parolee for Mrs. Pierpont." (Nathalie de Castro Pierrepont was a philanthropist and a friend of the Kennedys from Palm Beach.)

Whether the paroled cook ever found her way to the Pierrepont homes in Florida or Short Hills, New Jersey, is unclear, but Eunice did arrange at least one ill-fated placement through Alderson. "One of them I got work in my father's office," she said. "That didn't work out very well."

Eunice went to Alderson in January 1950 to research the needs of in-carcerated women with an eye toward helping them transition back into society and find jobs when their sentences were served. She planned to write a magazine piece about women in prison in hopes of sparking more public interest in rehabilitation. Her six-week stay at the prison was facil-itated by James V. Bennett, the director of the US Bureau of Prisons from 1937 until 1964, and a Kennedy family friend. He visited Alderson and met with Eunice there to discuss her findings.

Her presence was mutually beneficial: Eunice got access to the staff and inmates for her research, and the prison gained access to the Kenne-dys' social and political networks to help find jobs for Alderson's parolees. Eunice said as much in a letter to her father on February 1: "They very rarely let someone come in here who is allowed full recourse to any of their material, meetings, etc. They are doing all of this for me because they think I want to work out some plan for the parolees. When I have that plan worked out, it will be the time to write, and I am convinced that a talk or article containing such a plan plus my own observations on prison life can sell."

Ethel Kennedy thought Eunice's research project "was just the cover story"—that the Justice Department had asked her to go into the prison to gather information about illegal activities there, the specific nature of which Ethel never knew. "There was something amiss at Alderson," she said. But there is nothing in the archives of the Justice Department or the Bureau of Prisons, or in Bennett's papers and oral history on file at the John F. Kennedy Presidential Library, to suggest that Eunice was on a mission for federal law enforcement.

The research explanation also aligns more closely with Eunice's inter-est in the social causes of delinquency. That is the focus of her handwritten notes from Alderson, preserved in the files of James Landis, a lawyer who had succeeded Joe Kennedy as chairman of the Securities and Exchange Commission. In private practice by 1950, Landis, a former dean of the Harvard Law School, counted Joe as a client and a friend. A year before Eunice went to Alderson, Landis advised her on how to conduct prison research, sending her a copy of the book *Five Hundred Delinquent Women* by Sheldon and Eleanor Glueck, a husband-and-wife team of criminolo-gists whose work focused on juvenile delinquency. "Ever since the begin-ning, the world has been hunting for the cause and cure of crime and with very little success," Landis wrote to her.

The boarding school–like campus that Eunice encountered at Alderson was little changed from the original fourteen cottages that first opened as the Federal Reformatory for Women in 1928, the culmination of years of lobbying by activists, outraged by the sexual exploitation of women being confined in men's prisons and county jails across the country.

Built on more than five hundred acres of farmland less than a mile west of the town of Alderson, the prison camp on the Greenbrier River had a female warden, female matrons, and no fences or armed guards. Each cottage, equipped with a kitchen and segregated by race, housed thirty women, incarcerated for crimes as minor as bootlegging and as serious as treason.

The prison, designed for rehabilitation, operated a laundry, a garment factory, a leather shop, a bakery, and a vegetable and dairy farm. It trained women in skills officials hoped would lead to gainful employment when they were released. Its seamstresses produced uniforms, shirts, pajamas, aprons, medical gowns, and other items for the prison and several government agencies.

Nina Kinsella was the new warden when Eunice arrived on January 17, 1950. A native of Salem, Massachusetts, she had been an assistant to the director of the US Bureau of Prisons, supervising the inspection of county jails. Kinsella, who began her career at the Massachusetts Department of Correction, was "rather a simple, direct, frank, businesslike good woman, not charming, no airs, but nice," Eunice wrote in her diary.

Eunice lived with the warden during her stay, writing regularly to her father about the inmates and her thoughts on how best to help them. Joe sent steaks, lamb chops, and a canned ham at Eunice's request to thank the warden for "being awfully nice to me in addition to feeding me three meals a day!!!" She signed each letter with a different serial number, mimicking those assigned to inmates on their arrival at Alderson.

Her first week at the prison prompted fresh appreciation of her own life of privilege, from something as simple as being able to buy herself a $28 portable radio in the prison store to the complexity of the life stories she was hearing every day. "Dearest Daddy," she wrote on January 21. "Excuse pencil, but no pens here at the institution, as we are afraid the girls might do something with them besides writing!! All I can say after this week is 'My God, but I'm lucky.' I have been assigned 3 girls as my wards. They arrived Thursday, and I am responsible for their orientation and adjustment during their first week here. 1 is in for the numbers racket

(9 years; so stay away from numbers), the other for stealing a car. She is only 20 and comes from a family of 9. Very attractive and such a likeable kid with an IQ of 120. The other one is in for forgery. Also young and a nice kid. I'm convinced that some kind of a plan must be developed which help the kids from the day they leave the institution until after they have lived in their community for two years. Such a plan the warden here and all the officers and Jim [Bennett] say would be the biggest and most important contribution to this criminal field that has taken place in the last decade. I'm learning plenty, and I'm convinced now I know plenty you don't know, Pa! Tell Mother to send any extra records or clothes or anything here. How well, how useful such things will be. Much love. Write me. We don't get any outside news here."

Eunice knew there was precedent for partnerships between the public and private sector in correctional facilities. At the Justice Department, she had watched a similar sponsorship program for juvenile delinquents take shape at the National Training School for Boys. Long a small outreach program, it had been foundering until 1948, when the school joined forces with federal agencies to recruit businesses and professional men to serve as mentors to the incarcerated boys. She wanted to do the same thing for women; maybe to provide for them the mentoring her own father had denied to her.

Nina Kinsella and Jim Bennett shared Eunice's conviction that, without transitional assistance, women released from Alderson were in danger of relapsing into criminal behavior. "Most of the girls have nobody," she wrote in her notebook. "The girls haven't committed crimes because they want to be evil, rather because they haven't learned acceptable social ways of behavior." They needed sponsors just as much as the boys at the National Training School.

Initial overtures to women's service groups produced discouraging results. "The sponsor program did not move along as I had hoped," Julia Gorman Porter, a member of Alderson's advisory board and a Democratic Party activist from San Francisco, wrote to Bennett in January, noting the lack of sympathy for inmates among the women's business and professional groups she had hoped to interest in mentoring released prisoners.

Eunice was so eager to recruit sponsors because most inmates were poor, isolated, and estranged from their families, without the support they would need to thrive on the outside. Parole officers might find work for women when they left prison, but to succeed, Eunice wrote in her notebook, they "need people to get to take a personal interest in them, as they all feel 'I've had a record and people won't bother with me, advise me, etc.'"

To her surprise, she found most inmates at Alderson cooperative, hardworking, generous with one another, and able to maintain a sense of humor despite their circumstances. They were inventive as well, finding creative ways to make moonshine out of orange peels and other cast-off foodstuffs. But Eunice saw anger and depression, too, and "lots of sex among the girls," who braided bracelets for one another or carved each other's initials on their arms or legs with a razor. "Don't come between them, or they will kill you," she wrote, making a note to herself to "find out how many become sexually peculiar in prison."

The Alderson inmates were quieter and more composed than the women she had met in her tours of county jails, who were most memorable for the "high-pitched voices, the yelling, and the dirty jokes." At Alderson, she "never heard any vulgar or cheap words. In fact, one girl whom I was trying to tell to help more girls said, 'Miss Kennedy, you talk tougher than me.'"

It was not unusual for women to balk at leaving Alderson when they had completed their sentences, so afraid were many to return to violent husbands, sexually abusive fathers, negligent parents, dependent children, or the street life of prostitution and substance abuse that had landed them in prison. Eunice appealed to Bennett, for instance, to help one woman, who had distinguished herself in the prison infirmary, find a job in a hospital lab in a city far from her abusive adoptive mother. If she was going to succeed on the outside, it was her environment, more than the young woman herself, that needed to change, in Eunice's view. She promised another inmate, "a cute girl with black, curly hair" who was headed to Washington, DC, to finish school, that she would call and help her when she returned to Georgetown.

She recorded one poignant departure when an inmate named Joanna Morris took her leave of Alderson after three years of working on the prison farm. She was "all dressed up in the new navy-blue suit the bureau had made her. She looked so pretty," Eunice wrote. "The girls called to her, 'Keep your head up, Joanna. You sure look better than when you were plucking feathers off the turkey.'"

Impressed by the women's resilience and their concern for one another, Eunice saw their imprisonment as an opportunity to teach them everything from parenting skills to shorthand. In every face, she saw promise, from the sixteen-year-old car thief who was in solitary confinement for attacking a matron with a hairbrush, to the drug dealer who had gotten away for years with selling narcotics and running numbers by paying off the police. In every relapse, she saw societal neglect, from the drug addict convicted of stealing jewelry to support her habit, to the twenty-four-year-old mother of three who found her lawyer "by sticking her finger blindly on a list."

The wasted potential enraged her. "If this child had been guided wisely at 14 through 18, she wouldn't have wasted her time and married this jerk she married," she wrote of a twenty-year-old incarcerated for stealing a car with her husband. "I don't advocate prisons for young people," she wrote. "I only say that some girls learn things in prison [job skills] that they never have a chance to learn anyplace else—a reason to make prisons better."

Her assessment of those in charge was decidedly mixed. She praised Kinsella for meeting with six or more inmates every day to hear their complaints. "This is good. Shows they don't fear the warden. Know warden is willing to help them," Eunice wrote. She was less impressed with the civilian advisory group whose meetings she attended that winter. "The group looks bewildered to me," she wrote, expressing a desire to get appointed to that panel one day herself.

Bennett tried to keep Eunice focused on practical solutions to the shortcomings she was documenting in her notebooks. "Jim Bennett asked what I was going to do with these women who are 45 years old and back here for the 2nd and 3rd time," she noted. "What trade am I going to teach them? What trades could be put up here? It was suggested better training for maids and housekeepers and a better course for cooks. He seemed only slightly interested."

———

The Kennedy name was relatively unknown in 1950, especially in rural West Virginia. It had been a decade since Joe was US ambassador to the Court of Saint James's. It would be two more years before Jack would run for the US Senate and a decade before he would be elected president. At Alderson, the celebrities were more likely to be the inmates themselves. Living in the brick cottages that year were convicted spies and gangsters' molls. Women whose names had appeared regularly in the nation's newspapers were now in Eunice's diary and notebooks.

Iva Toguri D'Aquino, a Los Angeles native known to Allied troops in the Pacific as "Tokyo Rose" for her radio broadcasts of Japanese propaganda, worked in Alderson's medical clinic. She had been convicted of treason, though later investigations found her program, *The Zero Hour*, largely innocuous. President Gerald Ford would pardon her in 1977. Mildred Elizabeth Gillars, of Portland, Maine, had been known to Allied forces as "Axis Sally," Hitler's singing propagandist, for her broadcasts from Berlin. She, too, had been convicted of treason.

Eunice was intrigued by them both, noting that the quiet and polite Tokyo Rose "will do anything. No job is too menial for her here." But Eunice was especially drawn to Velvalee Dickinson, the fifty-six-year-old owner of a collectable doll shop on Madison Avenue in Manhattan, who had landed at Alderson in 1944 for spying for the Japanese during the war. The FBI nicknamed her "the Doll Woman."

In the aftermath of Pearl Harbor, Dickinson had used the identities of her customers on the return addresses of letters she sent to a Japanese contact in Buenos Aires, Argentina, letters filled with coded messages about the status of damaged American warships. Typical was one reporting details about three "Old English dolls" being repaired at a "wonderful doll hospital" on the West Coast. FBI cryptographers determined which vessels and shipyard she was referencing in this and a half dozen other letters, all of which were returned to her unknowing customers because Dickinson's Japanese contact had fled Buenos Aires. The judge had imposed the maximum sentence of ten years and a $10,000 fine.

It is not clear why Eunice found the wartime spy a sympathetic figure. After all, one of her brothers had died in combat in Europe and another had been seriously injured by the Japanese in the Solomon Islands. Perhaps it was because Dickinson had graduated from Stanford University or because the older woman had worked for a time in social services in San Francisco. Maybe Eunice believed her assertion that it was her now-dead husband who had masterminded the espionage or that she thought everyone was entitled to a second chance in life. For whatever reason, Eunice took Velvalee Dickinson under her wing, helping to find her a job with Catholic Charities in New York City after she was paroled from Alderson in 1951, and maintaining regular contact with her for years thereafter.

Known after her release as "Catherine Dickinson," the former spy would attend Eunice's wedding in 1953—with a gift of monogramed stationary from Tiffany's—and, years later, she would come to Cape Cod to work as Eunice's administrative assistant. "She was a remarkable secretary," according to Ethel Kennedy, who learned that one of her own treasured childhood dolls, dressed as a Dominican nun, had come from Dickinson's Madison Avenue shop.

In September 1963 Eunice tried to secure a position for Dickinson in the United States Pavilion at the following year's New York World's Fair. Her efforts prompted an anxious typewritten letter from the former spy to Eunice. *"Will a special clearance* be necessary?" she asked, worrying that the State Department might have a role in hiring and do a background check: "I am certain you realize *why* I ask this question of you." It turned out the Department of Commerce was in charge, but it is unclear whether Eunice's intervention got a job at the World's Fair dedicated to "Peace Through Understanding" for the woman who spied for Japan during World War II.

It was not the spies but a gangster's moll who left a lasting impression on Sargent Shriver when he visited Eunice at Alderson. "I used to say that I am the only guy I know who went and courted a woman at a federal penitentiary," he joked years later. Eunice introduced him to Kathryn Kelly, the wife and coconspirator of the bank robber and kidnapper George "Machine Gun" Kelly. She was serving twenty-five years to life for the 1933 kidnapping of a wealthy Oklahoma oilman. Her mother, Ora Shannon, was serving alongside her, having allowed the Kellys to stash their victim on her farm until his family paid the $200,000 ransom. One matron complained to Eunice that Kathryn had "all the girls in the greenhouse under her control" and warned she should never be released because "she could ruin a lot of men, just like a snake." Kathryn and her mother would both be paroled in 1958.

Toward the end of her stay at Alderson, Eunice was invited to address an assembly of the inmates and staff. The topic was personal happiness, "your happiness as human beings here on this earth and particularly as women." It was less a speech than a sermon, one that would have made the Sisters of the Sacred Heart proud and might have made her father squirm.

Women needed to be strong and independent, she said, because it would be foolhardy to expect men to act in the best interests of women: "Perhaps you don't know, but in ancient Greece and Rome, which we think of as wonderful civilizations, it was common practice for a father to take a baby daughter and leave her out on a desolate mountainside to die because women were not wanted and did not have any rights." It was "Christianity that changed this because God and Jesus Christ said that every human being was important and had rights no one could take from them—and that included women," she said.

Her emphasis on the dignity of women was driven, in part, by the number of inmates at Alderson whose illegal activities had been perpetrated in conjunction with, or at the urging of, husbands or boyfriends. The woman who embezzled from her job at her boyfriend's behest. Another who was along for the ride when her husband drove a stolen car across state lines. Others, still, who sold their bodies or narcotics under orders from their husbands or their pimps. "It is the woman who will finally pay with tears and unhappiness and insecurity—broken lives, broken hearts," Eunice told the women of Alderson.

Her belief in the capacity of these women to succeed in spite of the control men exerted over them mirrored her own resolve to carve out a consequential life in her male-dominated family. "You are free and I am free to do what we want with ourselves and our lives," she said, perhaps trying to convince herself as well as her audience. "You and I are happy when we fulfill our natures—when we do what God intended us to do and to be. We are unhappy if we go against our nature."

They could not be happy, Eunice told the women, without accepting that God has a plan for each of them that did not involve crime or drug addiction or alcoholism or prostitution or "running around like animals" with multiple men. Promiscuity was immoral, Eunice said, but it was also against women's self-interest. "Study any one of the civilizations where men were allowed to have three or four wives and find out what happened to the women. They are stuck off in some corner of the house by themselves; they have no rights; their children are taken away from them. There is no court to protect them, and they become slaves—slaves to men."

In Christianity, she told the inmates, women could find validation to live full, honorable lives. "Men were ordered to respect women and to honor them. God himself dignified women more than any creatures he had ever made when he chose one of them to be his own Mother, so that today, it can be truly said that only one perfect human being has ever lived, and that human being is a woman: the Blessed Virgin Mary."

Growing up in a family where wives and daughters were marginalized, with a father and brothers who treated women as either disposable playthings or plaster saints, it is not surprising Eunice would conclude that a religious vocation offered a woman greater opportunity than the secular world to reach her full potential.

"You always felt she had a foot in both worlds," Ethel Kennedy said. "You could see her thinking about the spiritual part of the equation when she was talking about anything. It was like a light shining on her rationale. I just felt she was always thinking not of the problem at hand as much as how could it balance off in the next world. I thought that for many, many, many years. It was all encompassing. It was motivating. It was her whole being."

Eunice had written to James Landis throughout her stay at Alderson, sending him her raw notes to be typed and asking for "any suggestions of ideas I should develop or things I should look for that are not in my notes. I want to write a good article for the *Reader's Digest*." For whatever reason, she never did. Perhaps she felt preempted by Norma Lee Browning, a *Chicago Daily Tribune* reporter whose two-part series about life inside Alderson ran that June.

By then, Eunice was back in Washington trying to line up jobs and mentors for women soon to be released from the prison. She got a commitment from the president of the United Garment Workers of America to hire qualified seamstresses out of Alderson in factories near their hometowns. She had meetings in Boston, New York, Washington, and Chicago with women's clubs to generate more interest among educated women in mentoring the inmates.

On one trip to Chicago, at the end of April 1950, Eunice had an unanticipated encounter with a thief she would think of less kindly than she did the thieves she had befriended at Alderson. She and Sargent Shriver had attended a pre-wedding party at the Casino Club for Marshall Field IV, the publisher of the *Chicago Sun-Times*, and his bride-to-be, Katherine Woodruff. After Eunice had returned to the Ambassador East and gone to bed, a thief entered the suite through the door she had left unlocked and made off with two diamond and sapphire bracelets valued at $18,000 from her bedside table. Shriver, in a separate suite down the hall, reported that $29 had also been stolen that night from his dresser top, the losses a reflection of their contrasting financial stations in life.

What the police report did not say, according to Ethel Kennedy, was that Eunice had awakened when she heard the thief drop her mink coat on the floor. "She pretended she was asleep," Ethel said. The thief dropped the mink after he stuck his hand in a pocket and found "it full of half-eaten Jujubes."

Two weeks later, Eunice was a bridesmaid in Ethel and Bobby's wedding at St. Mary's Roman Catholic Church in Greenwich, Connecticut, resplendent in a strapless gown and wide-brimmed silk hat. As the honeymooners headed for Hawaii, Eunice decided it was time for her to make a move as well. She packed up her things in the Georgetown house and turned over the key to Jack.

At her father's urging, she headed west to Chicago, that most American of cities, where at midcentury the meatpacking plants were yielding to Ludwig Mies van der Rohe's glass-and-steel skyscrapers, Ray Kroc's revolutionary fast-food franchise McDonald's, and Hugh Hefner's *Playboy* empire. It was the city of Richard Wright's *Native Son*, of James T. Farrell's *Studs Lonigan*, and Saul Bellow's *The Adventures of Augie March*, a city whose soundtrack in the new decade would be shaped by rock-and-roll pioneer Chuck Berry, gospel singer Mahalia Jackson, and bluesman Howlin' Wolf.

At twenty-nine, Eunice set her course inland, making no commitments beyond volunteer social work for Catholic Charities. She took up residence in her father's hotel suite on the fourteenth floor of the Ambassador East, inviting Carl Sandburg's "City of the Big Shoulders" to show her what would come next.

SEVEN

CHICAGO

I looked all my life for someone like my father, and Sarge came the closest.

**—EUNICE KENNEDY'S TOAST AT HER WEDDING TO
R. SARGENT SHRIVER, MAY 23, 1953**

THE SISTERS OF the Good Shepherd had been ministering to Chicago's "wayward" women and girls for almost a hundred years in the fall of 1950 when Eunice found her way to their cloistered refuge behind an eight-foot brick wall just blocks from Wrigley Field.

"Welcome to Chicago!!! Now watch things hum," read the handwritten note in the suite her father kept at the Ambassador East hotel, where Eunice would live for much of the next three years, sometimes with her sister Jean, who took a job in the publicity department at the Merchandise Mart. The note was signed "Your Conservative Father," but Joe didn't write it; a mischievous Sargent Shriver did.

Eunice joined the House of the Good Shepherd as a volunteer at the request of Monsignor Vincent W. Cooke, the head of Catholic Charities in Chicago, who was familiar with her work with juvenile delinquents and incarcerated women. Eunice arrived in the Windy City as committed as ever to using her wealth and social status in service of troubled young women who had neither.

She had come to the right place.

Social work, the field Eunice claimed as her own despite little formal training, came of age in Chicago, a city whose teeming tenements and ethnic enclaves had long served as a living laboratory for those who labored to understand poverty and ameliorate its consequences. Prominent among them was a group of sociologists at the University of Chicago who used data collection and quantitative analysis to explain such social conditions as crime, family dysfunction, and racial tension. Known as the Chicago School, its research methods originated in the 1920s, relying on fieldwork and empirical evidence to add rigor to a discipline that had been dominated by armchair theorists and well-meaning, but not always well-informed, philanthropists.

For all the erudition of the fewer than one dozen learned men who constituted the Chicago School, their basic premise—that people and social conditions are best observed and understood in the context of actual neighborhoods and real families—was hardly news to the women who had been performing social service work in the city for the better part of a century.

It was in Chicago in 1890 that Jane Addams and Ellen Gates Starr founded Hull House, the nation's first settlement house, to serve the Italians, Germans, French Canadians, Irish Catholics, and Russian Jews of the city's west side, providing for the immigrant working poor a kindergarten, social clubs, lectures, and classes in English and the arts, not unlike the services Eunice helped deliver to residents of the Bowery and East Harlem in New York when she was a student at Manhattanville College of the Sacred Heart.

Like Eunice, Addams had been a wealthy young woman whose work with the less fortunate was as much a spiritual mission as a secular exercise in social reform. Neither woman proselytized, but both were driven by their faith—in the case of Jane Addams, a mix of her father's perfectionist Christianity and Ralph Waldo Emerson's transcendentalism—to improve the lot of the poor and the reviled. Addams had immersed herself in that cause, living and working at Hull House, her personal life of self-sacrifice indistinguishable from her professional pursuit of social justice.

Eunice was contemplating a similar, all-encompassing commitment. In Chicago, she sought out Catholic nuns whose work with female prostitutes, thieves, runaways, and delinquents predated Hull House by decades and was propelled, first and foremost, by the desire to save their souls. The Sisters of the Good Shepherd had been working in Chicago since 1859, repeatedly relocating after fire destroyed their convents. The first blaze was a suspected act of anti-Catholic bigotry; the last was caused by the Great Chicago Fire, which cut a swath through the city four miles long and almost a mile wide, in 1871.

By 1950, the nuns had been at West Grace and Racine Streets for almost a half century. The original four-story main brick building with its ornate chapel had been supplemented by annexes housing a commercial laundry, classrooms, and dormitories. In its earliest incarnation, the house sheltered abandoned and neglected girls as well as those deemed delinquent by the nation's first juvenile court, established in Chicago in 1899. Al Capone regularly dropped off bags of ill-gotten cash to support the Sisters' work in the 1920s. By midcentury, the House of the Good Shepherd was a designated reformatory for girls of all races and creeds, administered by Catholic Charities, subsidized by Cook County, and run by the nuns.

Eunice was in charge of program development and served as liaison between the Sisters and the criminal justice system. "I'd go to juvenile court and tell the nuns whether we should take a girl," she said, recalling the House of the Good Shepherd as a reformatory so lacking in direction and services that twenty-six girls had escaped, or tried to, in the six months before she arrived.

The high brick wall and the bars on the ground-floor windows signaled that the place was more jail than school. As forbidding as it looked from the outside, it was as grim within. School truants were housed alongside prostitutes and thieves, all of them supervised by cloistered nuns whose belief in self-discipline was matched only by their remove from the wider world.

In that sense, the house was the antithesis of everything Eunice was learning about rehabilitation in the social-work courses she audited at the University of Chicago and from the reformers she knew at prisons in Framingham and Alderson. "These girls, aged 12 to 17, were tougher and of a vastly different background than the average American girl," she noted in a summary she and Sarge wrote of her time in Chicago, "but they were, nevertheless, human all the way through. If given intelligent understanding, sympathetic planning for their futures, and an opportunity to improve themselves, they would respond."

She began by convincing judges from the juvenile court who committed delinquent girls to the House of the Good Shepherd for a minimum of twelve months to start sharing the girls' medical, psychiatric, and educational records with the nuns, "making it possible for them to create individual courses for each girl." She designed an orientation program to help newcomers make the transition to institutional living and a merit system to allow the girls to earn the right to leave the house to attend a movie or a baseball game or to visit their families.

She partnered, not for the last time, with the Chicago Park District to create recreational opportunities for the girls, many of whom learned to swim during twice-weekly excursions to municipal pools when they were closed to the general public. She recruited a volunteer from Elizabeth Arden to teach a beauty course, a teenage model to teach poise and manners, an instructor from the Art Institute of Chicago to teach drawing and painting, and a high school drama coach to direct two plays a year. She convinced two editors from the *Chicago Daily News* to supervise the production of a bimonthly newspaper, the *Shepherd Sun*, the first in the history of the institution. She conscripted young women from Saint Xavier College to come two nights a week to help the girls form their first-ever student government, a process that was "an eye-opener for the college girls," Eunice wrote. "For the first time, the college students have found out that the world is not all sweetness and light, and, according to their own faculty members, the experience has had a very broadening and deepening psychological and educational effect."

In their first election, the residents of the House of the Good Shepherd selected "as their leaders some of the toughest girls in the institution," Eunice noted. "These 'toughies' who were given authority have turned out to be the real disciplinarians of the place. For the first time, the nuns find that the basic problems of discipline are beginning to be handled by the girls themselves."

Relying on Sarge's contacts in Chicago, Eunice invited local celebrities, politicians, and newspaper columnists "to give the girls a better idea of what the world was like and the opportunities that existed for them if 'they went straight.'" Eunice even recruited her mother. Rose Kennedy stopped by one evening when she was visiting Chicago, to share stories of being the wife of an ambassador and the mother of a congressman.

As helpful as Sarge was to her in her work, Eunice continued to resist his romantic overtures. An attractive man, Sarge did not sit home alone. He dated a young widow, a wealthy socialite, and a "tall, curvaceous" model who worked part-time for the Merchandise Mart.

Eunice, too, went on dates; she was photographed in November at the opening night of *South Pacific* at the Shubert Theatre on the arm of Frederick G. Wacker Jr., a socially prominent Chicagoan.

The voluntary nature of her work and her own peripatetic disposition left Eunice free to travel, and she did, leaving Chicago frequently to host dinner parties with Jack in Washington, ski with Pat in Sun Valley, or visit her parents in Hyannis Port, New York, or Palm Beach. She was gone so often that a cousin she recruited to volunteer at the House of the Good Shepherd wondered why she saw Eunice so infrequently there.

In February 1951, for instance, Eunice and Jean embarked on a tour of the Middle East, visiting Egypt, Saudi Arabia, Israel, Turkey, Greece, and Lebanon. Like all Kennedy excursions, the trip was designed less for relaxation than education. The sisters met with royalty and titans of the oil industry and visited reform schools for juvenile delinquents and institutions for the mentally retarded.

Eunice was especially taken with German-born Queen Frederika of Greece, with whom the Kennedy sisters discussed the plight of children displaced during the recent civil war between the Greek government and Communist forces. The queen had established camps on some of the Greek islands to house 2,500 homeless boys, an effort that Greeks alternately praised as a rescue mission or denounced as an indoctrination scheme, depending on their political persuasion. In her written account of their meeting, Eunice evinced some skepticism about the queen's idyllic description of those camps. "I asked her if the boys didn't run off," she wrote, noting that the question elicited laughter from the queen.

The fate of girls was worse, Queen Frederika told them. "There are two types of girls: first are those kidnapped by the Communists; the others are those who went off with the Communists willingly. In either case, when a girl comes back to her family, she is disowned because she has lost her honor. That is the worst thing that can happen to a Greek girl. We started a camp for these girls on one of the islands. I do not know how it will turn out."

Eunice must have thought about her own work with incarcerated women and delinquent girls similarly shunned by society. Her experience certainly governed her response to the queen's declaration that "I am against reform schools and prisons for young people. I am going to try to do away with them completely." If the queen succeeded, Eunice noted dismissively, "she would revolutionize all the modern theories of penology and also put ten thousand case workers out of business in the USA."

The trip was long and the accommodations sometimes less than ideal. After a predawn flight from Beirut to Dhahran, where the sisters toured Aramco's oil fields and refinery, Jean wrote that "Eunice's face had the look of a permanent death mold as we drew alongside a prefabricated army barrack whose façade boasted the sign 'Saudi Arabian Government Hotel.' No, it wasn't the Palm Springs of the desert."

Things did not improve when they were invited to "tea" by a local emir and had their first exposure to strong, spice-infused Arabian coffee. "Despite the discomfiture caused by my thoroughly American tastes, I enjoyed watching Eunice, who can't sleep for a week if she even looks at a cup of coffee," Jean wrote. "What this must be doing to her system was driving my imagination wild." Jean could be forgiven her mildly sadistic glee; Eunice, seven years her senior, was notorious for bossing around her kid sister, often relegating her to baggage handler on their overseas jaunts.

No sooner had the sisters resumed their lives in Chicago—organizing an exhibit at the Merchandise Mart of French religious art, as well as benefits for the girls at the House of the Good Shepherd—than Joe summoned them to Massachusetts. Jack, bored with his safe seat in the US House—he had been reelected in 1950 with 82 percent of the vote—had decided to launch an upstart challenge to Republican senator Henry Cabot Lodge Jr., who would have to defend his seat in the fall of 1952. The contest had the feel of a family grudge match: Henry Cabot Lodge Sr. had defeated John "Honey Fitz" Fitzgerald in a bid for the Senate in 1916. It would be all Kennedy hands on deck.

After returning from his own fact-finding tour of Asia and the Middle East with Bobby and Pat, Jack would make a half-hour appearance on *Meet the Press* on December 2, 1951. He acquitted himself well on the popular TV interview show, agreeing with President Harry S. Truman on Korea but expressing reservations about US support for French colonial interests in Indochina. One of Eunice's jobs in the campaign soon became hauling a projector and a reel of that interview from living room to living room across Massachusetts. At the end of the film, Jack would arrive to speak, and Eunice would pack up her projector and move on to the next house party scheduled that night.

Responsibility for organizing the large formal tea parties that Eunice and Joe DeGug had initiated in 1946 fell to Polly Fitzgerald, a Kennedy cousin by marriage, who rented veterans halls and chandeliered ballrooms across Massachusetts and invited Democratic women to come meet the bachelor candidate, his mother, and his glamorous sisters. From New Bedford to Pittsfield, thousands came, sealing the tea parties as an iconic Kennedy campaign ritual to be reprised in Jack's reelection bid in 1958 and in his presidential campaign in 1960.

Joe installed twenty-six-year-old Bobby as campaign manager, dispatching Eunice to stand in for Jack whenever the candidate had to juggle competing events. "Eunice appeared at a luncheon that [Boston] Mayor [John] Hynes gave for Jack on Bunker Hill Day, June 17, but Jack was unable to attend," Joe wrote to Ted, who was stationed in Europe with the US Army after being suspended from Harvard for recruiting a classmate to take a Spanish test for him. "After lunch she wandered through the streets of Charlestown looking at the parade and made her usual hit." In fact, Eunice had marched in the parade in Jack's stead.

Ruth M. Batson, of Roxbury, a daughter of Jamaican immigrants, remembered that Eunice projected a charisma on the campaign trail not unlike Jack's. Guests had to be admitted in shifts to meet Eunice at the crowded party Batson hosted in the four-room apartment she shared at the Orchard Park housing project with her husband and three children. "She wore a big felt skirt with 'Kennedy' written all over the bottom," recalled Batson, who would become a prominent civil rights activist in Boston. "And to this day, people still comment to me on that party. Even those who were kids at that time remember the excitement of standing and looking on the outside. That was the magic of the Kennedys. People still say that they met Kennedy, *the* Kennedy, there, when actually they had met Eunice Kennedy."

Sargent Shriver came to Boston from Chicago to help in the campaign, moving into a three-bedroom apartment Joe rented at 84 Beacon Street, around the corner from Jack's nominal residence at 122 Bowdoin Street. Sarge, by now something of a surrogate son to Joe Kennedy, occupied the middle bedroom between Rose's room and Joe's. Soon enough, he was conversing with Rose in French and accompanying her to Mass. For a man who had spent fruitless years courting Eunice, the campaign propelled him into the bosom of the family, where his potential as a son-in-law could be assessed as easily as his acumen as a political operative.

Sarge's political skills proved immediately useful when Adlai Stevenson, the Democratic presidential nominee, made a swing through western

Massachusetts. The Kennedy campaign was worried that the Illinois governor might criticize Senator Joseph McCarthy, whose virulent anti-Communism had divided the country. The Republican from Wisconsin was popular with Irish-Catholic voters in Massachusetts and with the Kennedy family.

McCarthy was a frequent guest at Hyannis Port, where the Kennedy siblings teased him about his lack of athleticism, and he won the affection and political support of their father, who contributed to his campaigns. Joe would send Bobby to work for him in 1953 as an assistant counsel to the Senate Permanent Subcommittee on Investigations. At Eunice's birthday party in 1950, the Kennedy siblings "gave him the boat treatment, i.e. throwing him out of the boat, and then Eunice, in her usual girlish glee pushed him under," Rose recalled. "To everybody's concern and astonishment, the senator came up with a ghastly look on his face, puffing and paddling. The wonder of it all was that he did not drown on the spot because, you see, coming from Wisconsin, he had never learned to swim."

When Stevenson asked how he could help Jack during his visit to Massachusetts, Sarge suggested he refrain from mentioning McCarthy. "Up here, this anti-Communism business is a good thing to empathize," wrote Sarge. Jack would remain silent as McCarthy's investigative tactics became ever more reckless. He was in a New York hospital recovering from spinal surgery when he missed—or ducked—the Senate vote censuring McCarthy on December 2, 1954. His aide Theodore Sorensen had drafted a statement in support of the censure, but Jack never authorized him to release it.

Charles Bartlett, the Washington correspondent for the *Chattanooga Times* and a friend of Jack's, was on Stevenson's train bound for Massachusetts in 1952 and remembered, "There was a great rhubarb because there was a question of which of the girls would be allowed to go to meet Adlai's train. And Mr. Kennedy selected Pat as the most decorous and restrained of the girls, and Eunice was furious because she had to stay in Boston."

Joe might have sent Pat instead of Eunice to thwart the gossip columnists who had been speculating all year about a romance between Eunice and the governor after she was spotted at several social events the divorced Stevenson attended in Chicago. Eunice had dismissed the chatter as pure fantasy, noting that on all those occasions, she had been in the company of Sarge and Bill Blair. But that did not stop Bob Farrell from writing in his New York at Night column that "the Adlai Stevenson–Eunice Kennedy four-alarmer has been shelved until after election time," or Dorothy Kilgallen from reporting on December 27, 1952, "Adlai Stevenson's romance with Eunice Kennedy (daughter of former Ambassador Joe Kennedy) didn't wane after Election Day. Still very big, their friends say."

Five weeks later, Jack had been sworn in as senator, and Eunice was engaged to Sargent Shriver.

In the end, she had accepted him while attending church one Sunday morning in January 1953. "We sat through Mass, and when it was over, she said, 'Sarge, will you join me at the side altar over there?'" Sarge recalled. "She was pointing over to the left where there was an altar to the Blessed Mother. Eunice had a tremendous devotion to Mary, so I assumed she just wanted to say some special prayers. We walked up to the altar and knelt down side by side on the barrier in front of the statue. She said a prayer, and then she turned to me. 'Sargent Shriver,' she said, 'I think I'd like to marry you.' I nearly fell off the altar rail."

She told her parents the news before Sarge had the chance, leaving him to communicate with Joe and Rose by telegram to Palm Beach on February 4: "Am Furious At You Know Who STOP Typically She Did Not Allow Me To Be Present When She Told You The News STOP Despite This And Her Other Peculiar Ideas And Actions I Love Her More Than Any Telegram Could Say STOP Thank You Both For Making Her Possible For Me."

After seven years of courtship, Eunice had not suddenly seen the light. It took an intervention just short of the divine to bring the nearly thirty-two-year-old to the altar. It is a story that the Reverend Theodore M. Hesburgh of the University of Notre Dame shared with friends in private conversations for decades but declined until two years before his death, in 2015, to confirm publicly. "They are all dead now," he said. "It can't hurt anyone."

At thirty-five, Hesburgh was two years younger than Sargent Shriver in 1952 when he succeeded the Reverend John J. Cavanaugh, one of Joe Kennedy's closest friends and frequent houseguests, as president of Notre Dame. Hesburgh had gotten to know Eunice and Sarge on their many visits to campus to make religious retreats or to attend Fighting Irish football games. Among Hesburgh's more pressing assignments in his new post was a conversation Joe asked him to have with Eunice.

"I was not that personally close to the family in those days," Hesburgh recalled. "I was not in that clique. Father Cavanaugh was practically a member of their family. They sent a plane for him when Jack was killed, and he stayed up there at the Cape with Joe for six weeks. He was in bad shape after Jack died. They didn't need me for that."

What Joe did need in 1953 was for the charismatic young priest to dissuade Eunice from becoming a nun, a stubborn aspiration that threatened to complicate her father's ambitions for Jack. Eunice came when Hesburgh summoned her to Notre Dame, and, he recalled, they had a "frank and honest exchange. I told her she did have a vocation, but that her vocation was to be Sargent Shriver's wife and the mother of his children and to continue to do the work she was doing. I think I resolved it to everyone's satisfaction."

Whatever discomfort he felt serving as Joe's stealth messenger was mitigated by his deep regard for Sarge, an admiration he knew that Eunice shared. "He was the best, the very best of the bunch," said Hesburgh, who also held Eunice in high esteem. "I knew her not as well as I knew him, but she was a great gal. There are a lot of Kennedys. They come in all shapes and sizes. But who did the work she did? Who cared for Rosemary as she did? It took a lot of strength, I will tell you that. The men tend to outrank the women in that family, but she had as much or more to offer as any of them."

For her part, Eunice was coy whenever asked what took her so long to accept Sarge's many proposals. "I don't know what made me decide to marry him," she said at age eighty. "I guess I must have been in love. I did take my time, didn't I? Seven years is a long time."

She never spoke publicly of her foiled hopes for a religious life, and only rarely did she speak of it privately to those, like Mary Cunningham Agee, who shared her deep Catholic faith. Agee, a prominent businesswoman thirty years her junior, partnered with Eunice in an organization in the 1980s to help single women see their unintended pregnancies through to delivery. She saw in her older friend a wistfulness, but no regrets, about the road not taken. "She loved her children too much for that," she said.

In Hesburgh's view, the Shriver marriage was the most successful union in the Kennedy clan, a partnership of equals forged in faith and dedicated to advancing social justice. "Sarge was one of the very, very few people who could have married into that family and survived. The family tends to attract people who are hangers-on or who are looking for shared glory. Sarge kept his independence, which is not easy to do, since they tend to subjugate people," he said.

Three weeks before his marriage, Sarge wrote a note thanking Father Cavanaugh at the University of Notre Dame for his promise to keep the couple in his prayers every day until the wedding. "Please remember me to Father Hesburgh and the other priests who always have made our visits to Notre Dame such a pleasure," he wrote.

The wedding of Eunice Mary Kennedy and R. Sargent Shriver shut down traffic on Fifth Avenue in front of St. Patrick's Cathedral in Manhattan on May 23, 1953. Eunie's wedding was everything that Kick's, in a wartime London registry office, had not been. Francis Cardinal Spellman celebrated the Mass, assisted by three bishops, four monsignors, and nine priests. The Vatican sent a papal blessing. Christian Dior shipped her white gown of French Valenciennes lace and mousseline de soie from Paris. Tall candles illuminated the interior of the cathedral, which was perfumed by pale peonies and white orchids.

Pat served as maid of honor. Jean and their cousin Mary Jo Gargan and Bobby's wife, Ethel, were among the nine bridesmaids. Herbert Shriver was best man for his brother, and Jack, Bobby, and Teddy Kennedy were among the groomsmen.

The reception at the Starlight Roof and the Grand Ballroom of the Waldorf Astoria featured a fifteen-piece orchestra and an eight-tier wedding cake that required Eunice to stand on a chair to cut the first ceremonial slice. The 1,700 guests included Margaret Truman Daniel; Bernard Baruch; Supreme Court Justice William O. Douglas; Thomas J. Watson Jr., the president of IBM; former US Secretary of Labor Maurice Tobin; Colonel Robert R. McCormick Jr. of Chicago; the mayor of New York; and the governor of Massachusetts. Wisconsin senator Joseph McCarthy gave Sarge a silver ashtray inscribed "from one of those who lost."

Less conspicuous among the luminaries were former inmates of the Women's Federal Penitentiary in Alderson, including Catherine Dickinson. The World War II spy, once known as the Doll Woman, had been paroled in 1951, and Eunice had found her a job at St. Vincent's Hospital in New York through her contacts at Catholic Charities. "I am grateful to you for giving her a chance in spite of her long prison record," Eunice wrote to Monsignor James Lynch at the time.

Although Sarge had visited Eunice at Alderson and met "Machine Gun Kelly's wife and other such interesting people," as he told a reporter from the *Washington Post*, he was surprised to see former prisoners in the receiving line at his wedding reception. "He reports that he quipped to his new father-in-law, Joseph Kennedy, 'I hope you have double guards watching the wedding presents,'" wrote the *Washington Post*.

The cost of the wedding, estimated at more than $100,000, made a distant memory of the vow of poverty Eunice had so recently been contemplating. "What a wonderful opportunity for all the cheap gossips and envious tongue wagers!" Erich Brandeis, a syndicated newspaper columnist, wrote. "What vulgar display, they said, what waste of money! Why couldn't father Kennedy distribute the money among the poor and do some real good with it? I think the undertone was, why couldn't father Kennedy have given some of that money to *us*? A hundred thousand dollars for Eunice's wedding. I bet Joe Kennedy would give all his millions to have his son and daughter back"—a reference to the deaths in the previous decade of Joe Jr. and Kick.

If Sarge thought a monthlong European honeymoon would be a hiatus from the sometimes suffocating embrace of the Kennedys, he was mistaken. Twenty-one-year-old Teddy popped up on the same flight to Lisbon, Portugal, as the newlyweds, in pursuit of an actress he had just met. Pat met up with the couple in London for a round of parties attendant to the coronation of twenty-five-year-old Queen Elizabeth II, whom the Kennedy sisters had known as a little girl fifteen years earlier.

"The honeymooners are in great form," Pat wrote to Rose, who stayed in touch by telephone and cable to report on the "rather cold" weather on Cape Cod and on photographs from the wedding that she found "terrifically amusing . . . because some of you have your mouths wide open." She thanked Pat for telling her "where Ted was, as we have not heard a word from him and cannot understand it . . . It's very stupid not to have some idea where your children are."

Back in Chicago, the couple settled into separate bedrooms in their first apartment, on East Walton Street. "I had a roommate my whole life," Sarge told his children years later. "The first time I didn't have a roommate was after I married Eunice." To which their mother replied, "Sargent, you snore so loudly!" By midsummer, Eunice was pregnant with their first child, a boy they named Robert Sargent Shriver III, for his father, not for Joe, despite press reports that the baby would be called Joseph.

Pregnancy did not interrupt Eunice's work in Chicago, where the 175 girls at the House of the Good Shepherd were only one of her philanthropic concerns. Through Catholic Charities, she had met the city's archbishop, Samuel Cardinal Stritch, and learned of his efforts to build a home for mentally retarded boys. Stritch had been transferred to Chicago a decade earlier from Milwaukee, where he had worked closely as archbishop with the Sisters of Saint Francis of Assisi, the nuns who ran the St. Coletta School in Jefferson, Wisconsin, the institution where Rosemary now lived. In the unlikely case that Eunice did not know where Rosie was in 1949, when she helped her father find a doctor for her sister, she certainly would have learned of her whereabouts from Stritch.

The Franciscan sisters had sent a small band of nuns to Chicago in 1949 to establish school on land Stritch had purchased south of the city. In the early 1950s, they were operating out of a renovated farmhouse and barn inadequate for the needs of the 121 boys they served. Eunice introduced Monsignor Cooke of Catholic Charities to her father, and—at her behest—Joe committed $1.25 million from the Kennedy Foundation to help build a modern facility for 400 boys in Palos Park, an affluent village just southwest of Chicago. For the rest of her life, Eunice would lead fund-raising efforts to supplement that gift and defray operating expenses of the school, which was named for Joe Jr.

One of her brothers would always hold the title of president of the Kennedy Foundation, but from the first, it was Eunice who was most committed to the work of the charity her father had created in memory of her eldest brother. The foundation was financed with a quarter of the profits from the Merchandise Mart. Its earliest gifts had a random character: $25,000 for the Boys Club of Boston, $450,000 for Associated Jewish Philanthropies (perhaps to blunt the impact on Jack's career of Joe's widely perceived anti-Semitism), $150,000 for a skating rink in Hyannis. But with prodding from Boston's Archbishop Richard Cushing, for whom the care of "exceptional children" was a special concern, the foundation's focus soon shifted to mental retardation, with grants for such brick-and-mortar facilities as a children's hospital and a residential school in Greater Boston.

Eunice added Chicago to the mix. "We of the Kennedy Foundation are especially gratified that the new home will be open to children of all races and creeds—for mental deficiency strikes without regard to artificial barriers erected by the narrowness of men," she said in 1952 when delivering the first check, for $500,000, to the Archdiocese of Chicago. Identified in newspaper accounts that day as vice president of the foundation, a title she would hold for the rest of her life, Eunice told reporters, "Parents can be happy, too, that their children will be contented here. The agony of separation will be eased by the security of the mutual love between the children and the nuns who have dedicated their lives to this service."

Was Eunice thinking of her own separation from Rosemary, erased from the family a decade before? Had she eased that agony by making the 135-mile drive from Chicago to Jefferson to visit her sister in defiance of her father's dictum that the Kennedys have no further contact with Rosemary? Had Eunice been in a pew at St. Coletta when Archbishop Cushing flew west to dedicate the school's new chapel a few days after she returned from her honeymoon?

"I think of [a] family and of their home," he told the congregants. "It's one of the most wonderful homes to visit in all their neighborhood. It is a house full of children, but there is a gentleness, a sense of consideration, a ready deference, a quiet, kindly attitude in all the girls and boys of that household. And the reason? One of their sisters is an 'exceptional' child, and the others have grown up used to the fact that in all their planning, all their playing, all their speech and everything they do and are, they must take her into 'exceptional' consideration. And so she, more than the mother, more than the father, has been the refining influence in the family, producing an exceptionally Christ-like spirit in an exceptionally troubled family."

It is uncertain whether Eunice was at St. Coletta to hear Cushing tell the story of a family that might or might not have been her own. What is certain is that she was finding her life's purpose. Her father's preoccupation with Jack's career and her brothers' indifference to the daily operations of the foundation provided the opportunity she needed to make her mark in the family and in the world, and she took it.

Eunice grabbed the reins of the Kennedy Foundation and never let go. By the late 1950s, when her father began to think about shifting the foundation's mission from building schools and hospitals to funding scientific research into the causes of mental retardation, Eunice had positioned herself as the one he relied upon to direct those efforts. She could not make her father see her as he saw his sons, but by taking control of the family foundation, Eunice ensured that Joe Kennedy's fortune would finance her goals no less than those of Jack, Bobby, and Ted.

Her father would not make it easy for her. Unwilling to give a daughter complete authority in the foundation, he installed Sarge as executive director and often undermined her in meetings. Father and daughter met early on with Dr. Howard Rusk, a rehabilitation specialist in New York, to solicit his advice about how best to fund scientific research. When Rusk suggested broadening the mission to include mental illness as well as mental retardation, Eunice snapped, "I don't want to do that," and Joe barked at her, "You are too difficult!"

She must have been humiliated by her father's public rebuke, but Eunice was so eager to win his approval she recorded in her diary his verbatim critique of her performance, placing a star next to it. "Dad: 'You say mental retardation but what is it you want to do? Not just a project. Who, where can you find standards for research in the field? What basic knowledge do you have to do research? Where are the people, Eunice? You do not have any of this information. Dr. Rusk does.'"

Eunice set out to prove her father wrong, making her first trips to homes for mentally retarded children expressly to assess the research potential. In August 1958 she visited two Kennedy Foundation–funded sites in Massachusetts—a hospital in the Brighton neighborhood of Boston and a residential school in Hanover—describing them both as "a gold mine for research" and assuring Joe that "it is clear our Homes should be a rich, fascinating, and less expensive source for research."

Eunice craved her father's appreciation and was shattered when he withheld it. She was crushed when Joe rejected her request that he send her and Sarge to the Far East to look at schools there, a fact-finding mission to help in her work with the Kennedy Foundation and in his with the Chicago Board of Education, to which he had recently been appointed.

The rebuff brought on "her first stomachache since July," Sarge told Joe in an undated letter that suggested her chronic pain had some psychological origins. Abdominal pain is often a physical manifestation of stress. The kind of stomach ills Eunice battled all her life are sometimes attributed to what would later be called irritable bowel syndrome, a condition researchers have linked to anxiety. Whether the anxiety triggered the pain or the pain triggered the anxiety, the connection between mind and body in Eunice's case was clear to her husband.

In his letter to Joe, Sarge attributed Eunice's stomachaches to "her ever-present desire to be important in your mind & heart. As she often says, you are the greatest father in the world. You must know she has a 'father complex,' as the doctors sometimes say."

Worse, she took the rejection, "emotionally and psychologically," as evidence "that you do not want her to do the things that others do." Eunice needs "your approval and commendation and enthusiasm for this idea of hers," Sarge wrote. "The trip is only a symbol."

So certain was she of her father's genius and what he had to teach her that Eunice wrote down every management technique he proffered, no matter how banal. "If you go to a meeting for advice, don't knock down the other fellow's idea. You never get a hundred percent. If you do knock his idea down, you will lose his enthusiasm," he told her. "Dad says he is a trader. He gives something & he gets something," she wrote. If she hoped to make an impact in the field of mental retardation, he told her, she had to understand the issue thoroughly, not just promote research as a worthy cause. "Fellows who do that are out on their ear in a short time," he said. That would not happen to Eunice, who set out to learn all there was to learn about mental retardation.

———————

Whatever her complex motivation for wanting control of the Kennedy Foundation—ambition, anger, empathy, guilt, daddy issues, or some combination of them all—Eunice chose a cause ripe for the championing. History had not been kind to those with mental retardation. As late as the Renaissance, Christians feared them as soulless "changelings" corrupted by Satan. The lucky might have been tolerated in the fledgling republic of the United States as "village idiots," left to sleep in barns and eat table scraps; the greater number were locked away under conditions that shocked early reformers.

The most prominent of those was Dorothea Dix, from the Kennedys' native Massachusetts, whose statewide survey of the treatment of the mentally ill and retarded in 1841 resulted in a report to the legislature that described the "cages, stalls, pens" in which people were "chained, naked, beaten with rods, and lashed into obedience." She found those conditions replicated in her travels throughout the country, prompting her efforts to establish state asylums and schools for the retarded and the insane, the first of which were founded in Massachusetts.

That progress notwithstanding, the first half of the twentieth century was still fraught for those deemed mentally deficient. The eugenics movement advocated institutionalization and sterilization of those with mental retardation as the only way to protect the public from such "rapacious social ills" as the crime and prostitution attributed to those who had inherited "bad blood"—ideas that would find genocidal expression in the Nazi atrocities of World War II.

The theory that the mentally retarded sprang from "degenerate stock" and should be eliminated from the gene pool infiltrated the law as well as medicine. In the 1927 case of *Buck v. Bell*, the US Supreme Court ruled that a compulsory-sterilization law in Virginia did not violate the due-process rights of a young unwed mother, Carrie Buck, whom the state claimed was retarded, the offspring of a mentally defective mother, and herself the mother of a feebleminded daughter. "Three generations of idiots are enough," Oliver Wendell Holmes wrote in the majority opinion upholding the sterilization plan of the Virginia State Colony for Epileptics and Feebleminded, where Carrie Buck was confined.

The lone dissenter on the high court was Justice Pierce Butler, a member of the Catholic Church, which would vigorously oppose dozens of sterilization laws that proliferated in states across the country in the wake of *Buck v. Bell*—the decision named for a young woman who, historians have now concluded, was not mentally retarded at all.

While later research would confirm genetic factors in some forms of mental retardation, the condition is much more complex than eugenicists claimed, caused variously by prenatal infection or intoxication, pre- or post-natal trauma, brain disease, chromosomal abnormalities, metabolic and nutritional disorders, and a host of other influences, known and unknown.

Even as knowledge expanded, stigma continued to eclipse science. Most family doctors routinely urged parents to confine a child with mental retardation to a state institution at birth for the sake of their other children and their marriage. No less prominent a child psychoanalyst than Erik Erikson and his wife, Joan, did just that when their son was born with Down syndrome, telling their older children that he had died at birth.

Although experts then estimated that 1 percent to 3 percent of all babies born in the United States would be mentally retarded, the federal government played little role in what was still considered a private family matter. Asylums for the retarded, founded as a humane gesture, were little more than human storehouses at midcentury. Passage in 1946 of the Hill-Burton Act to provide hospitals with federal grants and loans for construction and modernization in exchange for offering services to the poor was of no help to institutions for the mentally retarded. Guidelines stipulated that funds go only to facilities that provided therapeutic, as well as custodial, care. Since the conventional wisdom held that there was no treatment for retardation, residents were warehoused in overcrowded and understaffed state facilities, restrained in cribs and cots, bound in straitjackets or tied in chairs, condemned to look through barred windows at often bucolic campuses to which they had little or no access.

Conditions at many institutions for the retarded mirrored those Eunice had seen in 1947 at homes for juvenile delinquents during her tenure at the US Justice Department. At asylums she visited for the mentally retarded, she wrote, "There was an overpowering smell of urine from clothes and from the floors. I remember the retarded patients with nothing to do, standing, staring, grotesque-like misshaped statues. I recall other institutions where several thousand adults and children were housed in bleak, overcrowded wards of a hundred or more, living out their lives on a dead-end street, unloved, unwanted, some of them strapped in chairs like criminals."

Those who chose to keep their sons or daughters at home, like Joe and Rose Kennedy, were either wealthy enough to afford the few available tutors trained to teach their children or took on that challenge themselves.

As early as the 1930s, parents began to push back, demanding help from policy makers in the care and education of their children. A White House Conference on Child Health and Protection declared in 1930 that mentally and physically handicapped children should be entitled to "appropriate measures to reduce [their] handicap, and training to become a useful member of society." Those noble intentions were soon overshadowed by the demands of the Great Depression and World War II. It was not until the postwar period that parents began to organize in earnest.

At the time, "It was not popular or fashionable to be interested in mental retardation," Eunice noted. "Mental retardation was like syphilis. No one mentioned it in polite society. A mentally retarded child was like a skeleton in the closet. Its mere existence was a shame. In some places, it was even considered a punishment for sin. Thousands upon thousands of children, and mothers and fathers, were suffering physical and mental tortures with little or no help from medical science, government, or even from their own families and friends."

Margaret V. Tedone's situation was typical. The West Hartford, Connecticut, mother of twins recalled the isolation she felt after one of her boys failed to recover at age two from a bout of viral encephalitis. "He was a beautiful-looking little boy. Unless you observed him for ten or fifteen minutes, you'd think there was nothing wrong with him," she said. Her pediatrician dismissed her concerns as the fretting of an anxious mother. A neurologist she consulted suspected brain damage, a diagnosis confirmed when the Tedones took their son to the Lahey Clinic in Boston.

"I have this handsome little fellow on my lap, my Thomas, and the doctor is at the desk with Thomas's file, and the doctor says, 'This boy has had extensive brain damage. There is nothing to do but place him in an institution.' That was all they ever told us, 'Put him away,'" Margaret recalled. "I hate that phrase even now; when somebody says 'Put that away,' I cringe. This was the attitude of the medical profession. I might just as well have left Thomas home and come with his file. He never looked at him. He never listened to his heart. He never examined him. What did we know? We were young kids, just out of the service."

Back in Connecticut, she visited the Mansfield Training School to assess what it could do for her son. The evolution of the institution's name reflects much of the history of mental retardation in the United States. Founded in 1860 as the Connecticut School for Imbeciles, it became the Connecticut Training School for the Feebleminded in 1915, before merging with the Connecticut Colony for Epileptics in 1917.

By any name, Mansfield, in 1950—and scores of state institutions like it across the country—still fell far short of Dorothea Dix's ideal of a humane refuge for the vulnerable. "I had never seen anything so awful," Tedone remembered tearfully more than six decades later. "I had never seen so many children like that, some very seriously retarded, some not so bad. Many of them were restrained. They didn't do anything for them." For all of its deficiencies, Mansfield had a waiting list so long that the state built another facility, in Southbury, to meet the demand.

Margaret Tedone kept her son at home but also resolved to join other parents to improve their children's lives. If medical and educational professionals could not help them, they would help themselves. In state after state, parents of mentally retarded children began reaching out to find one another, sometimes through advertisements in local newspapers, often through social workers who introduced them to one another. What began as play dates for their children and mutual emotional support became the National Association of Parents and Friends of Retarded Children, later the National Association for Retarded Children (NARC), an umbrella organization for all the parents' groups springing up across the country.

To break the ice, Margaret Tedone brought a chocolate cake to the first parents' meeting in Connecticut, which attracted twenty-two people to a living room in Hartford. In short order, those parents decided to raise money for a private classroom where their children—legally denied seats in public school—could learn. They asked their milkmen to distribute donation envelopes on their routes. They ran rummage sales. They sold lollipops on Main Street.

Gradually women who, Tedone conceded, "did not know how an idea became a law," honed their skills as advocates, writing grant proposals, meeting with newspaper editors and lobbying lawmakers for special education, training, and recreational opportunities for children who had been locked away in institutions or hidden indoors at home for too long. Tedone once followed a state senator into a men's room to secure his commitment to an education-funding bill. "If going in was bad, you should see what it is like when you are seen coming out of the men's room," she said, her mix of embarrassment and pride still vivid at age ninety-one.

She would not meet Eunice Kennedy Shriver until the 1970s, when President Gerald Ford appointed them both to the President's Committee on Mental Retardation, but by then, they had been on parallel tracks for twenty years. Neither had been groomed for a public life; both defied expectations. Margaret Tedone won a seat first on her local school board and then on the city council, an unanticipated political career that sprang from a mother's determination to fight.

———————

Motherhood took a different form on North Lakeview Avenue in Chicago, where Eunice and Sargent Shriver moved from their first apartment after the births of Bobby, in 1954, and Maria Owings Shriver, nineteen months later. It was a gracious space, on two levels, with the living area downstairs and the sleeping quarters above, with commanding views of Lake Michigan. The elevator opened onto a large foyer cluttered with toys and bicycles and the occasional trespassing chicken, rabbit, or beagle— all of which the Shrivers numbered among their pets. Mercifully for the housekeepers, the Shrivers' pony stayed stabled at Cape Cod, with the Kennedy horses.

"It was a wonderful playroom on a rainy day," Dorothy Schrot recalled of the vestibule where her son, Paul, and daughter, Karen, played with Bobby and Maria when they were not romping in neighboring Lincoln Park. Dorothy met Eunice long after she had met the Shriver children in the park, accompanied by a rotating cast of nannies. There was a shy Norwegian, a charming Irish girl, and a stern German, the last fired when the Shrivers caught her hitting the children. Bobby remembered only the German, who "whacked us around."

Eunice sometimes took the children to the park herself, and when she did, other mothers recognized her immediately. The Shrivers were often photographed on the social circuit, attending charity and cultural events in Chicago and sometimes in Washington and Hollywood, too. Pat had married the British actor Peter Lawford in 1954. Jack had married, too, only four months after Eunice and Sarge, his wedding to Jacqueline Bouvier attracting national news coverage and throngs of onlookers at the social event of the season in Newport, Rhode Island.

By the mid-1950s, Sarge was well known as president of the Chicago Board of Education and an officer of the Catholic Interracial Council of Chicago, as well as a manager at the Merchandise Mart. In addition to her work with the House of the Good Shepherd and Catholic Charities, Eunice, too, had cultivated a public profile as a consultant to Mayor Richard J. Daley's Commission on Youth Welfare and a trustee of the Menninger Foundation, headed by Dr. Charles F. Menninger and his two physician sons to oversee the family's private psychiatric sanatorium that treated well-heeled patients, conducted research, and trained psychoanalysts on a verdant hillside campus in Topeka, Kansas.

It was a warm spring or early summer day when Dorothy Schrot first saw Eunice in the playground. Dressed in a crisp pink linen shift, Eunice was the image of a society matron until "she sat right down in the sandbox with the children," endearing herself to Schrot, who was watching Karen and Paul from a bench nearby.

Little Karen was quite a talker, often ignoring her playmates to interrogate the mothers about the size of their apartments and the style of their furniture. She peppered Eunice with so many questions that Schrot began to feel uncomfortable. "I didn't approach her, because I knew she was a Kennedy girl, and I thought she must get very tired of people bothering them. Finally, she turned to me and said, 'Boy, this girl is really going to go far. She's a smart one!'"

That encounter led to others, including pony-cart rides in the park for Bobby's birthday party one year that also featured an underappreciated tuna casserole and a much better-received frosted cake. Once, when the damp grass threatened to thwart picnic plans, Eunice simply took off her mink coat, spread it on the ground, and invited Schrot and the four children to sit.

As unpretentious as she could be sometimes, Eunice could also be oblivious. After Maria had fallen from a swing, Schrot became alarmed when the little girl kept waking from a nap on the picnic blanket in obvious distress. "She'd fall asleep and wake up crying over and over," she said. "I told [Eunice] to take her to the doctor, that something must be wrong. She did, but not right away. She was not at all alarmed. Turned out Maria had a broken clavicle."

A neighbor, Catherine "Deeda" Gerlach, experienced a similar incident that she thought reflected her friend's lack of interest in things she considered skin-deep. When Maria took a tumble on a gravel path, Gerlach brought her home from the park, worried that her scrapes might leave a scar. "Eunice was never preoccupied with appearances. Maria had scraped her face all above her lip," Deeda remembered. "Eunice cleaned it off, but when Sarge came home, he took her to a hospital to get every piece of that gravel removed."

Rose remained a hovering—and often critical—presence in her daughter's life, finding fault with her parenting skills as well as her fashion sense. In a letter dictated to her secretary, Rose chastised Eunice for allowing Maria to "go up and down the elevator in her nightgown. I do not think that it looks very well. If I were to come into an apartment house and find a child thus, I would think the apartment a very strange one and the parents of the child very careless."

As scattered as her maternal attention could be, Eunice was a generous friend. Having introduced Deeda Gerlach to Bill Blair at a dinner party at the Shriver apartment, Eunice gently coaxed the relationship forward. Because it was the 1950s and Gerlach was going through a divorce, Eunice offered to chaperone them on their movie and dinner dates. The only problem was she couldn't stay awake past nine o'clock. "We would go to the movies, and we would get to one of our two favorite restaurants, and Eunice would say, 'I am so tired, you have to let me off duty,'" the future Mrs. Blair recalled. "We did all kinds of things together. Eunice was the least judgmental person I've known. She might have opinions, but they were never judgmental."

That was certainly her attitude toward delinquent girls from the House of the Good Shepherd, three of whom Bobby and Maria remember living with them for short stretches in Chicago and on the Cape, one after the other and sometimes two at a time. "I remember them being there, but it was never explained to me why they were there," Maria said of the girls who shared the Shrivers' dinner table and often babysat for the children.

In the scant official documentation that survives from that era, there is no record of formal foster placements with the Shrivers, according to archivists for the Sisters of the Good Shepherd. Although Eunice described the girls as "foster daughters," it is more likely that the arrangement was an informal one, with Eunice opening their home to young women in need of transitional housing after their release from the reformatory while they looked for work or arranged for further schooling. She had first seen the desperate need for foster parents when she worked for the Justice Department and, in a pattern she would repeat throughout her life, stepped in personally to fill the vacuum. "Many nights I'd be sitting there reading the paper or poring over work from the office, and the doorbell would ring," Sarge recalled. "I'd go to the door, and there would be a woman with a suitcase and a plaintive look on her face. 'Uh-oh,' I'd think. 'Another one of Eunice's girls.'"

Charles Bartlett, the journalist and a family friend, thought, "Eunice married a benign man. Not many husbands would put up with all that."

What struck Gerlach about the unconventional housing arrangement was how natural it seemed to Eunice, who was often indifferent to social conventions. "I never knew anyone else who did it, at that time or ever since. She would take these young women, teenagers, from prison and move them into the apartment and treat them like family. Sometimes there were problems, but she was amazing about that. They were part of the family," she recalled, still incredulous six decades later at how refreshingly dismissive her friend could be of social mores.

"I know that many people feel you shouldn't bring youngsters from a lower income group into an atmosphere that is completely strange to them economically. But I don't agree," Eunice said. On visits to Cape Cod, her foster daughters learned to swim, water ski, and sail. "One of the girls became especially interested in horses," she recalled. "They all enjoyed swimming. Such activities provide them an outlet for their energy, whole-some interests so important to their well-being."

In Maria's and Bobby's memories, both parents were away for much of their early years, campaigning for Jack or on fact-finding missions around the country for the Kennedy Foundation. "I don't think we experienced it as coming and going and chaos. It was just absence," Bobby said. "It was just the way life was."

When the Shrivers were at home, they often entertained, despite Eunice's aversion to cooking, small talk, and late evenings. Spared the drudgery of domestic chores by her trust fund, she was free to enjoy her own parties with company of her own choosing, under circumstances she alone would dictate. Bill Blair remembered the original way she orches-trated the end of one dinner party that had gone on longer than she liked. She turned up the music and had her guests form a conga line. Then she danced them straight to the elevator.

It was not unusual for an evening with the Shrivers to combine a so-cial and scholarly agenda. For years, the couple hosted an informal salon, not unlike the one Kick presided over at her house in London's Smith Square after the war. A voracious reader, Sarge would choose a topic in history, the news, or theology and distribute summaries for guests to read before they met in the Shrivers' apartment for supper and conversation. "We'd all have the same material, and we would get together and discuss it," Notre Dame's Father Cavanaugh recalled. "They were wonderful, in-teresting evenings." If the conversation went on too long, Eunice would simply slip off to bed without a parting word.

Often it was ill health that prompted her to end an evening early. Still plagued by stomachaches, sleeplessness, and weight loss, she was easily overcome by exhaustion. "Eunice is still improving every day," Sarge wrote from Chicago in an undated letter to his father-in-law. It is likely from the mid- to late-1950s because he also thanked Joe for the gift for her birthday of Union Carbide stock for Maria "in the nursery." Eunice, Sarge reported, "is not too strong as yet but still not complaining about being confined to her room . . . so you see she isn't herself."

She made a rare exception for late-night entertaining when Chicago hosted the Democratic National Convention in 1956. Bobby and Maria were sent to Cape Cod for a visit with their grandparents. Jackie, who was seven months pregnant with a daughter who would be stillborn, moved into the Shrivers' apartment, along with Ethel and Jean, who, three months before, had married Stephen E. Smith, a financial advisor to his family's barge and tugboat business in New York. Jack, Bobby, and Steve Smith stayed downtown at the Conrad Hilton Hotel, near the convention site, the International Amphitheatre.

Eunice and Adeline Keane, the wife of a Chicago alderman, served as chairwomen of the entertainment committee for the convention, planning cocktail and dinner parties, fashion shows, and staging *Jenny*, a satirical play with a female presidential candidate as its central character. "In less than half a decade, Eunice has become so much a part of Chicago life that she could be chosen for such a highly visible task, seeming like a real Chicagoan and not an interloper from the East," the *Chicago Daily News* reported.

The party's nominee, Adlai Stevenson, threw open the choice of vice president to the convention that year, and Jack mounted a spirited campaign to be named to the ticket. He nearly prevailed, not losing to Senator Estes Kefauver of Tennessee until the third ballot. As consolation, Stevenson asked Kennedy to place his name in nomination, a speech that elevated Jack's national profile and propelled him into the ranks of likely presidential candidates in 1960.

History would judge the loss of the vice presidential spot in 1956 as a win for Jack's career after incumbent President Dwight D. Eisenhower and Vice President Richard Nixon trounced the Stevenson-Kefauver ticket in November. Had Jack been on the ticket, his Catholicism might well have been blamed for contributing to the defeat.

The Chicago convention launched Jack on his path to the White House and sent Eunice back to the classroom to become a more diligent student of both US history and her brother's career. She enrolled in a twice-weekly evening survey course at Loyola University, placing a star next to her lecture notes on the "Golden Age of the Senate," the antebellum period considered a time of elevated deliberation and debate. Even as she studied the words of Henry Clay, Daniel Webster, and John C. Calhoun, she sent a flurry of letters to Ted Sorensen, Jack's aide and speechwriter, requesting copies of all of her brother's floor speeches and public statements, perhaps to see how well he stacked up against them and the senators featured in *Profiles in Courage*, the Pulitzer Prize–winning collection of essays that Jack and Sorensen had compiled while Jack recovered from back surgery in the mid-1950s.

In her regular notes to Sorensen soliciting additional reading suggestions, Eunice also asked him to critique the speeches she was delivering with increasing frequency on behalf of the Kennedy Foundation. "This is a copy of a speech I gave earlier today," she wrote Sorensen in February 1957. "Actually, I spoke off the cuff part of the time and added some details about the operation of the Home in Palos Park. It's certainly not the best—but I'd really like to get some suggestions from you about improving the style, etc. Please be frank!" Throughout her public career, admirers would note how much Eunice sounded like Jack. It was not accidental. She studied Sorensen's rhetorical flourishes in order to replicate them in her own speeches.

Her insecurities about her growing public role come through in her diaries from the 1950s, where she recorded, in meticulous detail, her siblings' techniques for ingratiating themselves in social situations and her father's often harsh criticism of her interpersonal skills.

A political career of her own might have been beyond Eunice's imagining, but she was already emerging as a leader in her own right. In South Bend, Indiana, a month before the election, Eunice had given her first major political speech for a Democrat who was not her brother. Stevenson could not win without women, she told the crowd at the University of Notre Dame. "A few years ago, a poll was taken in which sixty-eight percent of the mothers stated they did not want their sons to enter politics because it was too corrupt. That attitude has changed. Now they prefer to light one candle than curse the darkness," she said.

By 1959, she could tell the audience honoring her at a dinner for the Greater Boston Association for Retarded Children that the family foundation she steered had spent more than $12 million to build "recreation centers, hospitals, day care centers, custodial homes, [and] educational institutions," across the country. It was time to redirect those efforts into research to identify the causes of mental retardation and develop interventions to ameliorate its impact, she said, because it would be financially impossible to build enough institutions for the estimated hundred thousand babies born each year with intellectual and developmental disabilities.

Eunice dated the shift in the Kennedy Foundation's focus toward research to a walk down Park Avenue with her father in the late 1950s, when Joe asked Eunice and Sarge to take the lead and determine how the foundation could best fund an expansion of nascent scientific efforts in the field. In speeches over the next decade, she identified the year variously as 1956, 1957, or 1958. Whichever year it was, Sarge and Eunice began their work, in standard Kennedy fashion, by identifying experts who could help them frame their inquiries. Jerome Schulman, a pediatric neurologist who directed the child guidance clinic at Children's Memorial Hospital in Chicago, took them on site visits to institutions. Richard L. Masland, a neurologist and assistant director of the US National Institute of Neurological Diseases and Blindness, urged them to focus on prestigious universities to elevate the status of mental retardation as a research subject. George Tarjan, a psychiatrist and superintendent of the Pacific State Hospital in Pomona, California, introduced them to activists in the parents' movement eager to see more resources devoted to research.

Guided by their consultants, Eunice and Sarge met with Nobel laureates in medicine at Stanford, with geneticists and biochemists at the University of Wisconsin, with an expert in neuropathology at Harvard, with a distinguished child psychiatrist and a Nobel laureate in chemistry at UCLA, and with the head of pediatrics at Johns Hopkins University, Robert E. Cooke, who would become their closest advisor for forty years. In short order, they packed in meetings in twenty different cities, once hitting the University of Wisconsin, Yale, and Brandeis University in a single week.

What they learned appalled and motivated Eunice. There were 365 business schools in the United States but only 90 medical schools, none of which taught any courses on mental retardation or exposed students to the private and public asylums where the mentally retarded were segregated from society. Research scientists were focused on heart disease, polio, and cancer, in no small part because that was where the money was. The federal government appropriated $88 million for research on cancer and $80 million for research on heart disease in 1958, but only $10 million for mental retardation. This despite estimates that the condition affected as much as 3 percent of the population—six times as many people as epilepsy, ten times as many as tuberculosis, twenty times as many as polio, and fifty times as many as muscular dystrophy—Eunice told audiences across the country, noting that advocates for patients with those conditions had done a far better job at raising public awareness and private philanthropy than had champions of those with mental retardation.

Three months after giving birth to her third child, Timothy Perry Shriver, in 1959, Eunice told a Boston audience, "Mental retardation research has no status in scientific circles. It is the stepchild, or ugly duckling, or forgotten one. Why? Because doctors thought that nothing could be done, that the children would die very young anyhow, and that custodial institutions were the practical solution. But successful use of antibiotics is keeping the children alive. Research is coming up with new answers. Yes, the facts have changed, but the traditional attitudes and prejudices abide. These prejudices must be eradicated. We must prove that mental retardation is a fit area for scientific research."

The first proving ground would be at Massachusetts General Hospital, which accepted a $1 million grant from the Kennedy Foundation to set up a laboratory under the direction of its head of neurology, Dr. Raymond Adams, to research metabolic disorders at the root of mental retardation. It was the first lab of its kind in the world. Adams, who was also a professor of neuropathology at Harvard Medical School, linked the basic science research to clinical experience with residents of state institutions for the mentally retarded.

That, to Eunice, was crucial. Scientists needed to see what she had seen to understand the urgency of their research. "I have seen sights that will haunt me all of my life," she said of her visits during that period to state asylums. "If I had not seen them myself, I would never have believed that such conditions could exist in modern America."

————

Jack, meanwhile, was on the road as much as Eunice, campaigning for fellow Democrats and accepting speaking invitations all over the country. He was basking in the national recognition that made him a leading contender for the 1960 Democratic presidential nomination. He had been reelected to the Senate in 1958 with 73.6 percent of the vote, the largest margin of victory any US Senate candidate in Massachusetts had ever recorded.

In a note to her brother, Eunice seemed to recognize that her role in the family had changed. Her work at the Kennedy Foundation—the expertise she was developing, the contacts she was cultivating, and the largesse she was distributing—made her a valuable political asset. She was determined to be a player both in her brother's presidential campaign and in the White House administration she was certain would follow.

"Illinois is still for you," she wrote to Jack in 1959, "but you better keep in touch with me, or else you'll be sorry in 1960."

EIGHT

CONSULTANT TO THE PRESIDENT

Many expectant mothers get less attention from doctors than cows get from cattle breeders.

—EUNICE KENNEDY SHRIVER, 1962

T WAS IRONIC that Wisconsin would prove a crucial testing ground in Jack's bid for the Democratic nomination for president. After all, Joe had sent Rosemary to that upper Midwestern state, nestled between the Great Lakes and the Mississippi River, for the precise purpose of separating his lobotomized daughter from her siblings and his ambitions for them.

Archbishop Richard Cushing, who had been named a cardinal in 1958, had been prophetic in his advice to relocate Rosie far from home. Her transfer in 1949 from a New York psychiatric hospital to the St. Coletta School for Exceptional Children in Jefferson, then a city of fewer than four thousand people, had avoided the publicity that surely would have accompanied her institutionalization in Massachusetts. A passive press corps had accepted without question the explanation for Rosemary's absence from Jack's US House and Senate campaigns: she was teaching mentally retarded children at a Catholic school in the Midwest.

It remains unclear how much Rosemary's mother and siblings knew or suspected. It is certain, though, that her move to St. Coletta served Joe's

dual purpose of finding a supportive home for his daughter and eliminating a potential distraction from Jack's political ascendance. "The solution
of Rosemary's problem has been a major factor in the ability of all the
Kennedys to go about their life's work and to try and do it as well as we
can," he wrote to Sister Anastasia at St. Coletta on May 29, 1958. That was
Jack's forty-first birthday, and plans were well under way to make him the
nation's first Catholic president.

Now, three months after Jack declared his candidacy on January 2,
1960, the state known as America's Dairyland was crawling with Kennedys. In March Jack had won the New Hampshire primary with 85 percent
of the vote, but the Granite State had been no contest for a candidate from
neighboring Massachusetts. Unopposed in Nebraska and Indiana—most
of his potential Democratic rivals having skipped the primaries—Jack
needed a strong showing in Wisconsin against Minnesota senator Hubert
H. Humphrey to prove a Catholic could be a serious contender for the
White House.

A rural state with a largely Protestant electorate, Wisconsin was not a
natural fit for a wealthy, Harvard-educated Catholic. Joe called the state
"the crisis of the campaign." If Jack did not win there, "we should get out
of the fight," he wrote to a friend. The family descended en masse. The
Kennedys "are all over the state, and they look alike and sound alike,"
Humphrey groused. "Teddy or Eunice talks to a crowd, wearing a rac-
coon coat and a stocking cap, and people think they are listening to Jack. I
get reports that Jack is appearing in three or four places at the same time."

Jack did win Wisconsin, on April 5, polling 56 percent to Humphrey's
44 percent, but the bulk of his support came from heavily Catholic dis-
tricts, undermining the significance of the win. Noting how downcast her
brother was in victory, Eunice asked what the results meant. "It means
that we've got to go to West Virginia in the morning and do it all over
again," Jack said.

The day after Jack secured the nomination in Los Angeles in July, the
New York Mirror reported that "Jack's sister, Rosemary, shuns publicity.
Now forty, she teaches at a Catholic school for exceptional children in
Jefferson, Wisc." But by then, Joe had realized it would be impossible to
keep Rosemary's condition private much longer, especially since Eunice
had chosen as her life's work a very public advocacy on behalf of those
with mental retardation. With the Kennedy Foundation devoting its resources to that cause, and Rosemary's circumstances an open secret among

many parents who were active in the National Association for Retarded Children, Joe had already begun to change the story he told about Rosemary.

A day before the Democratic National Convention had convened, Joe, confident that Jack would be nominated on the first ballot, told *Time* magazine that Rosemary had been a victim of spinal meningitis as a child. The article did not specify the disabilities she suffered as a result, nor did it mention the lobotomy she had undergone at twenty-three, but it did say she now lived in a Wisconsin nursing home. "I used to think it was something to hide, but then I learned that almost everyone I know has a relative or good friend who has the problem," Joe told the newsweekly. "I think it is best to bring these things out in the open."

The timing suggests his motive was more of a defensive maneuver than a sudden impulse toward transparency. Texas senator Lyndon B. Johnson, in his own bid for the Democratic nod, had been telling reporters that Jack's health was precarious; that he suffered from Addison's disease and relied on cortisone injections to combat the debilitating effects of his adrenal insufficiency. The Kennedy camp denied that Jack had the disease he had been taking steroids for since 1947. Did Joe worry that Rosemary's condition might be the next Kennedy secret exposed? How many lies could a presidential campaign sustain?

Decades of cultivating journalists served Joe well. In a feature story about the Kennedys in the *New York Times* during convention week, the nation's newspaper of record reported, almost as an aside, "Rosemary is in a nursing home in Wisconsin," without providing any explanation. That same week, Joe met with John Seigenthaler, a political reporter for the *Tennessean* of Nashville who the next year would become an assistant to Robert F. Kennedy in the US Justice Department. "The story had just come out in *Time* that Rosemary had been mentally retarded," Seigenthaler recalled, quoting Joe telling him, "I don't know what it is that makes eight children shine like a dollar and one dull. I guess it's the hand of God. But we just do the best we can and try to help wherever we can."

In that interview, Joe gave Eunice the public acknowledgment she had long craved. Citing her work for the Kennedy Foundation, Joe told Seigenthaler, "Eunie knows more about helping the mentally retarded than any other individual in America." And she made certain her expertise found expression in Jack's campaign. In the library of the Hyannis Port house, Jack would run his speeches by his sister, and Eunice would press her brother to consider a more robust federal role in mental retardation research, in the related—and neglected—study of maternal and child health, and in juvenile delinquency. She had Dr. Robert E. Cooke, the head of pediatrics at Johns Hopkins and her chief medical advisor at the foundation, prepare background materials for Jack's use on the stump.

Eunice continued to make regular appearances in embroidered circle skirts at tea parties on the campaign trail with Pat, Jean, and Ethel—once annoying aides to Lady Bird Johnson, whose husband had become Jack's running mate, by balking at donning a ten-gallon hat on a tour of Texas—but her role as a behind-the-scenes policy advisor to her brother was unique among the Kennedy women. Jackie, who had suffered a miscarriage and a stillbirth before the birth of Caroline in 1957, was sidelined for much of the 1960 campaign by her pregnancy with John Jr.

When Jack narrowly defeated Vice President Richard M. Nixon on November 8, Eunice played an active role in the transition. She shoehorned two specialists on mental retardation onto the task force shaping Jack's initiatives on health and welfare. She chose Cooke, the pediatrician from Johns Hopkins, and Dr. Joshua Lederberg, a Nobel Prize–winning geneticist at Stanford, to balance the influence of Wilbur J. Cohen, an official from the US Department of Health, Education, and Welfare (HEW) who had been one of the architects of Social Security during the administration of President Franklin Delano Roosevelt.

"The Kennedy Foundation was worried that the well-being, the health of children in general, and the mentally retarded in particular, would be lost sight of with Wilbur Cohen's singular concern for the elderly," Eunice recalled, a fear that would prove unfounded. Cohen's mastery of the federal bureaucracy would contribute mightily to achieving her goals.

Jack set up his transition headquarters at the Kennedys' oceanside villa in Palm Beach, where prospective Cabinet nominees encountered the barely controlled chaos that also greeted Jackie when she arrived at the North Ocean Boulevard house in early December, having given birth to John F. Kennedy Jr. at Georgetown University Hospital two weeks after the election. The scene, one historian noted, looked like "a screwball comedy, in which several generations of an eccentric family trip over one another in a creaky mansion where the phones never stop ringing, doors never cease slamming, typewriters clack around the clock, doorbells sound perpetually, and guests never stop arriving and departing."

Eunice spent a week at St. Elizabeth's Hospital in Boston after the election, recuperating from what she later described as "nervous exhaustion" and "an operation," the nature of which is not described in available records. Her stomach pain, weight loss, and anxiety were exacerbated by the stress of a presidential campaign. It might have been during this hospital stay that Eunice was diagnosed with Addison's disease and began taking corticosteroids regularly, just as Jack had been doing since 1947. "She and Jack were physiologically alike," Sarge said. "Seeing how it's treated and what its effects are, it's like being a diabetic. As long as you have your treatment, you are in no more danger than a diabetic is."

By the following spring, she was taking a 25-milligram cortisone tablet every day, along with medication to help her body retain salt. "Please impress upon her that it is absolutely essential that she take both these medications each day. She could very well run into real trouble if she is without them for even the shortest period," Dr. George W. Thorn, the prescribing physician from Boston's Peter Bent Brigham Hospital, instructed his secretary.

It is difficult to get an accurate picture of Eunice's medical condition, because she saw many doctors in several cities for different complaints, and it is not clear there was any coordination among them. The previous spring, for instance, an allergist in New York had confirmed she was allergic to corn, cocoa, chocolate, pineapple, and strawberry. A year later, unhappy with a persistent runny nose and watery eyes, she saw Dr. Janet Travell, Jack's personal physician at the White House, who prescribed 8 milligrams of Cloro-Trimetón Repetabs for her food allergies, instructing her to take them two or three times a day. She also reported to Travell that the phenobarbital she was taking, apparently to address anxiety and chronic insomnia, made her "dull-headed." But she was well enough by December 16, after her postelection hospitalization, to be back on North Lakeview Avenue, hosting—with the help of two butlers and a maid—a supper party for twenty-four, including Pat and Peter Lawford, to celebrate the Chicago premiere of *Exodus*, the Otto Preminger film that costarred Lawford.

Even as she wrestled with her own health challenges, Eunice was weighing an expanded role for the Kennedy Foundation on Capitol Hill now that Jack would be in the White House. By marrying its philanthropic role to public policy making, the foundation could magnify its impact. Parents of children with mental retardation had few allies in Congress and in the nation's statehouses as they agitated for reform. A decade of parental activism had produced a patchwork of state laws, applied inconsistently and funded unevenly. They won access to federal funds to improve medical infirmaries at some institutions. They secured more special education classes in some public schools. But comprehensive reform remained elusive.

Parents and sympathetic policy makers in New Jersey and Arkansas were more successful than most. The parents group in New Jersey, led by Elizabeth M. Boggs, a chemist and mother of a severely disabled son, won passage in 1954 of an education bill that within five years nearly tripled the number of special education classes in that state. Boggs, one of the founders of NARC, in 1950, took the lobbying skills she learned in Trenton to Capitol Hill, working with Rhode Island congressman John E. Fogarty and Alabama senator J. Lister Hill to win passage of legislation in 1958 authorizing the first federal program to train teachers for children with mental retardation—a rare national initiative on their behalf prior to the Kennedy administration.

Boggs could not have predicted that the junior senator from Massachusetts, who had not bothered to attend the hearing at which she testified about the critical need for those teachers, would champion their cause a few years later as president of the United States. What Boggs had experienced outside the meeting of the subcommittee of the Senate Committee on Labor and Public Welfare on April 4, 1957, was "some resentment because I felt that even if they [the Kennedys] did not wish to admit publicly that this was a problem in their family, the least that the senator could have done would have been to attend to the [committee] business as any other sympathetic senator might have done. Now it's easy to say, and it may very well have been, is probably true, that he had other business to attend to, and there was a reason for his leaving the meeting at that time, but I couldn't help feeling that he was leaving to others a task which he could have very well lent his support to at that time."

In the Washington of the 1950s, the others to whom the task had been left included the heads of federal agencies with small programs to benefit those with mental retardation. Dr. Martha Eliot, chief of the Children's Bureau, encouraged states to apply for grants for specialized diagnostic clinics. Mary Switzer, director of the Office of Vocational Rehabilitation, directed more resources to the states for the development of sheltered workshops. Arthur Hill and Romaine Mackie, in the Office of Education, had no federal aid to offer but encouraged their counterparts in the states to allocate more funding for special education.

On Capitol Hill, activists counted on Congressman Fogarty and Senator Hill to advance the cause. As chairman of the Subcommittee on Appropriations for the Department of Health, Education, and Welfare, Fogarty was in a position to ask why Washington was not doing more to foster medical research and special education for the mentally retarded, and he did. "This is the first year I have asked this question, so it is a little something new, I know," he acknowledged when he put that challenge to Secretary Oveta Culp Hobby on February 8, 1955.

Along with NARC, other nonprofit groups joined the effort. There was the Association for the Aid of Crippled Children, the United Cerebral Palsy Association, the American Association on Mental Deficiency, and the Council for Exceptional Children. But the real work fell to parents determined to claim their children's right to full lives. Summer camps with names such as Happy Day, Rainbow, and Shady Nook sprouted in suburban backyards where, with the help of women's clubs and local civic organizations, volunteers taught children with mental retardation to run and climb and play together just as their brothers and sisters did.

The stigma had by no means fallen away, but there was gradual public acknowledgment of a condition that affected more than five million Americans. In 1950, after two decades of hiding her existence, Nobel Prize–winning author Pearl Buck wrote about Carol, her mentally retarded daughter, in *The Child Who Never Grew*. In 1953, after the two-year-old daughter of Hollywood stars Roy Rogers and Dale Evans died of complications from Down syndrome, Evans wrote a best-selling account of the couple's decision to raise Robin at home against medical advice.

David B. Ray Jr. was on the cutting edge of policy change as the first superintendent of the Arkansas Children's Colony, touted as "a noninstitutional institution" when it opened, in 1959. It was the first facility of any kind for the mentally retarded in Arkansas; until then, children and adults with mental retardation had been confined, as they were in many states, to the state mental hospital. Ray reimagined the model of custodial institutions then dominating the landscape: "massive buildings; boys and girls regimented into enormous dining rooms and sleeping areas; grounds enclosed by high fences; untrained people serving as house parents, attendants, and teachers; and limitations on visits by parents."

What Ray built in Conway, Arkansas, must have reminded Eunice of the cottage system she knew at Alderson. Designed as a small village, eight one-story dormitories housed 256 children, all of whom had access to education and vocational training as well as to softball, Scouting, fishing, and bicycling, recreational activities their brothers and sisters were certain to be enjoying at home.

East of Arkansas, at George Peabody College for Teachers in Nashville, a new doctoral program in psychology and mental retardation was also raising the public profile of these children. The National Institute of Mental Health, which directed most of its resources to the study of mental illness, had awarded a critical grant to the fledgling program run by Nicholas Hobbs.

Boggs, Ray, and Hobbs were barely known to Eunice Kennedy Shriver on the eve of her brother's presidency, but soon enough she would draw them into her orbit, along with Congressman Fogarty, Senator Hill, and scores of others, recruiting the best in the field of mental retardation for a mission most of them had been on already most of their adult lives.

The incremental gains they had achieved by the decade's turn were not nearly enough for Eunice. Despite the silence with which her own family dealt with Rosemary's condition, she was enraged by a congressional report on the nation's mental health challenges that failed even to mention retardation. She had called her father from her hospital bed in Boston in November 1960 to discuss how best to light a fire under the federal government her brother was about to lead. "Just lie down and get well, for God's sake, and when you come to Florida we'll discuss the subject and see what turns up," Joe told her.

When she arrived in Palm Beach a few weeks later, no less agitated, she and Jack met with Joe in their father's bedroom on the top floor of the mansion, with Eunice laying out for the president-elect what she had learned about the scope of the problem during her travels for the Kennedy Foundation. "The foundation can't go on trying to lick this problem alone; it's impossible for us to do it. It affects too many families in this country," Joe told his son, who, in turn, urged Eunice to "get hold of Mike Feldman [Myer "Mike" Feldman, a campaign aide who would become a deputy special counsel in the White House and Eunice's greatest ally] and see if you can get something going on it."

What Eunice got going in the next several months would become the unprecedented President's Panel on Mental Retardation, a committee of twenty-seven scientists, educators, doctors, lawyers, social workers, and parents charged with outlining a new role for Washington in biomedical and behavioral research and in the construction of community-based

facilities to deliver diagnostic, clinical, educational, vocational, and residential services for the retarded.

By securing Jack's commitment during the transition that December,
Eunice ensured that no time would be wasted when her brother took
the oath of office on January 20, 1961. She was bundled up in mink on
the East Front of the US Capitol that blustery Friday morning, the city
blanketed in eight inches of fresh snow. Eunice was seated closest among
the Kennedy siblings to her brother, the president, in the second row, behind Mamie Eisenhower. Jack's victory was theirs, too, and his brothers
and sisters descended on the White House as if still the rambunctious
kids they had once been at Hyannis Port. Despite spraining an ankle as
she boarded a plane from Chicago to Washington for the festivities, Eunice missed nothing that day. She filmed the inaugural parade on her
8-millimeter movie camera from the reviewing stand, flew through the
six floors of the executive mansion—stopping to bounce on the bed in
the Lincoln Bedroom with LeMoyne Billings, Jack's roommate from
Choate—and joined Ethel to pester Jack to sign stacks of photographs of
himself on his first day in the Oval Office. Eunice even asked him to sign
a White House menu. "To Eunice, whose work in Wisconsin and Ohio
made all this possible," he wrote, his wit on full display. Jack had lost both
states to Nixon.

Jack's ascension was a family affair. At Joe's urging, the president
named Bobby to his Cabinet as attorney general, despite legal experience
so thin he had never argued a case in court. "We'll make Bobby attorney
general so he can throw all the people Dad doesn't like into jail," Eunice
had joked at the start of the campaign. Jack arranged for a placeholder—
his old Harvard roommate Benjamin A. Smith II—to warm his US Senate
seat in Massachusetts until Ted, twenty-eight at the time of his brother's
inauguration, was old enough to run in a special election in 1962.

Eunice, too, would relocate to Washington that spring. When Jack
tapped Sarge to run the Peace Corps, her husband set aside his own political ambitions—Illinois Democrats had considered him a fine prospect for
governor—and the Shriver family took up residence in a seven-thousand-
square-foot rented house known as Timberlawn on Edson Lane, in Rockville, Maryland.

The 250-acre estate was a working farm with a full complement of
cows, sheep, horses, ponies, pigs, and chickens. There were open fields,
rolling lawns, and a pond filled with fish and snapping turtles. There

were barns, stables, kennels for the pack of family dogs, wooded riding trails, a swimming pool, and basketball and tennis courts.

Timberlawn was both an active family home and an extension of the office for both Eunice and Sarge. On any given day, friends and men being vetted by Sarge for posts in the administration could expect to be put through their paces by Eunice on the playing fields, in the pool, and on the basketball court. There was Art Buchwald, the syndicated political humor columnist, losing yet another set of tennis to his hypercompetitive hostess. There was Harris Wofford, a special assistant to the president on civil rights, falling off Sarge's prized Irish horse named Mickey. There was a group of Peace Corps recruits playing a spirited game of softball on the Bermuda grass lawn.

In the midst of it all were the Shriver children, thrilled after the relative confinement of a Chicago apartment to be released into a rambling, brick-and-shingled mansion, its cellar full of "snakes, rats, mice, and bugs," pests regularly dispatched by Womack Exterminators. Bobby was seven, Maria five, and Timmy almost two when the family moved to Timberlawn, which the Shrivers would lease, but never own, for the next eighteen years.

"Timberlawn was a magical place," Bobby Shriver said, recalling the acres of woods and a pasture full of Black Angus cattle. "There were cows out there, big ones. We are not allowed to go after them or do anything to them, but they were there, so, of course, we figured out how to play with them," he said. "There were horses, twenty dogs. For a kid, it was paradise."

For Timothy, the magic was in the "boat races" he and his mother staged on a stream in the woods. Each would slide a small stick into the current and cheer on the "boats" as they moved downstream. "I loved the ritual of the game: the long walk down the field holding my mother's hand, the passage from the open grass of the cow pasture into the shade of the huge Maryland oaks, the crunchy path across the leaves and twigs of the forest floor to the edge of the stream, and the furious search for high-quality boats that I could race against my resolute opponent, Mummy," he recalled. "We were all alone in the woods, Mummy and me: quiet beyond the reach of the hated phone, beyond the city, the cars, and all those people asking Mrs. Shriver what she wanted, when she wanted, and where she wanted it."

In those busy, heady White House years, the Shriver children mostly caught glimpses of their parents on the run, spending more time in the company of the governesses Eunice hired fresh from Manhattanville College of the Sacred Heart or imported from Ireland, after her friend Dorothy Tubridy had conducted a thorough screening. Ethel, an avid horse woman, had introduced Eunice to Dot, whose husband had been a jumper on the Irish equestrian team until his death in 1954 in a riding accident. They forged a friendship that lasted all their lives, one of the few close bonds Eunice formed outside the family. "She was more of a sister than a friend," said Tubridy, unable to talk without tears about Eunice even years after her death.

In 1961 Sarge was building the Peace Corps from scratch, recruiting a staff of energetic young people who were as likely to discuss work at home plate in a pickup baseball game at Timberlawn as at a conference table downtown. From an office at the Department of Health, Education, and Welfare, Eunice was orchestrating a monumental effort to turn small, disparate programs sprinkled through the federal bureaucracy into a comprehensive national assault on mental retardation. "It took me three days to figure out where the department of special education was, dealing with the retarded," she fumed. "It was just a laughing, roaring joke."

The public and the private were indivisible on the sprawling estate. In her planning notes for even her fanciest dinner parties, Eunice often included seating assignments for Bobby and Maria, designating a "lap" for Tim. Neil A. Drayton, superintendent of the Mansfield Training School in Connecticut, recalled a working dinner at Timberlawn for thirty experts in mental retardation who had been invited to Washington to confer with the President's Panel. He was in the first of a caravan of government vans to arrive at Timberlawn, where he was greeted that February evening by Eunice and the children, the latter three in nightclothes. Maria introduced him to her talking doll while Bobby raced among the guests and eighteen-month-old Timothy, who was born on August 29, insisted it was his birthday.

As memorable to Drayton was the family's 155-pound Great Pyrenees, whose paw "was the size of a small ham," and who, with a smaller canine companion, had the run of the place that night. Household records for those years identify the family dogs as Blackie, Houlihan, Kim, Lassie, Misty, Mustard, Molasses, Rocky, and Shamrock, aka Morning Glory, suggesting that only the favored few had access to Timberlawn's dining room.

Combining serious work with serious fun was a Kennedy calling card, and Timberlawn alternated with Hickory Hill, Bobby and Ethel Kennedy's McLean, Virginia, estate, as the site of the action. One winter the Kennedys trumped the Shrivers by keeping a sea lion named Sandy in the swimming pool for three months before donating him to the National Zoo. Stories about ugly-pet contests and three-legged races at Hickory Hill were legion—so prevalent, in fact, that Rose once chastised Bobby when word reached her in Paris that presidential advisor Arthur Schlesinger Jr. had landed in the pool fully clothed during a party. "It sounds harmless when you are talking about it, but the repercussions are not always favorable," the image-conscious Rose chided her then thirty-seven-year-old son, the chief law enforcement officer of the United States.

Rose had no such worries about Eunice. No matter how lively, gatherings at Timberlawn were likely to have a higher purpose. The agenda might be Eunice's; it might be Sarge's. Usually it was a combination of both, reflecting their remarkable personal and political partnership. He conferred with Dr. Cooke on research projects the foundation funded, while she organized drives to collect hundreds of books to send to Peace Corps volunteers across the world. Friends knew to slip their checkbooks into a coat pocket or an evening bag, just in case what the Shrivers advertised as a quiet dinner party came with a pitch to support a sheltered workshop or a summer camp for the mentally retarded.

Formal affairs alternated with more casual evenings at Timberlawn. Frank Mankiewicz, an administrator for the Peace Corps, remembered Eunice and Sarge wheeling out two portable black-and-white television sets so Peace Corps staffers could watch a 1961 NBC documentary on the international goodwill program that would become one of the Kennedy administration's most popular and enduring initiatives. In his thank-you note, Mankiewicz apologized for a contretemps during the party between himself and Adam Yarmolinsky, an aide to Defense Secretary Robert McNamara. Yarmolinsky was annoyed that Mankiewicz had taken a job with the Peace Corps, spurning an offer to join McNamara's staff. "The result, I fear, is that the Peace Corps will not be assigned a bomb shelter," he wrote to Eunice.

Mankiewicz praised the conversation as "lively" and the refreshments as "excellent" in his note, but the truth, he said, was that while the company was always stimulating, the food was usually dreadful and in short supply at the Shrivers' small gatherings. There was so little she could eat

Eunice poses with her first birthday cake on July 10, 1922, at Nantasket Beach in Hull, Massachusetts, where her grandparents Josie and John "Honey Fitz" Fitzgerald, the colorful former congressman and mayor of Boston, have a summer home.

2

In a rare moment of stillness, ten-year-old Eunice poses on the lawn at Hyannis Port where, despite a physical constitution so weak her brothers and sisters call her "Puny Eunie," she emerges as the dominant quarterback in the Kennedys' fierce touch football games.

3

Even at age four, Eunice is her oldest sister's most reliable playmate, helping Rosemary, who was born with intellectual disabilities, participate in the swim meets, tennis matches, and sailing races that dominate Kennedy summers at Malcolm Cottage, the home the family rented on Marchant Avenue in Hyannis Port before Joe Kennedy purchased the property in 1928.

Twelve-year-old Eunice, center, strikes a tough-guy pose in a family photograph in front of "the Big House" in Hyannis Port. Left to right: Joe Jr., Jack, Rosemary, Kathleen, Eunice, Pat, Bobby, Jean, Teddy, and Rose.

5

Eunice, often compared by her mother to her more vivacious older sister, triumphs over Kick on the family's tennis court at the Kennedys' Palm Beach estate on North Ocean Boulevard.

Joseph P. Kennedy and his youngest child, Teddy, greet Rosemary and Eunice when the sisters join the family in April 1938 in London, where Joe is the new US ambassador to the Court of St. James's, the first Irish-American to hold the post. Left to right: Rosemary, Joseph, Teddy, and Eunice.

6

7

Eighteen-year-old Eunice and her mother, Rose Fitzgerald Kennedy, prepare to depart from the US Ambassador's Residence in London for Buckingham Palace for her presentation as a debutante to King George and Queen Elizabeth on July 12, 1939. At her coming out party, days before, she and Jack stayed up until dawn, dancing the Big Apple alongside 225 guests until Rose called a halt to the festivities.

8

Eunice and her handheld movie camera greet her adored father at La Guardia Airport in New York City on a visit home from duties as US Ambassador to Great Britain to confer with President Franklin D. Roosevelt, angered by Kennedy's public talk of appeasing Hitler.

9

Taking a semester-long break from Manhattanville College of the Sacred Heart because of ill health, Eunice spends the winter of 1941 in Palm Beach trying to gain weight at the family's home. A year later she will transfer to Stanford University.

10

After a seven-year courtship—and some behind-the-scenes matchmaking by Joseph P. Kennedy—R. Sargent Shriver has reason to smile as Eunice cuts the first slice of wedding cake at the Waldorf-Astoria Hotel in Manhattan on May 23, 1953. Left to right: Patricia Kennedy, Eunice, Sarge, and Jean Kennedy.

11

In June 1953, Massachusetts Senator John F. Kennedy takes his fiancée for a sail off Hyannis Port with many of his siblings along for the ride. The couple will marry three months later. Left to right: Eunice Kennedy Shriver, Jacqueline Bouvier, Jean Kennedy, Patricia Kennedy, Edward Kennedy (bending), and Jack Kennedy (standing).

12

The Shrivers on June 19, 1964, at Timberlawn, the family's leased home in Rockville, Maryland, the scene of more impromptu parties and athletic contests than formal portraits during the thousand days of the Kennedy Administration. Left to right: Sarge; Timothy, 4; Maria, 8; Bobby, 10; and Eunice. In bassinet is four-month-old Mark.

Six months after the assassination of President John F. Kennedy, the Shriver family visits his grave on what would have been his forty-seventh birthday. Left to right: Bobby, Eunice, Sarge, Maria, and Timothy. She never discussed her brothers' murders with her children.

13

14

At forty-four, a month after delivering Anthony Paul Kennedy Shriver, her fifth child, Eunice plays touch football with eleven-year-old Bobby Shriver.

More comfortable in men's trousers and tennis shoes, Eunice gets accustomed to haute couture during Sargent Shriver's tour as US Ambassador to France. Here she poses for *Vogue* on a mosaic-tiled floor in 1969 in the entrance hall of the American embassy in Paris, wearing a Madame Grès evening gown. Behind her is a painting by Al Held.

16

During the Shrivers' sojourn in Paris, Eunice plays with the three youngest of her five children in 1969. Left to right: Eunice, Anthony, Timothy, and Mark in the Tuileries Gardens.

Twenty-five-year-old Anthony Shriver gives his mother, sixty-nine, a lift down the boardwalk across the marsh behind the Shriver house on Nantucket Sound in Hyannis Port in 1990.

17

18

The Shriver siblings surround their seated parents at a celebration of their mother's eighty-fifth birthday in 2006. Sarge is wearing a T-shirt emblazoned with a photograph of "Saint Eunice." Left to right: Bobby, Maria, Anthony, Timothy, and Mark.

Special Olympics athlete Loretta Claiborne (*l.*) and Maria Shriver (*r.*) embrace in front of the bier at the wake for Eunice Kennedy Shriver on Cape Cod at Our Lady of Victory Church in Centerville, Massachusetts.

19

A bagpiper leads Special Olympics athletes in the procession to Eunice Kennedy Shriver's funeral at Saint Francis Xavier Roman Catholic Church in Hyannis on August 14, 2009. Several Special Olympics athletes threw their gold medals into her grave as the coffin was lowered into the ground.

without physical discomfort that Eunice, who did not know how to cook, paid scant attention to the meals themselves. She also had trouble keeping chefs, many of whom did not get along with the women with mental disabilities Eunice hired to work in her kitchen. One chef chased Eunice out of the kitchen with a carving knife after she accused him of wasting her money by serving jumbo-sized hamburgers to Bobby Shriver and his friends.

But no one came to a Shriver party for the food, anyway. Speculation was always rife at the formal soirees that the president might drop in, as he did for the black-tie bash for sixty-four guests on February 13, 1962, to celebrate the marriage of the Shrivers' old Chicago friends Bill Blair and Deeda Gerlach. Eunice and Rose had attended their wedding five months before, in the chapel at Frederiksborg Castle in Denmark, where Blair was serving as US ambassador.

"In those days, it was always black tie and very glamorous in Washington," Deeda Blair said, admitting to some amazement that Eunice had pulled off such a grand party. "I couldn't believe—because things were helter skelter in Chicago—that it was so well done. The president came. She was probably the closest to Jack. He adored her."

To judge by the thank-you notes, the president's rival in popularity that night was the dance instructor who taught the guests the Twist, the current Chubby Checker dance craze. "What a fun, mad party—with a lovely savory stew pot of people, simmering and bubbling to full-flavored goodness," wrote Letitia "Tish" Baldrige, the White House social secretary. "It was such a gay dance-'em up party—almost came back again tonight, hoping there would be more." Senator Frank Church of Idaho pronounced the party "delightful" but expressed hope "there were no guests injured by a flying elbow in my eagerness to learn the Twist." Nancy Dickerson, the first female television correspondent, for CBS News, sent a telegram: "No Matter How You Twist It, The Party Was A Smashing Success."

As glamourous as their formal parties might be—the entertainment usually provided by the four-piece Ted Alexander Band, the food catered by Avignone Frères, and Hollywood celebrities whom Eunice and Ethel called "glitteries" sprinkled among the guests—the Shrivers were most focused on work. Their experience at the Kennedy Foundation made it easier to recruit members for the President's Panel on Mental Retardation; they already knew most of the top people in the field. They tapped

Dr. Leonard W. Mayo, the executive director of the Association for the Aid of Crippled Children, as chairman, and Dr. George Tarjan, from Pacific State Hospital in Pomona, California, as vice chairman. They asked Cooke, from Johns Hopkins, and Lederberg, from Stanford, to reprise their roles from the transition's task force on health and welfare. They enlisted public health officials, special educators, social psychologists, pharmacologists, psychiatrists, and speech pathologists and relied on the expertise of such consultants to the panel as Dr. Richard L. Masland, now director of the National Institute for Neurological Diseases and Blindness. "She assembled a very impressive group," Cooke recalled.

Even as she pulled together the panel, Eunice was also urging Jack to elevate the status of maternal and child health within the National Institutes of Health. Poor maternal nutrition and inadequate prenatal care were among the many suspected contributors to mental retardation, but neither those topics nor fetal development and premature birth were a priority of medical researchers in 1961. Eunice was determined to change that.

Cooke first floated the proposal for a National Institute of Child Health and Human Development during the transition, though the idea had circulated for years in the warrens of various federal agencies. The level of ignorance about maternal and infant health was profound. A lack of prenatal care and inadequate nutrition produced newborns with low birth weights and a higher risk of infant mortality. Most vulnerable were black women, who gave birth prematurely at three times the rate of white mothers and whose babies were twice as likely to die before their first birthdays. Those infant mortality statistics inflamed Eunice, whose speeches often included her observation that "many expectant mothers get less attention from doctors than cows get from cattle breeders."

An emphasis on maternal and child health had political appeal for a new president whose youth and vigor had been a hallmark of his campaign. It could serve as a counterpoint to Medicare, his proposed health insurance program for the elderly. But the idea ran into immediate resistance from federal agencies that feared an independent institute would diminish their own portfolios.

The biggest skeptic was James A. Shannon, director of the National Institutes of Health. He was blunt in a meeting with Cooke, deriding the notion that the health needs of children were distinct from those of adults. "Dr. Shannon, in no uncertain terms, informed us that there were essentially no major disease problems in children, and he gave us the impression that a good grandmother could provide most of the care required by infants and children," Cooke recalled. "Needless to say, my reactions to that encounter were anything but sympathetic."

Like so many of the medical professionals and activists agitating for more attention to be paid to children, Cooke had a personal stake in the fight. He had two daughters with Cri-du-chat syndrome, a genetic disorder marked by developmental and intellectual disabilities.

Jack used his administrative authority his first month in office to create a Center for Child Health to raise the visibility of pediatric health issues while he weighed whether to ask Congress to create a National Institute of Child Health and Human Development. He was cautious, asking his sister why he should invite the ire of NIH officials by arguing for creation of an institute none of them thought necessary. Sailing on Nantucket Sound that summer, Eunice reminded him of his and Jackie's own experiences: one child lost to miscarriage and another to stillbirth. Those common but little understood tragedies affected millions of American families, she told him, but they garnered the attention of precious few researchers. For Eunice, the conclusion was obvious: maternal and pediatric medical research promised breakthroughs for all children, not just for those born with mental retardation.

History would prove Eunice prescient. The NICHD pioneered interdisciplinary research in human development that integrated biomedicine with the behavioral and social sciences. No longer would the National Institutes of Health embrace only a "disease model" that studied cancer or heart disease or polio in isolation. Socioeconomic and cultural deprivation would also be considered as contributing factors to negative health outcomes.

A focus on human development throughout the stages of life incubated such new medical specialties as neonatology, which, in the years ahead, would pioneer fresh prevention and treatment approaches, eventually all but eliminating deaths from conditions such as hyaline membrane disease. That lung condition was the most common cause of death among premature infants when Jack signed the NICHD into law in 1962, claiming twenty-five thousand lives a year in the United States. Tragically, it would also claim the life of his own son, Patrick Bouvier Kennedy, thirty-nine hours after he was born five and a half weeks premature on August 7, 1963.

Creating the National Institute of Child Health and Human Development taught Eunice what feminists would spend the next two decades preaching: that the personal is political. She might have been unwilling to acknowledge, even to herself, that her grief and her guilt about Rosemary's plight fueled her passion on these issues, but she could hardly ignore that her brother's heartbreaking personal losses had softened him to her point of view.

The experience also provided her with crucial skills in congressional lobbying and simple horse trading. "When I reported to Mrs. Shriver that there seemed to be opposition to the new institute, she arranged for us to visit [Congressman] John Fogarty, first, and subsequently, [Senator] Lister Hill," Cooke recalled. "Fogarty began his attack on the proposal similar to Shannon's: that there were no major health problems or death-dealing disorders in children. After some discussion, he listened carefully to the presentation of the problems of mental retardation, cerebral palsy, and other serious defects resulting from prenatal and perinatal events. He also had great interest in the concept of normal growth and how that might be improved by such research efforts."

With support from Fogarty and Hill, the proposal gained ground with doubters on the Hill. Shannon's opposition evaporated after the Kennedy administration offered him a quid pro quo: his support for a new institute within NIH focused on maternal and child health in exchange for elevation of the Division of Medicine to the National Institute of General Medical Sciences, an expansion Shannon had long sought.

Those lessons would serve Eunice well once Jack formally convened the President's Panel on Mental Retardation on October 17, 1961, designating her a "consultant" to the group, which would not have existed without her. Later, she said it would have been unseemly for the sister of the president to be a voting member of his advisory panel—a perspective on nepotism clearly not shared by her kid brothers, the attorney general of the United States and the senator-from-Massachusetts-in-waiting.

After meeting with the panel in the Rose Garden, President Kennedy described its work as a moral obligation. "The manner in which our nation cares for its citizens and conserves its manpower resources is more than an index to its concern for the less fortunate. It is a key to its future," he said. "Both wisdom and humanity dictate a deep interest in the physically handicapped, the mentally ill, and the mentally retarded. Yet, although we have made considerable progress in the treatment of physical handicaps, although we have attacked on a broad front the problems of mental illness, although we have made great strides in the battle against disease, we as a nation have for too long postponed an intensive search for solutions to the problems of the mentally retarded. That failure should be corrected."

The panel was charged in its first year with formulating concrete recommendations that, in its second year, would be shaped into formal legislation. It was an ambitious timetable that many thought unrealistic. Eunice was not among them. "We were action oriented," she said. "The need was enormously urgent, and if you get a year, you can really do a lot if everybody really hustles. Why would you need more than a year?"

The chairman of the panel agreed with her. "I think most of us produce best when we are in a slight tension between the realities of the present and what we want to produce for the future. And these things keep pulling and pushing on you, and you come through, unless you break," Leonard Mayo said.

Dr. Edward Davens, a Maryland physician on the panel, said he and his fellow skeptics "had not reckoned with the fact that the president's sister was to be a consultant to the panel. Nor did [we] reckon with the sense of hurry and hard work within the administration. Never in my entire life have I worked so hard as during this particular year and never have I enjoyed myself so much. I would say that the intensity of the hours and the work and the effort was equivalent to an average three-year commission."

Judge David L. Bazelon, who sat on the panel as well as on the District of Columbia Circuit Court of Appeals, was also soon convinced. "There was great pressure, and I think in the end that was helpful," he said. Eunice was "like a spark plug. There's no doubt about the fact that she sparked it and made it spark."

Sometimes those sparks could singe, as Edwin R. Bayley learned when he was recruited from his press relations post at the Peace Corps to handle news coverage of the panel's first meeting with the president in the White House. "Eunice is not the easiest person in the world to deal with. She's insistent and, I felt, unreasonable," he said, expressing an exasperation with her relentless demands that her subordinates would echo in the decades to come.

Bayley had begged the third-string reporters stuck on the weekend shift at the White House to write something for their Sunday editions, and many did, but Eunice "envisioned interviews with every one of these famous people and pictures all over the papers," he said. Early Sunday morning, Bayley's phone rang before he was out of bed. "There isn't any-thing in the paper," a familiar voice chided him at the other end of the line. He tried to interrupt, but Eunice was "livid." Retrieving a stack of newspapers from his front stoop moments later, he was relieved to see a six-inch story about the panel inside the *New York Times*. Feeling vindi-cated, he dialed her back. "The story is in the *Times*; it's on page fourteen," Bayley told her. "Well, I know that little story, but I meant the big story," Eunice scoffed. "Why wasn't it on page one?"

When not dismissing her as "unreasonable," the political class wrote off Eunice as an annoying do-gooder with too much time on her hands. "The big problem was that mental retardation, with the people right around Kennedy, had a low priority," said Dr. Patrick J. Doyle, a pedi-atrician who worked on the issue in the White House. He was referring specifically to Kenneth O'Donnell and Lawrence O'Brien, aides to the president who were part of a group known informally as the Irish Mafia. "Sometimes you had the feeling that they were very condescending be-cause Eunice was involved, and that they were going along with you be-cause of this, not because they had any real substantive interest in what we were doing. I always had that feeling. I think most of us had that feeling. And, of course, Eunice Shriver, that didn't bother her, because she felt at least she was getting what she wanted out of it."

Academics took her no more seriously. "A lot of deans of medical schools, presidents of universities would say, 'Okay, we'll play the game with you, but we don't think that mental retardation's that important. We know it has political significance at the moment, just as polio had under Franklin [Delano Roosevelt]. We don't think it's quite this important, but we'll play the game," Doyle recalled.

Dr. Bertram S. Brown, a psychiatrist and special assistant to the presi-dent on mental health issues, said the National Institute of Mental Health was torn about how to respond to Eunice's demands. On the one hand, administrators ridiculed the initiative on mental retardation as if "all this was a hobby of Eunice's and not to be paid too serious attention," he said. "On the other hand, you can't offend the president."

No one knew that better than Eunice, but complaining to her brother was a trump card she kept in reserve, knowing, as Mike Feldman did, that "John F. Kennedy felt that on mental retardation matters, Eunice was the expert." The president "wasn't intimately familiar with the problems of the mentally retarded," Feldman conceded, so Eunice tutored Feldman, and they both briefed the president before his two meetings with the panel, a year apart.

More. Better. Faster. That was how Eunice defined what was necessary, and, with the appointment of Mayo as chairman of the panel, the work began in earnest. Mayo had the administrative skill and the conciliatory temperament that Eunice so conspicuously lacked. She had known Mayo since 1947, when she was at the Justice Department working on juvenile delinquency issues and he was chairman of the National Commission on Children and Youth.

Mayo's job was not an easy one, mediating disputes between biological and behavioral scientists about causes and prevention, between partisans of the mentally ill and advocates for the mentally retarded, constituencies mired in decades of mutual mistrust as they competed for scarce federal resources. At one meeting in Baltimore, "There was just one platitude after another being put on the table," Cooke said. "I know Mrs. Shriver's blood pressure must have gone up and down about a thousand times during that session." Elizabeth Boggs, too, recalled being "acutely aware of the need to keep these internecine, interdisciplinary fights under some sort of control so that they didn't paralyze people."

At her father's suggestion, Eunice asked former president Herbert Hoover for advice. After his presidency, Hoover had chaired two commissions, one in 1947 for President Harry S. Truman, and another in 1953 for President Dwight D. Eisenhower, on how to better organize the executive departments of the federal government. Joe Kennedy had served with him, and the men had become close friends.

Hoover had eased Eunice into Stanford in 1942 and had offered his counsel once before, in 1947, when she was trying to bring order to the Justice Department's initiative on juvenile delinquency. Eunice and Mayo met with Hoover on November 8, 1961, at his suite in the Waldorf Astoria, in New York, where he suggested assigning panelists to task forces, each focused on an area of expertise, to minimize conflicts. "If I had been around in 1928, I would have worked my head off to get you elected president of the United States, and you are the only Republican I ever met that I felt that way about," Eunice wrote in a note thanking Hoover for advice that did, in fact, reduce the squabbling.

Soon after the panel got to work, Eunice arranged for Jack to greet at the White House two sisters who were the 1961 poster girls of the National Association for Retarded Children. Sheila McGrath, of Arvada,

Colorado, was a victim of phenylketonuria, or PKU, an inherited genetic disorder that causes an amino acid to build up in the body and leads to mental retardation. Her younger sister, Kammy, was born with the same metabolic defect but developed normally because, in the two-year interval between the sisters' births, scientists had perfected a test to detect PKU, allowing early intervention to prevent brain damage. It was exactly the sort of scientific breakthrough Eunice wanted Jack to see could be replicated on other fronts with federal support.

A few weeks later, the Kennedy family suffered a setback that Mayo was certain would slow the work of the panel. After a round of golf in Palm Beach on December 17, Joseph P. Kennedy had a stroke that left him, at age seventy-three, mentally alert but mute and partially paralyzed. In a handwritten note two days later, Mayo offered Eunice his prayers "that your father may be restored to his full health & vigor. Should your mind and heart be too full to give us that in the next several days, be assured we will carry on as you would want us to."

Mayo underestimated Eunice. She would fly to her father's bedside and help coordinate a plan for his rehabilitation in New York with Dr. Howard Rusk, the expert Joe had chided her for interrupting at a meeting years before, but she would not slacken the panel's pace. There was a deadline, and she intended to meet it. Mayo distributed the workload among six task forces. He arranged regional meetings across the country to hear from parents and professionals and organized trips to the Soviet Union, the Netherlands, Sweden, and Great Britain to assess what other countries had to teach the United States. Eunice went to Holland and England.

Too little engagement was not the problem Mayo faced in Eunice; too much sometimes was. Mike Feldman "had several jobs, one of which was to tell Eunice, you know, when she had to stop," Boggs said. "Leonard told me on one or two occasions that when Eunice had been pressing a point, you know, beyond what seemed to be reasonable and that he, Leonard, really got up against it, he would get Mike Feldman to say that this was as far as she could go."

Eunice's private diaries are full of underlined instructions to herself to adopt a gentler management style—"Don't find fault with why people have or haven't done as I do," read one—but she could not help herself; she expected everyone connected to the cause to mirror her own sense of urgency.

One example of overreaching was her insistence on installing in the

White House a special assistant to the president on mental retardation. Theoretically, a White House point man would underscore the importance of the issue to Jack. But the appointment of Dr. Stafford L. Warren, the first dean of the School of Medicine at the University of California, Los Angeles (UCLA), irritated the regular White House staff and duplicated the efforts of sympathetic officials in the bureaucracy who would have budgetary responsibility for any new programs. When Warren proved less than adept at handling those internal politics, Eunice attributed the problem to his personality rather than to her overreach. "If we had to do it over, I'd try to get a different, younger, peppier guy," she said.

Her father's stroke had an unexpected consequence for Eunice, freeing her to rely less on his judgment and more on her own. She had learned early from Joe the importance of public opinion. To win the systemic change she envisioned on behalf of the mentally retarded, Eunice now decided to mobilize the sympathies of the American people, as well as the mechanics of the federal bureaucracy.

It was time to talk about Rosemary.

With her father's voice silenced, Eunice pushed the family to publicly acknowledge, if not fully describe, Rosemary's condition, and to use her story to humanize the plight of the mentally retarded. The president agreed that more candor, rather than the family's usual silence or obfuscation, made sense, according to Ted Sorensen, Kennedy's aide and speechwriter.

Nine months after her father's stroke, the *Saturday Evening Post* published an essay under Eunice's byline that would have been unimaginable even a year before. Actually written by David Gelman, a reporter on leave from the *New York Post* to work as a consultant to the Peace Corps, the essay told a wide general audience bluntly that Rosemary was mentally retarded. (The piece did not disclose that she'd had a lobotomy; the ghostwriter did not know that.)

Gelman recalled working on that piece as the most stressful summer of his life, mostly because he found Eunice to be "imperious and demanding." How he and his typewriter had arrived at the Big House in Hyannis Port, on July 14, 1962, was typical of how the family operated. In search of a writer, Sarge had asked Bill Haddad at the Peace Corps, himself a former *New York Post* reporter, to recommend the best magazine writer in the country. Haddad suggested Gelman, whom he had recruited to evaluate Peace Corps training programs at universities across the country. Gelman was surprised to get Haddad's call while at the University of California, Berkeley, in no small part because he had never written a magazine article in his career.

"I was to fly back immediately, forget anything else, rent a car at the airport, drive to Southbury, Connecticut, where I was to meet Sargent and Eunice Shriver at a training school for the mentally retarded," he recalled. It began badly. "You're late," Eunice snapped, the first and last words she spoke to him that day.

Gelman left Connecticut as abruptly as he had arrived. He had no idea the destination when the Shrivers bundled him first into a helicopter and then into a private plane bound for Hyannis Port. Eunice installed him and his typewriter on the wide porch facing the ocean and ferried boxes of notes and research studies and newspaper clippings for him to cull. She marked up draft after draft of the 4,500-word piece, complaining that his style bore too little resemblance to Jack's. "She wanted to sound like her brother," Gelman recalled. "The problem was, she wasn't her brother."

That her brother was the president of the United States was often driven home to Gelman when he was "gazing out to the sea for inspiration, or just to avoid writing, and I'd hear a voice all too unmistakable: 'Eunie? Eunie?' and he'd open the door, coming out to the porch, calling, 'Hey, Eunie, where are you? It's time to go sailing, Eunie.' And then the president would notice me. 'Is my sistah heah? Have you seen Eunie?' And I'd say, 'No, Mr. President, I haven't seen her this morning,' or 'Yes, Mr. President, she went that way.' One morning, near lunchtime, Pat Lawford came out on the porch, looking distraught and confused, and just wandered off across the lawn. Soon thereafter, Eunice appeared on the porch, looking worried. 'Have you seen Pat?' I said, 'She went that way.' Eunice then said, 'Poor Pat, she had terrible news today. Marilyn Monroe killed herself last night. Marilyn was a friend of Pat's. Pat feels just awful.' Then Eunice disappeared in search of Pat."

Gelman considered himself under "house arrest" for several weeks during which his only reprieve was a visit from his family, who stayed at a motel in nearby Dennis. "The owner of the motel got a huge kick out of announcing over the loudspeaker system, 'Mr. Gelman, Mr. Gelman, Sargent Shriver is here for you,'" he said of the car that arrived each morning, with or without Sarge, to return him to the Big House.

"Eunice ran it like a campaign," he said. "There was a brain trust of experts at the ready, and she kept piling boxes near me of material to cram into the piece. Everybody was really nervous about the piece. But she was determined to knock down all the competitor afflictions when it came to getting government funding."

The sanitized version of Rosemary's story received a warm reception when it appeared on September 22, 1962, less than a month before the Panel on Mental Retardation was set to make its recommendations to the president. The public gave the Kennedys credit for candor and compassion. Eunice gave Gelman a Sulka silk tie for his efforts.

The public's sympathy was one thing, but if Eunice wanted to generate political support for the spending program about to be unveiled, she would also need to enlist the nation's governors in her cause. The federal government might fund bold new initiatives for the mentally retarded, but the states would have to sustain or expand them as the need required in the years ahead. Closing barbaric institutions would be a hollow victory if the community services planned to replace them were inadequate to the task. She asked her brother to convene a White House Conference on Mental Retardation to win over policy makers in the states.

To her consternation, most participants were more interested in mental illness than in mental retardation. "Mrs. Shriver had a very strong feeling about the role of the state mental health agencies, mental hygiene agencies," according to Doyle. "She felt they had too long suppressed the retarded programs, and so she herself was quite opposed to the mental health people." But Eunice was nothing if not pragmatic. She would need an alliance with those officials if she was going to convince the states to better serve those with mental retardation, so she asked each governor to send a representative to the conference.

Four hundred participants gathered at Airlie House, in Warrenton, Virginia, to hear a keynote address from Sargent Shriver—Eunice's byline in the *Saturday Evening Post* did not translate into a starring role at the conference she'd convened—and presentations from Surgeon General Luther Terry and Mary Switzer, from the Office of Vocational Rehabilitation. Eunice arranged a reception at the White House, although Jack's schedule did not permit him to attend that social gathering or the conference itself. Instead, he addressed the participants at Airlie House by telephone hookup.

The panel, meanwhile, was in the final stages of drafting its report to the president. Mayo was in Turkey to speak to a meeting of the International Child Welfare Association when the behavioral and biomedical scientists came to blows over the wording of the section on research. He had promised his wife they would stop in Vienna on the way home to attend the opera. Instead, after a telephone call from Eunice at his hotel in Istanbul, Mayo skipped both his speech and the opera. "I don't want you to feel pressured to return," Eunice told Mayo. "But I think if you can't come now, we'll postpone our appointment with the president to give him the report." It was one of those moments, Mayo said, "when one knows instantly what one ought to do." He booked the next flight home to calm the combatants.

The final report contained more than ninety recommendations for federal action to aid the mentally retarded. The most significant urged Washington to adopt new health programs for women and children, to finance construction of university-affiliated facilities for research and for the "diagnosis, treatment, training, and custodial care" of the mentally retarded, and to close large residential institutions in favor of smaller homes in community settings.

The panel submitted its report to the president on October 16, 1962, a day before its self-imposed deadline. Kennedy arrived in the Cabinet Room five minutes late for the ten thirty morning meeting. "All of us were struck by his rather somber demeanor," Dr. Edward Davens recalled. "He was in an entirely different mood than at the meeting a year previously when he gave us our marching orders. He did not smile or crack jokes in his usual fashion; he was polite and reserved."

What Davens and the others did not know was that the president had come to the Cabinet Room from the Oval Office, where McGeorge Bundy, his National Security Advisor, had just shown him U-2 aerial surveillance photographs of Soviet ballistic missile launchers in Cuba. The panel had unknowingly witnessed the start of the Cuban Missile Crisis. The meeting on mental retardation lasted two hours, during which President Kennedy "discussed the recommendations intelligently" and "in a most informed way," according to Davens, who later marveled at the president's focus, given the international crisis about to unfold.

A month after the panel delivered its report, Eunice used the Kennedy Foundation's first international awards ceremony honoring achievement in research, service, and leadership in the field of mental retardation to highlight the panel's work. Adlai Stevenson, the US ambassador to the United Nations, was master of ceremonies at a black-tie dinner at the Statler Hotel attended by members of the Cabinet, the Congress, and the Supreme Court. Judy Garland sang. President Kennedy presented the winners with checks from the Kennedy Foundation and Steuben crystal sculptures of the angel Raphael cradling an infant.

Eunice saw to it that the Kennedy Foundation and the federal government worked in tandem on behalf of the mentally retarded in matters large and small. She often called on Bobby for help. Would the attorney general find out whether the National Park Service could lease seven to twelve acres of open land to the Recreation Department of the District of Columbia for use as a camp for the mentally retarded? He would. Could he secure an immigration visa for a Korean psychiatrist whose services were urgently needed by a new facility for the mentally retarded in North Carolina? He could. Would he make a dinner speech in New York City to the Association for the Help of Retarded Children? He would.

The expedited work of the panel gave the White House time to incorporate its proposals into budget recommendations for the 88th Congress, which convened in January 1963. Kennedy called for increased spending on existing programs in public health, welfare, education, and vocational rehabilitation to benefit the retarded. His legislative team drafted bills to address the major recommendations of the panel: to improve child and maternal health and to construct community mental health centers and group homes that would move mentally ill patients and the retarded out of psychiatric hospitals and large institutions back into the community.

In a message to Congress on February 5, President Kennedy said the future for those with mental retardation was far from hopeless. The American people, he said, "have an obligation to prevent mental retardation, whenever possible, and to ameliorate it when it is present." That goal would require a comprehensive effort to address "the social, educational and vocational lifetime needs of the retarded individual."

Eunice's focus turned toward getting the bills passed. In the course of her travels, she had toured the Children's Colony in Arkansas with David Ray Jr. Now she recruited him to come to Washington to help shepherd the legislation through Congress. The Children's Colony was in the congressional district of Democrat Wilbur Mills, the chairman of the House Ways and Means Committee, without whose support the bills would have no chance of passage.

Eunice had reason to think she would need all the help she could muster. The Democrats held only a razor-thin majority in Congress, and many southern Democrats were suspicious of their Catholic, Ivy League–educated playboy president. President Kennedy's legislative initiatives on education, tax cuts, and civil rights were stalled. But Eunice had Sarge, who had cut his teeth on Capitol Hill in 1961, lobbying to keep the Peace Corps independent from the Agency for International Development, which distributed foreign aid for the US State Department. Then he had personally talked to no fewer than 350 lawmakers, impressing them at lunch, in their offices, or in elevators, "with evangelical zeal for his mission," in the words of Anthony Lewis of the *New York Times*.

Sarge and Eunice now turned those skills to the mental retardation bills. At times they found themselves working at cross purposes with the president's own staff. Kenneth O'Donnell and Lawrence O'Brien had done nothing on the Hill to help the cause of keeping the Peace Corps independent, and they proved just as indifferent to the cause of mental retardation. The president's aides chastised Doyle and Warren for recruiting a Republican congresswoman—Catherine May from the state of Washington—to help mobilize GOP support for the bills, despite the fact that she personally delivered a half dozen votes.

While Eunice's team worked the halls of Congress in June 1963, she enjoyed one of the perks of being the sister of the president of the United States. She and Jean accompanied Jack on a trip to Europe, during which he delivered his historic "Ich bin ein Berliner" speech in Berlin and visited the Kennedy homestead in County Wexford, Ireland.

Characteristically, Eunice did not leave her work at home. David J. Fischer was a consular officer in Frankfurt, Germany, assigned to assist members of the presidential party with special requests. Eunice asked to visit facilities for the mentally retarded. She was especially impressed by one. "Dr. Schmidt, your work is so fabulous. I want you to go to the American Embassy. I want you to visit America and go to the embassy, and we'll take care of it," Fischer remembered her telling the director. "Even though I was a junior officer, I knew we couldn't just hand out VIP visitor programs to everybody we liked, so I translated this into German saying, 'Dr. Schmidt, you're doing such a wonderful job. I hope one day you'll be able to visit the United States.' He answered in German, thank God, not in English. He said, 'That's not what she said, and I'll see you in your office Monday morning.' Which is what he did." Dr. Schmidt got his visa.

Back in the United States in early July, Eunice reluctantly agreed that the construction bill tailored to the needs of the mentally retarded should be consolidated with legislation aimed at replacing state mental hospitals with community mental health centers. Gunnar Dybwad, the executive director of the National Association for Retarded Children, sent her an indignant letter, the point of which, he wrote, "can be put quite plainly in the vernacular: is we is or is we ain't in support of the keystone of the President's Program—a clear differentiation between mental illness and mental retardation?" Despite her mistrust of psychiatrists and the mental health bureaucracy, she knew a single bill stood a better chance of passage, and she headed back to Capitol Hill to sell the combined legislation. Everyone worked hard to win those votes, Doyle said, but Eunice and Sarge "deserve the credit for most of it."

She kept Jack abreast of legislative developments during weekend sails on Cape Cod, a routine that kept her staff on its toes. Ray remembered the first time the White House telephone operator called him out of a movie theater on a Friday night with instructions to call Eunice immediately. "I'm getting ready to go to Hyannis Port," she told him. "I'm going to see the president tomorrow. Now, give me an up-to-date report on the legislation." From that point forward, Ray always carried the latest report with him when he left the office on Friday. Eunice's "tremendous contribution," he said, "was when the president was somewhat relaxing at Hyannis Port on a weekend to be able to talk to him about mental retardation, about the legislation."

McGeorge Bundy, the president's National Security Advisor, recognized a confidence, a competitiveness, and an impatience in Eunice that had been forged by the same forces that had shaped her brother: "the combination of energy and pain as physical phenomena." Both siblings had "to live with pain, to cast it aside," to accomplish their goals, but Eunice had to do it in what was "very much a man's world," Bundy noted. "She's had extraordinary weapons, but she has used them . . . Eunice has done a job, that would make any professional woman proud, of making mental retardation respectable."

Manhattanville College of the Sacred Heart was proud, awarding its former student an honorary degree on October 22. Two days later, President Kennedy signed the Maternal and Child Health and Mental Retardation Planning Amendment to the Social Security Act, which would grant $265 million in federal aid over five years to support programs for the mentally retarded. "She's one of the best lobbyists I ever had," he said of Eunice at the signing ceremony for the bill. Vice President Lyndon B. Johnson sent her a note after the ceremony: "I was inspired this morning. I was proud. It must be a great day for you." Seven days later, President Kennedy signed the Mental Retardation Facilities and Community Health Centers Construction Act, finding his sister at the back of the crowded Cabinet Room to hand her a second presidential signing pen in a week, this time for legislation that would provide $330 million over five years for planning and for new buildings to serve the same newly enfranchised population.

There would be precious little time for Eunice Kennedy Shriver to savor those victories, to bask in her beloved older brother's high regard. On November 22, 1963, she was having lunch with her husband and four-year-old Timmy in the dining room of the Lafayette Hotel, a few blocks from the White House, when Sarge was called to the telephone. President Kennedy had been shot in Dallas.

Dr. Joseph T. English, the medical director of the Peace Corps, was waiting for them in Sarge's office on Connecticut Avenue when the Shrivers arrived. English knew from wire service reports that the president had been shot in the head. He worried how Eunice would react if the injuries proved fatal, as he expected they would. She had come into town that morning for an appointment with her obstetrician; at forty-two, she was six months pregnant. Sarge had steadied her when she faltered briefly as they left the restaurant, "but nothing can overcome Eunice," he said later, crediting her strength to her deep Catholic faith.

When a Peace Corps staffer relayed the bulletin from United Press International that the president was dead, Eunice knelt, dry-eyed, and asked Sarge and English to join her in saying the rosary. On their knees in Sarge's office, they recited the prescribed prayers for Jack, the Catholic doctor self-consciously aware that he, alone of the three, was unable to pull a set of rosary beads from his pocket.

After arranging for Timmy to be returned home, the Shrivers headed with English to the White House to confer with Bobby and Ted about arrangements for the next few days. Bobby would meet their brother's coffin and Jackie at Andrews Air Force Base. Sarge would begin to plan the funeral. Ted and Eunice would fly to Hyannis Port to be with Rose and Joe.

Hearing their plans, English slipped away to the White House medical office to get some sedatives for Eunice. He instructed Ted to give her the pills on the plane to stave off hysteria when the awful news finally registered. Ted would return the pills to English three days later at the president's funeral, telling the well-intentioned physician, "Right medicine, Doc, wrong girl."

PART THREE

IN HER OWN RIGHT

NINE

FROM CAMP SHRIVER TO SPECIAL OLYMPICS

You know, Eunice, the world will never be the same after this.

—CHICAGO MAYOR RICHARD DALEY, JULY 20, 1968

SIX WEEKS INTO the new year, the winter days were lengthening and grief was loosening its grip on a nation still mourning the death of President John Fitzgerald Kennedy.

Time had not stopped on November 22, 1963. Since the year turned, Republican senator Barry Goldwater of Arizona had declared his candidacy for president of the United States. The paperback edition of *The Feminine Mystique*, by Betty Friedan, had become a best seller. The Beatles had appeared live on *The Ed Sullivan Show*.

That life goes on, even in the face of tragedy, was a lesson the Kennedy siblings had learned long ago. The deaths of Joe Jr. and Kick and the damage done to Rosemary did not prepare them for Jack's assassination, but those early losses—and the family's innate fortitude—steeled them to survive the blow.

By February, Eunice was dividing her time between Kennedy Foundation headquarters and a small office at HEW, where she monitored the application of the mental retardation laws. Sarge was wrapping up a monthlong tour of Peace Corps sites in Asia and acting as an emissary for

President Lyndon B. Johnson to the leaders of Iran, Turkey, Afghanistan, India, Jordan, Nepal, Thailand, Pakistan, and Israel, where he delivered a letter from the new president to Pope Paul VI, who was on a pilgrimage to Jerusalem. Even Bobby, for whom Jack's death had triggered an existential crisis, returned, forlorn, to the Justice Department to serve in the Cabinet of a man he loathed. Their contempt was mutual and of long standing. LBJ had dismissed Bobby as a "grandstanding runt" since he worked for Joe McCarthy in the Senate, and Bobby, in turn, had mocked the often-coarse vice president from the Texas Hill Country as Uncle Cornpone.

But Jack's death had altered the political landscape for the Kennedys. There would be no more spontaneous drop-ins at the White House for Eunice, no more midnight strategy sessions in the Oval Office for Bobby. They were, as Sargent Shriver told a friend, a "palace guard now without a palace."

Johnson delivered his first State of the Union address on January 8, 1964, while Sarge was still abroad. Declaring his intention to mount "an unconditional War on Poverty in America," Johnson told the joint session of Congress that his aim was "not only to relieve the symptoms of poverty, but to cure it and, above all, to prevent it." He asked Sargent Shriver to lead that charge, a vote of confidence in his Peace Corps director and a snub of his attorney general, who had discussed just such a program with Jack in the weeks before the assassination.

Sarge was a reluctant conscript. His heart was in the Peace Corps, a promising but fragile experiment that still needed a guiding hand. LBJ dismissed that concern, pressing his notably energetic administrator to do both jobs at once. To decline would be a dereliction of duty. To accept could trigger the antipathy of JFK loyalists, especially Bobby, for whom anything beyond token cooperation with Johnson amounted to a betrayal of the slain president.

Sarge had deferred to the Kennedys' political interests time and again since he first signed on as Joe's deputy at the Merchandise Mart. He had turned down an invitation to write speeches for Adlai Stevenson's 1948 gubernatorial campaign, at Joe's direction. He had spurned calls from Illinois Democrats to run for governor in 1960, when his father-in-law insisted that Jack's campaign take precedence. He had left Chicago, where his work on the Board of Education and the Catholic Interracial Council would have provided a platform from which to launch his own political career, to run the Peace Corps for Jack.

Now the president of the United States was asking him to direct the greatest expansion of social programs since the New Deal, two key elements of which—job training for at-risk youth and national service—the Kennedy closest to him had been proposing for almost two decades. It is hard to imagine Eunice doing anything but encouraging Sarge to accept the job. "It's a terrific compliment that Johnson would ask you to do it," she told him.

In his State of the Union speech, Johnson had called for more training "to put jobless, aimless, hopeless youngsters to work on useful projects," a federal commitment Eunice had been advocating since her work in the Justice Department seventeen years earlier. She had read the work of Richard Cloward and Lloyd Ohlin, two Columbia University sociologists who argued in 1961's *Delinquency and Opportunity: A Theory of Delinquent Gangs* that social conditions, more than individual pathology, triggered delinquent behavior, a perspective Eunice had long espoused herself. She might even have known Ohlin, who was studying for his doctorate in sociology at the University of Chicago during the same period she was auditing graduate courses there in its School of Social Work.

Certainly, since 1947, she had been preaching a layman's version of the "opportunity theory" that Ohlin and Cloward advanced in their book. *Evil* and *pathological* were not words she applied to the teenagers she'd met at the National Training School for Boys in Washington, the women she'd known at the federal penitentiary in Alderson, or the girls she'd counseled at the House of the Good Shepherd in Chicago. For Eunice, it was the deprivation in which they lived, the dysfunction with which they were surrounded, the economic and educational opportunities they were denied that bore the greater responsibility for their crimes.

It is no surprise, then, that it was Eunice who had convinced Jack to issue an executive order on May 11, 1961, establishing the President's Committee on Juvenile Delinquency and Youth Crime, an issue in which he had shown as little interest as he had in mental retardation. Just as she pushed her brother to confront the comprehensive needs of the mentally retarded, she pressed him to approach juvenile delinquency as a symptom of economic and social inequality, requiring the response of the whole community, not just law enforcement. A corps of volunteers, devoting a year or two to national service, could provide job training and social services to at-risk teenagers, in Eunice's view.

Jack agreed, putting Bobby in charge of the initiative; within months, he produced comprehensive legislation to address the problems of "youth unemployment, poor housing, poor health, inadequate education, and the alienation of lower-class communities and neighborhoods." The Juvenile Delinquency and Youth Offenses Act of 1961 authorized $10 million a year for three years for innovative state and municipal pilot projects to be administered by community-based nonprofits.

To Eunice's dismay, her idea for a domestic service corps had not survived congressional negotiations on that bill, but now the new president was calling for the creation of a "National Service Corps to help the economically handicapped of our own country as the Peace Corps now helps those abroad." Whatever Bobby's personal pique at Johnson and however deep Eunice's Kennedy loyalty, she welcomed a role for Sarge that advanced her agenda even as it enhanced his career. If anything, Eunice was perceived—by her sister-in-law Jackie, at least—as too ambitious for her husband's advancement. Recalling Bobby's reluctance to serve as Jack's attorney general, Jackie had contrasted his reticence with "Eunice pestering Jack to make Sargent head of HEW because she wanted to be a Cabinet wife."

Ethel Kennedy thought that characterization was "a little bit of a denigration. I'm sure she thought that Sarge deserved it," she said. Eunice was certainly less interested in the social cachet of having her husband in the Cabinet than in the political leverage it would afford her to advance the issues she cared about most.

Bobby, still reeling from his brother's death, was in no state to object to what he saw as Johnson's usurpation of the antipoverty issue that the Kennedy brothers had begun to address through the juvenile delinquency prevention grants. Frank Mankiewicz was the director of Peace Corps operations in Latin America and stationed in Peru when Sarge added the antipoverty initiative to his portfolio. Back in Washington for meetings with Sarge, he accompanied his boss to the attorney general's office to talk about the War on Poverty. "That's how I met Robert Kennedy," said Mankiewicz, who would become his press secretary months later. He remembered how deep the circles were under Bobby's eyes, his eyes themselves reddened from lack of sleep. His suit hung too loosely on a gaunt frame that hinted at how much weight he had lost since the assassination.

"I remember looking at his wrists coming out of his shirt, so thin, and him not saying very much, kind of nodding. 'Is this what President Kennedy would have wanted?' he asked. And Sarge said, 'I think it is.' God, he was absolutely shattered."

Eunice was certain Jack would have approved. Hadn't she, with his encouragement, made poverty, delinquency, and voluntary service the focus of at least a half dozen speeches in the last three years? "I think my speech on the Domestic Peace Corps went over very well," she had written to Jack after delivering a commencement address on June 2, 1962, at Santa Clara University, in California, where she was awarded an honorary doctorate. "They are all crazy about you out there *but* slightly less than they are about Doctor Shriver."

It was the first time the Jesuit university had ever granted an honorary degree to a woman. "To receive a degree from a men's university is a new experience for me as it is for Santa Clara," she told the graduates. "All of my life I have been taught that men are the dominant sex, that it is men who go to the best colleges, that it is men who make the memorable speeches and run for public office. I therefore congratulate the president and faculty of Santa Clara for striking this new blow for freedom and for equality, although I am withholding any announcement of my candidacy today."

Even as Eunice reveled in the public recognition, she remained beset by self-doubt. In a letter from Hyannis Port to Sarge at Timberlawn a few weeks later, she worried that the Kennedy Foundation was insufficiently "dynamic" and that the director she had hired to run the office did not give "every moment to the foundation work"—an expectation that was as typical of Eunice as it was unrealistic. "The foundation still lacks something, attention & drive & creative spirit that Wally gives to the Mart, you give the Peace Corps, Bobby gives the Justice Dept. etc.," she wrote, her inclusion of Wally Ollman, the manager of her father's Merchandise Mart in Chicago indicative of how much she tied success to the person in charge. She wanted to make as big an impact in her job as the men did in theirs, and for Eunice, the meter was always running.

She transmitted her sense of urgency to the graduates of Santa Clara, telling them to put their education to use where it was most needed. Choose a cause. Make a plan. Their education was not designed to give them "an economic advantage in the life struggle," she told the graduates. They had not read the Greeks to ponder the "mysteries of pure scholarship or the delights of abstract discourse." They were called, instead, to action. "It is not enough to lend your talents merely to discuss the issues and deplore their solutions." They needed to find better answers. By training as social workers or probation officers. By volunteering at mental hospitals and institutions for the mentally retarded. By assisting in public school classrooms. "In short," she said, "there is a world of opportunity for those with the courage to act."

That was how she and Sarge lived their own lives, the private sphere indistinguishable from the public. He had barely assumed his new duties as Johnson's director of what would become the Office of Economic Opportunity (OEO) when Eunice gave birth to Mark Kennedy Shriver, on February 17, 1964, the first of their children to carry the Kennedy name. President Johnson sent flowers. Economist John Kenneth Galbraith sent huzzahs from Harvard. Actress Carol Channing invited her to New York to see *Hello, Dolly!* when she was back on her feet. Illinois congressman Dan Rostenkowski, pronouncing himself "green with envy," wrote to solicit the secret to producing sons: "After thirteen years of marriage, all I've got to show for it is four daughters!"

Mary Switzer, the head of the Office of Vocational Rehabilitation, crocheted a sweater, a domestic gesture Eunice celebrated in her acknowledgment: "The fact that you made it makes me think I shouldn't put it on my son, but in a special box marked 'She rehabilitates a hundred thousand people a year, and still makes handsome sweaters for beautiful babies!'"

Whether from complications of Mark's delivery, nervous exhaustion, or a flare-up of gastrointestinal problems, Eunice was readmitted to the hospital one month later. She was hospitalized again in August and yet again in October, but the available record is mum on the nature of her illnesses.

Whatever their cause, her ailments barely slowed her down in what was proving to be an eventful year. Sarge's expanded role in the Johnson administration led to press speculation that the president might ask him to join the ticket in the fall. Anthony Lewis of the *New York Times* wrote that his qualifications included a "deep personal commitment to social justice and equality" and a reputation as a "hard-headed practitioner of economy in government." Johnson did not discourage the rumors, telling reporters, "I regard Sargent Shriver as one of the most brilliant, most able, most competent officials in the government. I regard him as my real confidant."

Selecting Sargent Shriver as his vice president would have provided Johnson with the Kennedy aura without the complications of an actual

Kennedy. But, given the rules of political primogeniture in the Kennedy family, there was no opening for Sarge. "Just as I went into politics because Joe died," Jack had once said, "if anything happened to me tomorrow, my brother Bobby would run for my seat in the Senate. And if Bobby died, Teddy would take over for him." There was no room in that succession plan for an upstart brother-in-law, especially since a vice presidential perch would put Sarge in a more advantageous position than Robert Kennedy as a future presidential prospect.

"I never got the feeling that Sarge was a full partner in that family, and I felt very close to him; I admired him very much," Mankiewicz said. "But when I started working with Bob, Sarge was never part of the picture. *Dismissive* is a good word. He was kind of 'rah, rah' for them."

Nicholas Katzenbach, an assistant attorney general in the Justice Department, agreed: "I don't think Sarge was a real Kennedy. They didn't really think of him as a Kennedy. I don't know, I imagine they thought Sarge toadied up to President Johnson much too much, would be my guess. He got on pretty well with President Johnson as far as I could make out."

Talk of the vice presidency shook Bobby out of the torpor that had enveloped him since Jack's death, forcing him to wrestle with his own political future. If staying on as attorney general under Johnson felt untenable, given the antagonism between them, how could he advance himself as a candidate for vice president, as so many in the party were urging him to do? He could count on a win if he ran for governor of Massachusetts, but his interests and experience lay in Washington. In a private meeting in the Oval Office, Johnson quashed any hope Bobby might have had about being his running mate. Days after receiving a tumultuous ovation at the Democratic National Convention in August, in Atlantic City, New Jersey—delegates applauded for twenty-two minutes before letting him introduce a memorial tribute to his slain brother—Bobby resigned from the Cabinet to run for the US Senate from New York.

Eunice campaigned for both brothers that fall. She was an especially important surrogate in Massachusetts, where Ted was running for his first full term in the Senate from a hospital bed. On June 19, after voting for the Civil Rights Act that Jack had crafted and President Johnson had guided to passage, he was flying to the state Democratic Convention in Springfield in a small plane when the twin-engine Aero Commander 680 crashed during a storm. The pilot and a Kennedy aide were killed. Ted, pulled from the wreckage by his fellow passenger, Indiana senator Birch Bayh, had broken his back. He would spend five months in New England Baptist Hospital and easily win reelection with the help of his sisters and his wife of seven years, Joan Bennett Kennedy.

In New York, Eunice recalled for voters Bobby's childhood in Bronxville to counter charges from incumbent Republican senator Kenneth Keating that he was a carpetbagger, with tenuous ties to the Empire State, having just moved his family into a house on Long Island. But she used those speeches to advance her agenda as much as her brother's candidacy. Why did New York need Bobby in the United States Senate? To make sure that Washington renewed research funding for the Albert Einstein School of Medicine at Yeshiva University, one of the new federally funded centers for the study of mental retardation. Why was his presence on the national stage so crucial? To fight for more federal money to train special education teachers, for innovative educational models, for even more university-affiliated research centers to tackle the problem of mental retardation.

"If our requests, if our recommendations, are to become law, we will need friends in the House of Representatives and in the Senate," she told one audience. "We will need men like Robert Kennedy, for we can be sure that Senator Kennedy will want to carry to completion the programs that President Kennedy inaugurated. We want in Washington representatives and senators who will assure that our goal will be realized: that wherever a retarded person lives, there will be services available to him." Bobby supported those causes but they were less central to his agenda than to Eunice's.

Her campaign speeches were a tacit acknowledgment of her changed circumstances. In deference to the Kennedys, President Johnson had appointed his own Committee on Mental Retardation, but by 1965, he would relocate its work to HEW from the White House. His interest was genuine—the man he chose to be his vice president, Minnesota senator Hubert H. Humphrey, had a three-year-old granddaughter with Down syndrome—but the urgency of the Kennedy years was gone.

Dr. Patrick Doyle, a deputy assistant for mental retardation in the White House under Dr. Stafford Warren, felt the change in status immediately. "After the assassination, the federal agencies no longer felt they had to pay too much attention to us. There was quite, you know, quite a difference before and after," he said. "I left a month after the assassination because I could see the writing on the wall—that we were in a holding action and that the office could be disbanded at any moment. It's to Mr. Johnson's credit that he kept it going as long as he did."

When Warren finally turned out the lights in his White House office on May 30, 1965, no one thought to tell Eunice, with predictable results. "Mrs. Shriver called me Sunday morning after reading in the *New York Times* that Dr. Warren has resigned and that his responsibilities would be assigned to an assistant secretary in HEW," Wilbur Cohen, then undersecretary at HEW, told Secretary John Gardner. "Mrs. Shriver indicated extreme annoyance that she had not been consulted on what was going to happen and couldn't find out anything definite. She was so upset I wasn't able to complete a sentence in the conversation. She said she was going to talk with President Johnson about the situation." But surrendering control to the federal bureaucracy would have been inevitable, no matter who was in the White House, thought Leonard Mayo, the man who had chaired President Kennedy's Panel on Mental Retardation, because of the coordination required among the multiple agencies responsible for carrying out the new programs.

As Warren saw it, Eunice just "didn't want to have anybody not a Kennedy come in to develop an image in mental retardation. This was a Kennedy show, Kennedy Foundation show, presidential show, and a Shriver show."

There was a place in Washington—at the opposite end of Pennsylvania Avenue—where Eunice's influence had not waned. The Democratic landslide in 1964 that had sent Bobby and returned Ted to the Senate created liberal majorities in both chambers that the party was determined to preserve in the 1966 midterms. The Democratic Study Group, the liberal caucus on Capitol Hill, had 175 members, all of whom wanted Bobby Kennedy to campaign with them and cut TV ads for them that year.

Bobby had filmed several spots for colleagues in the Capitol's television studio one morning when an aide arrived to tell him that Eunice had called to remind him there was a noon meeting across town for trustees of the Kennedy Foundation. Scores of his colleagues were still lined up to shoot campaign spots with him. "Let me ask you, Frank," he said to

Mankiewicz, his press secretary. "If you had to offend 170 Democratic members or Eunice, what would you do?"

Mankiewicz did not hesitate: "I'd go to the meeting." The junior senator from New York laughed. "Yes, no question," Bobby said, promising the waiting congressmen he would make their campaign ads with them on another day.

"I am sure if he had a meeting with the president, he'd have done the same thing," Mankiewicz said. "'Sorry, Mr. President, but Eunice says there's a board meeting.'"

In family and foundation matters, Bobby deferred to Eunice, but he did not confer with her on policy, as Jack had done. Their brother had relied on both of them as advisors, but Eunice and Bobby did not have the same relationship.

President Johnson still took her calls, and her allies on Capitol Hill still fought to reauthorize the laws she had propelled to enactment, but the going got tougher. Rhode Island congressman John E. Fogarty considered the bills President Kennedy signed a month before his death "the most forward-looking pieces of legislation in the field of retardation that had ever passed the Congress." By 1965, he was just "trying to make sure that we give them every dime they ask for under this authorization."

It took vigilance. On December 12, 1967, after attending a White House signing of amendments to the mental retardation laws, Eunice wrote to LBJ to suggest that the change "authorizes for the first time federal funds to begin a program of recreation and physical education for mentally retarded and physically handicapped youngsters"—an interpretation that William D. Casey, an assistant director of the Bureau of the Budget, did not share. But Casey was wrong. There *was* a provision for $10 million earmarked for physical fitness and recreation. Eunice knew it was there because she'd had Ted insert it.

In speeches across the country, she emphasized the mounting research, and her own anecdotal evidence, that physical activity improved the motor skills and intellectual capacities of children with mental retardation. The government had to do more. "Not only can the retarded, with proper training, learn to run and throw and swim—sometimes as well as normal children—but physical education and recreation actually improves their intelligence," she said.

The emphasis on physical activity for the mentally retarded reflected a further evolution in the Kennedy Foundation's focus. The family philanthropy that had begun by building schools and hospitals for mentally retarded children, which had shifted to funding scientific research, now added recreation and physical fitness to its concerns.

An accomplished athlete herself, Eunice had marveled at Rosemary's proficiency as a swimmer when they were children. She had seen scores of boys and girls develop similar skills in her own backyard. Since 1962, Eunice had opened Timberlawn to mentally retarded children for several weeks of outdoor play in late spring and early summer. The impetus had been a call from a Maryland mother asking why—with all the attention the White House was lavishing on mental retardation—was there no place to send her child to summer camp. It was the sort of practical problem Eunice responded to best. There was a need, so she filled it. She lived in Maryland, after all, and there were all those acres of open space just outside her back door.

She began with three dozen children from private homes and local institutions, recruiting students from local Catholic high schools to coach them in horseback riding, tennis, softball, basketball, and swimming, the last of which she often taught herself, once jumping into the pool fully clothed when there was no one close at hand to soothe an anxious child.

It was only in retrospect that her own children saw Camp Shriver as something unusual. In the moment, a field full of scores of boisterous children—some in wheelchairs playing catch, others in protective helmets banging their heads against the trees—was just life with Mummy. Bobby, Maria, and Tim would meet the cars and yellow school buses as they pulled into the driveway and join the solemn recitation of the Pledge of Allegiance during the daily flag raising. They had no idea who their playmates were or why they were there, but, Tim said, "What child would not love going down to the arts and crafts building or riding a pony or driving a go-cart? In our case, it just happened to be in our backyard."

John "Sandy" Eiler, a physical education instructor whom Joe had hired before his stroke to teach his grandchildren to swim and play sports in Palm Beach and Hyannis Port, signed on to run the makeshift operation Eunice called Camp Shriver. He relied on volunteers, some as young as fifteen, to supervise children with a wide range of mental and physical disabilities. Some were local teenagers such as Joan Hosmer, who, years later, brought the "joy and enthusiasm" she says she experienced at Camp Shriver to her job as principal of Our Lady of Mercy elementary school in nearby Potomac, Maryland.

Some of Eiler's other staffers came from Lorton Reformatory, in Virginia. "In retrospect, I think some of it is kind of horrifying," Bobby Shriver said. "They got off the prison bus and looked after 'special' folks during the day, and then got back on the prison bus and left. Nothing happened, but it's a little out there. She was very determined, so if she didn't have the counselors she wanted or if she wanted to make a statement about prisons, she would just do it."

Some of the inmates working at Camp Shriver were serving long prison terms. Ernest Johnson was twenty-two years old and had been sentenced to twelve years to life for kidnapping. But he was also a freshman in the prison's Lorton Federal City College. "I'll be back on the street one day," he said. "While I am going to jail, I must establish something." For her part, Eunice wanted the racially and economically diverse campers to interact with counselors who came from "all strata of society. The Lorton men have been very impressive," she said. "They have a lot of compassion for these children."

Whether she was reckless or naive, Eunice was consistent. She regularly brought home delinquents for a meal with the family at Timberlawn or for days at Hyannis Port. Her youngest child, Anthony, remembered an especially belligerent pair of boys who arrived on the Cape with her one summer in the 1970s from Washington, DC. His mother installed the much bigger boys in his room, instructed Anthony to teach them to swim and sail, and then promptly left for a weeklong business trip. "They'd beat me up," Anthony said. "She'd just roll with it. I had to roll with it. People are survivors right? There was not to be any complaining. She'd be, like, 'Aren't you lucky you have a sailboat? Aren't you lucky you have this beautiful house?'"

Eunice was reflexively passing along her father's dictum to the next generation: "There'll be no crying in this house." Sarge provided the necessary balance. When a young Bobby Shriver began to cry after getting hurt during a touch football game at the Cape one summer, his Uncle Bobby scolded him, "Kennedys don't cry!" Sarge gently lifted his son off the grass and told him, "It's okay, you can cry. You're a Shriver!"

There was a method to Eunice's organization of Camp Shriver. Her goal in introducing typical high school students to mentally retarded children was to normalize those interactions. Teenagers who were initially anxious around their young charges relaxed as they played. Ann and Mary Hammerbacher, eighteen-year-old twins, were among them.

"We had no idea what it would be like. We'd never met any retarded children," Ann said after that first summer. "None of us really had any experience. To tell the truth, all of us were a little afraid."

Kathleen Kennedy Townsend, Bobby and Ethel's oldest daughter, found working at Camp Shriver made her see her aunt in a new light. "What was amazing about her to me when I was a camp counselor, she would play in the pool with them. She would play ball with them. It wasn't like 'I am running the camp, and you do the work.' She physically liked doing the work herself," Townsend recalled. "That struck me as really wonderful and amazing. The other thing that struck me was the first day of camp, we all did 'Hava Nagila' [the Israeli folk song and dance, "Let Us Rejoice"], and I remember thinking, 'Where did this come from?' It is kind of funny. It was pretty extraordinary. We would end the day with 'Taps,' which was kind of special. It's a great spirit that has you end your day with 'Taps.'"

Bobby, Tim, and Maria learned soccer and volleyball alongside the campers, who were as likely to be black as they were white, a not-insignificant fact in 1962 in Maryland, where life was largely segregated. Black children had been welcomed in Eunice's home since she and Jack first set up house in 1947 in Georgetown, where she regularly brought juvenile delinquents, black and white, home for dinner. That practice continued in Chicago, where she and Sarge got to know leaders in the black community through his work on the Catholic Interracial Council. In 1967 she made inquiries about taking a black foster child into their home, but the idea never came to fruition because a new career opportunity would take them out of the country.

———————————

A typical day at Camp Shriver—"Where Everybody Is Somebody"— began at eight in the morning with a discussion of problems encountered the day before by the counselors, each of whom was assigned a single camper. At nine the counselors greeted each arriving child with a handshake followed by the flag raising, the Pledge of Allegiance, the national anthem, and an opening prayer. Morning individual or group activities included crafts, soccer, pony rides, swimming, croquet, badminton, and time on the swings or slides.

In 1962 three-year-old Tim Shriver liked to race Wendell, a nine-year-old hyperactive boy. Eight-year-old Bobby Shriver made model airplanes with Raymond, at fourteen the oldest of his single mother's eight children. Maria Shriver bonded with a girl named Leila and insisted that her friend was not mentally retarded. "I think she just wanted to come to camp," Maria told her mother.

For her part, Eunice professed to see little difference between the campers and her own children. Watching Tim and Wendell race down a hill, she pronounced them "evenly matched" and noted that they "both picked up their clothes—with some prodding—after swimming; both caught and threw a ball with the same ability, although Wendell kicked much better than Timothy. Both had the same table manners. Sometimes they would throw the food and would then have to go without dessert." Veronica, who liked to play with Bobby, "can't read but paints better than Bobby," Eunice noted, and his friend Raymond "learned to post and canter on Bobby's horse in a week. I taught Bobby at the age of six. He took several weeks."

Because she focused on what her campers could do rather than on what they could not do, her counselors did the same. "I believe the children should be called 'exceptional' because if they were retarded they wouldn't be able to play games or do much of anything," a sixteen-year-old Catholic schoolgirl told Eunice. "I find they have many abilities I didn't think they had."

Some of the campers' mothers made similar discoveries. Shirley Bulka of Kensington, Maryland, was stunned to see her son, Michael, riding horseback on parents' visiting day. "To see him not just sitting atop for a walk around but actually controlling the pinto, making turns, taking a can off one post and putting it on another," she told Eunice, "was thrilling beyond words and an opportunity he would otherwise have never had."

Eunice, of course, saw it the same way. "Many of you are asking yourself, was it worthwhile? Did I really do anything for my child? And my answer to you is a very strong yes," she told her counselors at the close of one camp session. "Some of you have gotten your child into the water when he was too frightened before. Maybe he didn't learn to swim, but the important point is to take the first step. His parents or his gym teachers who thought he just couldn't learn much now see that he can learn the preliminaries of swimming. Your teaching has had a radar effect . . . You have helped both the parents and the child."

She urged them to return the following summer and encouraged them to volunteer during the winter with mentally retarded or underprivileged children in Washington, DC. "God offers to every mind its choice between truth and repose. Take which you please—you can never have both," she told them, quoting Ralph Waldo Emerson. Her counselors, as well as her own children, got the message: repose was not an option.

Eunice often brought professional athletes to Camp Shriver, knowing that they, in turn, would attract press attention to her cause. Joey Giardello, the middleweight boxing champion, might be sparring with a child on the lawn, while his eleven-year-old-son, Carman, who had Down syndrome, ran football drills in the pasture with Bobby Mitchell of the Washington Redskins and Jim Brown of the Cleveland Browns, or learned to hit a baseball from Stan Musial of the St. Louis Cardinals.

For all of the fun, the camp was in Tim's words "superdisruptive and superchaotic." On a single day in 1965, Mary Lou Norton, one in a long line of Eunice's revolving assistants, was calling Roosevelt Grier of the Los Angeles Rams to remind him he was due at Camp Shriver; shipping the dog Peter Lawford had left at Timberlawn back to California; wrapping presents for the Shriver children to take to a friend's birthday party; driving Rose Kennedy to the White House for a Rose Garden ceremony; and "soothing Ethel, the laundress, when a black snake brushed her foot while she was ironing in the basement."

Adding to the tableaux at Timberlawn were all the serious men in suits and ties gathered around the dining room table with Sarge, roughing out ideas for how preschool education, legal services, job training, and even foster grandparents might help break the cycle of poverty. Briefcases of the men from the Office of Economic Opportunity shared floor space with wet towels, archery bows, baseball mitts, and badminton rackets dropped by campers rushing to and from the bathroom.

Children brought their lunch to camp every day, but Eunice provided the gallons of milk they devoured before hurrying off to afternoons of softball, kickball, or more time on horseback and in the swimming pool. She led the march to the flagpole every day at two forty-five for the closing ceremony. By three o'clock, the only children left at Timberlawn were Bobby, Maria, Tim, and their little brothers, Mark and Anthony Paul Kennedy Shriver, the latter of whom was born in 1965, when Eunice was forty-four years old.

"There was no division between our lives and the camp. No lines. No boundaries," Tim said. "There was no question that she was on a mission and we were on the mission with her, but she didn't have motherhood and wifehood and professional-hood separate. They were all the same. Her brothers' political careers. Her husband's career. Her own career. Her children's lives."

The seamlessness with which the Shrivers moved between his work and hers had benefits for both. The idea for Head Start sprang from research the Kennedy Foundation helped fund at Peabody College in Nashville, where the psychologist Susan W. Gray had determined that early intervention could improve the IQs of mentally retarded children. If preschool could have a positive effect on the cognitive development of mentally retarded boys and girls, Sarge wondered, wouldn't early education also improve the performances of poor children?

That question led the Shrivers to Syracuse University, where Dr. Julius B. Richmond, a pediatrician, and Bettye Caldwell, an early-childhood educator, were studying the development of infants and toddlers in poor families by placing half of their charges in what amounted to an early day care center. The stimulation of that educational setting, they concluded, yielded discernible cognitive benefits for children reared in poverty.

That was a revolutionary idea in the mid-1960s, when the prevailing view was that any early separation from the mother would be detrimental to an infant or toddler, and kindergarten was not even offered in 60 percent of the states. When Eunice visited their Children's Center, "she asked a lot of questions, very good questions," Caldwell recalled. "Her main concern was always mental retardation, but she recognized that early intervention could make a difference. She saw it as prevention, maybe even cure. That doesn't sound like much now, but back then, experts did not think anything was happening in the brain before language developed. She was a visionary about early childhood education. At a time when the experts insisted that child development began at age three, she recognized that our work with infants was just very important."

Sarge hired Richmond in 1965 as the first director of Project Head Start, which began as an eight-week summer program with a few thousand participants, staffed by volunteers. Widely hailed as the most successful of Johnson's antipoverty programs, Head Start, by its fiftieth anniversary, had served more than thirty-two million children in what had become a year-round, full-day preschool program.

Caldwell became a professor of education at the University of Arkansas at Little Rock and at Fayetteville, where she directed the Center for Early Development and Education. She continued to be a resource for

Eunice for the next two decades, helping to shape her views on the benefits of quality child care centers, the necessity for comprehensive education of teenage parents, and the need for government either to subsidize child care for working mothers or pay a salary to poor mothers who stayed at home to raise their children.

Those were radical ideas, especially for Eunice, a woman who, against all evidence, saw herself as a traditional suburban matron. She was never that, but neither was she a charter member of the National Organization for Women (NOW), which declared in its founding document in 1966 that "the time has come to confront, with concrete action, the conditions that now prevent women from enjoying the equality of opportunity and freedom of which is their right, as individual Americans, and as human beings."

One of those "conditions" was the primacy of motherhood in women's lives. "With a life span lengthened to nearly 75 years, it is no longer either necessary or possible for women to devote the greatest part of their lives to child-rearing; yet childbearing and rearing, which continues to be a most important part of most women's lives—still is used to justify barring women from equal professional and economic participation and advance," read the statement from NOW, drafted in part by its first president, Betty Friedan.

McCall's and *Ladies' Home Journal* had both excerpted *The Feminine Mystique*, Friedan's explication of the frustrations of well-educated suburban housewives denied equal participation in the workforce and in public life—what she called "the problem that has no name."

Eunice heard in the feminist critique a denigration of motherhood; the suggestion that it was a bore and a burden. "It is a very respectable attack," Eunice wrote in *McCall's*. "It wears gloves. It is made in the most sophisticated and respectable national magazines. It is heard in the best circles. Some of the attackers are women of fame and distinction. I am sure they think they are doing us a favor."

But her defense of motherhood revealed a curious lack of self-awareness, a disconnect between the words she wrote and the life she led. "A career girl may have her news clippings and take pride in the fact that she has done what men can do. But no award or achievement can be equal to the moment when a child turns to his mother as the one person in the world on whom to rely," she wrote.

Is that how Eunice saw herself? As a nurturing maternal presence always at the ready to guide or comfort one of her children? Where, in that description, is the daughter who took control of her family's charitable foundation? Where is the sister who goaded her brother, the president, and cowed the men controlling the purse strings on Capitol Hill into committing millions of dollars to combat mental retardation and juvenile delinquency? Where is the mother who was as at home in the office, on the campaign trail, or on far-flung missions for the Kennedy Foundation as she was at Timberlawn—the mother who regularly left her children in the care of the household staff in order to pursue her professional goals? Wasn't Eunice a career girl, too?

She was in the eyes of her niece Kathleen Kennedy Townsend. Her generation had great fun sailing, swimming, and riding with their mothers, she said, but "my mother didn't raise children; my aunts didn't raise children. They have governesses to raise children." And, in the estimation of her younger brother Robert F. Kennedy Jr., "Eunice Shriver would probably have made as good a president as anybody in our family," a view echoed in a headline about her that appeared in the March 1976 *Ladies' Home Journal*: "The Kennedy Who Could Be President (If She Weren't a Woman)."

Arthur Schlesinger Jr., the historian and advisor to President Kennedy, observed, "Whoever she was, she could never be satisfied simply being a wife and mother. She quickens things; she galvanizes people," he said. "How could that energy be latent?"

In one perhaps more candid interview, Eunice acknowledged thinking that "most mothers are happier if they do some work consistently outside their homes. But I don't pose this as the way of life for all women. I realize that many, many mothers can't go away and leave their children, and I have no desire to set myself up as an example in this. I've someone dependable to leave them with so I can manage."

Her children knew only that she was away a lot and never sat down when she was at home. When she headed to her bedroom for the night, she locked her door behind her to be sure there were no interruptions in her nightly struggle with insomnia. Sleeping pills helped, but Anthony remembered hearing her behind the closed door every night on the telephone, usually with Lem Billings, Jack's Choate roommate who was akin to a tenth Kennedy sibling, so close was he to the late president's brothers and sisters.

It was to Sarge that the Shriver children more often turned for nurturing. Timmy was six in 1965, after the arrival of Mark and Anthony, when his dad replaced the king-size bed in his bedroom with two twins and invited his middle child to bunk with him. Tim did until he was a teenager. "I watched him listen to the news every morning and curse the often horrible news of men lost in Vietnam, and I learned to want to stop the horrors of war like him," Tim recalled. "I watched him cling to his rosary in bed every night, and I learned to want to quiet my mind in those beads just as he did."

Before heading to the office or the airport, Sarge slipped notes in his perfect cursive script under his children's bedroom doors, encouraging one to do his best on a test, praising another for her insightful remark at the dinner table the night before, telling them all he would be thinking of them wherever his work was about to take him. They knew their mother loved them ferociously, but public, or even private, emotional displays did not suit her personality.

"They definitely had their gender roles mixed up," Maria Shriver said.

Bettye Caldwell thought that Eunice was, like so many women of their generation, caught between the image of womanhood imposed on them by religion, society, and the dynamics of their own families and the much more complicated women they knew themselves to be. "She never got her due within or outside of the family," in Caldwell's view. "She always stood deferentially on the sidelines when Mr. Shriver was with her, but I always felt she was the visionary and he was the implementer."

Eunice's ideas about gender equality were developing along with the country's. At the urging of Esther Peterson, the director of the Women's Bureau in the US Department of Labor, Jack in 1961 had appointed a President's Commission on the Status of Women, chaired by former First Lady Eleanor Roosevelt. It was an unexpected move for a president who did not have a single woman in his Cabinet, as had each of his three immediate predecessors. The commission's 1963 report *American Women* called for government-supported child care centers and job training for so-called displaced homemakers whose children were grown or who needed to support themselves after divorce. It would be a decade before the ideas promoted by *American Women* became mainstream. The report did lead to passage of the Equal Pay Act of 1963, although fifty years after its enactment, female full-time, year-round workers still made only 80 cents for every dollar earned by men.

———

Camp Shriver ended each year in late June, when Eunice and her five children left the Maryland farm for summer on Cape Cod. But if anything, Eunice's frenetic pace intensified at the Cape, where summer vacation meant daily sailing races, swim meets, and baseball games, some organized, some spontaneous, all competitive, and none confined to the children alone.

"She was the most competitive person I have ever met in my life," Ethel Kennedy said of Eunice, recalling the picnics she and her sister-in-law would throw together whenever the weather was good. Eunice would pile her brood into her twenty-seven-foot Wianno Senior sailboat, called *Head Start*, and Ethel would load her gang into her identical boat, the *Resolute*. "She'd have a boatload of children, and so would I. We'd go to Great Island. It was maybe a mile or two; we'd sail there. But there was another island, Egg Island, that would come up and go down depending on the tides. We'd get in our boats, and immediately that competitive spirit would kick in. You could see her getting the sails up to get out of there. But then she'd wait for me to get kind of close to Great Island, and then she'd run me up on the island. She was just outrageous."

Being run aground by her sister-in-law was as predictable as Tuesday night dinner at the Shrivers'. Each family was assigned a night to cook, and everyone dreaded Tuesdays. "It was the same meal every Tuesday— the exact same meal—chicken, peas, and mashed potatoes," Ethel recalled. "Eunice always had a cook, but it was always the same meal. I'd call her up in the morning and say, 'Now, Eunie, not tonight!' And then she'd get distracted and start talking about what was going on in the news. Food was not on her radar screen."

Neither, apparently, was paying her bills. A letter from Sarah Anderson, of Hyannis, was typical of those that arrived regularly from vendors who had not been paid. Eunice had not replied to an earlier certified letter from Anderson, asking that the housekeepers she had engaged more than a month earlier to clean the Cape house be paid. Eunice's assistant had apparently asked for an itemized bill before payment would be made. "They did not have any secretary on the job to itemize their labor," is the curt way an insulted Anderson replied.

As indifferent as she was to the help, Eunice was more attentive to her children in Hyannis Port than she could be during the school year. She sailed and played tennis with them, rode horses with them through cranberry bogs, and played water polo with them in the pool at the Big House. She chased them outside if she caught them watching TV on a sunny day. She was delighted by them, grateful for them, proud of them, and as emotionally reserved with them as her mother had been with her. She was not a hugger, though she was more available to her younger sons because, busy as she was, she was around more than she had been when Bobby, Maria, and Tim were small. "I'm a huge fan of my mother's, but I'm a different kind of mother," Maria said. "My mother didn't touch me, but you can't give what you didn't get."

She was not big on heart-to-heart talks, either—none of her children recalls her discussing their uncles' assassinations with them. They absorbed their family history by osmosis. "If something came on the TV about that, the TV would go off. If somebody asked about it, boom, she'd walk out of the room. I never talked about that ever in my whole life," Anthony said. "If you are ten years old, and that keeps happening, you think that's something your mom does not want to talk about. We are not the kind of family that sits around and talks about stuff like that."

They could not remember their mother ever telling them she loved them or inviting them into her bed to snuggle—a marked contrast to their father, with that spare bed and open door. Eunice assumed her children were as confident in her love as she had been in Rose's. What was the need for ostentatious displays of affection? She grew up hearing from her father that "Kennedys don't cry." Neither did they emote.

"In our family, we grew up in an environment where you don't spend a lot of time being reflective and thinking and trying to figure stuff out," Anthony said. "There was not a lot of time for that kind of stuff, and, sometimes I think that is not so good, but that is who she was. There was no sitting back and worrying 'Are you happy? Are you sad? Let's talk it through. Let's cuddle about it.' There was none of that kind of stuff. It was 'What's the plan today, what are we doing, let's get going, get to work.'"

In May, for three years running, the plan included a Maryland-registered Shriver Horse Show to Benefit the Mentally Retarded. The proceeds from the hot dog and lemonade sales and the parking fees went to the Lieutenant Joseph P. Kennedy Jr. Institute in Northeast Washington, whose students were regulars at Camp Shriver. The Shriver children competed on the professionally designed course, as did their Kennedy cousins and many of the children from the institute who had learned to ride and jump at Timberlawn.

Michael R. Gardner, a Georgetown University student hired to exercise Sarge's horse every day, was skeptical. "Mrs. Shriver, are you sure this is a good idea? After all, registered Maryland horse shows are not casual country fairs; everything will have to be done right," he said. "Do you really think it will work?"

Eunice waved off his worries. "Of course it will, Mike," she said. "The only thing those boys at the Kennedy Institute need is some help, and they'll be terrific. You wait and see. This show will be a great eye opener because we'll get all the press out here, and they'll see what's possible if you just give retarded teenagers a chance."

As they got older, Bobby and Maria helped by forming a "Committee of Volunteers" from Bobby's school, Landon, and Maria's school, Stone Ridge Country Day School, to work the hamburger stand and the cake stand to feed spectators who came to see riders eighteen years of age and younger compete for trophies. The most prestigious trophy was donated by attorney Edward Bennett Williams, one of the owners of the Washington Redskins. The Redskin Cup was especially prized because it was presented each year by a member of the Redskins football team.

Eunice's high expectations for her own children are evident in the letters she wrote to their teachers asking for summer reading lists and her rare, not-always-welcome supervision of their homework. Eunice saved a very short story written with some creative spelling by her son Bobby, apparently early in grade school. "Once upon a time, there was a meen, meen Ladye. The Layde's name was Eunice. This Layde Eunice had a very nice boy. His name was Bobby. But Eunice was very meen to the boy. She made him do three-page stories, two arithmetic pages a night, and if he did not do it, he would get this," he wrote, adding an illustration of a spanking. "And the Bobby couldn't sit down for a week. One day when he had nothing to do, he poisened his mother. And this he did. But he lived happily ever after (and no storys)."

Bobby might have included his grandmother in his grim fairy tale had he been aware of Rose's note to his mother about some mischief she had witnessed while visiting Timberlawn. "Bobby hid the tools of the chauffeur because the chauffeur did not take him down the street to buy crayons," Rose wrote to Eunice. "Do not tell Bobby I said so, but I did not know if it was a very good idea to encourage. It seems that Bobby should have asked the chauffeur to get the crayons when he was passing the store coming home from school."

Eunice did not see everything but she did see time passing, as only parents can, as she watched her children grow. She saved hundreds of pages of penciled notes scribbled across her lifetime in spiral notebooks, on loose-leaf paper, on legal pads, and on random scraps of paper, most about professional meetings she chaired, dinner parties she attended, conversational gambits she tried to emulate, and advice from her father. She wrote little about her children. But one wrinkled scrap of paper, covered in Eunice's distinctive hen scratching, was an exception to the usual fare. Buried in a batch of news clippings in an uncatalogued box of personal papers, it captured the poignancy of a mother's recognition of the fleeting nature of childhood and a glimpse of how constant physical activity was the glue that bound Eunice to her children.

Under the heading "Bringing Up Children," she wrote: "There is a change with teenagers—Maria is 12, Bobby 13—that you just give them orders and make plans for them and make life pleasant for them. The fun and benefits of child & parent are to do things together that are fun; e.g. today, Maria and I went swimming & I pretended I was a porpoise & rode her all through the waves. We laughed and laughed. We went bike riding— Anthony, Mark & Maria & me at the lake front. Anthony still wants to stay with Mummy. Mark will go off with Maria & Tim, but not always. Today, went out on the boat with me & grandpa instead of going swimming. Easter egg hunting great fun for the children even without Easter."

At the Cape, as in Washington, her other children were never far from her thoughts. Plans to improve the next season of Camp Shriver began as soon as the last one ended, so there was always work to be done. Hers was not the first or the only such camp in America; parents had been hosting smaller backyard programs for a decade. But Eunice had larger ambitions than most camp directors. Of the approximately 230 day camps operating nationwide for the mentally retarded in 1962, few were under the auspices of a public agency. Eunice sought to change that.

What began at Timberlawn with approximately three dozen children in 1962 attracted more than a hundred campers in 1966. By then, six similar camps, seeded with grants from the Kennedy Foundation, had sprouted across Maryland and the District of Columbia. More popped up around the country after she brought municipal and state recreation officials and the wives of US senators to Timberlawn to show what these children could do if given the chance. She sent all her guests home with a promise that, if they designed similar camps in their own communities, the Kennedy Foundation would help fund them.

Her conviction that sports could build self-confidence in a mentally disabled child sprang not only from the anecdotal evidence unfolding in her backyard. As early as 1958, James N. Oliver had published results of his study in England demonstrating that exercise improved classroom performance for children with mental retardation. Eunice recruited him to be a consultant to Camp Shriver, as she did William H. Freeberg, whose work at Southern Illinois University focused on the physical education needs of the retarded, and Frank Hayden, a professor at Ontario's Western University, who researched sports and fitness activities for children with mental retardation. After Freeberg conducted a two-day conference presenting empirical data extolling the benefits of physical activity, the Kennedy Foundation hired him to train camp directors and municipal park workers around the country.

One of the first takers was the Chicago Park District, the oldest and one of the largest park networks in the United States.

In 1965 Anne McGlone was twenty-one years old, one of ten park workers from Chicago sent to Carbondale, Illinois, to learn from Freeberg, financed by a $10,000 grant from the Kennedy Foundation. "I had never even seen a retarded child, but I believed what Dr. Freeberg taught us: that every kid can learn to participate in sports and that by learning to swim or bowl, they will be able to enjoy being part of their families," she recalled almost fifty years later, when she was Justice Anne Burke of the Illinois Supreme Court. "He taught us how to adjust our teaching style but to have high expectations."

Working at West Pullman Park, the young Anne McGlone learned that "teaching retarded children isn't an 'Everybody-line-up-on-this-side' proposition. They are too active to stand still in a group. You can't even say, 'Form a circle,' because they don't know what a circle is." She improvised, recruiting as junior counselors the park bullies who teased her campers so that "they got invested in these kids, too." Word spread, and more parents brought their children to the park to play under Anne McGlone's supervision. In 1967, after she staged a production of *The Sound of Music*, McGlone was confirmed in her belief that these children had the potential to participate fully in all the rituals of childhood.

"Before I knew it, I had a hundred kids," she said. The play's success made her wonder what else her students could do to show off their skills. She asked Freeberg whether it was realistic to think they could compete in a citywide track meet. At his urging, she wrote a proposal for a track-and-field competition and submitted it to Eunice at the Kennedy Foundation for funding.

"The next thing I knew, we were going to Washington because she wanted to meet with us," Justice Burke remembered. For a young woman, not far removed from the classrooms of Maria High School and the tutelage of the Sisters of Saint Casimir, it was an intimidating prospect, meeting a member of America's royal family. But politics was central to her life. She was engaged to Edward M. Burke, the son of a Chicago alderman who would be elected to the same seat himself one day. She worked for a park system in which Mayor Richard J. Daley, a longtime Kennedy ally, took enormous pride.

Having read that Eunice wore Pierre Cardin dresses and had her hair styled by Kenneth, in Manhattan, she fretted as much about what she would wear as what she would say, an apprehension she could have spared herself had she known the lack of interest Eunice took in her appearance. "I remember I didn't have my glasses on at first, and I thought, 'Wow, she is pretty fashionable with those striped stockings,'" the justice said. "When I did put my glasses on, I realized those were runs, not stripes. I immediately relaxed. What a relief that she was just a regular person."

Eunice was not that, but she did recognize a good idea when she heard one. She had proposed something similar in a 1965 speech in Dallas, envisioning "a national tournament of athletic contests, among teams of mentally retarded children," and she had revisited the idea, using the identical language, a year later in a speech to the National Education Association in Washington. She suggested Chicago think bigger.

In the revised eleven-page proposal for a National Olympics for the Retarded that McGlone and Freeberg submitted to the Kennedy Foundation on January 26, 1968, they anticipated participation by five hundred athletes above the age of eight, mostly from Illinois, "in view of the fact that transportation will be difficult." The competition—a baseball throw, fifty-yard dash, hundred-yard dash, relay race, high jump, standing broad jump, swimming, and ice skating—would be held on a summer Saturday at historic Soldier Field on the Chicago lakefront. A temporary shallow pool and a small ice rink would be installed. Housing and meals would be provided for out-of-town participants and their chaperones. Lunch would be served to all athletes on the day of competition. A doctor, nurse, and ambulance would be on site. They calculated that the event would cost $28,250. Eunice gave them $25,000.

The money "came with strings," Justice Burke said. Eunice dispatched Frank Hayden from the foundation to Chicago to help organize the games, but his presence caused some tension with the Chicago Park District workers who thought this was their show. "He was a great help, but nothing was ever good enough or big enough. I was just a young woman. I was just trying to put a fun day together that would show what my kids could do," Justice Burke said. "My vision was never for national or international games. I didn't have the experience or the connections to think globally. She had bigger ideas."

By the time Eunice flew to Chicago to meet the press at Mayor Daley's office on March 29, 1968, the young park worker detected subtle changes in the program. It was now to be called the Chicago Special Olympics, a title that reassured her the Chicago Park District would retain pride of authorship. "It is our hope that the Chicago Special Olympics will stimulate more recreational programs and athletic competition for the retarded, not only in Illinois and throughout the Midwest but across the United States," Eunice told the news conference, echoing the objective spelled out in McGlone's original proposal.

The Kennedy name attracted attention: an event planned for five hundred drew almost a thousand athletes from twenty-three states and Canada, and a roster of celebrity coaches that included James Lovell, the astronaut; Jesse Owens, the Olympic track star; Rafer Johnson, the 1960 Olympic gold medalist in the decathlon; George Armstrong, the captain of the Toronto Maple Leafs; Stan Mikita, the center for the Chicago Blackhawks; Paul Hornung, the former Green Bay Packers halfback; boxing champion Joey Giardello; and Olympic figure skating champion Barbara Ann Scott.

The Daley machine scrambled to ensure that there would be enough box lunches for the athletes and enough beds at the LaSalle Hotel for all the participants and their guests. Daley's son, the future mayor Richard M. Daley, served as a driver, ferrying guests to and from the field.

Only a few hundred spectators were in the stands of the 61,500-seat stadium when seventeen-year-old Philip Weber carried the Special Olympics torch into Soldier Field to light the forty-foot Flame of Hope. Eunice would say years later, when Special Olympics regularly drew capacity crowds, that most parents in 1968 had not yet learned to be proud of these children.

The US Navy Band led the parade of athletes onto the field, where hundreds of blue and yellow balloons with their names attached were released. "The Chicago Special Olympics prove a very fundamental fact," Eunice told the crowd. "The fact that exceptional children—retarded children—can be exceptional athletes. The fact that through sports they can realize their potential for growth."

It was what she said moments later that shocked the Chicago Park District organizers. "I wish to announce a national Special Olympic training program for all mentally retarded children everywhere," Eunice said. "I also announce that in 1969 the Kennedy Foundation will pledge sufficient funds to underwrite five regional Olympic tryouts . . . the winners of those trial meets, and of hundreds of others like them, will participate in another International Special Olympics in 1970 and every two years thereafter."

It was the first her Chicago partners had heard of her plan, and they felt blindsided. But in truth, it was less hostile takeover than excited impulse on Eunice's part. By her quick calculation, there were one and a half million other mentally retarded children all over America who should have access to games like those unfolding in Soldier Field. "I decided out there in Chicago that we should have every state do this sort of sports event every year," she said, oblivious to the anger her presumption engendered in those who felt a proprietary interest in the idea, having worked so hard to stage those first games.

"She didn't think about people's feelings if it moved her closer to her goal," Burke said. "Everyone in Chicago admires what she did; just don't get up in Chicago and say Eunice Kennedy Shriver started the games. The Chicago Park District did that."

Tact was not one of Eunice's virtues, but ideas are also slippery things; they won't easily be owned. Vice President Hubert H. Humphrey might have felt similar dismay reading that the idea for the Peace Corps originated with John F. Kennedy. Hadn't Humphrey introduced a bill for a "Peace Corps" to send "young men to assist the peoples of the underdeveloped areas of the world to combat poverty, disease, illiteracy, and hunger" in June 1960, four months before JFK floated the same idea in a speech at the University of Michigan? Hadn't he first introduced Peace Corps legislation as a senator from Minnesota in 1957 and 1958? Hadn't Congressman Henry S. Reuss of Wisconsin proposed a comparable "Point Four Youth Corps" in 1959?

Timing matters in politics. In 1957 "many senators, including liberal ones, thought it silly and an unworkable idea," Humphrey wrote in his autobiography. In 1961, "with a young president urging its passage, it became possible, and we pushed it rapidly through the Senate."

Justice Burke eventually came to the same conclusion, but she donated her correspondence with Eunice and the Kennedy Foundation about the "National Olympics for Retarded Children" to the Chicago History Museum. And in 1995 she had their contents inserted into the *Congressional Record* to make certain the role of the Chicago Park District in the origins of Special Olympics would never be erased.

Who thought of what when turned out to be less important than what happened in Soldier Field that summer Saturday. Six hundred athletes went home with medals, and an idea, whatever its origin, was made manifest on the playing field. "Here were people who weren't getting all the help they could, and yet as a group they had accomplished so much. It really hooked me," Rafer Johnson said after witnessing the first games. "I know you can't get where you want without interest from other people, so I just jumped right in. I wanted to help Special Olympics grow."

Mayor Daley saw something more. Turning to Eunice on the reviewing stand that day, he said, "You know, Eunice, the world will never be the same after this."

TEN

AN AMERICAN IN PARIS

If couples want to limit their families, they should know how to do so, in accordance with the dictates of their conscience. But they should not be forced—by either government programs or social pressure—to follow any particular course.

—EUNICE KENNEDY SHRIVER, 1965

THE TRIUMPH IN Soldier Field came at a turbulent time in American politics, in the middle of a traumatic year that tested the nation's faith in its leaders and in itself.

Robert F. Kennedy began 1968 as he had ended 1967, debating whether to challenge a sitting Democratic president over his escalation of the war in Vietnam. Opposition to the war was mounting, fueled by televised scenes of clashes in the streets of Saigon in late January and early February after North Vietnamese troops rolled through US and South Vietnamese forces during the Tet Offensive.

On March 16, four days after Minnesota senator Eugene McCarthy exposed President Johnson's vulnerability with a strong showing in the New Hampshire primary, Bobby entered the presidential race. He declared his candidacy from the same Senate Caucus Room where Jack had initiated his own. Two weeks later, LBJ announced he would not seek reelection.

Suddenly the notion of a Kennedy restoration sounded less implausible. No one was more excited by the prospect than Eunice, but there were complications. Before abandoning his reelection bid, Johnson had flirted again with the idea of Sargent Shriver as his running mate. Sarge was better known in 1968 than he had been in 1964, with a burnished reputation for steering the antipoverty program through rocky political and fiscal shoals as Vietnam siphoned off more and more of the federal budget. But the threat of an RFK candidacy loomed even larger for Johnson. If Bobby did run, Johnson did not want his savvy Office of Economic Opportunity director on his nemesis's campaign team. Before Bobby entered the race, the president asked Sarge to become his ambassador to France.

"LBJ was tickled that he could hold a Kennedy brother-in-law out of the race," according to Joseph A. Califano Jr., the president's top domestic advisor. "To him, the appointment of Shriver as ambassador to France was made in heaven."

Donald Dell, a lawyer and former professional tennis player who had resigned his post at the Office of Economic Opportunity to work for Bobby's campaign, drove out to Timberlawn to get Sarge to change his mind. Eunice arrived home when he was in midpitch. "We are going to Paris as the ambassadors," she told Dell, a close friend and Mark's godfather, as well as her husband's former colleague.

Bill Blair, the Shrivers' friend from Chicago, got pressure from Eunice's sisters. "It was Jean and Pat who called me and said, 'Please talk him out of it. He ought to stay here and work in Indiana for Bobby.' They pleaded with me, and I said, 'No, he is entitled to his own life.' And Eunice was supporting him; she was all for him going," Blair said. "There was always a tension there. Bobby was always the one they were concerned about. There was always some jealousy of Sarge coming into his own."

The tension between Sarge and Bobby dated back more than a decade, from Bobby's time working for Senator Joseph McCarthy on the Senate's Permanent Subcommittee on Investigations. Sarge's contempt for the Wisconsin Republican's reckless anti-Communist crusade led Bobby in the 1950s to dismiss his brother-in-law as a liberal Boy Scout and the family's house Communist.

Some of Bobby's advisors resented the Shrivers' decision, but, Ethel Kennedy insisted, she and Bobby understood. "He's smart. He's imaginative. He's energetic. He gets along with people," Ethel recalled thinking. What better qualities were there for an ambassador?

The Shrivers were due in Paris in May. Should Sarge abandon his
pledge to Johnson and stay to help Bobby? Could he defend as US ambassador Vietnam policies his brother-in-law would be denouncing on
the campaign trail? Would Eunice remain at home to campaign for her
brother or go to Paris to support her husband?

Sarge himself was unsure of some of those answers, telling the Senate
Foreign Relations Committee he could not say what he would do if Eunice
pressed him to come back to help her brother. "That's an iffy question,"
he answered. "It depends on what happens—on what she feels, what the
[State] department feels, what I think."

Eunice had no such ambivalence. She would campaign for Bobby in
April in Indiana and join Sarge in May in Paris, where peace talks between the United States and North Vietnam were set to begin. If contradictions were inherent in that choice, it was immaterial to Eunice, for
whom loyalty would always trump consistency.

She and Bobby were not as close as she and Jack had been, although
their families often vacationed together, skiing at Waterville Valley Resort
in New Hampshire, deep-sea salmon fishing in the Pacific Northwest, and
white-water rafting down the Colorado River. There was, perhaps, some
envy of the relationship her younger brother had forged with Jack, first
as manager of his campaigns and then as his closest advisor in the White
House. Those were roles she might have played herself had they not been
foreclosed to her as a woman.

Eunice had less sway with Bobby than she had had with Jack, as well.
Bobby "deferred to her on family matters, but he never consulted her on
policy," according to Frank Mankiewicz, his press secretary. He did not
ask her to review his speeches, as Jack had done, or seek her advice on legislation. Jack and Bobby were "two completely different human beings,"
she said once. "All this business about Jack and Bobby being blood brothers has been exaggerated."

But as much as Eunice had revered Jack—with whom she shared
both a love of politics and a life of chronic illness—her personality more
closely resembled Bobby's. Jack was charming, a born leader; Bobby was
tough, more dogged worker than natural politician. And it was with
Bobby that Eunice shared a well of moral outrage when confronted with
social injustice.

In 1965 Bobby reacted just as Eunice had years before on her first visits
to institutions housing those with mental retardation. On an unannounced

stop at the Willowbrook State School, a facility on Staten Island, New York, the senator saw residents "living in filth and dirt, their clothing in rags, in rooms less comfortable and cheerful than the cages in which we put animals in a zoo." He described the place as a "snake pit," and his outrage prompted the state to initiate a five-year-improvement plan, one that was never fully realized in the twenty-two years before Willowbrook finally closed in 1987—a symbol of society's indifference to its most vulnerable members.

Bobby's impatience—with Willowbrook, with racial inequality, with the carnage in Vietnam—sprang from that same sense of urgency that, in the 1960s, was driving young people into the streets to protest. "Older people say, 'We're getting things done.' That's the way older people want it to be," Eunice told reporters covering Bobby's campaign. "Look at history. When a young man speaks for a whole new position, his ideas are unrecognized. I think they will understand in about twenty-five years what he is talking about, what young people are talking about today. These ideas will be in vogue then. Whether Bobby wins or not, and I believe he will, someone has to recognize this consensus, this generation."

But Eunice herself was not entirely comfortable with the generational changes unfolding in the sixties, a decade that was looking markedly different at its end from how it had at its beginning. Along with the expansion of civil rights and overdue attention to pressing social issues came a breakdown in the established order: a diminution of the family as the foundational unit of society and an embrace of casual sex and recreational drugs that she thought alarming. The availability of oral contraceptives had accelerated changing views of both sexual mores and motherhood. If she found the traditional role of wife and mother limiting, and her vigorous public endeavors confirm that she did, she was unsettled by an emerging feminist alternative that did not place motherhood at the heart of a woman's life.

The centrality of motherhood for Eunice was less a reflection of her experience than an expression of her Catholic faith. It was Mary she strove to emulate, not Rose. Her lifelong devotion to Mary of Nazareth was grounded in her belief that the divine grace that elevated a simple teenage girl to become the mother of Jesus was accessible to all who opened themselves in faith and in love, as Mary had, to being an instrument of God's will on earth. Eunice would have agreed with Rose, who said once that when she held an infant in her arms for the first time, "I used to think that what I said and did to him could have an influence not only on him but on all whom he met, not only for a day or a month or a year but for all eternity—a very challenging and exciting thought for a mother."

Eunice's vision of Mary transcended that traditional idea of motherhood, however. "She talked about Mary as a refugee, as an unwed mother, as a widow, as the mother of a felon. Mary as an undocumented alien in Egypt," recalled the Reverend Richard Fragomeni of the Shrine of Our Lady of Pompeii in Chicago, a family friend who served as a consultant on *Mary, Mother of Jesus*, a made-for-TV movie about the Blessed Virgin that Eunice and Bobby Shriver produced in 1999. "Mary isn't just some statuary. She is engaged in the pain of life."

Engaged and conscious of her second-class status as a woman, Eunice might have added. The Reverend Donald MacMillan, the Catholic chaplain at Boston College, was taken aback by a question Eunice posed after he celebrated Mass one summer Sunday at Our Lady of Victory Church in Centerville, Massachusetts, one of the two churches Eunice frequented on Cape Cod. "How do you think the Blessed Mother felt at that Marriage at Cana when Jesus just looked at her and said, 'Woman, do this'?" she asked Father MacMillan. "Well, it's a translation," he replied carefully. "The way we hear it in English may not be the way she heard it in Aramaic."

Mary Cunningham Agee, a business executive who shared Eunice's faith and friendship, thinks the thirty-four depictions of the Madonna that Eunice displayed in her home "[say] something about her love of the image of mother and child that cuts across all religions. The depth of her faith as it relates to the Blessed Mother is that there is a universality about the maternal instinct that will save the planet, that would save the world. It isn't intellectual. It's deeply emotional."

Like the Catholic Church itself in the 1960s, Eunice was trying to reconcile an ancient faith with a modern, secular culture that was challenging basic assumptions about the role of women and the nature of life. Why couldn't there be altar girls as well as altar boys? Why did nuns not have policy-making roles in the Vatican? Why were only men, not women, allowed to be priests and deacons? She was already asking those questions in 1962 when the reform-minded Pope John XXIII convened the Second Vatican Council.

"When women were not given much space, she was determined she was going to have space," said the Reverend J. Bryan Hehir, professor of the Practice of Religion and Public Life at Harvard and secretary for health care and social services in the Archdiocese of Boston. "She had the faith of her mother, but she was not going to play the role of her mother; that's for sure. She was going to do it a different way." Eunice was, in the words of her daughter, Maria, a "maternal feminist."

As early as 1964, when Ted and Bobby were both running for the US Senate, she and Sarge invited a group of Catholic theologians to meet with all of them in Hyannis Port to discuss the morality and meaning of abortion. It was not an idle inquiry. Efforts were gathering steam in state legislatures across the country to decriminalize nineteenth-century abortion laws in the name of public health. Estimates of the number of illegal abortions performed in the United States ranged widely from 200,000 to 1.2 million—medical societies put the best estimate at 1 million—but even the smaller number indicated a serious national health challenge.

Scholars at the American Law Institute in 1962 had drafted a template to revise criminal statutes to permit abortion if a physician believed "there is substantial risk that continuance of the pregnancy would gravely impair the physical or mental health of the mother, or that the child would be born with grave physical or mental defect, or that the pregnancy resulted from rape, incest, or other felonious intercourse."

While the theologians meeting in Hyannis Port agreed that abortion was immoral, they were divided about whether endorsing government regulation of the procedure amounted to approval of abortion in certain circumstances. Abortion was a sin, but should it be a crime? Neither Bobby nor Ted stayed long at that meeting—Mankiewicz said abortion was not on RFK's radar in 1964—but the questions raised by the theologians would influence Eunice and Sarge through decades of legal and legislative battles to come.

The Reverend Richard A. McCormick, a Jesuit theologian who attended that session on Cape Cod, later described abortion as "morally problematic, pastorally delicate, legislatively thorny, constitutionally insecure, ecumenically divisive, medically normless, humanly anguishing, racially provocative, journalistically abused, personally biased, and widely performed." His opposition did not preclude that acknowledgment of the complexities of the issue.

Eunice's interest in women's reproductive choices were shaped as much by her work and experience as her religion. She had exposed herself to the struggles of incarcerated mothers in federal prison and pregnant girls in juvenile detention, and, in doing so, had broadened her world-view. By the midsixties, she was no longer the sanctimonious young woman who in 1951 had written to editors of *Reader's Digest* to protest publication of "a laudatory account of the life of Margaret Sanger," the founder of the nation's first birth control clinic. Perhaps, Eunice had written then, the editors should commission an article "based on our Lord as the 'Father of self-control and self-control clinics.' Christ when faced by beggars and middle eastern slum conditions worse than anything Margaret Sanger ever saw did not dispense prophylactics but penance. Penance raises the spirit, and Christ knew that the development of the spirit was the only way to free man from slavery to the body. That's why Catholics oppose birth control and plug for purity and continence. The latter develop self-control, elevate the mind to spiritual matters, and, by increasing man's control over his body, permit him to free his mind and soul from slavery."

By 1965, Eunice considered birth control a private matter. Writing in *McCall's* magazine three months before the US Supreme Court declared unconstitutional a Connecticut law that banned the use of contraceptives by married couples, she all but anticipated its ruling. "If couples want to limit their families, they should know how to do so, in accordance with the dictates of their conscience," Eunice wrote. "But they should not be forced—by either government programs or social pressure—to follow any particular course."

Her motivation was exactly the opposite of those who had challenged the Connecticut statute in *Griswold v. Connecticut*, but the effect was the same. Estelle Griswold, the executive director of the Planned Parenthood League of Connecticut, wanted the government out of the bedroom so that women could limit the size of their families. Eunice wanted the government out of the bedroom so that women could have as many children as they wanted.

It was preposterous, she told a Georgetown University audience, for increasingly vocal advocates of population control to attribute the country's social ills to family size. "With drug stores full of contraceptive devices, limiting the population is no challenge. If poor people had fewer children, would it really solve the problem? Isn't that the easy way out of the problems of slum relief and the problems of despair and unemployment?" she asked. Those were provocative questions that resonated as much with liberal activists as with conservative Catholics in the sixties.

"Ours is not a problem of scarcity. It is a problem of lack of will and lack of distribution. We live amid plenty if we could only bring it forth," she said. "The real challenge is to mobilize our resources, to use them more fully, to spread them to all who deserve them, whether it is two hundred million or three hundred million or even more."

For Eunice, the deserving included those likely to be born with mental retardation, a population she feared would be targeted for abortion if the procedure was decriminalized. Why were policy makers rushing to relax the nation's abortion laws instead of strengthening the social safety net to support mothers with low incomes and mothers with disabled children? In one of the odder philosophical alignments of the era, Black Power activists agreed with that argument, likening government advocacy of birth control and abortion to promotion of "black genocide."

"She would say, 'You mark my words, in ten years we are going to have liberal abortion bills,' and she was so upset about it," Ethel Kennedy recalled.

Eunice was not unaware of the often tragic circumstances that led women to seek abortions. She visited England when she was a consultant to the President's Panel on Mental Retardation early in the decade and saw babies born with deformed or missing limbs to women who had taken a sleeping pill during their pregnancies that contained the drug thalidomide. At her urging, President Kennedy had appealed to Americans to empty their medicine chests of pills secured from foreign pharmacies— thalidomide was widely available in Europe but had not been approved for use in the United States. She was mindful, too, of the rubella pandemic between 1962 and 1965 in Europe and America that had led to the births of tens of thousands of babies with blindness, deafness, heart defects, or mental retardation.

Eunice's moral opposition to abortion was steadfast, but she was not without sympathy for women in dire situations, Ethel Kennedy insisted. "If you talk to some poor overworked mothers and find out that they have to have another child and they just can't do it. They barely can feed the ones they have. Life isn't easy all the time. I can't bear saying this because it sounds so trite, but in the midst of all her own pain—and I think she was always in pain—she was able to feel other people's pain," Ethel said of Eunice.

In endorsing the use of contraceptives as "a matter of conscience," Eunice was reflecting the thinking of most Catholics. Pope John XXIII had established a commission in 1962 to review the Church's prohibition on the use of artificial methods of birth control. His successor, Pope Paul VI, expanded the panel to fifty-eight cardinals, bishops, scientists, lay people, and theologians, including Protestants. In its preliminary report, in 1966, the panel overwhelmingly recommended lifting the ban on birth control. But dissenting bishops and priests on the commission convinced Pope Paul VI to keep the ban in place. In July 1968 he issued the encyclical *Humanae Vitae* (*On Human Life*), reaffirming the prohibition on contraception, a directive widely ignored then and now by a majority of American Catholics.

Adoption by Colorado, California, and North Carolina of less restrictive abortion laws in 1967, and plans by twenty-eight other legislatures to consider similar changes based on the American Law Institute model statute, heightened Eunice's desire for more clarity on the issue. In February Bobby Kennedy had endorsed the idea of decriminalizing New York's law, which allowed abortion only if a woman's life was in jeopardy. He did so despite a pastoral letter issued by the eight Catholic bishops of New York calling on Catholics to use "all their power" to oppose those efforts as "a new slaughter of the innocents." In June the American Medical Association dropped its long-standing opposition to abortion, adopting a resolution that endorsed its use to preserve the life or health of the mother, to avoid the birth of a baby with an incapacitating physical deformity or mental deficiency, and in cases of rape or incest.

The heightened activity prompted Eunice to ask the Harvard Divinity School to partner with the Kennedy Foundation to sponsor what they called the First International Conference on Abortion. The three-day symposium would meet in the nation's capital at the Washington Hilton Hotel during the first week in September.

The interdisciplinary conference was another expansion of the mission of the Kennedy Foundation. From building schools and hospitals, to funding scientific research, to developing recreational programs, Eunice went where her instincts and the needs of children with mental retardation led her. Advances in medicine were making it possible to find fetal defects in earlier stages of pregnancy, Eunice knew, "but at the same time, just as new tests are developed to discover these defects of the fetus in utero, work is going on in research laboratories around the world seeking ways to repair or prevent those defects before the baby is born." She feared the law would move faster than the research.

The seventy-three participants at the invitation-only conference included doctors, lawyers, judges, philosophers, ethicists, biologists, social scientists, educators, clergymen, and theologians of many denominations. Americans dominated. Men outnumbered women. Oregon senator Mark O. Hatfield and philanthropist John D. Rockefeller III, who was interested in population control, were there. So were US Supreme Court Justices Abe Fortas and Potter Stewart and US Solicitor General Erwin N. Griswold. Radcliffe College president Mary Bunting and Notre Dame University president the Reverend Theodore Hesburgh attended. So did Norman St John-Stevas, a Conservative member of the British Parliament. TV journalists Eunice trusted—Barbara Walters and Frank McGee—were there, too.

Much of the conference wrestled with philosophical questions about when life begins and legal and medical arguments about the appropriate role of lawmakers and the courts in personal decisions about reproduction. There were two women on a fifteen-member panel exploring the medical implications of abortion. There were no women on the fourteen-member panel examining the ethics of abortion, and none on the panel, which included US Supreme Court Associate Justice Potter Stewart, exploring the legal ramifications of the issue.

The *New York Times* praised the organizers for having "made a contribution to rational, healthy discussion in an area of human decision too long ruled by emotional and religious prejudices." But the National Organization for Women dismissed the forum as a "smokescreen" by religious leaders with "the most reactionary opposition to abortion reform." Noting how few women participated, Ti-Grace Atkinson of the New York chapter of NOW said the conference "amounted to an erudite panel of dogs discussing the nature of cats."

Eunice knew that, whatever the law might say, the decision to abort or to carry a pregnancy to term would always come down to the woman— and Eunice was not interested in hectoring her. She said as much in the dedication to *The Terrible Choice: The Abortion Dilemma*, a compilation of the proceedings of the Washington conference that was published in 1968. She dedicated the book "to all mothers to be or in being." To them, she wrote, "Doctors may advise you, ministers or priests or rabbis may counsel you, lawyers may tell you your rights; but—when the advisors have finished and gone their ways, only you, the mother, will make the final decision on abortion. Pray God that your decision be wise and honest and just and loving—and may this book help you in your moment of truth."

Pearl Buck, the Nobel Prize–winning author and the mother of a daughter with mental retardation, wrote the introduction to the book, at Eunice's request. "I had firm views on the subject, and I was pleased that she did not ask me what those views were," Buck recalled. "I assumed that as a Roman Catholic she would probably not approve of abortions, but, I, too, did not inquire. I was happy to do what she asked me to do. As it happened, we were in agreement, although I felt she would have accepted disagreement, honest soul that she is."

Eunice had walked past the daily protests that Lana Clarke Phelan and others from the California-based Association to Repeal Abortion Laws had staged outside the Washington Hilton, carrying signs that said "End Butchery" and placards that displayed the knitting needles and coat hangers that would become enduring symbols of illegal abortion. Still, she had been shocked to read that while Arthur J. Goldberg, the US representative to the United Nations, was delivering final remarks in the Hilton ballroom, the protesters were holding a class across town on self-induced abortion. This was a form of political activism beyond Eunice's experience or imagining.

As much as she would miss the excitement of Bobby's campaign, so much of the social unrest roiling the country was beyond her understanding. Maybe 1968 was not the worst time to move abroad. At Sarge's farewell party that April, skits performed by his OEO colleagues poked gentle fun at Eunice's dilemma. "My Bobby lies over the ocean, my Bobby lies over the sea / Oh, how can I campaign for Bobby, when Bobby is so far from me," they sang.

"Of course," she wished she could play a more extended role in her brother's campaign, she told the *Washington Post*. "But what Mr. Shriver is doing is important, too. He will be working on problems that bear on international peace. You certainly cannot have peace [in Vietnam] without France." Just as significant to Eunice was that Sarge had given Johnson his word. "He made his commitment, a very firm one, to the president before Bobby announced. We think it is a great opportunity," she said.

Rose had urged them to go to Paris. Remembering her own star turn as the wife of a US ambassador in London, she told Eunice and Sarge the experience would be exciting for them and broadening for the children. Eunice would need to dress better and to work harder on her French pronunciation, especially of the word "Versailles," which, Rose said, Eunice mangled regularly. "I mean these criticisms always to be constructive, and

I know that you are using the word so often, so you will want to have a perfect accent," Rose wrote. "Also be sure to pronounce *Champs-Élysées* correctly."

Appearances simply did not matter to Eunice the way they did to Rose, according to her friend Deeda Blair, herself a fashion icon who appeared annually on lists of the best-dressed women in the world. "She would say, 'My mother came home again and said, "Why can't you be like Deeda and wear fine clothes and have your hair done?"'' That just wasn't Eunice; she just didn't think about things like that. She had to when she was in Paris, but it didn't last long thereafter. Some of her costumes were beyond belief. Somebody would have given an embroidered sweater with glitter on it, and she'd pair it with some old pants that were torn. She'd sometimes get herself together if she had to make a speech. But it was just a matter of total indifference to her. Her mother cared passionately. Pat was well dressed because she lived in Hollywood. Jean was neatly dressed, but not memorable. Maybe it was a reaction. Why spend your time doing that? It's not lasting or important."

No detail was too small to escape Rose's attention, however. In a note informing Eunice that she had ordered her two pairs of white nylon gloves from Bonwit Teller for her to wear with her suits and coats, Rose instructed her daughter that "they are supposed to be worn a little wrinkled rather than perfectly straight." If Eunice remembered to wear the gloves at all, she was unlikely to have paid much attention to how they were meant to be worn. She preferred comfort to style. Her husband knew as much, reminding Rose that "we have made a deal. You're to be on hand in Paris for at least the first month to get things organized. I don't want that fancy china on the table with the wrong tablecloth or flowers, and somebody has got to organize the counting of the sheets and pillowcases."

Sarge would need his own talents to warm the chilly relationship that existed between France and the United States in 1968. Since his election as president of the Fifth Republic in 1959, Charles de Gaulle had sought a Europe independent of American influence. Shriver's predecessor, Charles "Chip" Bohlen, had warned Sarge he could expect to be ignored by Élysée Palace. De Gaulle was an outspoken critic of US intervention in Vietnam, urging the Johnson administration as early as 1964 to withdraw its troops from the former French colony embroiled in what France now, belatedly, saw as civil war between the Communist North and the US-backed South. De Gaulle, Sarge hoped, would see the peace talks about to begin as a promising sign that the United States was retreating from its misadventure in Southeast Asia, as France had done in 1954, leading to a thaw in relations.

For her part, Eunice was as good as her word, giving Bobby the month of April before joining Sarge in Paris come May. She travelled with Ethel on a four-day swing through Indiana that her sister-in-law remembers most for the contents of Eunice's luggage. "We were in Indianapolis, campaigning, and Eunice had this huge suitcase, really big, and I put it up on the luggage rack at the hotel, and I said, 'Eunice what did you pack?' and she said, 'I don't know. I just threw it in.' I unzip it, and there was a nightgown and a slip and a pair of stockings in this enormous suitcase!"

Eunice wore the same dress for four days, but she opened a campaign office in Fort Wayne, hosted a tea in Lafayette, and visited a sorority at Purdue University. She was impressed by the students' concern about the war, urban renewal, and civil rights, but she had a question for the women of Pi Beta Phi house: "Why aren't there any Negro members in the sorority?" There was some stammering in response. "They said, 'Well, there are only four hundred Negroes in an enrollment of twenty thousand' and that Negroes didn't want to belong. But they didn't really have an answer," Eunice said.

Race was on her mind, as it was on everyone's that spring. On April 4 the Reverend Dr. Martin Luther King Jr. had been gunned down in Memphis, where the civil rights leader had gone to support the city's striking sanitation workers. King's assassination unleashed a wave of violent protests in more than a hundred cities across the nation. Indianapolis had remained calm, perhaps because of an emotional appeal by Bobby Kennedy on the night of King's murder. From the back of a flatbed truck, he shared with a black audience the news he had just learned. There was an audible gasp when he told the gathering that King had been shot and killed.

"For those of you who are black and are tempted to be filled with hatred and mistrust of the injustice of such an act, against all white people, I would only say that I can also feel in my own heart the same kind of feeling. I had a member of my family killed, but he was killed by a white man," Bobby told the crowd.

Indianapolis did not riot, but the "violence and lawlessness" Bobby decried that night were becoming the stuff of daily newspaper headlines, generated as often on college campuses as in urban slums. On April 30 the New York City police used tear gas and nightsticks to clear academic buildings seized by Columbia University students protesting the Vietnam War and the university's plans to build a gymnasium in a neighborhood park. Scores were injured in the melee and more than seven hundred arrested.

Sarge encountered an even more radical spirit when he arrived in Paris, where students, in full revolt, on makeshift barricades in the streets surrounding the Sorbonne, were joined by unionists who had called a general strike in solidarity. Marches and skirmishes with police continued for two weeks, until de Gaulle announced new elections and hinted that he would use the military, if necessary, to restore order.

In the United States, an inchoate rage as the war dragged on coexisted with a more restrained antiwar movement that hoped, through the campaigns of Eugene McCarthy and Bobby Kennedy, to bend the political system to its will. Activists who cut their hair and shaved their beards to "get clean for Gene" and students who left school to knock on doors in Oregon for Bobby wanted to win the White House, not burn it down. A similar tension coursed through the civil rights movement, with King's philosophy of passive resistance and civil disobedience under challenge by the more militant Black Panthers.

There was an electrical charge in the atmosphere that spring, a sense of possibility—but also of dread—that anything could happen. On June 5, in Los Angeles, it did.

Bobby had just beaten McCarthy in the Democratic primary in the most populous state in the nation. Addressing a cheering throng of supporters in the ballroom of the Ambassador Hotel, Bobby vowed to press on to the Democratic Party's nominating convention, in late August. "Now it's on to Chicago, and let's win there," he said.

Minutes later, as Robert F. Kennedy walked through the hotel kitchen on his way to a waiting press conference, a twenty-four-year-old Palestinian named Sirhan Sirhan, aggrieved by the candidate's support for Israel, stepped from the shadows and fired multiple rounds from a .22-caliber revolver, striking Bobby in the head and neck. He died twenty-five hours later.

Eunice was in Paris entertaining Ted's wife, Joan, at the ambassador's residence when the call came. There were prayers, not tears. "We sat in the house, saying rosary after rosary after rosary," Timothy Shriver, then nine, recalled.

Joan Kennedy and the Shrivers arrived at New York's LaGuardia Airport in time to meet the plane carrying the body of Robert F. Kennedy home for a solemn high requiem mass at St. Patrick's Cathedral and burial alongside his brother in Arlington National Cemetery. Aides to Bobby shoved Sarge aside when he tried to help move the coffin to a waiting hearse, as if his perceived political slight of RFK pertained in any way to the larger injustice confronting them all on that airport tarmac.

The family would move forward from Bobby's death with the same resolve it had shown less than five years earlier when it was Jack the Kennedys had been left to mourn. It was not stoicism that got them through, Ethel said; it was faith. The family was secure in the belief that there is a heaven and that the brothers had reunited there, with Joe Jr., with Kick, and with everyone who had gone before. Ethel, pregnant with her eleventh child, displayed a grace that was inexplicable to those without comparable faith. Eunice showed the same calm. "She was happy for her family in heaven; she was so cheerful because she knew that there was another life," Ethel said of the faith the sisters-in-law shared even in the depths of their grief that awful summer.

In the essay she contributed to a private collection of family remembrances of Bobby, Eunice could have been describing herself as well as her younger brother: "He grew out slowly. He was a lonely, very sensitive, and restless youngster . . . his brothers had so many talents, people were always telling Bobby how exceptional his brothers were. One had such a sharp wit, charm, and intellectual ability; another was so handsome and vigorous, all the women adored him; another was a fine athlete with an extraordinary disposition, making everyone laugh and feel gay with life. Later, when Bobby grew up, he always felt close to those who were not outstanding and talented, who were unpraised or a little ignored." The same might have been said of Eunice.

In Ethel, Bobby had found a partner who valued him as his family had not, Eunice wrote. "[A]ll the love and appreciation for which she seemed to have an infinite capacity came pouring down on him forever after. He blossomed. Ethel told everyone he was the best, the finest, the smartest at everything." Eunice could have written the same words about Sarge's devotion to her.

Her faith and Sarge's support explain how a smiling Eunice could mount the reviewing stand in Soldier Field and preside over the first Chicago Special Olympics only six weeks after Bobby's death. "As she crisscrossed the Atlantic Ocean, she must have experienced joy and excitement and great sadness," marveled her son Mark. He could only guess; she never talked about it.

She tapped into the grief Bobby's campaign workers were feeling as well, urging them to come to Chicago and redirect their pain in service of others. Scores answered her call, including Rafer Johnson, who had helped subdue Sirhan Sirhan in that hotel kitchen. "I was just shattered. I was lost like everyone else," the 1960 decathlon champion said of the weeks after the assassination. Answering Eunice's summons? "That was my return to a life," he said, a life Johnson would spend devoted to the athletes of Special Olympics.

Sarge had flown from Paris to Chicago with Eunice for the games and was as surprised as anyone at the impressive display of athleticism on the field. "I was the original number one skeptic of Special Olympics. I didn't believe it would ever work," he conceded.

But work it did, and Eunice carried the success at Soldier Field back to Paris, where she set out to upend French ideas about what children with mental retardation could do. She had natural allies in de Gaulle and his wife, Yvonne. Their daughter, Anne, had been born with Down syndrome in 1928. Despite physical disabilities that made it difficult for her to walk, Anne had lived her entire life at home with her family, though largely out of public view. She died, at twenty, of pneumonia, and in her memory, her parents opened the Château de Vert-Cœur, a private facility for girls with disabilities, near Versailles. De Gaulle credited Anne with saving his life from a would-be assassin in 1962, when a bullet meant for him was deflected by the metal frame that held a photograph of his daughter he carried with him always.

Just as she had on her Maryland farm, Eunice opened her home to children with mental retardation from local institutions. But home now was the ambassador's residence, an imposing stone mansion on the Avenue d'Iéna, in the Sixteenth Arrondissement, more typically the setting for formal teas and diplomatic soirees. Now, inside the iron gates, visiting dignitaries encountered a pile of bicycles by the guard shack, an American station wagon on the cobblestone driveway, and black truck tires scattered across the marble foyer as part of an obstacle course to strengthen the coordination of mentally retarded children. Outside, the once-manicured lawn had been transformed into a badminton court and play space for two of the family dogs, Shamrock and Lassie, that made the trip to Paris with the family. A well-used trampoline dominated a corner of the garden under a shade tree.

Several members of the household staff quit in protest of the chaos, but the Shrivers had brought more compatible help from home. Richard Ragsdale, the chauffeur and jack-of-all-trades known as "Rags," came from Timberlawn with his wife and daughter. The Shrivers engaged a series of governesses for the four children who had accompanied them to Paris. Fourteen-year-old Bobby arrived after finishing up his school year at Landon, in Bethesda. He would later enroll at Phillips Exeter Academy, the elite boarding school in New Hampshire.

There was some "private seething among State Department personnel" when four new positions were added to the embassy staff at a time when other diplomatic outposts were cutting personnel, according to the *Washington Star*'s society columnist Betty Beale. "My wife is a very active person," Sarge explained of Eunice's need for her own bilingual foreign service officer.

Eunice taught physical education every Monday at the External Médico-Pédagogique, a nearby institution for the mentally retarded, using techniques taught to her by Frank Hayden, now the director of physical education and recreation at the Kennedy Foundation. She had brought her own equipment to Paris: two chinning bars, three softballs, twelve two-by-four blocks for marking relay courses, a hundred-foot cloth tape for measuring fields, a hundred-foot rope for jumping, masking tape, a yardstick, and a stopwatch. In addition to teaching the children calisthenics, she led regular discussion groups at the ambassador's residence for their teachers and parents with invited experts who explained the latest genetic research and the therapeutic value of sports.

It was an unusual role for the wife of an American envoy, especially in a country that did not share the US penchant for volunteerism. The French had been aware of this peculiar American proclivity since at least 1835, when Alexis de Tocqueville, in *Democracy in America*, described the proliferation of civic associations he encountered in touring the United States. The idea of volunteerism remained a foreign concept when the Shrivers arrived in Paris in 1968.

Eunice proposed to change that by recruiting French teenagers to work in facilities for mentally retarded children. She encountered immediate resistance from the unions, which saw in her plan a scheme to deprive workers of paid employment, and from the larger society, which still stigmatized these children as hopeless cases. She began slowly, demonstrating to balky administrators what could be done, with a dozen American college students volunteering one or two days a week at their institutions during a junior year studying in Paris. Soon the value of an extra pair of hands became evident, as volunteers assisted children in the swimming pool, on the jungle gym, or on the swings.

In less than a year, the number of volunteers grew to more than one hundred, in more than twenty-five institutions or recreational centers in and around Paris. The majority were French. Ellen Varmus worked for two years with Eunice from a desk in the ambassador's residence to establish this Franco-American corps. It was a demanding but inspiring job for the Wellesley College graduate, who had completed a tour with the Peace Corps in Niger, where she and another volunteer had worked in a small health program designed to reduce infant mortality in the villages near Lake Chad. The hours were just as long in Paris, and the sense of mission as pronounced.

Varmus did not share the annoyance of some of the governesses and other assistants Eunice engaged. Yes, their employer's expectations were often unreasonable, her manner brusque, and her tone dismissive, but in Varmus's experience, Eunice worked as hard as anyone she hired. In the process, she created a spirit of volunteerism in a country where one had not existed before. "It wasn't as though she was behind the scenes, organizing and making phone calls," Varmus said. "She was on site. She was enthusiastic. She was communicating with the kids and the volunteers. She was a very, very hands-on and wonderfully participatory woman."

Young and single, Varmus did not mind the long hours. "Maybe if I'd had more of a life, I might have resented it. But I loved her spirit. I loved her energy," she said, recalling that if work kept her at her desk past seven in the evening, Eunice would invariably show up at her elbow with a glass of wine for her. "I loved that gesture."

She admired, too, the way in which the Shrivers complemented one another: "Her mind ran in such wonderful and exciting directions—some of it was just crazy—she would go so far afield and have such ambitious thoughts," she recalled. "We had regularly scheduled meetings with Sargent Shriver. She would go there and the purpose seemed to be to throw all her ideas out there: 'I am thinking of this. I am thinking of that. I want to go here, and I want to do this.' He would be the one who would rein her in. She trusted his judgment." The opposite was true as well. When his idealism got the better of him, it was the pragmatic side of Eunice that kept Sarge grounded in realpolitik.

Eunice's impatience often imposed needless stress on her staff, but

it got results. She had been in France only months when she convinced
the government's Ministry of Youth and Sports to welcome five Kennedy
Foundation experts for a three-day conference on physical education for
those with mental retardation. Eight hundred people attended. To deepen
the exchange of ideas, she arranged for the Kennedy Foundation to send
ten French officials to the United States to visit sheltered workshops and
the new group homes that were beginning to replace the large, inhumane
institutions that had dominated the landscape for so long. She made certain her brother Ted welcomed the delegation to Capitol Hill.

Her overworked staff was invited to the cocktail parties and intimate
dinners the Shrivers hosted regularly for visiting Americans, some famous and some not. Ellen Varmus rarely attended, but she remembered
being thrilled to meet tennis great Arthur Ashe, who was a regular at
those soirees. In their informality, those evenings replicated the discussion
groups the Shrivers had assembled in Chicago and at Timberlawn. Wherever they lived, they could not pass up any opportunity to put together
interesting people around their dining table.

Donald and Carole Dell were at one dinner party in Paris at which
Eunice made everyone write a poem. Arthur Ashe was there that night,
too. "Is she kidding?" he asked Carole, who knew she wasn't. "I thought
it was fun. She passes out paper and pencils and puts the poetry in a bowl,
and you had to pick one out and guess who wrote it," she recalled. "She
was always challenging you to do better or to do more."

Twenty-four-year-old David Mixner was shocked to find an invitation from the Shrivers to a dinner party when he arrived in Paris on his
first trip to Europe. Mixner was an antiwar activist who had worked for
McCarthy's presidential campaign in 1968 and who, along with hundreds
of others, was beaten by police on the streets of Chicago at the Democratic National Convention. Almost a year after Vice President Hubert
H. Humphrey narrowly lost the election to Richard M. Nixon, Mixner
helped organize Moratorium Day, a national day of demonstrations on
October 15, 1969, that drew millions of Americans into the streets to protest the war in Vietnam.

"Someone had told them I was coming. I have no idea who," Mixner
said of the Shrivers, who welcomed him to the ambassador's residence in
his rumpled suit. The mansion "could have been a museum piece, but the
Shrivers had made it warm and homey. There were signs of the kids everywhere, family photographs all around," he remembered. "Mrs. Shriver

knew how awkward and out of place I felt, and she made me feel that her home was my home."

Among the guests that evening was Coretta Scott King, the widow of the Reverend Dr. Martin Luther King Jr. "You could find anyone around their table. That's the kind of people they were. They loved ideas. They were enormously intelligent and insightful and genuinely curious," he said, noting that "no one got a free meal. You were expected to participate, and everyone did. Mrs. King was the star of the show that night."

At the end of the evening, the guests held hands around the piano and sang "We Shall Overcome." When he returned to his hotel room, Mixner said, "I wrote in my diary that Bertrand Russell quotation from his autobiography because it perfectly captured the unconditional love for humanity that I felt at the Shrivers' table: 'Three passions, simple but overwhelmingly strong, have governed my life: the longing for love, the search for knowledge, and unbearable pity for the suffering of mankind.'" Twenty years later, when he ran into Eunice on a street in Hyannis Port, he began to introduce himself, when she cut him off. "Oh, I know you," she said. "You were at our home for dinner in Paris."

Paris was not all work and serious talk for the Shrivers. There was plenty of play, with vacations in the South of France, and visits to Marc Chagall's studio near Saint-Paul-de-Vence and to the palace of Prince Rainier and Princess Grace, in Monaco. "We've had concerts by Yehudi Menuhin, ski instruction from Jean-Claude Killy, dances with Brigitte Bardot," Sarge wrote to his father-in-law in Hyannis Port. "I became Godfather to Jane Fonda's baby [Vanessa, her daughter with first husband Roger Vadim], and Eunice danced with [French prime minister Maurice] Couve de Murville. Is it any wonder Eunice never wants to go home!"

Home came to them. The movie stars, whom Eunice and Ethel called their "glitteries" or "sparklies," stopped by when they were in Paris: Harry Belafonte, Yul Brynner, Julie Christie, Vanessa Redgrave. There were always visiting Kennedys coming and going. Kathleen Kennedy Townsend, Bobby and Ethel's eldest child, went to France to celebrate her birthday in 1969. "They gave me a wonderful time in Paris," she said, recalling a minor mishap when she and a friend borrowed Eunice's blue convertible. "I am such a terrible driver. I stalled out on the Champs-Élysées. Many people would not lend their niece their convertible."

But her aunt was not like many people, she said. "What made Eunice special is that she would talk to you. She was curious about our lives. She didn't seem as strict as my mother was. My mother had very set ideas about things. Eunice was less strict, much less judgmental. You could talk to her. She'd ask questions. She was more open to ideas, more open to what kids were doing and thinking."

Jackie Kennedy was much in the news the first year the Shrivers were in Paris. Four and a half months after Robert F. Kennedy's assassination, Jack's widow married Aristotle Onassis, a wealthy Greek shipping magnate twenty-three years her senior. The marriage afforded her the security she sought for herself and her children in the wake of the murders of Jack and Bobby. But because Onassis was divorced, her marriage incensed conservative Catholics, who poured out their anger in the fifty to sixty letters Rose received every day that fall. "They are for the most part critical of Jackie, but full of praise and admiration for me and for the dignity with which I have faced all the tragedies," she wrote to Eunice on October 29, nine days after the wedding, which Pat and Jean attended, on Skorpios, Onassis's private island in the Ionian Sea. "I am rather fed up on the whole thing," Rose wrote. "I don't know whether the Vatican issued some statement calling Jackie a public sinner, or whether it was some priest whose name remains ambiguous. But the expression has been used in all the news media."

French newspapers and magazines were enchanted by the Shrivers. They covered the bike rides of the new American ambassador and his family around Paris, Sarge's match in the French tennis championship, Eunice's visits to institutions for children with mental retardation in Menton and Forcalquier, and her ribbon cuttings in Rambouillet and Angers at town squares renamed in memory of President Kennedy. They described the hockey sticks and baseball mitts and children's toys littering the open spaces of a formal residence transformed into a family home. They noted Gilbert Stuart's portrait of George Washington, on loan from the Boston Museum of Fine Arts, displayed alongside a Jackson Pollock from the Guggenheim Museum, and Eunice's growing collection of paintings of the Madonna and Child hanging opposite Sarge's modern art by Robert Graves, Hans Hofmann, and Josef Albers.

The art competed for attention with dozens of Kennedy family photographs on display in every room. The décor proved too much for President Nixon's aides H. R. Haldeman and John Ehrlichman, who toured the residence in advance of the president's visit to Paris, in 1969. Nixon was to host a dinner honoring the de Gaulles at the ambassador's residence on

March 1. But spying the Kennedy photographs, the statues of the Blessed Mother, the red and pink dining room, and what the *Washington Post* described as a "a multicolor Jasper Johns painting the size of a Volkswagen bus," the president's men swapped the Shriver's furnishings for more traditional American décor, flying antiques into Paris from Washington "to change the tone." The president even spurned the talents of the residence's French chef and instead served the de Gaulles Kansas beefsteak and baked potatoes he brought with him on Air Force One.

Eunice was unfazed. "That was perfectly all right with me," she said. "I've travelled enough with presidents to know that they do get what they want."

Nixon's advance men had insisted that the Shriver children remain upstairs during the black-tie dinner, but when the de Gaulles arrived, Madame de Gaulle immediately asked after them, and the children were invited down to greet the guests. "I just remember my mother being so incensed that we were not allowed to come down to the state floor," Tim recalled.

A reticent public figure, Yvonne de Gaulle had been coaxed by Eunice the previous December to attend a televised Christmas party with music and puppeteers she hosted at the ambassador's residence for children with mental retardation. Michael R. Gardner, who had taken care of the family's horses at Timberlawn, was a houseguest at the time and "marveled at Mrs. Shriver's media savvy in recruiting the French president's wife to help open the minds and hearts of French citizens who hid their developmentally disabled children from public view."

President Nixon had asked Sarge to remain in Paris after the change in administrations, but Sarge was less and less comfortable in his post the longer the war dragged on and peace talks stalled. Eunice, too, was feeling her lack of influence. Despite the distance, she had stayed on top of developments in Washington. When John A. Volpe, the US secretary of transportation and a former Massachusetts governor, visited in June for the Paris Air Show, she sent him home with a message for the new HEW secretary, Robert Finch: increase the budget for the Division of Mental Retardation.

The Shrivers flew to Florida in July to witness the realization of President Kennedy's promise to send men to the moon by the end of the decade. They were at Cape Kennedy to watch the launch of the *Apollo 11* spacecraft carrying Neil Armstrong and Buzz Aldrin to the surface of the moon. Already back in Paris when the lunar module touched down, their attention was diverted by news that Ted had driven his car off a bridge on Chappaquiddick Island, off the coast of Massachusetts, and not reported the accident for ten hours. His passenger, twenty-eight-year-old Mary Jo Kopechne, had drowned.

The Shrivers headed for Hyannis Port, where Kennedy political retainers were gathering along with the family in the wake of the accident. Eunice helped draft the nationally televised seventeen-minute speech Ted made on July 25, an expression of regret and responsibility that clarified little about what actually happened that night but included a direct appeal to the voters of Massachusetts to advise him on whether he should remain in the Senate "after this most recent tragedy." Eunice had talked Ted out of his plan to promise never to seek the presidency. He pled guilty to leaving the scene of an accident and received a two-month suspended sentence. Letters and telegrams poured in urging him to stay in Washington. The next year, Massachusetts voters reelected him with more than 62 percent of the vote.

Sarge began to contemplate his own political options now that their French sojourn was, he had resolved, nearing its end. His desire to serve in elected office had been repeatedly derailed when the Kennedy family decided it conflicted with the ambitions of one of his brothers-in-law. Most recently, Hubert Humphrey had considered Shriver as a running mate in 1968, following Bobby's assassination, but the family's desire to keep the road clear for Ted to make a future presidential bid helped prompt Humphrey to select Maine senator Edmund Muskie instead. Sarge would explore a run for governor of Maryland, where the Kennedys had no political interests, when the Shrivers returned home in the spring of 1970.

There would be one more fraught trip from Paris to Hyannis Port before then. On November 18, 1969, Joseph P. Kennedy lay unconscious and near death in his second-floor bedroom overlooking Nantucket Sound while his family gathered. The Shrivers came from Paris. Ethel came from Washington, as did Ted and Joan. Jean and Stephen Smith and the now-divorced Patricia Lawford came from New York. Jacqueline Kennedy Onassis flew in from Greece. His twenty-eight grandchildren would fill the pews of the simple white clapboard church in Hyannis named for St. Francis Xavier for a funeral Mass offered by Richard Cardinal Cushing of Boston and Terence Cardinal Cooke of New York at the altar Joe had donated so many years before in memory of his oldest son and namesake, killed in the war he had tried to prevent.

Only Rosemary, the fifty-one-year-old daughter Joe had not seen or spoken of in more than a quarter century, was missing, living in the private ranch house he had built for her and the nuns who cared for her on the grounds of St. Coletta.

"I don't believe he is without faults," Ted said in his eulogy, quoting an essay Bobby had written about their father in *The Fruitful Bough*, published privately for the family in 1965. "But when we were young, perhaps because of his character or the massiveness of his personality, they were unobserved or at least unimportant."

Perhaps that was true for his sons, whose political success was the focus of his enormous energies and his considerable fortune. But for his daughters, Joseph P. Kennedy was a beloved but more complicated figure. Pat told her children he had held her back from reaching her full potential because he thought a business or legal career was unseemly for a woman. Jean told hers he had thwarted her ambition to become a doctor because, he said, "that's not a suitable profession for a woman." Among the sisters, only Eunice had managed to forge a career of consequence, tapping Joe's deep financial resources—and perhaps his even deeper paternal regrets—to spare those born with mental retardation the fate that had befallen Rosemary.

Now the patriarch's death at eighty-one would free Eunice to bring Rosemary back into the heart of the Kennedy family after her long and lonely exile.

ELEVEN

MATERNAL FEMINISM

The fetus has all the ingredients of human life from the moment of conception on, and it is merely a question of development and not essence that changes.

—EUNICE KENNEDY SHRIVER, 1970

T HE FAMILY DOGS Lassie and Shamrock had already arrived from Paris and taken up residence in their old kennel at Timberlawn when Sarge and Eunice and the four youngest Shrivers returned to the Rockville, Maryland, estate on March 27, 1970. The family's travel had been delayed a day by stormy weather and a nationwide work slow-down by air traffic controllers.

Their eldest son, Bobby, was there to greet them that Good Friday, having returned from Exeter for spring vacation at Hickory Hill with Ethel Kennedy and his eleven cousins. The front embankment at Timberlawn was freshly planted with pansies, and the bedrooms of the seven-thousand-square-foot house were newly laid with wall-to-wall carpeting. Richard "Rags" Ragsdale, the handyman Sarge called his "Top Man," had orchestrated the placement of the family's furniture and artwork, which had arrived from Paris just the day before.

The Shrivers made an easy transition back into the Washington social swirl that spring. Tennis and ugly-pet contests at Hickory Hill. Swimming at Deeda and Bill Blair's pool on fashionable Foxhall Road in Northwest Washington. An evening at the Shoreham Hotel's Blue Room to hear singer Jack Jones. A night of comedy with Dan Rowan and Dick Martin of TV's popular *Laugh-In* at the Shady Grove Music Fair, a theater-in-the-round in Maryland owned by Lee Guber, the husband of Eunice's friend, Barbara Walters, the television journalist, whose older sister had mental retardation.

In May there was less frivolity than there might have been at the Washington premiere of Art Buchwald's play *Sheep on the Runway*. The antiwar comedy by Eunice's good friend and favorite syndicated columnist opened the day after Ohio National Guardsmen killed four students at Kent State University during a demonstration against the US incursion into Cambodia. The Shrivers joined Ethel Kennedy and Coretta Scott King at a memorial service for the slain students days later at the New York Avenue Presbyterian Church. Ted Kennedy spoke and Judy Collins sang. The family assembled again in early June at Arlington National Cemetery for a candlelight folk Mass to commemorate the second anniversary of Robert F. Kennedy's death.

Typewritten memos dictated by Rose to her secretary resumed their regular appearances in the mailbox at Timberlawn, advising Eunice on household management or chastising her for a breach of etiquette by her or one of the children. "Now is a good time to buy sheets on sale," read one. "I use hem-stitched only for the family and regular sheets for the help." Another expressed dismay that Eunice had not restored the family's New York apartment to its proper order after hosting a cocktail party for doctors doing research on mental retardation. "I would appreciate it if you would see that the liquor is put away properly," she wrote.

In another, Rose corrected Eunice's grammar. "Be careful of the inscriptions in books you autograph. I noticed 'on which' was written in your longhand, and it was wrong. 'With whom I could not live without' should be 'without whom I could not live.'" She expressed shock in yet another note that Eunice's children had not owned up to breaking a glass coffee table at her house. "I think if when they destroy anything here or anyplace else, they would tell the owners about it," she wrote. "Children have been coming here for forty years, and this has never happened before."

Rose calmed herself enough to fly up from Palm Beach that spring to attend a reception at the Washingtonian Motel in Gaithersburg, Maryland, sponsored by the Friends of Sargent Shriver to test the waters for his anticipated campaign for governor of Maryland. More than 1,200 supporters, many of them former Peace Corps volunteers or colleagues from the Office of Economic Opportunity, paid $7.50 to munch on hors d'oeuvres and mingle with the Shrivers that night. But as Sarge spoke to voters across the state in the weeks that followed, his ambivalence about challenging incumbent Democratic governor Marvin Mandel became as clear as his discouraging poll numbers.

Instead, Sarge accepted the entreaties of more than a hundred Democratic congressmen to lead the effort to improve the party's prospects in the 1970 midterm elections. He attracted a staff of old Kennedy hands and new blood to the office on K Street that became headquarters of Congressional Leadership for the Future. Mike Feldman, Eunice's troubleshooter on mental retardation in the White House when Jack was president, signed on, as did Edward Bennett Williams, the prominent Washington attorney. "It will be very good, in the final analysis. The whole basis of it is to have great men in public office, and if he isn't to be one of them himself, the next best thing is to help find them," said a disappointed Eunice, who had urged Sarge to make the run despite the long odds, her conviction firm that there was no higher calling than elective office.

One of the newcomers Sarge hired was Michael Novak, a Catholic theologian and political philosopher whose book *The Experience of Nothingness* Sarge had taken to quoting at the dinner table. Novak, his wife, and two small children moved into the four-room guesthouse that, with the owner's permission, the Shrivers had built for Rose's visits at Timberlawn. The two couples spent evenings sitting on the back porch of the main house while the children drove go-carts, rode horses, or did cartwheels on the lawn.

Eunice bet Novak $5 one evening that he would not last until the fall. "Sarge is very impatient with speechwriters," she warned. Eager for a smoke as the sun was setting, Novak pulled a pack of Tiparillos from his pocket. "Does a gentleman dare offer a lady a cigarillo?" he asked Eunice, mimicking a television commercial for the short, mild, narrow cigar with the white plastic tip. She sneered, pulling a fat ten-inch stogie from a table drawer and lighting it up. "She smiled and looked at me with complete contempt," Novak recalled.

With her men's trousers, her Cuban cigars, and her role as quarterback in the family's touch football games, "she wasn't exactly like any other mother you'd ever seen," said her daughter, Maria. "As a young girl, I didn't actually know how to process her appearance much of the time, because most of the mothers were dressed up and neatly coiffed." When Eunice, on the other hand, arrived to pick Maria up at the Stone Ridge School of the Sacred Heart "in her blue Lincoln convertible, her hair would be flying in the wind; there usually would be some pencils or pens in it. The car would be filled with all these boys and their friends and their animals. She'd have on a cashmere sweater with little notes pinned to it to remind her of what she needed to do when she got home. And more often than not, the sweater would be covering a bathing suit, so she could lose no time jumping into the pool to beat us all in a water polo game."

If Eunice defied categorization, she also modeled commitment. That summer, when Maria was fifteen, her mother sent her to Tunisia on a service project. "I'd call to complain that there was no running water, no toilet, and I was sleeping with five men, and she'd say, 'I don't want to hear one more yip out of you. Get your job done and don't come back until you're finished,'" Maria said. "I've heard, 'I don't want to hear one more yip out of you' a lot."

Novak found Eunice "indomitable, for sure. I always used to say that she had my vote as the Empress of the World; the one woman meant to rule things. She got things done, as disorganized as she was. She knew to hire good people who could bail her out. She was tough minded, as tough minded as they come—more intense than cold-blooded. She did not take imperfection kindly; she really expected a lot of you, and she didn't mind letting you know when you failed."

Novak defied her expectations, staying through Election Day, sprinkling Sarge's speeches with quotes from the French philosopher Pierre Teilhard de Chardin, even though Eunice complained it made her husband sound pretentious. "Why can't you do it like my father?" she scolded Sarge after one speech. "My father knew how to talk in a way that the man in the street would understand." In truth, she, too, was a fan of the Jesuit paleontologist, her copy of *Building the Earth* full of underlined passages and dog-eared pages. She just wore her erudition more lightly than her husband did.

Perhaps thanks less to his theological references than to his punishing travel schedule—Sarge visited thirty-two states in four months—Democrats retained their majority in the Senate and picked up twelve seats in the House.

Eunice's focus at the Kennedy Foundation expanded, too, from organizing the second International Special Olympics, in Chicago, in August 1970, to responding to the rapid changes in the nation's abortion laws. The movement to decriminalize abortion that had begun a decade before in the name of public health had evolved while she was abroad into a referendum on women's rights. Feminists now were demanding the repeal of all restrictions on abortion. No effort to achieve full equality in the workplace or the home would succeed, they argued, without women having control of their reproductive lives.

Public opinion surveys found a growing number of Americans supported broader availability of abortion, at least in the early stages of pregnancy. Forty percent of respondents to a Gallup poll in November 1969, for instance, supported "a law which would permit a woman to go to a doctor to end a pregnancy at any time during the first three months." But the National Organization for Women was lobbying for unrestricted access to abortion.

Hawaii became the first state to agree, in March 1970, followed by New York, in April; Alaska, in July; and Washington, in November. Unlike the three other states, New York did not require a woman to be a resident to secure an abortion. It permitted abortion without restrictions until the twenty-fourth week of pregnancy, when a fetus was considered sufficiently developed to survive outside the womb. Governor Nelson Rockefeller credited "women's liberation" and "the wives of the Senate and the Assembly" for passage of the bill that Terence Cardinal Cooke condemned as a "threat to our state and our country" and "a direct assault on the sanctity of human life and the welfare of our society."

A three-judge federal court panel had been scheduled to hear arguments about the constitutionality of New York's restrictive 1830 abortion law when repeal made the legal issue moot. Courts had already struck down abortion statutes in California, Wisconsin, and the District of Columbia, and similar lawsuits were pending in several other states. Thirteen state legislatures were considering bills to repeal abortion laws without conditions; eleven had already eased restrictions on the procedure.

In 1970 opposition to abortion came from some on the political left as well as those on the religious right. The argument from the left was that abortion was no less a human rights issue than capital punishment, euthanasia, or the war in Vietnam. That was the position of Richard John Neuhaus, the Lutheran minister and civil rights activist; of social critic Michael Harrington, the author of *The Other America*, which had helped shape the War on Poverty; of Mark Hatfield, the antiwar Republican senator from Oregon; and Jesse Jackson, the civil rights leader. The solution to unwanted pregnancies was not abortion, these progressives argued, but more government support for pregnant women, a streamlined adoption process, and federally funded child care.

The idea that a fetus was less than human and so unworthy of protection made no sense to those who believed life begins at conception. In an April letter to her sixteen-year-old son, Bobby, at prep school in New Hampshire, Eunice expanded on a telephone conversation they had begun the night before. "I do not say that the fetus is a completely developed person, but neither is a baby one-year-old, neither is a boy of 5," she wrote. "The point is that the fetus has all the ingredients of human life from the moment of conception on, and it is merely a question of development and not essence that changes. Why should a doctor be permitted to do an abortion at 24 weeks, yet if the baby is born at 28 weeks and the doctor kills it, he is up for murder?"

She put her money where her principles were by supporting Birthright, an organization founded by a Canadian grandmother to provide direct financial aid to pregnant women, and by deploying the resources of the Kennedy Foundation to encourage wider public discussion of the ethical challenges posed not just by abortion but also by the rapid advances in medicine, genetics, biology, and technology that "can have an irreversible effect on our human future."

Twelve hundred people attended a symposium she sponsored called "Choices on Our Conscience" in October 1971 at the Shoreham Hotel, in Washington, DC. The conference brought together scholars, ethicists, lawyers, doctors, and medical researchers. It represented yet another pivot for the Kennedy Foundation, this time toward the study of the intersection of biology and ethics, or what would in the next decade become the academic field of "bioethics."

The centerpiece of the conference was a nine-minute film re-creating the decision-making process that led to the death of a mentally retarded newborn at Johns Hopkins Hospital. The baby was born with Down syndrome and an unrelated life-threatening, but easily corrected, obstruction between the stomach and small intestine. The parents, unwilling to raise a child with mental retardation, refused permission for the surgery. The infant was placed in a bassinet in a dark corner of the hospital nursery and left alone to starve to death. It took fifteen days.

Roger Mudd of CBS News moderated the panel discussion that followed among Michael Harrington, Harvard Law School professor

Paul A. Freund, Yale Divinity School professor James M. Gustafson, Minnesota senator Walter Mondale, and the social psychologist Sidney Callahan. That night, after dinner at the Shrivers' home, participants drafted a letter calling for an examination of the ethical implications of medical practice and scientific advances, specifically to address whether "some persons, especially the powerless and helpless, such as infants, the sick, the retarded, the elderly, have rights that stand in need of defense." It became known as the Timberlawn Statement.

"Now, too late, that surgeon has discovered that several foster families would have been willing, even eager, to give that child a home," Eunice said in one of the many speeches she made about the case. "Now, too late, that surgeon says that if he had known this at the time, he never would have acceded to the parents' wishes. Now, too late, he agrees that a life could have been saved. Not the life of a totally normal child, perhaps, but a good life, a happy life, a life that no one had any right to take."

It was not an isolated incident. The case reflected the not-uncommon view that a child with mental retardation was not fully human. In 1968 Joseph Francis Fletcher, an ordained Episcopal priest who taught Christian ethics at Harvard Divinity School, wrote in *Atlantic Monthly* that there was "no reason to feel guilty about putting a Down syndrome baby away, whether it's 'put away' in the sense of hidden in a sanatorium or in a more responsible lethal sense. It is sad, yes. Dreadful. But it carries no guilt. True guilt arises only from an offense against a person, and a Down's is not a person."

It was not until 1984 that withholding lifesaving medical treatment from a disabled newborn was considered child abuse under the law. President Ronald Reagan was spurred to sign the "Baby Doe" amendment to a federal child abuse statute after parents in Indiana refused permission to fix an easily corrected obstruction in the esophagus of their infant, who had been born with Down syndrome. The newborn died.

"Even after the first stirrings of the international human rights movement in response to Nazi horrors, the mid-twentieth century was a quiescent, even legally apathetic period," recalled Stanley S. Herr, a lawyer who led the charge for legal rights for the disabled. "The courts were silent. The legal profession was unengaged. The law on mental disability was a backwater, and its tributary on mental retardation was its most stagnant pond."

For Eunice, abortion represented an existential threat to the mentally retarded. In the argument that abortion should be an option in cases of fetal deformities or mental retardation, she heard echoes of early-twentieth-century eugenicists advocating sterilization and institutionalization to rid society of "defectives." In the use of amniocentesis for prenatal diagnosis of chromosomal abnormalities, she saw a risk not only to fetuses with Down syndrome but also to scientific research on mental retardation. Why study a condition that could be eliminated through abortion? That New York City doctors performed 168,000 abortions in the twelve months after the state legalized elective abortion convinced Eunice that easy access to the procedure had turned abortion into a form of birth control for any woman who found herself inconveniently pregnant.

In response to those perceived perils, the Kennedy Foundation donated $1.35 million in 1971 to Georgetown University to establish the Kennedy Institute of Ethics. The grant endowed two faculty chairs and financed the establishment of the Bioethics Research Library, the world's largest collection of resources in bioethics. Its first director, André Hellegers, an abortion opponent and a professor of obstetrics and gynecology at Georgetown University Hospital, said his aim was to "bring expertise to the new and growing ethical problems in medicine today."

To Eunice, that meant a search for practical answers applicable in the real world. "She's very impatient in conversation about an idea," recalled Harris Wofford, who worked as an advisor to President Kennedy on civil rights and with Sarge at the Peace Corps. "She wants to wrap it up quick. Her brother had some of that quality, too, the president, but it was quite different. The impatience of Jack was that he didn't want to be bored. She really wanted the answers."

To get them, she hit the books. The Kennedy Foundation agreed to finance research in medical ethics at Harvard, including the development of courses to be taught throughout the university, from the college level to the medical school. Arthur J. Dyck, who held a joint faculty appointment in the Harvard Divinity School and the School of Public Health, administered the new Kennedy Interfaculty Medical Ethics Program. Dyck became her ethics tutor, discussing theories of social justice in weekly one-hour seminars conducted by telephone between Eunice's home in Maryland and his in Massachusetts. "She asked very intelligent questions. She did something I like very much, and something that I always was encouraging students to do, bring the stuff right into the warp and woof of real life," he said.

They studied the Harvard philosopher John Rawls, whose *A Theory of Justice* had just been published. By emphasizing the transparency of the process by which decisions are made, Rawls failed, in her view, to stress the special vulnerability of the weak: the mentally retarded, the frail elderly, or the developing fetus. Instead, Eunice came away from her semester-long tutorial believing that society should provide "additional protection and compensatory benefits to those who are rendered powerless by physical, mental, or social forces beyond their control. Instead of simply seeking guarantees that mentally retarded youth will have equal access to recreational activities, the foundation, through Special Olympics, has made it possible for the retarded to have their own athletic program."

Critics would later find fault with her approach, seeing paternalism and segregation where Eunice saw protectiveness and support, but in the early 1970s, she was ahead of most of the country in thinking about those questions at all. And nothing about these matters was theoretical to Eunice. After returning from Paris, she had assumed responsibility for Rosemary.

It is unclear from available records when in the 1960s Eunice first visited Rosie at St. Coletta, but she spent the 1970s, and the rest of her life, reintegrating her sister into the family that had abandoned her. "Eunice has taken over the supervision of Rosemary, who is retarded," Rose wrote in her diary, "and so her parents know that she will be well cared for after their demise."

Eunice made regular trips to Wisconsin—sometimes with her mother, more often without—to consult the doctors and therapists she hired to work with Rosie on her mobility and speech deficits. She supervised construction of the swimming pool that Rose instructed administrators to build on the campus, financed by Rosemary's trust fund. Eunice also brought Rosemary and the nuns who cared for her to Hyannis Port, Palm Beach, and Maryland for extended visits several times a year, comfortable in her sister's company in a way that Rose was not. "Of course, I would like you to be here, since she relates to you so well," Rose wrote to Eunice about a planned Easter visit with Rosemary at Palm Beach in 1975.

"I remember thinking she looked just like Mummy, but she didn't talk as much," said Bobby Shriver. Rosemary spoke only a few words; "Eunice" was one of them. After Joe's death, the Kennedy siblings would see Rosemary in Hyannis Port for dinner at the Big House or at the Shrivers' house nearby on Atlantic Avenue on a bluff overlooking Nantucket Sound. Jean would sometimes bring Rosemary to New York for Thanksgiving, but it was Eunice who became the primary caretaker of their sister.

Anthony was five in 1970. He cannot remember a time when Aunt Rosemary was not part of his life, swimming alongside him in a pool or holding his hand on long, silent walks. She was a respite for the youngest Shriver from the frenetic pace of the rest of the clan. "She was very impaired, but she had a spirit about her," he said. "You don't always have to talk to bond with someone, I find. Especially when you are in a hustle-and-bustle society, sometimes I think you really appreciate the peace and tranquility that comes from just being in the room with another human being, and someone smiling at you, and being with you as a companion, and feeling the love, without them saying that they love you."

If he was curious about Rosemary's story, he did not ask his mother, no more than he asked about the assassinations or the losses of Joe Jr. and Kathleen. There was "a culture of silence" in the family about painful events, Anthony said. "It was not something that we discussed. We grew up with people with disabilities all around us, and she was another disabled person we happened to have in our family. There's Rosemary, and there's Johnny, and there's Jimmy, and they are all in the backyard."

Rose, unable to accept the damage that had been done to her oldest daughter, could not talk about the lobotomy. "She was progressing quite satisfactorily but circumstances developed by which she was further retarded, and so it is very difficult at times to become reconciled to her present state," she wrote to the Reverend Robert Kroll at St. Coletta, adding that she tried "to accept God's holy will." She left the lobotomy out of her memoirs *Times to Remember* in 1974 as well, although Eunice took pains to explain to Robert Coughlin, Rose's ghostwriter, that what Rose called Rosemary's "accident" was brain surgery gone tragically awry.

Eunice often worked from home when Mark and Anthony were young, but the politics of abortion and the emerging fight for expanded educational opportunities for those with mental retardation just as often sent her into the city to map strategy with congressional allies. By 1972, abortion had become a public policy issue that politicians could not duck. Although Republicans had been in the forefront of efforts to decriminalize abortion—it was Ronald Reagan, as governor of California, who signed legislation liberalizing that state's abortion law in 1967—now the GOP saw an opportunity to lure socially conservative Catholics away from the Democratic Party, itself under pressure from feminists to support abortion rights.

Ted Kennedy, once an opponent of abortion, would soon abandon the public position he had staked out in 1971, when he wrote, "Wanted or unwanted, I believe that human life, even in its earliest stages, has certain rights which must be recognized—the right to be born, the right to love, the right to grow old. When history looks back to this era, it should recognize this generation as one which cared about human beings enough to halt the practice of war, to provide a decent living for every family, and to fulfill its responsibility to its children from the very moment of conception."

Public attitudes were changing along with state abortion laws. In 1972 more than 80 percent of Americans agreed that abortion should be legal to protect the health of the mother and more than 70 percent in the case of rape or birth defects. The issue would take center stage in the presidential campaign that year, one that would unexpectedly find R. Sargent Shriver on the national Democratic ticket as candidate for vice president with George McGovern, the senior senator from South Dakota.

Sarge was not George McGovern's first, or even second, choice for vice president. He was his seventh. McGovern settled on Shriver after being rebuffed by several senators—including Ted Kennedy—who recognized the Democrats' dim prospects that fall. McGovern had doomed his candidacy when he first selected Missouri senator Thomas Eagleton as his running mate without knowing that he had received electroshock therapy for "nervous exhaustion." When the news broke in July, Eunice and Sarge sent Eagleton a telegram urging him to stand firm: "Don't Quit. Make this a plus for the people of the country. You are a great candidate. Your record is superior in every way. Please, please don't give up." But McGovern concluded that the stigma surrounding mental illness made Eagleton a political liability, and he dropped him from the ticket eighteen days after picking him.

McGovern was saddled as well with the accusation that he was the candidate of "acid, amnesty, and abortion." That mischaracterization of his positions on the legalization of marijuana, draft evasion, and abortion, ironically, originated in an unattributed quote during the primaries from a "liberal senator" to Robert Novak, the syndicated columnist. Novak later identified the senator as Eagleton.

McGovern's actual position on abortion was that he was open to some loosening of restrictions but thought the issue was best left to the states. President Nixon's reelection campaign was able to capitalize on the alliterative slur and paint McGovern as a radical leftist, in sympathy with what much of the country saw as the excesses of the sixties.

Shriver was no one's idea of a radical. After the 1970 election, he had become a partner in the law firm of Fried, Frank, Harris, Shriver & Kampelman, his first job in the private sector since he worked for Joe Kennedy at the Merchandise Mart. He brought glamour to the ticket, with his good looks and his Pierre Cardin suits and Gucci loafers—to say nothing of the coterie of Kennedys who campaigned for him, none of whom worked harder than Eunice.

"She had really wanted Sarge to do well when he ran in 1972," recalled Colman McCarthy, a family friend who was then a columnist for the *Washington Post*. "Teddy was not particularly gracious to Sarge, and I never really understood how Eunice reconciled her allegiance to Sarge and to her brothers. There were pluses and minuses into marrying into that family, and the minus was that they kept you down. Sarge could have been governor of Illinois or governor of Maryland. Who knows how it might have turned out?"

Eunice missed Sarge's first campaign trips that August because she was in Los Angeles for the Third International Special Olympics, where 2,500 athletes from eight countries and all fifty states competed for six days. "In these days of commercialism, when great athletes compete for gold as well as glory, we've almost forgotten the real meaning of sports. Sports as play. Sports as grace," she told the crowd, praising the courage of the girl from Tennessee with an artificial leg who won the long jump event, the boy from Colorado who ran his three-hundred-yard dash on crutches, and the blind boy from California "who followed the voice of his coach to the finish line."

In only a few years, with a modest financial investment, she had marshalled the energy and resources of mothers and fathers, who had once been ashamed of their children, to create an unprecedented athletic and philanthropic phenomenon. Organized by a lean staff of paid professionals, Special Olympics was fueled state by state by the enthusiasm of volunteers who raised money, coached athletes, and recruited sponsors to provide everything from the venues to the buses that transported the athletes to and from local, state, and regional games.

The field was larger than it had been in Chicago for the second Special Olympics two years before. Rafer Johnson was back, as were dozens of celebrities, volunteers, and professional athletes serving as coaches. The games attracted world-class athletes—Olympic downhill skier Suzy Chaffee, Boston Celtic Dave Cowens, Olympic swimmer Donna de Varona, heavyweight boxer and Olympic gold medalist George Foreman, former

Dallas Cowboys quarterback Don Meredith—and half of Hollywood seemed to be on parade at the games at UCLA: Johnny Carson, Lorne Greene, Michael Landon, Jack Benny, Bob Newhart, Jean Stapleton, and stars of the hit TV shows *The Mod Squad* and *Rowan & Martin's Laugh-In*.

The French team returned, disappointed that the presidential campaign would preclude a stopover at Hyannis Port on the way home. Ellen Varmus, Eunice's former assistant in Paris, had accompanied the French athletes and their coaches to Chicago in 1970 and recalled their visit to Cape Cod following those games as a "homecoming of sorts. I come from a very informal family, and they were the same way," she said of the extended clan who had been eager to play baseball on the lawn at the Big House with the French Special Olympics athletes.

Flush with the success of the Los Angeles games, Eunice was on the beach at Hyannis Port with her Irish friend Dot Tubridy when she decided, on impulse, to join Sarge on a campaign trip to the Midwest. She threw a sleeveless flowered shift over her bathing suit, brushed the sand off her feet, hopped into the car, and headed to the airport. She was wearing the same dress that evening at the opening of the McGovern-Shriver headquarters in Detroit and again the next morning at a press conference in the office of Mayor Roman Gribbs. In her haste, she had forgotten to pack a bag.

"She did what she wanted to do when she wanted to do it," said Lucille Larkin, her press secretary during the campaign. "I admired her because she was a spectacular politician. She would pick up the phone on the plane and call ahead to talk to all the local politicians. She knew everybody, and she really worked it. She wasn't intimidated by anybody."

Bob Schieffer, who covered the campaign for CBS News, remembered Eunice as the most impressive political strategist he had ever seen in action, and the most intense. "One day she cornered me on the campaign plane to make sure I understood one issue or another. Her finger was right in my face until I realized she had grabbed the lapels on my jacket to be sure I was paying very, very close attention to what she was saying," he recalled. "Oh, I was."

Gary Hart, McGovern's campaign manager, called her "inexhaustible." She "laced her political speeches with anecdotes, improvisations, and spontaneous humor. She also seemed unintimidatable. She would go almost anywhere in search of voters and was not easily put off by precedents or tradition."

Some places were more welcoming than others. After a full day of campaigning across Maryland with Baltimore City Councilor Barbara Mikulski, she found herself in a tug-of-war over a microphone at a Democratic rally with Joseph J. Staszak, a state senator from east Baltimore. Staszak, a "Democrat for Nixon," refused to let her speak even though she had been invited to the event. Eunice seethed as she shook as many hands as she could grab on her way out of the hall. "That's not politics," she said. "They were rude about it as if they resented us coming, as if they were too fearful to say hello. It's their loss."

Wherever she appeared, she talked to voters about the need to reinforce the family as the nation's central social unit. "She felt we could do nothing without strong families. That's what you need to help children," said Mikulski, a former social worker and later a US senator from Maryland. "She was very much interested in every aspect of social issues, but she was always asking the kind of questions about the day-to-day issues that families were facing."

The campaign meant more chaos than usual for her own family. There were babysitters and household staff to try to create some sense of normality, but the Shrivers were always on the road, and "some of the staff were crazy," according to Anthony, who recalled with particular vividness a chain-smoking, profanity-prone kitchen aide named Goldie whose mental retardation was compounded by a hair-trigger temper. "She could get really violent. She'd throw your food on you," he remembered.

Richard Ragsdale was the stabilizing influence, the Shriver siblings agreed. "I had an incredible relationship with Rags," Anthony said. "He was a big figure in my life. He was officially the driver, but he was the driver, the handyman, the babysitter. He drove me to school. He picked me up at school most of the time. He'd take the dogs to the vet with me. He'd buy the food with me. He'd wake me up every morning. In a lot of ways, he was my best friend when I was a kid."

Lucille Larkin remembered going to Timberlawn to pick up Eunice for a campaign swing and finding her and Maria "running across the lawn in a footrace." The house was a mess, with decorations from the previous Christmas still on display outside, cold cereal spilled on the kitchen counter, and Eunice's suitcase still unpacked. But there was also this "wonderful image of the two of them laughing like crazy, trying to beat each other, these long skinny legs and their hair flying," she said.

The years of travel—for political campaigns and Kennedy Foundation causes—came at a cost once the children hit adolescence. It led to some troublesome behavior, especially in Hyannis Port. "Most of what we did, she had no idea," Anthony said of his mother. "If you give kids boats, and you have charge accounts so you can get gas, and you have a lot of energy, and you are fourteen years old, you can create a pack, a gang mentality." Some got away with more than they should have. "Unfortunately for us, because we are Kennedys, people allowed us to do things they would not normally allow people to do," Anthony said.

As his older brother Bobby had learned in the summer of 1970, more license did not mean less scrutiny if you attracted the attention of the police. There were nearly a hundred reporters and seventeen television cameras staked out at the Barnstable District Courthouse when Bobby Shriver and his cousin Robert Kennedy Jr., both sixteen, were placed on probation for possession of marijuana. The pair had been pinched with a number of other teens in Hyannis Port in a police sting operation. The two Bobbys were part of a crowd that called itself the Hyannis Port Terrors, or the HPTs. Mostly they engaged in the sort of mischief that often happens in summer resort towns after the sidewalks roll up. They untied skiffs from the docks. They threw water balloons and firecrackers at cars from atop Sunset Hill. They shoved potatoes into the tailpipes of cars stopped at red lights on Main Street.

For Bobby Shriver, the hijinks ended abruptly. Seeing his arrest reported on the front pages of the *New York Times* and the *Washington Post* was a private and public humiliation. "I had let my family down; I dishonored my father's name, and my mother's name," he felt. But his parents stood by him, calling him, in a public statement, "a joy and a pride to us. We will help him in every way to reestablish his sense of responsibility for himself and for others, his dedication to high ideals, his personal self-confidence and dignity."

Christopher Kennedy Lawford, Pat's oldest child, who engaged in a more prolonged experimentation, and with harder drugs, with Bobby Kennedy Jr., said that after the marijuana arrest, "My aunt Eunice yanked Bobby Shriver away from us before you could say 'straight and narrow.'" Bobby himself said the experience scared him, and he was more than ready to keep his distance from the HPTs. He and his father flew to California after the court hearing. There were no lectures or recriminations, just the two of them, far from Hyannis Port, playing punishing sets of tennis in the California sunshine. It was "the story of my father saving my life," he said. His father's embrace was "how I always saw manliness and strength," as impressive as any campaign for national office.

Eunice went where the campaign sent her in 1972, but wherever she went, she built in visits to institutions for the mentally retarded, often to the irritation of the McGovern staff. "She didn't care," her press secretary said, especially after it became clear the ticket was headed for defeat. "She'd be down on the floor, doing sit-ups, so completely herself."

She worked hard with Sarge on his speeches, especially one on the role of the family in society, which he gave frequently that fall. Eunice sent it to Bettye Caldwell, an early childhood education specialist at the University of Arkansas, and Caldwell took the opportunity to urge her and Eleanor McGovern, the presidential nominee's wife, to project a more modern image of political wives. "There are thousands if not millions of women in America today who object to the image of the president's wife being that of a vacuous female whose only concern is whether she has the right clothes for every occasion," she wrote. "Both your husband and Mr. McGovern have spoken of their admiration for their wives and have endorsed your playing a significant role in American life. My feeling is that this theme could be even stronger." Eunice underlined that paragraph in Caldwell's letter twice.

Eunice rarely campaigned with Sarge, but when their paths did cross, Lucille Larkin got a glimpse of the Shrivers' intimate partnership. Once, late at night, at an airport motel somewhere in the Midwest, she rustled up some tea and toast for Eunice, whose stomach was giving her trouble again. She walked into their room to find them sprawled across the bed "laughing like hell about stuff that happened during the day. I was embarrassed. It was really sweet. He had his hand on her shoulder. It was like they were eighteen, even though she looked eighty," said Larkin, a reference to Eunice's premature facial wrinkles, the result of a lifetime of unprotected sun exposure on the sea and the slopes.

She could not have been more beautiful to Sargent Shriver, as a campaign speechwriter learned when what he thought was a clever quip reached Sarge's ears. "Where's Eunice?" someone had asked. "Upstairs ironing her face," the soon-to-be-unemployed staffer replied.

Sarge "was totally devoted to her in every sense of that word," noted their daughter, Maria. "A man who marveled at everything she said and everything she did. He didn't mind if her hair was a mess, if she walked around in a wet bathing suit, if she beat him in tennis, or challenged his ideas. He let her rip and he let her roar, and he loved everything about her."

She loved him no less, said her friend Carole Dell, but Eunice was not the demonstrative type. "It must have given her such confidence as a woman to have someone love her so much," Dell said. "She was passionately loyal to him. She would have jumped in front of a train for him, but you didn't see that. She didn't have to show it, because he was showing it all the time. When somebody dotes on you like that, I think you become a little complacent."

The end of the campaign, in which the Democrats carried only Massachusetts and the District of Columbia, did not lessen the pace of activity at Timberlawn. After a family Christmas trip to Israel, Sarge returned to his international law practice, where he spent weeks away on trips to Moscow representing, among other clients, the billionaire American industrialist Armand Hammer. The son of Russian immigrants and the head of Occidental Petroleum, Hammer had considerable business interests in the Soviet Union. Eunice bore down on two new initiatives at the Kennedy Foundation: a program of character education for schools, being developed by Lawrence Kohlberg at Harvard, and a network of Life Support Centers to encourage pregnant teenagers to have their babies by providing them with comprehensive prenatal care and academic support.

The first such center had barely opened at Johns Hopkins Hospital with a three-year, $300,000 grant from the Kennedy Foundation, when the US Supreme Court issued its landmark ruling in *Roe v. Wade*, an abortion case from Texas. In a 7-to-2 decision on January 22, 1973, the high court held that a woman's right to terminate an unwanted pregnancy was constitutionally protected under the due process clause of the Fourteenth Amendment. The state's interest in protecting fetal life, the justices ruled, was limited to the late stages of pregnancy when a fetus could survive outside its mother's womb.

Things could not get worse, Eunice thought, until they did. On April 10 a front-page story in the *Washington Post* revealed that the National Institutes of Health was contemplating research on live, aborted fetuses. Such research was taking place in Europe, and an NIH advisory board had suggested it could be done in the United States as long as the fetus was no older than twenty weeks, weighed no more than one pound, and was no longer than ten inches from crown to heel. In cases of an abortion resulting in a live birth, the fetus rarely survived more than a few hours, so the window for such research was small.

In a matter of hours, Eunice had contacted scientists, ethicists, and religious leaders to denounce the use of federal funds for live fetal experimentation. She put two hundred Catholic schoolgirls from the Stone Ridge School of the Sacred Heart, including her seventeen-year-old daughter, Maria, on buses to the NIH's Bethesda headquarters, where they demanded, and got, a meeting with Dr. Charles Lowe, the scientific director of the National Institute of Child Health and Human Development, on whose original advisory board Eunice once sat.

Lowe assured the protesting students gathered in Masur Auditorium that the NIH had no plans to fund such studies, ducking a student's pointed question about why the advisory board would have drafted guidelines for live fetal research if it was not under consideration.

The US Conference of Catholic Bishops reissued its call for a constitutional amendment to reverse the *Roe* decision, with John Cardinal Krol of Philadelphia expressing shock that live fetal research was even under discussion. "If there is a more unspeakable crime than abortion itself, it is using victims of abortion as living human guinea pigs," he said.

Eunice echoed his outrage in a letter to the *Washington Post*, comparing such research to the recently revealed Tuskegee Syphilis Study by the Public Health Service, which, for forty years, had examined the effects of untreated syphilis on black men without ever disclosing to them that they had the disease. "The fetus is being studied in these situations because it is human. Otherwise we would not be discussing standards to safeguard the fetus," she wrote. "We have no such safeguards for tonsils or the appendix."

Not everyone she tried to rally was sympathetic to her point of view. "If I shared your philosophical position that the early fetus is indeed a human being, of course I would share your sense of outrage that it should be the object of experimentation," wrote Joshua Lederberg, a Nobel Prize–winning geneticist at Stanford whose research was being funded, in part, by the Kennedy Foundation. "In fact, as you know, I do not hold this view, and my moral distress is focused on the misery that will be perpetuated if we do not learn more about prenatal and genetic disease, so that we may better help future generations."

There was no simple way to reconcile those competing interests. In response to the public outcry about both the Tuskegee experiments and talk of live fetal research, Eunice urged Ted to sponsor legislation, which Congress passed, creating the National Commission for the Protection of Human Subjects of Biomedical and Behavioral Research, the first national body to shape bioethics policy in the United States. "The commission will focus the most creative minds in the nation on the complex moral, ethical, and religious problems and will help clarify them both for society as a whole and for the individual investigator," he said. "The commission is designed to help us find the critical balance required to satisfy society's demands for advancement of knowledge while abiding by [the rights] of its individual members."

The eleven-member panel was chock-full of Eunice's friends, including Dr. Robert E. Cooke, her closest advisor since she took charge of the Kennedy Foundation. Just as she had dragged the neglect of the mentally retarded out of the shadows a decade earlier, she now nudged the discussion of bioethics from her Timberlawn drawing room onto the national stage. If the other trustees of the foundation—Ted, Pat, and Jean—objected to this new direction, there is no record of any dissent. They were marginally involved in the foundation. Only Jean had sought and received funding from the foundation. In 1974 she created a program called Very Special Arts "to promote the inclusion of people with disabilities in the arts, education, and culture around the world."

Neither the *Roe* decision nor the NIH's research protocols politicized the abortion issue; state legislatures had been wrestling with the question for a decade. But by adopting the feminist view that abortion was a private decision to be made by pregnant women, the Supreme Court ruling heightened the risk for politicians who equivocated. At stake were the votes of newly empowered women who saw abortion as a fundamental right and those of religious conservatives who saw abortion as an abomination. Democrats, including Ted Kennedy, who had opposed legalizing abortion, now swore to uphold the law. Republicans, including Ronald Reagan, who had supported decriminalizing abortion, now called for a constitutional amendment to outlaw it.

For Eunice, the political jostling obscured the moral dimension at the heart of the issue for her. She battled it out with Ted behind closed doors, but she stood by him in his campaigns, never hesitating if asked to draw a distinction between his view on abortion and her own. She was a realist about the political calculations the Democrats were making, but Eunice never reconciled herself to her party's embrace of abortion rights. Instead of taking to the streets with antiabortion demonstrators, she chose to fight behind the scenes to limit the impact of *Roe*, to encourage women to bring their pregnancies to term and to fight for more government assistance, especially for pregnant teenagers, before and after the birth of their babies. That battle, in her view, promised more concrete results than a prolonged, longshot effort to pass a constitutional amendment banning abortion. "I came to the conclusion," she said, "that no one—not even if the Lord came down Himself—could get through a constitutional amendment to override the Supreme Court decision in favor of allowing abortion. All you can do is encourage life support centers for teenage mothers and their infants."

At her behest, in September 1975, Ted and Indiana senator Birch Bayh proposed the National School-Age Mother and Child Health Act to "encourage coordination and improvement of existing services, as well as the provision of new services where necessary." The emphasis was on providing care to expectant mothers, rather than family planning services, which were already funded under the Public Health Service Title X Family Planning Program. The $30 million measure called for the integrated delivery of health, educational, and social services, modeled on the pilot Life Support Center designed and funded by the Kennedy Foundation at Johns Hopkins. Bayh's original version was even called the Life Support Centers Act.

As was so often the case, public credit for the bill went to Ted, not to Eunice, who had drafted it. "Mrs. Shriver Backs Kennedy in Pregnant Teen-Ager Plan," read the *New York Times* headline above a two-paragraph story recounting her testimony before the Senate subcommittee her brother chaired. The bill, opposed by President Gerald Ford as duplicative of existing programs, never made it to the floor of the House or the Senate for a vote, but Eunice had staked out her position in the abortion fight. She would be back on the Hill, revisiting the issue of teenage pregnancy after the 1976 presidential election sent a Democrat, Georgia governor Jimmy Carter, to the White House.

She may have failed to win President Ford's support for her legislative efforts on behalf of pregnant teens, but she had more success enlisting him in the promotion of Special Olympics. Ford appeared in black tie, on March 9, 1975, as honorary chairman of Eunice's biggest event yet on behalf of her program of competitive athletics for those with mental retardation: a one-hour television special on ABC featuring Barbra Streisand. The live program, hosted by Dick Cavett from the John F. Kennedy Center for the Performing Arts, was followed for those in the Washington theater by the movie premiere of the new Streisand musical, *Funny Lady*.

It was the first of many movie premieres Eunice arranged to benefit Special Olympics. In 1978 she would seek out Jay Emmett, the president of Warner Communications, for fund-raising advice, recruiting a lifetime supporter. "Back then, she did not want to ask for government money because Special Olympics was her baby, and she did not want to cede control," he said. He offered to premiere *Superman*, raising $350,000 from the black-tie events attended by President Jimmy Carter and other dignitaries in Washington, and Lauren Bacall and dozens of other movie stars in New York. She then put Emmett on the board of Special Olympics, "ensuring that I'd keep producing for her," he said. "No one ever said Eunice Shriver was not a smart lady."

In addition to elevating the public profile of Special Olympics, the 1975 *Funny Lady* premiere produced an anecdote, perhaps exaggerated by time and repetition, which defines Eunice Kennedy Shriver for the friends and family who revel in recounting it—as she herself often did. Having stayed too long at the Kennedy Center to watch Streisand's dress rehearsal, the tale goes, Eunice asked "Rags" to bring from home the designer gown she intended to wear that evening. But unable to decipher how to put on the intricate, multipiece dress, she abandoned the effort only minutes before she was due onstage to introduce President Ford. When an unsuspecting patron entered the ladies' room where Eunice was unsuccessfully wrestling with her red chiffon Oscar de la Renta, Eunice demanded she surrender her gown. "I'm Eunice Kennedy Shriver, and I have to get out there and introduce the president of the United States," she is reputed to have told the thoroughly intimidated woman, who promptly disrobed. In most retellings, Barbara Walters finds the unidentified woman shivering in her slip during intermission.

Walters does not remember the incident, but Ethel Kennedy insisted it occurred, perhaps with an usher in the role of rescuer of the reluctant dress donor. "An uglier dress was never made. It was brown, and it had big purple tulips with green stems. I remember because it was so unspeakably ugly," Ethel said, still aghast decades after the sight of the "pleated gold lamé cummerbund" that completed the costume.

Apocryphal or not, the story was vintage Eunice: the mix of moxie and entitlement, a combination that could charm and appall in equal measure.

———————

Eunice would be called on to summon all her charm and connections that fall when Sarge launched a campaign for the Democratic nomination for president, a quixotic effort by a man who had never been elected to public office. Eunice tried to recruit Dorothy Day, the social activist with the Catholic Worker Movement, to endorse Sarge. "I, an anarchist," the astounded Day wrote in her diary, where she committed to praying for him instead.

Sarge was driven by a sixties idealism that was out of sync with a decade drained of its optimism by the Watergate scandal that had forced the resignation of President Nixon in 1974 and the Vietnam War that had claimed more than fifty-eight thousand American lives before the North Vietnamese seized Saigon in April 1975.

Sarge was the ninth Democrat to enter the race when he announced his candidacy on September 20, 1975, a year after Ted, chastened by his oldest son's battle with cancer, his wife's alcoholism, and the public's lingering doubts about Chappaquiddick, made a "firm, final, and unconditional" decision not to run. He remained aloof from his brother-in-law's campaign, however, as he had four years earlier during Sarge's bid for vice president. "I've declared that I am not supporting any Democratic candidate before the convention," Ted told reporters. "But if my sister Eunice should decide to run, I might have to reconsider."

The rebuff extended to many old Kennedy hands, who remained bitter about Sarge's decision to go to Paris instead of work for Bobby in 1968. "You didn't even mention my last name," Eunice scolded Ted after her brother introduced her during a dinner speech in Boston in the middle of the Massachusetts primary campaign.

Laurence H. Tribe, a professor of constitutional law at Harvard Law School, was issues director for Sarge's campaign. His phone rang regularly in the middle of the night. "Larry," Eunice would begin, "what are you doing about the third point in the economic plan? Have you called Henry Kissinger yet? Have you looked at my notes on the abortion speech?" Sarge, Tribe said, "was a poet and an idealist. She kept trying to bring him down to earth. She had a nice hard-rock pragmatism matched with a flaming intensity that balanced his airy idealism. We shared a concern for the disadvantaged, but she knew I supported reproductive rights."

Abortion had emerged as an unexpectedly contentious issue in Democratic primary contests, beginning in Iowa, where three candidates—Birch Bayh, Frank Church, and Sargent Shriver—opposed a constitutional amendment to ban abortion. Pro-life voters found their way to the least-known of the contenders, Jimmy Carter, whose comments on the issue managed to sound more conservative than his actual position. As Carter told a meeting with six Catholic bishops, he opposed abortion but had yet to see a constitutional amendment banning it that he could support.

Shriver's position was that *Roe* was the law of the land. As president, he would uphold it but also invest more federal resources to support women who chose to bring their pregnancies to term.

Eunice "was firm in her convictions but not beyond approach on the subject," Tribe remembered. "She respected the other point of view, even if she could never share it. I have considerable sympathy for her pro-life view; her feelings for the rights of the unborn grew from the same very humane impulses that made her care so deeply about people with disabilities."

Eunice campaigned especially hard in the Bay State, knowing a loss in Kennedy country would be the death knell of Sarge's candidacy. "Wherever she goes, people seem to see momentary flashbacks of an era before two of her brothers were assassinated, before Vietnam, before racial turmoil in northern cities, before Senator Kennedy's accident at Chappaquiddick," the *New York Times* reported after Eunice spent a day shaking hands at subway turnstiles and shipyard gates. "She reminds people most of President Kennedy and their hard-driving father. 'She could have been a tycoon,' says a family counselor. 'She could have been another Joe Kennedy.'"

Sarge came in sixth in Massachusetts, after placing fifth in Iowa, and winning only 9 percent of the vote in New Hampshire. He was determined to mount one last stand, in Illinois, but even his most loyal supporters were ready to end it. At a strategy session with his inner circle, at Timberlawn, Eunice was uncharacteristically quiet when campaign aides Mickey Kantor and Harris Wofford gave voice to what many in the room were thinking but reluctant to say: it was time to quit. "After the meeting, Eunice came to me and said, 'Mickey, you have got to be even stronger; you have to really go at him. He respects your political judgment. We have got to surround him here on this,'" Kantor recalled. "She was not averse to going to other people to get him to move in another direction." She said much the same thing to Harris Wofford.

For what he described later as sentimental reasons, Sarge did compete in Illinois in March. After placing third, he dropped out of the race. A few weeks later, when Eunice called Dorothy Day to invite the Catholic social activist to visit Hyannis Port that summer, the defeated candidate's wife struck Day as despondent. "She is reading my books. Bedside books, she calls them," Day wrote in her diary. "She is not a happy person. 'Do you believe in heaven and hell?' she asked me. 'Why?' Driven by some sense of duty and the responsibility which goes with wealth and her family's experience in politics. And what tragedy . . . and how brave a family. With the violence of our day and kidnappings so prevalent, resentment of the rich so strong, I marvel that they do not live in fear, but they have faith, the Faith."

In the new president and Joseph A. Califano Jr.—his secretary of Health, Education, and Welfare—Eunice found a receptive audience for her anti-abortion views. Carter, an evangelical Christian, and Califano, a devout Catholic, opposed abortion except to save the life of the mother. Carter was an unknown quantity to the Washington establishment, but Eunice knew Califano well from the Johnson administration, when he was LBJ's chief domestic policy advisor and Sarge was running the War on Poverty. She had nicknamed him Donut Arms after he proved a consistently unreliable receiver during touch football games at Timberlawn.

They were both regulars at the weekday late afternoon Mass at Holy Trinity Catholic Church in Georgetown. Entering the sanctuary, Califano remembered, he would see what he took to be a homeless woman alone in a back pew, her hair wild, her coat askew, and sundry possessions and papers spilling out of overstuffed bags. It always took a beat or two before it registered that he was looking at Eunice Kennedy Shriver.

Questions about abortion had dominated Califano's confirmation hearings. In the wake of *Roe*, HEW had authorized Medicaid, the joint state and federal health care program for the poor, to pay for abortions. Estimates of the number secured with Medicaid funds were as high as three hundred thousand. That figure galvanized abortion opponents, and in 1976 Republican congressman Henry Hyde of Illinois attached an amendment to the HEW appropriation bill prohibiting the use of federal funds "to perform abortions except where the life of the mother would be endangered if the fetus were carried to term."

Before the Hyde Amendment could take effect, a coalition of abortion-rights advocates secured an injunction from a federal judge blocking implementation of the restrictions. When the US Supreme Court ruled on June 20, 1977, that a constitutional right to abortion did not imply an obligation on the part of the federal government to pay for the procedure, a contentious social issue was joined with a fundamental question of equity.

President Carter ignited a firestorm when he acknowledged that the Hyde Amendment created a two-tier system in which women of means could secure an abortion and poor women would be denied access to a constitutionally protected medical procedure. "Well, as you know, there are many things in life that are not fair, that wealthy people can afford and poor people can't," Carter said. "But I don't believe that the federal government should act to try to make these opportunities exactly equal, particularly when there is a moral factor involved."

Carter was echoing a sentiment similar to one President Kennedy had expressed in 1962, when US Army reservists protested their orders to go to Vietnam after having already completed a tour in Berlin. "It's very hard in military or in personal life to assure complete equality," President Kennedy said. "Life is unfair." But Joe Califano knew instantly that Carter had struck a discordant note, an impression confirmed by a deluge of indignant phone calls and letters. One exception was Eunice, who wrote Califano to say, "In terms of the equity argument, I think the president's answer is satisfactory." It was, he said, "one of the few times I can recall disagreeing with the political judgment of this extraordinary woman."

The real inequity, in Eunice's view, was that all fetuses could not be protected. "It is unfortunate that in the present situation the rights of the unborn can be protected only in some cases," she wrote. "The Supreme Court has created a form of economic inequality that is regrettable, but would there be truly greater equality if even more of the unborn had their lives terminated? Would it be more moral if all the powerless were put at risk?" Inequity was the price that had to be paid to reduce the number of abortions. It was a price, of course, that no one in her social circle would ever have to pay.

Watching the intractable debate between two sides convinced of their own righteousness, Eunice thought she saw a middle ground—one that would not resolve the equity issue but would provide broader access to abortion to those dependent on Medicaid. As Califano recalled, "In July, unknown to the public, to most of the antagonists prowling the halls of Congress with roses and hangers, and, indeed, to most congressmen and senators, a secret compromise remarkably close to the agreement the House and Senate would reach in December was beginning to take shape in the mind of Eunice Kennedy Shriver."

She drafted some preliminary language and called Califano at HEW to get his reaction. "We've got to face the rape and incest argument," she told him. "We also have to deal with serious damage to the mother— physical damage, not this fuzzy psychological stuff. I'm sending this over to you, personally and confidentially, and you can use it as your own."

Califano had no intention of getting in the middle of the congressional wrangling over the Hyde Amendment, but he also knew his phone was not the only one Eunice would be calling that day. She had too many contacts on the Hill to rely on Califano alone. Her language—prohibiting the use of federal funds for abortion except in cases of rape or incest or where necessary to save a mother from death or grave physical damage to her body—found its way into an amendment proposed by Senator Warren G. Magnuson of Washington, himself an abortion-rights proponent. "When I heard about his proposal, I suspected the fine hand of Eunice Kennedy Shriver," Califano said.

It was an imperfect compromise, but enough of one to win passage in the $60 billion HEW appropriation bill President Carter signed on December 9, 1977. Eunice had estimated that the revised Hyde Amendment would result in no more than fifteen hundred Medicaid-financed abortions a year. She was not too far off, according to Califano. During the first sixteen months after the Hyde Amendment took effect, "only 92 Medicaid abortions were funded for victims of rape or incest. The overwhelming majority of Medicaid-funded abortions—84 percent of the 3,158 performed—were to save the life of the mother; 522 were to avoid severe and long-lasting health damage to the mother."

It was only after the Hyde Amendment language was resolved that Califano remembered how his telephone conversation with Eunice had ended the previous July. "Joseph, when we get over this, we need a teenage-pregnancy bill," she told him. "I'm getting Teddy to introduce it, and I want the two of you to work together on it."

The nation was then in the grip of a minor panic about an alleged epidemic of teenage pregnancy in the United States, a problem subsequent scholars have concluded was overblown—less the result of sober analysis than an emotional reaction to sexually permissive behavior among young people. Public debate pitted those who favored providing access to contraceptives to teenagers against those committed to funding services for pregnant girls, as though those options were mutually exclusive.

Ellen Goodman, a syndicated columnist at the *Boston Globe*, argued the case for birth control in a column on June 14, 1977, noting that "we have chosen to pretend that we can prevent teenagers from being sexually active rather than protect them from the worst consequences—pregnancy." Eunice was incensed by what she interpreted as Goodman's suggestion

Representative John F. Kennedy with Eunice, twenty-five, in the Georgetown house they shared in 1947 during his first year in the US House and hers at the Justice Department working on the issue of juvenile delinquency. By all accounts, she made a better impression in Washington than did the bored freshman congressman from Massachusetts.

Eunice served as co-chair of the entertainment committee of the Democratic National Convention in 1956 in Chicago where her brother, Jack, the junior senator from Massachusetts, made a credible but unsuccessful bid for vice president on the ticket with Illinois Governor Adlai Stevenson. Left to right: Jacqueline Kennedy, the senator's wife; Jean Kennedy Smith, the senator's sister; and Eunice on August 14, the second day of the convention.

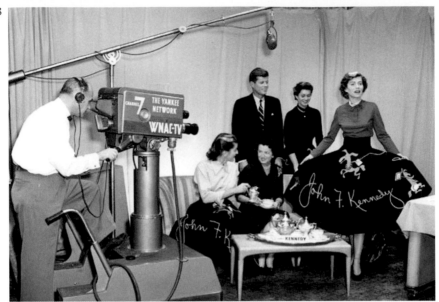

While her younger brother Bobby tried his hand as campaign manager, Eunice was relegated to modeling the poodle skirt she and her sisters wore during Congressman John F. Kennedy's campaign for the US Senate from Massachusetts in 1952. Left to right: Pat and Rose, seated; Jack, Jean, and Eunice.

Representative John F. Kennedy looks on as volunteers pin corsages on, left to right, Eunice, Pat, and Rose, in advance of a reception for women voters during JFK's 1952 campaign for the US Senate. Eunice and Cambridge City Councilor Joseph A. De-Guglielmo hatched the idea for the iconic tea parties during Jack's first congressional campaign in 1946.

It is emblematic of her behind-the-scenes role in shaping social policy during the Kennedy Administration that Eunice is barely visible in this photograph of President Kennedy meeting with the President's Panel on Mental Retardation at the White House on October 18, 1961. Present: Dr. Robert E. Cooke (*far left*); Abraham Ribicoff, Secretary of Health, Education, and Welfare (*third from left*); Eunice Kennedy Shriver (*at back, behind Secretary Ribicoff*); JFK (*front, center*); Deputy Special Counsel to the President Myer "Mike" Feldman (*far right*); Dr. Leonard Mayo; Dr. Lloyd M. Dunn; others unidentified.

Eunice, in 1962, opened a camp at her Maryland estate to teach sports to children with intellectual disabilities. At a time when segregation was the norm, Eunice is seen here instructing black children, as well as white, how to swim.

President John F. Kennedy finds his sister Eunice at the back of the Cabinet Room to hand her the last ceremonial pen he used to sign the Mental Retardation Facilities and Community Mental Health Centers Construction Act of 1963. The legislation, the last he would sign into law, was as much her triumph as it was his.

On June 16, 1964, during a Rose Garden ceremony, President Lyndon Baines Johnson introduces Eunice to discuss the progress of the national program on mental retardation she helped to draft and President Kennedy signed into law eight months before.

8

9

Eunice ran the family's charitable foundation for fifty years, but Jack, Bobby, or Ted always held the title of president. Here, New York Senator Robert F. Kennedy on March 18, 1965, presents Yeshiva University president Dr. Samuel Belkin with a foundation check for $1.45 million for a mental health center. Left to right: Sargent Shriver, Dr. Belkin, Rose Fitzgerald Kennedy, Senator Kennedy, and Eunice.

10

In April 1968, Sarge and Eunice watch a satirical presentation by his staff at the Office of Economic Opportunity in Washington before he heads to Paris as the new US Ambassador to France. Eunice will join him after a swing through Indiana, where her brother Bobby is campaigning for the Democratic presidential nomination.

11

Eunice Kennedy Shriver imported the American idea of volunteerism to Paris when Sargent Shriver became US ambassador to France in 1968. Here she plays ball in Paris in 1969 with an institutionalized boy who hopes to participate in Special Olympics in Chicago in 1970.

12

Eunice, in her familiar campaign role as supportive sister or loyal spouse, listens while her husband, Democratic vice presidential nominee Sargent Shriver, takes center stage on September 13, 1972, in Houston, Texas. Democratic presidential contender Senator George McGovern will lose resoundingly two months later to incumbent Republican President Richard M. Nixon.

13

Senator Edward M. Kennedy of Massachusetts running hard to keep up with his sister Eunice on the Ellipse in Washington on February 6, 1975, after she kicks off a national 3,182-mile fund-raising run to benefit Special Olympics. Ted would advance her agenda on Capitol Hill for the next thirty years.

14

Fascinated by celebrities and eager to enlist them in her cause, Eunice arranges for Special Olympics athletes to practice with the New York Cosmos at Giants Stadium in East Rutherford, New Jersey, on June 21, 1977. Left to right: Eunice and Pelé (Edson Arantes do Nascimento), the team's forward, and an unidenti-fied Special Olympics athlete.

15

Eunice talks with champion boxer Muhammad Ali prior to the unveil-ing of a US postal stamp commem-orating Special Olympics in August 1979 at the World Summer Games at the State University of New York at Brockport, where more than 3,500 athletes competed from every state and more than twenty countries. The fifteen-cent stamp featured an illustration of a smiling athlete clutching a gold medal.

16

When she was not coaching Special Olympics athletes herself in everything from skiing to swimming, Eunice was cheering them on from the sidelines. Here she encourages a runner across the finish line at a meet in Arizona in 1983. Her motto for Special Olympics—"Let me win, but if I cannot win, let me be brave in the attempt"—turned her father's obsession with winning on its head.

President Ronald Reagan in 1984 presents Eunice Kennedy Shriver with the Presidential Medal of Freedom—the nation's highest civilian honor. Her husband, Sargent Shriver, received the same honor in 1994 from President Bill Clinton, making Eunice and Sarge the only husband and wife to receive individual Presidential Medals of Freedom.

President Clinton and First Lady Hillary Rodham Clinton listen as Eunice Kennedy Shriver, right, speaks at the thirtieth anniversary celebration of Special Olympics on December 17, 1998, at the White House. For more than four decades, she influenced presidents on the rights and needs of those with mental disabilities.

Special Olympics partnered with the Nelson Mandela Children's Foundation to host an eighty-fourth birthday celebration in Polokwane, South Africa in 2002 for Mandela, one of dozens of global leaders she convinced to adopt Special Olympics. Eunice Kennedy Shriver sits with South African Special Olympics athlete Matsobane Mojapelo and former President Mandela.

20

Eunice's portrait by artist David Lenz is unveiled at the National Portrait Gallery in Washington, DC, three months before her death at age eighty-eight on August 11, 2009. The painting includes five persons with intellectual disabilities who have benefitted from Special Olympics and Best Buddies. Left to right: Airika Straka, Katie Meade, Andy Leonard, Loretta Claiborne, Eunice Kennedy Shriver, and Marty Sheets. The setting is a beach on her beloved Cape Cod, not far from the Shriver home in Hyannis Port.

that "short of locking the entire teenage population in their rooms, the only thing adults can do is to 'help' them avoid the most permanent and disastrous consequences."

In a rebuttal, published three weeks later, Eunice called Goodman's premise "shocking and demeaning—to parents because they are dismissed as failures; to teenagers because the implication is that they are without values (or that what sexual values they do hold are nothing but raw plea-sure principles). Nowhere do I hear a suggestion that teenage intercourse can be controlled, that teenagers themselves might want to control it. So-ciety itself may be encouraging teenage sex and then hypocritically con-demning its results."

Califano appointed a task force to examine the issue, naming Sargent Shriver and many of Eunice's allies to the panel. Its report recommended that the federal government fund a network of "Teenage Pregnancy Cen-ters based on the model at Johns Hopkins University"—the very one de-signed and funded by Eunice and the Kennedy Foundation.

The Carter administration then sent to Capitol Hill the Adolescent Health, Services, and Pregnancy Prevention and Care Act of 1978. It was, in essence, a revival of the National School-Age Mother and Child Health Act that had not gotten off the ground in Congress three years earlier. Eunice was "so well connected within HEW that I got her revision of my draft testimony in support of the bill before I even received the draft from departmental staff," Califano recalled.

Dr. Stuart Shapiro, an aide to Ted who focused on health care pol-icy, said the senator's staff called the measure "the Eunice bill." His boss "could have cared less over the substance of it" but required him to work with Eunice on it. Shapiro had to negotiate the space between her opposi-tion to abortion and Ted's public support of *Roe*. "I was dead center in the middle constantly," he recalled. "She'd write a speech for him; I'd change the speech; she'd change it back. He'd call me to come to the house, and it was very difficult to keep her out of the legislative, day-to-day politics."

Testimony on the bill reflected the tension between family planning advocates and those focused on providing services to pregnant teenagers. Eunice was firmly in the latter camp, seeing in the bill a tool to reduce abortion. She took vocal exception when HEW deputy assistant secretary Peter Schuck was quoted in the press saying that the legislation would allow states to distribute funds to clinics that performed abortions as long as they also provided prenatal and postnatal care to pregnant teenagers. "I certainly have not worked on this bill for three years under the assumption that abortion services would be provided under this bill," she told Califano in a scorching letter.

She went straight to Capitol Hill, and did what she did best.

Her method never varied, according to Tom Songster, who worked for Eunice for more than three decades at the Kennedy Foundation. She drove, ignoring speed limits and stop signs on Pennsylvania Avenue. She parked wherever she wanted at the Capitol, sometimes on the grass or the sidewalk. She led the way, through the entrance, past the receptionist, straight into the office of whichever senator or congressman she was buttonholing that day. Songster carried her bags, stuffed with briefing books full of facts and figures and one-page handouts containing a succinct summary of the bill, the amendment, or the appropriation for which she was soliciting support.

Once inside, she ignored the proffered chair and instead edged her hip onto the member's desk so that she was eye to eye with her prey. "We are going to do this," she would tell him—it was almost always a him. "I am counting on you to do this." Tom Songster does not recall anyone ever saying no to her. "You learned that 'no' was not in her vocabulary," he said. Besides, "She wasn't asking him. She was telling him." Eunice never stayed longer than fifteen minutes. "These are busy people," she said, ever reverent of those elected to public office.

She had followed the same script in 1973 to win support for the Rehabilitation Act, which barred discrimination against the disabled by any federal agency or private concern receiving federal funds. She did it again in 1975 on behalf of the Education of All Handicapped Children Act, which for the first time guaranteed access to a "free and appropriate" education to the eight million disabled children in the country between the ages of three and twenty-one, half of whom were receiving inadequate services, and one million of whom were receiving no education at all. She returned time and again to the Hill to champion amended and reamended versions of that special education law, now called the Individuals with Disabilities Education Act (IDEA).

"She was the grand dame. No one could turn Eunice Kennedy Shriver down," said Senator Orrin Hatch, the Utah Republican. "She was very forceful. You'd succumb to her charm or to her argument. When she was on one of her self-appointed assignments, she was fierce. She also knew that Teddy and I had a great political relationship. There were times, when he was being downright stubborn, I'd say, 'Careful. I am going to see Eunice.' And he'd say, 'No, no, don't do that.'"

Her well-honed skills shaped the Adolescent Health, Services, and Pregnancy Prevention and Care Act of 1978. "Due in large measure to her lobbying on the Hill, when the bill was eventually enacted, no abortion services were funded under it," according to Califano.

———————

Whether from overwork or the chronic illnesses that afflicted her, Eunice was hospitalized a number of times at the end of the 1970s. Ted's office felt compelled to issue a statement in 1978 denying reports in the New York press that his sister had suffered a heart attack. The denial had not caught up to Thomas J. Watson Jr. before the former president of IBM sent Eunice an antique music box along with some unsolicited advice. Seven years her senior, Watson had retired in 1971 after a heart attack. He wrote, he said, because of his "profound admiration" for her.

They had known each other for twenty-five years, sharing a love of skiing and sailing. He had renewed his pilot license since he retired, jogged a mile every day, and skied in Vail, Colorado, every winter. "Once in a while, one deserves to pause—reflect—and take satisfaction from what one has done," he wrote. "Today might be a good time to wind up this little antique and look backwards and realize how much you have done for everyone connected with you and how much inspiration and example you've been to all your friends."

He must have known, even as he composed his heartfelt handwritten letter, that looking backward and slowing down were not part of Eunice Kennedy Shriver's genetic makeup. "Like you, I was brought up to do my best, but I never included staying alive as one of my goals," he wrote. "You can do a great deal and still stop short of grinding yourself down. Think about it!"

If she did think about it, Eunice chose to ignore his advice, maybe because she knew that Thomas J. Watson Jr. was more like her than he cared to admit. In 1979 he came out of retirement to serve as US ambassador to the Soviet Union.

TWELVE

PROTECTING THE PRESENT,
SEEDING THE FUTURE

If you want to understand Eunice, you need to understand two things: faith and family.

—DOT TUBRIDY

BRIGHT ORANGE SURVEYOR'S tape marked the end of an era on Edson Lane. Timberlawn had been sold, and its rolling lawns and open fields, its deep woods and riding paths would be carved up to accommodate 550 houses on lots no bigger than a half acre. A wood harvester on the tennis court would chew up the felled trees, the resulting thirty-foot piles of chips bound for a paper mill. Magic Mountain Drive would run straight through the swimming pool.

The Shrivers had decamped for their new home on Foxhall Road, in Northwest Washington, by the time the demolition crew knocked down the stables and the kennels and the small cottage they had built on the rental property for Rose. The mansion would remain, incongruous in its grandeur alongside the new subdivision, where houses were priced between $175,000 and $200,000.

Only Mark and Anthony were still at home, enrolled at Georgetown Preparatory School, a short walk from Timberlawn but a forty-minute drive from their new home called Avondale. Bobby was twenty-five, a student at Yale Law School. Maria was twenty-four, a writer and producer at Baltimore's WJZ-TV, where she was forming what would become a lifelong friendship with the cohost of the station's local talk show, a young woman named Oprah Winfrey. Tim was an undergraduate at Yale.

Timberlawn held so many memories. Dinners with President Kennedy. Camp Shriver. The junior horse shows. The house tours guided by Joanne Woodward and Cloris Leachman to retire Sarge's campaign debts. The fund-raisers for Cesar Chavez and the United Farm Workers. The Connemara ponies imported from Ireland. Sarge and Eunice's anniversary parties.

"I don't think I've really been a very good parent," Eunice had joked with guests who came to celebrate their twenty-fifth wedding anniversary the year before. "I can remember when Bobby went off to Yale as a freshman, he called one evening. He said, 'Mom, I don't have anything to talk to these boys here about. You never talked at the table at dinner about the kinds of subjects Grandma talked about: the war, politics, et cetera. I have only three subjects: abortion, the fetus, and pregnant teenagers, especially thirteen-year-old pregnant teenagers."

The Shrivers' new home was a thirty-room mansion next door to Bill and Deeda Blair. It had once belonged to Nelson Rockefeller, the former governor of New York and vice president under President Ford. The Shrivers would live at Avondale until 1986, when they built a custom-designed Colonial Revival on almost seven acres in Potomac, Maryland, equipped with an elevator so Rosemary would not have to climb the stairs during her frequent visits.

They had barely unpacked on Foxhall Road when politics summoned Eunice and Sarge back to the road. In October, they attended the dedication of the John F. Kennedy Presidential Library, in Boston. When Eunice rushed up to President Carter before the ceremony and grabbed his arm, Ted turned to Dan H. Fenn Jr., the director of the new library, and whispered, "Got to be mental retardation or teenage pregnancy."

Eunice and Sarge were back in Boston, in the city's historic Faneuil Hall on November 7, 1979, for Ted's announcement that he was, at last, a candidate for president of the United States. It had been a long wait for Eunice; she had sent her baby brother a telegram in 1962 after seeing him interviewed on TV, demanding to know why "you refused to answer the question whether you were going to run for the presidency."

He had gotten off to a rocky start in an interview with CBS correspondent Roger Mudd, stumbling through his answer about why he wanted to be president. The interview ran on November 4, 1979, the same day that Iranian students seized the US Embassy in Tehran, taking fifty-two Americans hostage and elevating President Carter's stature as a leader during an international crisis.

Eunice traveled with her brother to Iowa and New Hampshire, often appearing in place of Ted's wife, Joan, who was living in Boston, pursuing graduate studies in music education. When Eunice was unable to substitute for Joan at a big fundraiser in New York, Ted called Pat and begged her to fill in. To Pat's protests that her hair was a mess and she had nothing suitable to wear, Ted thought instantly of a solution which he presented between bouts of laughter. "You go dressed like you are now, with your hair just like it is, and everybody will think you're Eunice," he told Pat.

Eunice was with him in Dubuque when demonstrators protested his support of abortion rights and his evasiveness about the accident on Chappaquiddick. "Character is enormously important in a campaign, and I would like to make it very clear that I think he has an enormous amount of character," she told the crowd. "My younger brother, in terms of our own personal life, has shown an enormous personal responsibility for our family." In those few sentences, the *New York Times* reported, "Mrs. Shriver deftly recalled the family's sacrifices while reminding people that Chappaquiddick was not the only test of moral fiber."

It was to Ted's role as surrogate father to the children of their two slain brothers that Eunice was alluding that day. She had tagged along on the camping trips to western Massachusetts and excursions Uncle Teddy organized to Civil War battlefields in Virginia and Pennsylvania and to Revolutionary War landmarks in Massachusetts and New York. Her love for Jack was akin to hero worship; her love for Ted—eleven years her junior—was less complicated, more maternal. Jack made her think. Ted made her laugh. "He's had a hard time because he has had to do it all on his own. President Kennedy had my father and Joe Jr.; Bobby had all three. But Teddy's been without all of them for a long time," she said.

Her sympathy was broad enough to embrace Ted's estranged wife, whose problems with alcohol always got more press attention than did the senator's own. Eunice had sent a blistering letter to the *Washington Star* for invading Joan's privacy in 1976 when it reported private conversations shared by a patient who had been in a rehabilitation program with her. She chided the *Chicago Tribune* in 1985 when it serialized excerpts from a book written by Joan's former secretary, "who posed as a friend only to make money by peddling gossip," in Eunice's view.

"Who in our family was the personification of the social gospel but Eunice?" asked Patrick Kennedy, the youngest of Ted and Joan's three children and a former congressman from Rhode Island. "Not only in the public acts with Special Olympics but in the unknowable private acts of generosity she showed my mother. She would come by our house all the time even when my mom was struggling, intoxicated, and Eunice would not turn away, and everyone else did."

Her protectiveness was especially fierce in the face of any criticism of her parents. She excoriated the *Washington Post* for publishing an excerpt from Gloria Swanson's 1980 autobiography, in which the actress described her years-long affair with Joe. Calling it "warmed-over, 50-year-old gossip," Eunice overlooked the obvious fact that Swanson was in a unique position to know. She wrote a similar letter to the *New York Times* to protest its review, more than a decade later, of *JFK: Reckless Youth*, calling the biography by Nigel Hamilton a "grotesque portrait of our parents."

It was as though her role and her father's had now reversed. "It's a strange thing," Joe had written in 1951 to Congressman John W. McCormack of Massachusetts, the future speaker of the House, "that the only thing that seems to even disturb me is something said about my children. Nothing ever said about me has ever bothered me five minutes."

It was a special Kennedy skill Eunice had mastered: the ability to simultaneously know and not know inconvenient truths that contradicted the family's carefully curated narrative. It took talent to sell the story line as hard as she did in the face of so much evidence to the contrary. Rose's marriage was the "happiest part" of her mother's life, and the closeness her parents shared inspired all their children "to revere the values of home and family," she wrote to the *Post*—her father's affairs, Jack's reckless infidelities in the White House, and Ted's ongoing womanizing notwithstanding.

"You do that to be safe," Maria Shriver said. "You do that to protect yourself. You believe it to be true, and there is absolutely nothing that someone could say that would deter you from that belief system unless you actually sit back and begin to question all your beliefs, the story that you live in, the family that you were raised in. I have spent quite a bit of time doing that, so I believe she absolutely could have. She was sharp. She needed that to be true because when you idolize somebody, you want somebody to be what you want them to be. You see them as such and will not allow anything to deter you from your belief about who that person was, and she definitely had that about them [her father and Jack]. She did not entertain anything that would deviate from that story line."

To ignore the contradictions at the heart of her family's story was to cast herself as the naïf, a role ill-suited to a woman as astute as Eunice. But it was the only posture that allowed her to preserve the exalted stature she assigned to the father who overlooked her and the brother who was stolen from her. To be fair, the paradoxes were too much for most of the country to comprehend as well. "Where else but in gothic fiction," Clare Boothe Luce said of the Kennedys, "where else among real people could one encounter such triumphs and tragedies, such beauty and charm and ambition and pride and human wreckage, such dedication to the best and lapses into the mire of life; such vulgar, noble, driven, generous, self-centered, loving, suspicious, devious, honorable, vulnerable, indomitable people?"

Eunice's impulse was to shield, not to judge. When Ethel could not deal with one or more of her recalcitrant sons, they turned up on the Shrivers' doorstep, sometimes staying for a week, sometimes for a year. When Pat's son Christopher Lawford got busted for heroin possession in his first year at Boston College Law School, it was Eunice who showed up at his arraignment and met with his lawyers. When Jean's son William Kennedy Smith was accused of rape after a night of drinking with Uncle Teddy at a bar in Palm Beach, it was Eunice who told the media scrum in the courthouse lobby that the family stood behind him.

"Eunice had the Kennedy ambition to save the world and was fully equipped to do it. For the time being, I was the world, and she was going to save me," Christopher Lawford recalled. "I remember her saying to me in a fit of frustration as we sat in my lawyer's office, 'We're so goddamned good at taking care of everybody else's problems, but absolutely lousy at looking after our own.'"

Did she wonder why? Would she have agreed with her nephew Patrick Kennedy, who became a mental health advocate after confronting his own dependence on drugs and alcohol? It was the price, he said, of harboring secrets, of fostering denial, of trying to bridge the gulf between myth and reality without ever confronting either one. The family was not perfect; Eunice knew that and, increasingly, the American people knew it, too. But for Eunice, for reasons she was loathe to explore, the façade had to be maintained. Joe Kennedy's dictum, "It doesn't matter what you are; it only matters what people think you are," had to be obeyed.

Eunice could take that directive to ludicrous extremes. Long after their mother was no longer lucid—she died at 104 in 1995—Eunice and Ted would bundle Rose into a wheelchair and roll her around outside the Big House in Hyannis Port within range of the zoom lenses of photographers assembled to record whichever birthday the matriarch was marking. "When she goes out, which is often, she wants to wear an attractive coat, checking carefully to see if the colors are right for her," Eunice told credulous reporters, so often complicit in Kennedy mythmaking, before her mother's 100th birthday.

She could also turn against her own if she feared they might cast an unflattering light on the family. When Jean's adopted daughter, Amanda Kennedy Smith, a doctoral candidate at Harvard in the 1990s, compiled Joseph P. Kennedy's correspondence into a well-received volume, *Hostage to Fortune*, Eunice tried to obstruct her path. She fought to exclude letters exchanged between Rosemary and their father even though the letters had already appeared in Rose's memoirs, *Times to Remember*. She wanted to exclude a letter from Joe Jr. to their father in which he endorsed the Nazi policy of forced sterilization of "undesirables," a discordant note inconsistent with Catholic teaching and the family's role as champions of those with intellectual disabilities.

She saw herself as the keeper of the flame, regulating the strength at which it burned to ensure that the legacy was not singed. The transparency that history requires was of less import than the preservation of the myth. Certainly the Kennedys had reason to mistrust the motives of some who tried to peel back the layers of their lives—not every journalist or historian had treated them fairly—but Amanda was her niece. And Eunice might have trusted her father's instincts for self-preservation more. Joe Kennedy believed in not writing "anything down that you wouldn't want published on the front page of the *New York Times*." His letters were about Franklin D. Roosevelt and Winston Churchill, not Gloria Swanson.

Eunice was even frostier when Amanda, at Ted's request and with the approval of the committee that oversaw access to Joe's papers at the John F. Kennedy Presidential Library, began to assemble a volume of family photographs for publication. The project was an invasion of privacy, she told her niece, demanding that Amanda remove from her proposed book 90 of the 302 selected photographs, many of which had been previously published and thirty-three of which were news service photographs depicting her father or brothers in their public roles in public places. She also insisted Amanda not include a photograph of Jean with their father on the lawn in Palm Beach despite the fact that Jean, who had finished a five-year tour as ambassador to Ireland for President Bill Clinton, had no objection to its publication.

Exasperated by Eunice, who enlisted Caroline Kennedy and Pat Lawford in opposition to her book, Amanda abandoned the project two years after Ted asked her to undertake it. In a letter to her uncle, Amanda declared herself "mystified and bewildered" by the "anger which has been directed at me and my mother," an anger that further chilled Jean's already cool relationship with her sister. In a separate letter to Eunice, Amanda expressed her "disappointment and, frankly, disgust" at her aunt's actions. "Thinking over your interactions with me regarding the letters and photographs over the last decade, I am struck by the uncalled for pettiness, imperiousness, arbitrariness, and suspicion with which you've treated me."

Twelve years later, after Eunice's death, Caroline Kennedy published a book of photographs from the family's private collection, called *Rose Kennedy's Family Album*.

There were some family events over which Eunice simply had no control. Ted and Joan filed for divorce after he lost the nomination to President Carter, who, in turn, lost the White House to Ronald Reagan. Ted returned to the Senate, where he spent the next three decades cementing his reputation as a champion of the vulnerable, fighting for those with disabilities, to his sister's delight, and continuing to oppose restrictions on public funding of abortion, much to her dismay.

When he went off the rails in the years after the divorce, partying a little too publicly, Eunice kept the code of silence, even within the family. Anthony Shriver was an undergraduate at Georgetown in the 1980s and would often run into his uncle and Senator Christopher Dodd of Connecticut at neighborhood watering holes. "I saw a lot of Teddy's bad behavior when I was in college," he said of meeting up with his uncle in bars and polishing off the night back at Ted's home in McLean, Virginia.

"There would be parties there until three in the morning. I'd wake up at eight thirty the next morning, and he'd be on the news giving a speech in the Senate. He had enormous energy and an ability to keep going," Anthony remembered. "But I'd mention it to her: 'Say, you know, last night I was out with Teddy, and this happened.' She'd say, 'Did you see that speech he gave on the floor of the Senate? It was so great, Anthony. Let's get that, and let's go talk to him about it.' She had an incredible relationship with him, and I think he adored her. She really loved him to death. He was enormously helpful to her and her legislative efforts on the Hill."

Claudia Ingram Weicker, then chief of staff of the Subcommittee on Labor, Health, Human Services, and Education of the Senate Appropriations Committee, said it was not unusual to hear from Eunice on matters large and small when Ted was the ranking Democrat on the panel. "She was a great advocate of abstinence education," Claudia said, recalling Ted's instruction to leave that line item intact. "He had no compunction about saying, 'This is what Eunice wants.'"

Stanley B. Jones, another legislative aide, recalled how insistent the senator was that Eunice be kept informed of the status of any bill in which she had expressed a particular interest. "I remember one night calling Eunice after some battles on the Senate floor to brief her on what had happened, standing in a phone booth at a campground," he said. The subject of the legislation is lost to time, but Jones never forgot his urgent search for a telephone as he drove to join his family on vacation in Pennsylvania. "All the way up there I'm thinking, 'Where in hell am I going to call Eunice from?' Because he'll see her probably this weekend and wanted her to have been called."

At the Kennedy Foundation, Eunice was focusing her efforts on integrating her concerns about teen pregnancy, mental retardation, and values education into a program she funded called Communities of Caring. The school-based project, launched in 1981, was operating at sixteen sites by 1982 and in more than 1,200 public and private schools by 2017. Its aim, to integrate ethical values into teaching across the curriculum, grew out of Lawrence Kohlberg's research at Harvard on moral development, much of it funded by the Kennedy Foundation. The program trained teachers and administrators to frame everything from classroom discussions to playground conflicts in terms of a school's shared values of "caring, respect, responsibility, trust, and family" to create an environment that would discourage early sexual experimentation and bullying of classmates with intellectual disabilities, and, in the process, build a nurturing community.

There were those at the Kennedy Foundation who thought Eunice would have benefitted from that training herself. She was not an easy boss. She installed a buzzer on the wall next to her desk to summon her secretary, its ear-piercing pitch shattering nerves as well as the silence in a suite of offices small enough to beckon her assistant with a well-modulated voice.

Working for Eunice meant always being on call. In an era before cell phones, Steven M. Eidelman, who did two tours as executive director of the Kennedy Foundation, bought an exercise bicycle after she complained she could not reach him when he was out jogging. Erika Hagensen, who filled the post during Steve's interregnum, stopped taking meetings outside the office, inviting people from the Hill or federal agencies to share a brown bag lunch at her desk, so Eunice could always find her. Renee Dease, who worked for her for almost thirty years, kept her Saturday nights free in case Eunice needed her to pass hors d'oeuvres at a party.

Given Eunice's insomnia, her calls could come at midnight or at five o'clock in the morning. Had Renee put sugar in her tea earlier in the day instead of the soothing honey Eunice preferred? Is that why she had stomach cramps? Had Steve seen the story in the *New York Times* about proposed changes in Social Security benefits that would hurt those with disabilities? Had Tom Songster finished revising the training manuals for Special Olympics coaches?

Not everyone could stand the strain. "I knew she was a strong Roman Catholic," said Gillian Healy, who appealed to Eunice's Christian sense of mercy. "'Mrs. Shriver, I am a believer in Jesus Christ, who is my Lord and Savior,'" she said one morning, "'and, during this past week, it has been necessary for me to go to the church next door, on my lunch hour, to get through each day working for you. I don't believe anyone should be working for you under these conditions.' There was silence for a while. Then the conversation continued, without her acknowledging there was even a problem."

She made employees long for a boss who was merely mercurial in her demands. By one count, Eunice went through twenty-one assistants in four years, one every few months. It wasn't just that she was short-tempered and impatient, expecting a task to be done before she'd finished assigning it. Her attention was so scattered and her agenda so full that few could keep up with her.

There was the time she sent an assistant to buy a table she had admired the day before in an antique shop on Connecticut Avenue. No, she didn't know the name of the shop. How hard could it be to find? Hard, her harried assistant discovered when she finally located the shop on Wisconsin Avenue and learned that Eunice had not been there the day before but three weeks earlier. Triumphant at the success of her search, the assistant was confounded by her outraged boss, who accused her of wasting the afternoon.

There was the time she instructed a new secretary to retrieve some papers from her car. The assistant asked what kind of car she drove and where it was parked. "You'll find it," came the clipped response. Her secretary could not locate an attendant to direct her to Eunice's designated parking space in the multilevel garage, but, it turned out, that would not have helped. After wandering among the floors, she spied a car at a crooked angle in the travel lane with the driver's door wide open. Eunice's car. She retrieved the papers and quit the job.

Lisa Derx came to interview with Eunice despite the employment agency's warning about the high turnover rate among her assistants. "I asked her in the interview, 'Why is that?' She said, 'Well, I think a lot of people aren't used to working as hard as we work here.' So, I immediately thought, 'Okay, it's the workload; it has nothing to do with her,'" Derx recalled, laughing at the memory of her younger self.

Eunice hired her when she learned Derx had worked for the Securities and Exchange Commission. "My father worked there," Eunice told her.

"I know. He was the first chairman," Lisa replied, earning a broad smile from her new boss, who was apparently unaware there was a portrait of Joe Kennedy hanging in the SEC offices that would have been hard for Lisa to miss. "I know I got the job because I knew who her father was," said Derx, who still does not know why she lost it thirteen months later. The conversation went something like this:

> **Derx:** Mrs. Shriver, is there something I did that you don't like?
> **Eunice:** No, you're terrific.
> **Derx:** Okay. Should I have done something that I didn't do?
> **Eunice:** No, no, you're terrific.
> **Derx:** And yet you want me to leave?
> **Eunice:** Yes.
> **Derx:** Well, Mrs. Shriver, I'd like to thank you for the opportunity to work with you.
> **Eunice:** Yes, fine. Now what can I do to help you get a job?
> **Derx:** You are firing me, but you want to help me get a job?

Renee Dease saw a gentler side of Eunice. She had not finished high school when she began working at the Kennedy Foundation in 1978. Eunice enrolled her in an adult education program a few blocks from the office. When, discouraged by the math requirements, she began to skip classes, Eunice marched her to Franklin School, an imposing brick building in

Northwest Washington every day after work. "Mrs. Shriver talked to the director so she could get me a math tutor," recalled Dease, who went on to earn her diploma and her associate degree.

When, a few years later, Dease found herself overwhelmed by exhaustion with no obvious cause, Eunice had Dr. Robert Cooke, the foundation's chief medical advisor, arrange a complete workup at Georgetown University Hospital. Dease had lupus. "To work with her, you had to get to know her, to understand her family values," she said. "I know so many of the people who quit, but when you talk about her, they will still smile. They knew under the surface what she was really about. She always had the attitude of doing for people."

Connie Garner saw beneath the exasperating surface, too. A pediatric and neonatal nurse practitioner and educational policy specialist, Garner served as policy director on disability issues for Ted. He often dispatched her to sort out medication issues for Eunice, who was notoriously non-compliant about taking the right dosage of sleeping pills, pain medication, or the corticosteroids necessary to regulate her hormone levels. Ethel Kennedy remembers no rhyme or reason to her pill-taking regimen. "I saw her take so many you couldn't count them," she said.

Eunice's children worried about her health and her reliance on pills to sleep at night and to jump-start her in the morning. "She was a working addict, people would say today," said her son Bobby. It could hardly have been otherwise, he said, of a generation of Kennedys who were so practiced in denial and repression.

There was, in Maria Shriver's view, something "obsessive in the family about not talking about things. That naturally breeds agitation, anxiety, restlessness. When there is no outlet for any of that, what do you do? You have all of this stuff inside of you, and where do you put it? Do you eat it? Do you drink it? She channeled it all toward work."

Maria chose death as the subject of her first children's book, *What's Heaven?*, "because there was no discussion of that in my house. So you end up later in life—not even later in life, earlier—going, 'Wow, nobody is talking about this, and everybody is rolling over that.' I actually wanted to be a different kind of mother in that respect because I wanted to find out who was in there. I wanted to know each of my children intimately because I wanted to know my mother intimately." Her mother "wouldn't have that" until "at the very end, she didn't have the walls up anymore."

Garner, a rare woman unintimidated by Eunice, said not taking her pills or taking too many of them "was Eunice's way of rebelling against being sick." It was a dangerous form of denial. If Eunice's blood pressure dropped too low—which it would when she frequently got dehydrated or failed to eat—she would get dizzy and pass out.

But Garner also saw a softer side when she spent time working with Eunice on legislation impacting those with intellectual disabilities, an issue personal to them both. One of Garner's seven children had been left with lifelong disabilities after contracting viral encephalitis. "At our first meeting, she said, 'Tell me about your daughter; tell me about Ashley.' So, I told her I was so sad because I just went Christmas shopping, and I started out with the twenty-four months to thirty-six months at Toys "R" Us and realized she couldn't do that. So I had to back it up to the next aisle. By the time I was in twelve months, I was in tears. 'Oh, no, no, no,' she says. 'It's not about the toys and what she can't do. That's not where you start. It's about what she can do. You start there and go forward, not the other way around.'"

Eunice told Lisa Derx something similar when the younger woman asked her if she didn't get discouraged by the incremental nature of social progress. "You don't look at it that way," she told Derx. "People see someone who is paralyzed who can move only his little finger and they think, 'That is so sad.' But God doesn't look at it that way. He thinks, 'Are you doing everything you can with that little finger?'"

That was her approach with Rosemary. When she visited Hyannis Port or Washington, Eunice took her sister sailing and swimming, to Mass and to the shops—sometimes whether Rosemary wanted to go or not. Sister Juliane, one of the nuns who accompanied Rosemary on her trips east from Wisconsin, bristled at what she interpreted as her unrealistic expectations. "Eunice has no compassion for human weakness," she complained once.

But there was another way to view Eunice's behavior. William P. Alford, a professor at Harvard Law School and a longtime member of the board of Special Olympics, recalled a week he spent in Hyannis Port with the Shrivers that overlapped with a visit from Rosemary. "I got to see Mrs. Shriver interact with her sister, and that's really when I knew one hundred ten percent what kind of person she was," he said. It took him a few days to puzzle out what he was witnessing. "Every day, for hours, Mrs. Shriver would sit there with flashcards, as you might with a child, and say, 'Rosemary, this is a dog. Repeat after me: dog.' I think most people would have long since given up on the possibility of her learning anything new."

At first, he thought the exercise was a manifestation of Eunice's doggedness, her faith that persistence yielded rewards. But by the time his stay ended, he had reconsidered. The goal, Alford thought, was not a concrete result at all. "It was just an expression of love, affirming the dignity of the other person, showing you care. Even if she can't articulate, at some visceral level, Rosemary can see that her sister loved her. That kind of lay at the heart of Special Olympics, not just about her sister, that you don't give up on anybody, that everybody has gifts."

Dot Tubridy, Eunice's longtime friend from Ireland, who for decades accompanied her on campaign swings and Special Olympics trips, said, "If you want to understand Eunice, you need to understand two things: faith and family."

Eunice spoke to her adult children daily, sometimes multiple times a day. If one of them called when she was in a meeting, she excused herself to take the call. She interrupted friends at breakfast to tell them to turn on the TV—Maria was on the *CBS Morning News*—or at dinner to remind them Bobby was producing the opening ceremonies of the International Special Olympics, airing live from Notre Dame, in Indiana.

She sent them clippings from the *Hoya*, Georgetown's student newspaper, about the fifty classmates Anthony recruited for his new Big Buddies program to pair students with children with intellectual disabilities, in much the way that the Big Brothers and Big Sisters programs matched mentors with fatherless boys and motherless girls. She bragged about Tim's work with an after-school program in the New Haven public schools and Mark's ideas for combating juvenile delinquency in Baltimore.

In ways large and small, the Shriver children were following their parents' example of public service, from Sarge's organizing the Peace Corps and the War on Poverty, to Eunice's role in the founding of the National Institute of Child Health and Human Development and Special Olympics. They had been exposed to no other way to live, even during family vacations. A beach destination did not mean lying in the sun, Mark said, recalling "vacations" to Panama and Nicaragua that involved cutting sugar cane and meeting with Catholic missionaries living out liberation theology in their work with the poor. Their mother's odd but favorite phrase, whether she was chasing her children off the couch or urging them to volunteer in a soup kitchen, was "Get on to yourself!" Get moving. Seize the day. Contribute.

It could be exhausting, the pressure of those expectations. Her children spent much of their young adult lives trying to learn how to slow down, to appreciate stillness as much as they value productivity. "She was not warm and fuzzy," Bobby Shriver said of his mother. Had she been, "I am sure it would have made my life more easygoing, more calm. I would know how to take a vacation—that would have been good, if they had taught us how to go on vacation—but I did learn how to get to work."

When, as a city councilor in Santa Monica, California, he became an activist on behalf of homeless veterans, Bobby recalled the shiver of fear whenever he heard on the news that a vet had died on the streets anywhere in the United States. He would think, "'My mother is going to find out about that, and she will hold me responsible for it because she thinks I am in charge of this issue and I have to deliver.' It's a little crazy," he acknowledged. "But that's the way we grew up."

Each of the Shriver siblings volunteered at the games and organized fund-raisers to support Special Olympics. Working in music and film production in Los Angeles, Bobby mined his talent and his Hollywood connections to produce a television special, *Victory and Valor: A Special Olympics All-Star Celebration*, and a series of holiday albums called *A Very Special Christmas*, featuring such artists as Bruce Springsteen, Madonna, U2, Bon Jovi, Stevie Wonder, and Whitney Houston, raising millions of dollars for his mother's cause.

Anthony apprenticed himself to her. The job that Eunice found for Lisa Derx after firing her turned out to be down the hall with Anthony, where the newly minted college graduate was planning to expand Big Buddies. Derx accepted a temporary position to help organize a conference about his nascent idea, following the Kennedy and Shriver strategy of beginning any new enterprise by assembling the experts in the field. Twenty-five years later, the name had changed slightly but Best Buddies International had become a global nonprofit organization, based in Miami, with Anthony as its chairman, his wife, Alina, its vice president of art and merchandise, and Lisa Derx its Washington-based vice president for governmental relations.

Derx never did figure out why Eunice fired her, and Anthony suggested it was best not to try. His mother's motives were often a mystery better left unplumbed. Sue Swenson learned that one morning when, as executive director of the Kennedy Foundation, she was instructed to fire the entire staff. "My father told me every now and then you have to fire everybody just to get people's attention," Eunice told her.

An astonished Swenson replied, "Mrs. Shriver, your father was a man of his times, and if he were alive now, he would know that is not a good management technique. She went 'Harrumph' and turned around and walked out of the room. Last I ever heard of it."

Until she fired Swenson. "This isn't going to work anymore," Eunice told her one day out of the blue. "I'm running this place. I don't want you running it." Swenson came in as usual the next day and the next, making herself inconspicuous while continuing to do the job. "It took some time" for Eunice to accept her, Swenson said, but Eunice never took her off the payroll.

Those who stayed developed a thick skin and a sense of humor. Ela Work laughed when she remembered the days she wanted to strangle her boss. But she worked for Eunice for ten years in the 1970s, a decade she treasures for the energy and excitement generated by Eunice's sense of mission. "I can get along with anyone. I understood her impatience. She wanted to do so much," Work recalled. "She used to say, 'I should have been born a boy; I could have done so much more if only I had been a boy.'"

One assistant exploited Eunice's attention deficits for personal gain. Pamela Jo Luna, whom everyone called Lucy, worked as her personal secretary from October 1981 until January 1983. In those sixteen months, she used Eunice's credit cards to purchase about $60,000 worth of furniture, diamonds, clothing, and a trip to Switzerland. She wrote another $40,000 in checks on two of Eunice's bank accounts.

Her office mates were stunned by Lucy's arrest, but, some conceded, her mink coat should have been a tip-off. What secretary, earning $18,000 a year, wore a $6,000 fur to work? Eunice was unaware when she hired Lucy that she was on probation after pleading guilty to theft from a credit union in Alabama. For her fresh crimes, she went to prison. "After, Mrs. Shriver would say, 'Well, how about that? She sure fooled me,'" Renee Dease remembered.

Lucy Luna was a signal that Eunice needed help juggling the dual responsibilities of Special Olympics and the Kennedy Foundation. If she was going to make Special Olympics truly international, she would need the skills of someone who had spent much of the last decade negotiating deals in places as challenging as Moscow. In 1984 Sargent Shriver became president of Special Olympics, retiring fully from his law practice two years later to focus on the global mission of an enterprise that had begun in his backyard twenty-two years before. He was back where he had begun with Eunice in 1947, when he worked at her side at the US Justice Department, her partner now, as he was then, in furthering their shared vision of social justice.

He arrived at an expansive time for Special Olympics. By the mid-1980s, its programs had spread to more than fifty countries. Four thousand athletes attended the 1983 Summer Games, in Louisiana. The United Nations declared 1987 the International Year of Special Olympics.

In the office, Eunice and Sarge were a study in contrasts. Dapper and charming, he was impeccably dressed and unfailingly polite. He would no more shout at a secretary than Eunice would offer to make the morning coffee run. But they were an impressive team. Eunice remained founder and chairman of Special Olympics, but having Sarge on board meant she could focus on the foundation and the goals that increasingly preoccupied her: reducing pregnancy rates among teenagers, aiding women who wanted to carry their pregnancies to term, and preserving and expanding federal protections and services for people with intellectual disabilities.

In Mary Cunningham Agee, Eunice found a younger, like-minded partner in one of those endeavors. Cunningham had come to Eunice's attention, and the world's, when she resigned from Bendix Corporation in 1980 amid rumors of an affair between the married twenty-nine-year-old and her equally married forty-three-year-old boss, William Agee, the chairman and CEO. Both denied the affair, and working women across the country expressed outrage that the rumor had cost the Harvard Business School graduate her job and left Agee in the corner office. Two years later, when both were divorced and in other jobs, Bill and Mary reunited and soon married.

The loss of their first child to a late-term miscarriage prompted Mary to create the Nurturing Network, a financial and emotional support system for women with unplanned pregnancies who were seeking an alternative to abortion. Eunice embraced the idea when she met Mary and Bill on Cape Cod, where the Agees maintained a home in Oyster Harbors, not far from the Shrivers' house in Hyannis Port.

The two women had much in common. Both considered themselves practical idealists more interested in concrete results than public protests. Outlawing abortion did not strike either of them as a realistic goal; reducing it was. "I am not carrying a placard. I am not fighting a cause, other than for the woman who has no other option and wants to give birth to her child," Agee said. "Without politicizing it, we wanted to say, 'We are here for you. It is going to take more money. It is going to take more time, but we will take the walk with you,' without in any way disparaging the other option. That's not what we are about."

Both women were admirers of Joan Chittister, a Benedictine nun and social psychologist who wrote and lectured on the hypocrisy of isolating abortion as a moral issue from the challenges surrounding an unintended pregnancy. "I do not believe that just because you're opposed to abortion, that that makes you pro-life," Sister Joan said of the antiabortion activism of some social and fiscal conservatives. "In fact, I think in many cases, your morality is deeply lacking if all you want is a child born but not a child fed, not a child educated, not a child housed. And why would I think that you don't? Because you don't want any tax money to go there. That's not pro-life. That's pro-birth. We need a much broader conversation on what the morality of pro-life is."

In helping Agee get the Nurturing Network off the ground, Eunice found a kindred spirit. Both had a special reverence for the Blessed Virgin Mary. Both were devoted to Mother Teresa. The Kennedy Foundation had honored her in 1971, eight years before the Catholic missionary gained wide recognition when she was awarded the Nobel Peace Prize for her work with the destitute in Calcutta. Both had contemplated becoming nuns as young women.

In Eunice, Agee saw a soul shaped by loss and forged in suffering, a woman who knew she could not change the past but believed she could influence the future. "When suffering comes into your life, you basically have a choice. You have to decide, 'Am I going to feel sorry for myself?' You can completely self-destruct. I think what she did [when confronted with what happened to Rosemary] was so much more constructive than that. The fact of it, she shut off. She knew her own psyche enough to know that if she kept revisiting it, she would not be able to do the higher calling. 'There are people here and now today for whom I can do this,' she thought. And that's what she chose to do."

Eunice relied on prayer and religious ritual, as well as work to redirect that pain, said her son Tim: "We prayed the rosary as a family on many occasions, and I remember hearing my mother dedicate the prayers again and again to the repose of her brothers' souls, intimating that our grief could be channeled through the beads and converted from pain to peace."

In Joan Chittister's work, Eunice saw an explication of her own struggle to live a life of consequence in a patriarchal world. The lot of too many women, as Sister Joan described it, was to be "tolerated in life and often loved" but "seldom respected for themselves, for their opinions, for their talents, for their perspectives." That was the life Eunice might have led had she not pushed her way into the rooms where decisions, and history, were made.

By the mid-1980s, Eunice's work was being widely celebrated. In 1984 President Ronald Reagan awarded her the Presidential Medal of Freedom, the nation's highest civilian honor. In the years ahead, hers would be the first image of a living woman to appear on a commemorative silver dollar coin, sold by the US Treasury Department to benefit Special Olympics; she would be inducted into the National Women's Hall of Fame in Seneca Falls, New York, and her likeness—surrounded by Special Olympics athletes—would hang in the National Portrait Gallery in Washington, DC, the first commissioned portrait of an individual who had not served as a US president or First Lady.

Even as her siblings celebrated her Medal of Freedom at a White House luncheon, something of a family insurrection was brewing about the future of the Kennedy Foundation. The other trustees—Ted, Pat, and Jean—insisted that its assets of about $16 million be made available for projects unrelated to mental retardation, including the John Fitzgerald Kennedy Presidential Library, the Robert F. Kennedy Memorial, the Kennedy Center for the Performing Arts, even the renovation of the Big House in Hyannis Port. In their view, Eunice and Sarge had already steered the foundation in new directions by funding ethics programs at Harvard and Georgetown, where scholars were studying issues related only tangentially to mental retardation.

Eunice resisted their demands. "Whatever assets of the foundation are siphoned off for other purposes, even laudable family purposes, such grants reduce the capacity of the foundation to fulfill its primary function," she argued.

But was it their father's intention to make mental retardation the exclusive focus of the foundation? Or had Eunice hijacked the foundation when Joe turned over the reins to her and Sarge a few years before his stroke? Her siblings, who had paid scant attention at the time, expressed skepticism. Certainly that was how Eunice interpreted her father's wishes, and, she noted, the need was still great for the family's charity to fill this role. "No other foundation or private agency contributes in any significant way to meeting the problems of mentally retarded children and adults," she wrote. "The objectives of the Joseph P. Kennedy Jr. Foundation for the next ten years should remain fixed as they have been for the past twenty years."

Her siblings were unmoved. Their father's will had been ambiguous, stipulating only that the foundation's resources be spent "to fulfill its dedicated purpose," without defining what that purpose was. "Our first and principal conclusion is that the foundation should be a family enterprise and support all of the areas of charitable interest held by family members with a special emphasis on mental retardation," they argued. "Because it has always been the policy of the family to generally limit the foundation to funding mental retardation programs, the family's other efforts have suffered for it."

Rose shared Eunice's perspective on Joe's wishes. In an undated memo, marked "Notes for Steve Smith," Jean's husband, who served as a financial advisor to the family, she wrote, "Do not use Mr. Kennedy's money for outside interests which he has already earmarked for mental retardation. The money he put aside for mental retardation he felt should be used solely for that. Otherwise if it were distributed among other charities and other interests, it would not have the influence on mental retardation which he felt in his own heart was the reason for its existence."

She had expressed a similar perspective as early as 1969 in a letter to Eunice, Pat, Jean, and Ted in which she urged them to spend their own money to help retire the campaign debts from Bobby's 1968 presidential run. "I am sure you can all afford it, as your father told me that you all had much more money than he ever expected," she wrote. "I am writing this only because my conscience dictates that money should not be deducted from the sums allocated for mental retardation or charity." For Pat, Jean, and Ted, the phrase "or charity" was key.

That Eunice had special influence with her mother is clear from Rose's correspondence with her other children, all of whom had to be reminded to visit their sister at St. Coletta. Jean came in for an especially harsh rebuke after she complained about Eunice. "With reference to Eunice, she has been a source of great joy and consolation through the years because she keeps in constant touch with Rosemary," Rose wrote. "You remember I asked you to go see her when Eunice was in Paris, but you said you could not make the effort—a great disappointment to me."

Rose insisted she did not play favorites. "I love all my children and have never shown any favoritism," she said, although she conceded that her children "all think Eunice is my favorite. Maybe she is . . . just a bit. If she is, it is because she is the hardest worker. She has helped me so much in my work with the retarded."

Eunice had also bent to Rose's wishes when, in 1971, it was her mother who wanted to use the resources of the Kennedy Foundation for a pet cause. Manhattanville College was in need of funds. "Mother felt that so many members of the family had attended Sacred Heart Schools, including Manhattanville, that it would be extremely unfortunate if the Kennedy name were missing from the current effort being made by Manhattanville to raise money nationally," Eunice wrote to Pat, Jean, and Ted. The foundation gave the college $100,000.

Eunice's resistance to change at the Kennedy Foundation a decade later was not just about power, although certainly she had grown accustomed to running the show. The greater threat was a loss of focus. The research community had not cared about mental retardation until Eunice aimed at the problem her father's fortune and, later, federal resources. Victims of AIDS or domestic violence or drug addiction deserved energetic advocates, she acknowledged, but the Kennedy Foundation had led the way on mental retardation. She was unwilling to abandon that cause no matter how worthy other causes might be.

In truth, the cause was already being diluted by the loss of an important revenue stream. In 1973 the money that had flowed into the Kennedy Foundation from the Merchandise Mart in Chicago was rerouted to Eunice, Pat, Ted, Jean, Jackie, and Ethel. Why that change occurred four years after Joe's death is unclear. But Rose appears to have disapproved. "I want to impress it upon you that your father thought out the financial arrangements very carefully, and he decided that a percentage [25 percent, as it were] should be given to the foundation," she told her children and daughters-in-law. "I feel very strongly that if your income increases, even in spite of inflation, you should still continue to feel conscientiously obliged to give a certain amount to the foundation because that was your father's wish."

Money generated by prudent financial investments and the stars who contributed to the *A Very Special Christmas* albums, produced by Bobby Shriver, raised millions for Special Olympics, but the Kennedy Foundation would cease to be the transformative force it once was. Special Olympics would play that role.

To loosen Eunice's grip on the foundation's purse strings, her siblings insisted on involving the next generation in charting its direction. "If one believes in charity and family," they wrote, "the role of the grandchildren should be part of any long-term strategy and mission."

That was an idea Eunice could embrace. She offered any Kennedy grandchild who could produce a viable proposal $50,000 to get the project off the ground. She provided professional supervision, from planning to implementation, to foster success. But she did not make it easy. She required that each project be completed within a year and that it be undertaken in partnership with an existing organization, so the grandchildren would learn how to work within a community, not outside of it.

Marty Krauss, a professor at Brandeis University whose research explored the impact on parents and siblings when a family member has intellectual disabilities, was on the committee Eunice appointed to review the proposals: "I think it wasn't just about mental retardation. I think it was, 'Do these kids get what it takes to be in public service?' I think she wanted them to have some real experiences where they had to produce something. So she was really demanding. They didn't all get funded. Some of them were really sketchy."

The most successful programs were designed by Mark Shriver, John F. Kennedy Jr., and Kathleen Kennedy Townsend.

Kathleen affiliated with the Kennedy Krieger Institute in Baltimore to help low-birth-weight babies avoid developing intellectual disabilities. "It turns out if you give them a lot of attention, they are going to be okay," she said. "We set up this special house next to Kennedy Krieger where mothers would live and learn how to pay more attention to their children."

Eunice loved that project because it affirmed her belief in the power of mothers to change the trajectory of a child's life. Victoria Reggie Kennedy remembered with anger the pediatric neurologist in New Orleans who told her sister that her son, born with disabilities, would never walk or talk. "We were in such despair," Ted's second wife recalled. "I called Eunice, and she said, 'You tell your sister not to believe that doctor. You tell her never to give up, never to stop fighting. I believe in mothers.' And the doctor was wrong. My nephew is thriving."

JFK Jr. partnered with existing nonprofit groups to create a program he called Reaching Up. Targeting the high turnover rate among low-paid direct-care workers in the field of mental retardation, Reaching Up steered grants to workers to pay for tuition, books, transportation, child care, and other expenses, on the theory that more education would lead to a bump in salary and position and more committed caregivers. After his death in a small plane crash off Martha's Vineyard in 1999, Reaching Up joined with the City University of New York to establish the John F. Kennedy Jr. Institute for Worker Education.

Mark Shriver, fresh out of the College of the Holy Cross, was working as an assistant to Maryland governor William Donald Schaefer at a time when the state was closing large juvenile detention centers. Little preparation had been done, however, to help offenders transition back into the community. Mark designed what he called the Choice Program, to supervise and mentor troubled kids. Working out of an old janitor's closet in a public school in Baltimore, he hired new college graduates as caseworkers to check in daily with kids who had been referred by the state's Juvenile Services Administration. It was hard work for little pay, but it met his mother's criteria for a community-based start-up. It must also have stirred memories of her own work with juvenile delinquents when she was not much older than Mark.

"I really admired her efforts to bring these kids along," said Marty Krauss, who supervised many of the projects. "I think she would have to say that, in the long run, it was not successful" in fostering a commitment in the next generation of Kennedys to those with mental retardation. "None of them has picked up the spark, except her own kids, but, then, they grew up with it."

Kathleen Kennedy Townsend later applied the lessons she learned in Baltimore to a statewide initiative she developed to make community service a high school graduation requirement. At Eunice's urging, she partnered in 1993 with the state rather than have her Maryland Student Alliance stand alone. "She taught me it is much easier to grow something if you have institutional support," Kathleen said. "It allowed me to have the blessing of the state Department of Education in Maryland, but I had my own 501(c)(3), which allowed me to hire and fire and raise my own money and do my own curriculum development outside the department. I got the best of both worlds: their credibility and my own independence. That really came from Eunice, because she knew about structures and how to get things done."

Tim Shriver, too, was working with young people. He had returned to New Haven after doing graduate work in theology and education at

Catholic University and, in May 1986, marrying Linda Potter, a lawyer with whom he had shared an even longer courtship than his parents did. After an ecumenical wedding in the chapel of Georgetown University— Paul Moore Jr., the Episcopal bishop of New York, represented Linda's religious tradition, and the Reverend Richard Fragomeni represented Tim's—Linda would work on child neglect and abuse cases at Yale Legal Services, and Tim would teach nonviolent problem-solving strategies to teenagers in one of the city's most violent neighborhoods.

Tim was the second of the Shriver siblings to wed. A month before, Maria had married Arnold Schwarzenegger, the bodybuilder and Hollywood action movie hero. That wedding brought the paparazzi back to Hyannis Port, to snap the famous guests emerging from Saint Francis Xavier Church, national political figures eclipsed by the likes of Grace Jones, Andy Warhol, Oprah Winfrey, Jacqueline Kennedy Onassis, Quincy Jones, Andy Williams, and Barbara Walters. Maria wore Christian Dior, as her mother had thirty-three years before. Her wedding cake was a replica of the one served at her parents' wedding reception.

A life in California meant a life far "from the madness of the whole Kennedy thing," Maria said. But there was no escaping the madness of the whole Shriver thing. Her mother, a master at mixing celebrity and philanthropy, promptly recruited her son-in-law as "honorary weight-lifting coach" for Special Olympics and used his movie premieres, beginning in 1988, with *Twins*, to raise funds for the games. Years later, when Schwarzenegger served two terms as Republican governor of California, his mother-in-law made certain that his austerity measures did not include cuts in services to Californians with intellectual disabilities.

Shriver and Kennedy weddings and political campaigns came in quick succession in the next few years. In 1992 Ted married Victoria Reggie, a Washington lawyer, a week before Mark Shriver wed Jeanne Ripp, a classmate from Holy Cross. Ted and Mark were both on separate campaign trails two years later, Ted in an unexpectedly tough reelection fight against Republican Mitt Romney, the son of former Michigan governor George Romney, and Mark in a successful bid for a seat in the Maryland House of Delegates. He would not be the first of his generation to take the plunge. Joseph P. Kennedy II, Ethel's eldest son, had been a congressman from Massachusetts since 1987. Patrick Kennedy was a state representative in Rhode Island, and Kathleen Kennedy Townsend was on the Maryland ballot, too, running for lieutenant governor.

"Eunice and I would go door-to-door," her friend Carole Dell recalled of Mark's campaign. "People would nearly have a heart attack when they saw Eunice at their front door: 'I'm Eunice Shriver. Are you going to vote for my son?'" Eight years later, when Mark made a failed bid for Congress, he had to break the news to his mother that he would be running as an abortion rights supporter. She asked only that he talk to Pennsylvania governor Bob Casey, who, along with Eunice and Sarge, had signed an advertisement in the *New York Times* in 1992 calling for a "New American Compact" to reconsider the abortion issue. "No sooner did I agree to call him than my phone rang," Mark recalled. "It was Governor Casey. My mother did not waste time." Mark did not change his mind, "and my mother respected that."

Through it all, Special Olympics kept growing, even as the health challenges confronting its founders were mounting. The Shrivers had recruited Doug Single, the athletic director at Southern Methodist University, to serve as president and CEO after Sarge underwent heart bypass surgery and radiation for prostate cancer in 1988. In 1991 Eunice nearly lost her own life when her car collided with a van at high speed, the only speed at which she drove. Her car was totaled, and she was cut out of the twisted metal by first responders. She had cuts all over her body, internal injuries, two broken arms, and a shattered hip and elbow, but she survived the crash.

Her only concession to her injuries was to work more from home, where much of her focus in the next several years was on preserving hard-won gains for those with mental retardation and seeding the future with the next generation of advocates. Perhaps the most important lesson she had learned in Washington was that all battles won are but temporary victories. She sprang into action during the Clinton administration, for example, when the federal government interpreted a law designed to rein in welfare spending as a license to cut benefits for more than 95,000 children with disabilities. Most of the low-income children losing benefits under the Supplemental Security Income program—78,600 of the 95,180—had mental disorders, including mental retardation.

She was in the Roosevelt Room of the White House in short order, protesting the tougher eligibility standards for benefits that families needed to pay for social services, for alterations to houses to accommodate children with disabilities, and to offset wages lost by parents who stayed home to care for those children. She brought with her Jonathan M. Stein, general counsel of Community Legal Services, in Philadelphia; Martha Ford, from the Consortium for Citizens with Disabilities; and Guy McKahnn, a pediatric neurologist who was director of the Kennedy Krieger Institute.

They met with Elena Kagan, then Clinton's deputy assistant for domestic policy, who would later be appointed to the US Supreme Court by President Barack Obama. They described two children denied benefits; one with cerebral palsy, learning disabilities, and depression; the other with mental retardation and the AIDS virus. Eunice stopped in the Oval Office on her way out to underscore her dismay.

She then took her case to Capitol Hill, where confirmation hearings were about to begin for Kenneth S. Apfel, Clinton's nominee to head the Social Security Administration. Making the rounds of Senate offices, she lined up key senators from both parties, including Republican John Chafee of Rhode Island, and Tom Daschle, the Democratic minority leader from South Dakota, to challenge the cuts as inconsistent with congressional intent. "If Eunice Shriver was at your door, she wanted something important," said former senator Tom Harkin of Iowa, himself long a champion of disability rights. Apfel vowed to launch a thirty day review of the benefit cuts as soon as he took office. Three months later, he concluded the administration had erred and urged those denied benefits to reapply.

In a letter to the *Washington Post* praising Apfel's decision to take "positive steps toward restoring benefits for some of the children who were unfairly denied aid," Eunice gave no hint that she had played any role in the Clinton administration's change of heart.

She followed a similar script a few years later when President George W. Bush proposed cuts to a Housing and Urban Development program that awards grants to nonprofit organizations to expand supportive housing for individuals with severe disabilities. The program was a regular target of budget cutters in Democratic and Republican administrations alike.

"Get that nice man on the phone I always talk to at parties," Eunice told Steve Eidelman, then running the day-to-day operations of the Kennedy Foundation. "The one who likes to swim and loves the opera." She meant Karl Rove, deputy chief of staff and the president's senior advisor. Rove took her call. "She trucks over to see Karl Rove with a couple of experts. Congress restored the funds, and she talked about it with President Bush at a Christmas party," recalled Eidelman. "It was amazing to watch."

When Eunice was not lobbying herself, she was training others to follow her lead. She could not transfer to them her famous name, but she could give them the skills necessary to keep up the fight. The Joseph P.

Kennedy Jr. Fellowships she created brought to Washington professionals and volunteers for an intensive yearlong internship in public policy. She placed fellows on Capitol Hill and in federal agencies, all with an eye toward cultivating leaders who would remain in Washington or return to their home states armed with the necessary political knowledge and skills to benefit those with mental retardation.

Experience had taught her that some of the most effective advocates—from Elizabeth Boggs to Connie Garner—were mothers of children with disabilities, so she looked especially hard for applicants with leadership qualities who fit that description and would benefit from a crash course in the intersection of public policy, disability advocacy, and the political process.

That was how she had met Sue Swenson, who began their relationship as a Kennedy Fellow and later returned to run the foundation under Eunice's watchful eye. Eunice almost didn't select her as a fellow, in 1996, because Swenson refused to use the phrase "mentally retarded" to describe the status of her son, Charlie, who had profound disabilities. Having fought so hard in the 1960s to force more than one state to create a Department of Mental Retardation, Eunice did not want to retire the phrase. She worried a change in nomenclature would tempt lawmakers to divert money and attention to other uses. But the word "retarded" had become an ugly slur, just as the terms "moron," "idiot," and "imbecile" had decades before. The phrase gaining traction in the advocacy community, "intellectual and developmental disabilities," was too vague for Eunice.

Swenson, who had been active in the Minneapolis schools on disability issues, won her over, but she had less success convincing Eunice that the term "mental retardation" was demeaning. Sue fulfilled the long-term goal of Eunice's fellowship program, becoming commissioner for developmental disabilities in the US Department of Health and Human Services under President Clinton and assistant secretary for the Office of Special Education and Rehabilitative Services at the US Department of Education under President Obama.

Eunice chose Sharon Lewis as a Kennedy Fellow after the mother of a daughter with intellectual disabilities described the Teddy Bear Rally she organized at the Oregon state capitol to protest planned cuts to medical and social services for infants and toddlers. "We made a template and had families write stories of a child that they know who benefitted from early intervention services, both kids with and without disabilities," she recalled. "We had an incredibly overwhelming response, and we were able to fill the capitol steps with teddy bears, thousands from all across the state." Their efforts saved the threatened programs.

It was a story tailor-made for Eunice, who cared most about results that improved the lives of families in a concrete way. The Kennedy Foundation assigned Lewis to work with Senator Chris Dodd on the Senate Subcommittee on Children and Families, where she witnessed Eunice's "art of vehement persuasion" in her advocacy of everything from the reauthorization of Head Start to the Higher Education Act. "Oh, we heard from Eunice quite a lot," said Dodd, the Connecticut Democrat. "She always came armed with information and left with a commitment from us to do whatever she wanted."

The Higher Education Act, known in 2008 as the Higher Education Opportunity Act, made students with intellectual disabilities eligible for federal financial aid to help cover the cost of college. "Mrs. Shriver really saw access to college and lifelong learning as the next frontier," Lewis said of an idea unimaginable when Eunice began her work on these issues in the 1950s. But what hadn't been unimaginable then? The right to a public school education? The right to services from birth to age three? The right to live in a neighborhood, not an institution?

Like Sue Swenson, Sharon Lewis made good use of her experience as a Kennedy Fellow. She became the senior disability policy advisor to the US House Committee on Education and Labor and, later, the commissioner of the Administration on Intellectual and Developmental Disabilities under President Obama.

There are scores of advocates, administrators, lawmakers, and scholars in positions across the country shaping policy on disability issues who might never have followed that path had Eunice Kennedy Shriver not brought them to Washington and trained them in the nuts and bolts of lobbying and lawmaking so that they could continue the battle she could not fight forever. And there was no question whom she had in mind to lead that fight into the next century. Connecticut governor Lowell Weicker, one of the nation's most impassioned disability-rights advocates, had persuaded Tim Shriver to run the 1995 Special Olympics World Games in New Haven. By then, nearly one million athletes in more than one hundred countries around the world were participating in Special Olympics, including in the People's Republic of China and the former Soviet Union. That year, there would be a Special Olympics marathon for the first time and health-screening centers where athletes could access free dental care and hearing exams or be fitted with eyeglasses. There were panel discussions on the social, psychological, legal, and spiritual dimensions of living with intellectual disabilities. There were clinics in nutrition and injury prevention. New Haven in 1995 was a long way from Chicago in 1968.

Tim raised $34 million from private sources and filled the eighty-thousand-seat Yale Bowl. President Clinton opened the competition that was known as the Games of Inclusion, reflecting a stronger emphasis on the integration of those with intellectual disabilities into the wider community. Special Olympics had been drawing criticism from a new generation of parents who said the games stigmatized the athletes they claimed to champion by separating them from athletes without disabilities. Why shouldn't a child with intellectual disabilities play on the same team as the boy without disabilities who lived next door? How would the stigma ever be erased if children with disabilities were segregated in "special" competitions?

Special Olympics took the reproach to heart, forming Unified Sports in 1988, for athletes with and without disabilities to play together on the same teams, first in bowling, softball, and volleyball. It would not satisfy those critics who saw the very existence of Special Olympics as a bar to full integration, but it was a beginning that, within a few years, would attract more than one million athletes with and without disabilities to compete together in Unified Sports.

Loretta Claiborne, a Special Olympics athlete who had been winning gold medals in track events since she first began participating in the games in 1970, became Tim's mentor as he planned and executed the New Haven games. She would become something of a celebrity ambassador for Special Olympics as time went on, speaking across the country about the power of sports to change the lives of those with intellectual disabilities. Claiborne revered Eunice and Sargent Shriver, but she also knew they could not run the organization forever.

"Why don't you move to Washington and take over Special Olympics?" Claiborne asked Tim at the conclusion of the New Haven games. "You should go to Special Olympics. I think that's the place for you." Tim demurred politely. He and Linda and their children were happy with their lives. "The last thing on my list of career goals was to succeed my mother and father in a Washington, DC, office, working full-time for Special Olympics," he said.

One year later, he moved to Washington, DC, to do exactly that.

EPILOGUE

Love gave me confidence, and adversity gave me purpose.

—EUNICE KENNEDY SHRIVER, 2007

THOUSANDS OF TWINKLING lights illuminated satin ribbons of purple and sapphire draping the ceiling of the dinner tent where projectors flashed images of peacocks and lions onto the white canvas walls. Round tables, dressed in crisp linen and topped with rose centerpieces, were set to receive the more than nine hundred guests who had paid $600 apiece to dine on seared jumbo sea scallops and spicy lamb-shank tagine.

Beauty queens in rhinestone tiaras and Cirque du Soleil acrobats in clown face circulated in the entrance hall of the hosts' sixteen-thousand-square-foot mansion, greeting men in black tie and women in designer dresses. Jazz musician Kenny G carried an autographed saxophone that would be auctioned for $9,000 later in the evening. Randy Jackson guarded four backstage passes to a taping of *American Idol*, which would fetch $64,000 after feverish bidding by fans of the TV talent show. Robert De Niro held court. The honoree was Her Highness Sheikha Mozah bint Nasser Al-Missned of Qatar. Sales of tickets and auction items would raise more than $3.35 million for Best Buddies, the nonprofit organization

Anthony Shriver had founded two decades before in his Georgetown University dorm room.

The mix of Hollywood celebrity, Arab royalty, and Washington politics was a cut above the usual charity event in the Federal City. But the blend—two parts glamour, one part calculation—was the signature cocktail of the hostess welcoming guests from a mahogany armchair at the foot of the foyer's circular staircase.

Every strand of her usually wild, tawny hair was tamed into a neat pageboy, with her red nail polish and lipstick a bright flash of color against her black crepe Armani pantsuit and white pearls. No one who bent to kiss her cheek or shake her hand on the evening of October 18, 2008, could remember Eunice Kennedy Shriver ever sitting still so long. Time had done what a lifetime of chronic illness, near-fatal car crashes, and a succession of family tragedies could not: slowed the step of the most energetic of Joe and Rose Kennedy's nine children.

Even at a diminished eighty-seven, *formidable* was still the adjective most often applied to Eunice Kennedy Shriver. It was as though her deceptively frail frame embodied all the gales she had weathered during a lifetime sailing on Nantucket Sound. As though her taut muscles had absorbed the tension from the strings of every racket she wielded like a weapon on tennis courts from Hyannis Port to London, from Palo Alto to Paris. As though she knew, in a way others did not, that every play counts, whether in a game of touch football on the lawn at Cape Cod or in a round of arm-twisting on Capitol Hill.

This was to be the last gala Eunice and Sarge would host at their Potomac, Maryland, home. Washington Fine Properties had listed their 6.84-acre estate for sale at $11.8 million. Five years earlier, on the eve of their fiftieth wedding anniversary, Sarge had resigned as chairman of Special Olympics after a diagnosis of Alzheimer's disease. In a letter to friends, he reassured them, and himself, that Eunice was still going strong. "I would gladly scrap any work of my own simply to watch her in action! Age has neither dimmed her anger at injustice nor her humor in overcoming any obstacles the foolhardy throw across her path," he wrote. "What a joy to be part of her whirlwind!"

But the whirlwind, too, was decelerating. A series of strokes had sapped her strength, just as Alzheimer's had shrouded his memory. In 2000 she was recovering from surgery to remove part of her pancreas when a case of sepsis sent her into intensive care. The Reverend Richard Fragomeni, a family friend, flew from Chicago to administer the last rites, the Catholic blessing before death. He offered daily Mass at her bedside. Her children read to her in shifts. They and her doctors were stunned when she emerged from a coma, frail but resilient. "This is a proud family," said Father Fragomeni. "Giving the impression that you are invincible was required."

She survived another car crash, a year later, a few days before her eightieth birthday, with a broken leg and an unbowed spirit, just as she had earlier survived a house fire that damaged their home and a storm that flooded the tent and sent tree limbs crashing onto her guests' cars at Sarge's eightieth birthday party. She had been working from home on September 11, 2001, when hijacked airliners slammed into the World Trade Center, the Pentagon, and a field outside Shanksville, Pennsylvania. "Keep working. Don't send anyone home. Too much to do," she told Sue Swenson in a call to the Kennedy Foundation that its director quietly ignored.

She would go to Dublin, forty years after she'd visited Ireland with President Kennedy, for the first summer Special Olympics held outside of the United States. She would go to South Africa to hear President Nelson Mandela embrace Special Olympics in a country where it was still common to consider a baby born with intellectual disabilities a cursed child. She would go to Poland to promote Best Buddies in a place where children with intellectual disabilities were still segregated in special schools, with little or no contact with peers without disabilities. She would go to the White House to celebrate her birthday with President George W. Bush and First Lady Laura Bush at a dinner honoring Special Olympics. She would go to Shanghai to see the Chinese celebrate the children that they, too, had hidden away in warehouses for far too long.

By 2008, there was no more pretense. Eunice Kennedy Shriver had taken her last foreign trip, opened her last Special Olympics games, harangued her last congressional committee. Her son was proving a worthy successor. As skilled in the boardroom as his father, Tim attracted major corporate sponsors. As adept as his mother on Capitol Hill, he steered passage of the Special Olympics Sports and Empowerment Act of 2004, authorizing $15 million per year over five years to spur further expansion of Special Olympics worldwide.

No one but Eunice called the athletes "special friends" anymore. The paternalism of the past was yielding to a culture of self-determination, giving power to those with intellectual disabilities to advocate for themselves, to make their own decisions about their lives. But changing times and her slowing step would not stop Eunice from sharing that journey with them.

On this Saturday night, as on every other night of her goal-oriented life, Eunice was looking forward, not back. The Twentieth and Grand Finale Best Buddies Ball could not simply trumpet its success. Best Buddies had to grow, as Special Olympics had grown before it, expanding into places in the world—Africa, Asia, the Middle East—where too many of those with intellectual limitations still lived in the shadows. By 2008, Best Buddies had brought 350,000 young people together through programs at 1,300 middle school, high school, and college campuses around the world; Special Olympics had expanded to more than 170 countries and 3.5 million athletes and continued to grow.

Eunice still credited her brother Jack, the visionary president, and her husband, Sarge, the persuasive lobbyist, with passage of the landmark legislation that first committed the federal government to the cause and care of those with intellectual disabilities, in 1963. Jack was "marvelous," his commitment "fantastic," she said. "He couldn't have done more." Sarge was "crucial," and "the country, the retarded, my family, and I owe him an unbelievable debt of thanks for changing and enriching millions of lives."

As for her own contributions, Eunice said little, dismissing out of habit the idea that Rosemary had inspired her life's work. Hadn't she pooh-poohed that notion publicly for almost five decades, convinced that the key to being taken seriously was to politicize, not personalize, the needs of those with intellectual disabilities?

"I knew that this work had to be Jack's if it was to be successful," she told her son Tim. "The way to make things happen in Washington was for people to see this issue as important to Jack. It had to be an *important* issue, not a family issue. I never wanted people to think that what President Kennedy was doing was about Rosemary. Then they would have dismissed it as a personal matter. It wasn't. It was about the outrageous neglect. It was about the outrage. I wanted all those experts to face the injustice of it all and not write us off."

Her cause had been about the injustice of it all and about Rosemary, too. It had also been about Eunice, a woman who would not be written off. Not by her father. Not by history. "In a strange way, perhaps, my life also includes being lucky in the adversity I encountered," she said at a program honoring her at the John F. Kennedy Presidential Library in 2007. "I am lucky that I experienced the sting of rejection as a woman who was told that the real power was not for me. I am lucky that I saw my mother and my sister Rosemary treated with the most unbearable rejection. I am lucky that I have had to confront political and social injustice all over the world throughout my career. You might say, 'Why are you lucky to have had such difficult experiences?' The answer is quite simple: the combination of the love of my family and the awful sting of rejection helped me develop the confidence I needed to believe that I could make a difference in a positive direction. It's really that simple: love gave me confidence, and adversity gave me purpose."

Her family had been the source of the love and the rejection both, and the culture that now showered her with accolades was the same one that earlier had barred the door. "When I was a little girl, I wanted to go to Notre Dame, but I couldn't because it was an all-male school," she said with a mischievous smile when the university awarded her its Laetare Medal for service to society. "Today Notre Dame is trying to make it up to me by giving me this medal, and I accept it on behalf of all the women . . . who never had a chance to go to Notre Dame."

She had reared her own daughter to go anywhere and be anything she dreamed she could be. She coached Maria to beat her brothers at tennis. She made sure she went along with them to Baltimore Orioles games. She haunted bookshops whenever Maria published a new book, moving them to the front of the display tables. If a manager complained, her daughter said, "She'd tell him to go right back behind the desk where he belonged and be quiet."

She refused to conform, confounding those who tried to pigeonhole her. "She was a woman who didn't choose, and women are often told you have to choose to be this, or that, this kind of woman, you have to dress this way, talk this way, you have to have one opinion. Well, Mummy wasn't like that; she didn't choose," Maria said. "She let all the different parts of her go out, and that's what made her unique. She didn't allow herself to be tamed, or contained. She achieved herself, her true authentic self. The very same woman who made grown men quake in their boots when she stepped foot on Capitol Hill was the very same woman who spent quality time with each and every one of us, making us feel loved, making us believe in [ourselves]."

The mother who had been so self-contained that Maria would not have dreamed of crawling into bed with her until she was dying had a gentler relationship with her grandchildren —"building sandcastles, looking for leprechauns, looking for mermaids," her daughter said. In the end, "she didn't choose between being strong and soft, complex or simple."

For the last big gala she was to host, Eunice and Anthony had selected the evening's honoree with care. The sheikha had embraced Eunice's cause as chair of the Qatar Foundation for Education, Science, and Community Development and as a special United Nations envoy for education. If honoring the Qatar royal with a leadership award in a capacious backyard tent topped with a tiny minaret could open more doors across the Arab Peninsula, Eunice was happy to transform her home into a scene from *The Arabian Nights*.

While her guests sat down in the big tent to dessert of baklava tarts garnished with pistachios and figs, Eunice slipped upstairs. It had not been so long ago that she told her friend Carole Dell how glad she was she had installed an elevator in the house. "The only reason I put it in was for Rosemary," she said, "and who would ever know that I'd need it?" Rosemary had died, at eighty-six, three years before, with her brother and sisters at her bedside at St. Coletta.

Eunice was tucked in bed when Lowell Weicker, the former US senator and ex-governor of Connecticut, knocked on her door. The father of an adult son with Down syndrome, Weicker had been a friend and ally through dozens of battles on behalf of those with intellectual disabilities. He lost his bid for reelection to the Senate before the Americans with Disabilities Act passed in 1990, but he was one of the chief architects of the landmark law barring discrimination against those with physical and intellectual disabilities.

His was not a social call. Eunice had summoned him from the party to discuss the Americans with Disabilities Amendments Act and the Prenatally and Postnatally Diagnosed Conditions Awareness Act, both of which President Bush had just signed into law. The ADA amendments had broadened the definition of disability in response to several decisions by the US Supreme Court that had restricted application of the original law. The latter bill strengthened the informed-consent process for prenatal testing to ensure that mothers received more detailed information about such conditions as Down syndrome. That bipartisan bill was cosponsored by conservative Kansas Republican senator Sam Brownback and Ted, once again doing the bidding of his big sister, who—having fought for the medical advances that had increased the average lifespan of a person with Down syndrome from nineteen to sixty years—was appalled that 90 percent of such fetuses were being aborted in the United States.

Eunice's failing health had been apparent when Brownback met with her months earlier. "She said, 'Is Teddy being helpful? Is Teddy working with you and helping?' I would say, 'Yes, he is, but you can always help us more and push him more.' And she did," Brownback recalled.

Upstairs in her bedroom, she peppered Weicker with questions. Both bills were important wins, but Eunice worried about the future. Enacting a law did not guarantee its permanence, she well knew. How often had she gone back up to the Hill to fight for a measure to be reauthorized, for adequate funds to be reappropriated?

Would the results of the presidential election in a month strengthen or weaken their hand? Would Barack Obama protect their hard-won gains? Could Sarah Palin, John McCain's running mate, put politics aside to work with Democrats to benefit her son with Down syndrome? How deep was their bench in Congress? On whom would they rely when Iowa senator Tom Harkin or Maryland congressman Steny Hoyer or Utah senator Orrin Hatch retired?

The two old friends did not talk that evening about the precarious state of her health or about the brain tumor that had kept Ted away from those recent votes in the Senate and the evening's festivities in Eunice's backyard. Death would claim both Eunice and Ted ten months later, only days apart, in the bright light of a last Cape Cod summer, their funerals a final, fitting contrast between the public life of a Kennedy man and a Kennedy woman. Ted would lie in repose at the John F. Kennedy Presidential Library before a requiem Mass in Boston's grand Marian basilica and burial beside his martyred brothers at Arlington National Cemetery. Eunice would be buried from a simple white clapboard church on the Cape where, in a spontaneous act of love and gratitude, several Special Olympics athletes threw their gold medals into her grave as her coffin was lowered into the ground.

On this autumn evening, however, death was not on Eunice's agenda. She had little use for idle chatter about the things she could not change. Instead, while hundreds of revelers outside were bidding up the price of trips to Paris and Hawaii to benefit Best Buddies, Eunice Kennedy Shriver was propped up in bed, notepad on her lap and pencil in her hair, asking what was for her always the most important question: "What's next?"

ACKNOWLEDGMENTS

A job offer from a US attorney general. A love letter from a Conservative member of Parliament. A wedding gift from a World War II spy. A diary entry about Joe McCarthy. A thank-you note from Jacqueline Kennedy Onassis.

Thirty-three boxes of uncatalogued letters, documents, diaries, and memoranda provided a window into every period of Eunice Kennedy Shriver's life. For granting me unrestricted access to their mother's private papers, I owe the greatest debt to Bobby, Maria, Timothy, Mark, and Anthony Shriver. They were as generous with their trust as they were with their time in sharing memories of their mother.

In addition to Mrs. Shriver's children, her extended family, friends, and professional colleagues answered my questions and offered their perspectives on the woman and the times she helped to shape. Among the many to whom I owe special thanks are Mary Cunningham Agee, William Alford, Sister Dorothy Bell, Deeda Blair, Ann McGlone Burke, Joseph A. Califano Jr., Geri Critchley, Renee Dease, Carole Dell, Lisa Derx, Christopher Dodd, Arthur Dyck, Steven Eidelman, Dr. Joseph English, the Reverend Richard Fragomeni, Connie Garner, David Gelman, William Haddad, Erika Hagensen, Tom Harkin, Orrin Hatch, Gillian Healy, the Reverend Bryan Hehir, Mickey Kantor, Marty Krauss, Ethel

Kennedy, Patrick Kennedy, Vicki Reggie Kennedy, Lucille Larkin, David Lenz, Sharon Lewis, the Reverend Donald MacMillan, Colman McCarthy, Mav McCarthy, Barbara Mikulski, David Mixner, David Phelps, Dorothy Schrot, Tom Songster, Scott Stossel, Sue Swenson, Margaret Tedone, Kathleen Kennedy Townsend, Laurence Tribe, Ellen Varmus, Barbara Walters, Lowell Weicker, Harris Wofford, and Ela Work. To those who spoke with me on background, I am equally in your debt.

One consequence of researching a book over many years is that several of those who assisted are no longer here to accept my thanks. I remember with gratitude the conversations I had with William McCormack Blair Jr., Bettye Caldwell, Dr. Robert E. Cooke, Jay Emmett, Frank Gifford, the Reverend Theodore Hesburgh, Frank Mankiewicz, Michael Novak, and Page Huidekoper Wilson.

I had the good fortune to spend many research hours in the company of archivists at the John F. Kennedy Presidential Library and Museum in Boston. Karen Adler Abramson, Stacey Chandler, Michael Desmond, Sharon Kelly, and Stephen Plotkin were knowledgeable, helpful, and gracious guides. Their assistance was matched only by that of their former colleagues, Tom Putnam, who served for sixteen years with distinction at one of the finest presidential libraries in the National Archives system, and Tom McNaught, who for seventeen years led the John F. Kennedy Library Foundation with equal charm and intelligence. They lent a hand and an ear when they were needed most.

Archivists and librarians from Mrs. Shriver's convent school in London to her university in Palo Alto, California, helped me in my quest, and I thank them all: Diana Bachman, Bentley Historical Library, University of Michigan; Jennifer N. Christy, House of the Good Shepherd Archives, Chicago; Judith S. Engelberg, Joseph P. Kennedy Jr. Foundation Archives, Washington, DC; Spencer Howard, Herbert Hoover Presidential Library and Museum, West Branch, Iowa; Jenny Johnson, Special Collections & University Archives, Stanford University; Christina Violeta Jones, National Archives, College Park, Maryland; Carol Leadenham, Hoover Institution Archives, Stanford University; Ellen M. Shea and Jennifer Fauxsmith, Schlesinger Library, Radcliffe Institute, Harvard University; Joel Shedlofsky, Archives of the Sisters of the Good Shepherd, St. Louis; Stephen Spence, National Archives at Kansas City; Barbara Vesey, Archives of the Society of the Sacred Heart, London; John R. Waggener, American Heritage Center Archives, University of

Wyoming; and Lauren Ziarco, Manhattanville College Archives, Purchase, New York.

I am particularly indebted to Tab Lewis at the National Archives in College Park, Maryland. When one of his colleagues dismissed as folly my suggestion that the archives might yield a record of Eunice Kennedy's pro bono work in the Justice Department in 1947 and 1948, Mr. Lewis stepped in to guide my successful search. It was an act of kindness and a lesson in persistence.

My family, friends, and colleagues have been souls of patience, listening to more stories than warranted and providing more helpful feedback during the research and writing process than I had any right to expect. Susan Trausch and Mark Feeney deserve special thanks for reading the manuscript with an editor's sharp eye for errors in fact and inconsistencies in tone. Larry Tye supplied advice and wisdom born of his distinguished career as a biographer of, among others, Satchel Paige and Bobby Kennedy. Maura Jane Farrelly, chair of the American Studies Program at Brandeis University, offered suggestions and a reliable shoulder throughout, as did Charity Adams-Brzuchalski, Beth Bernstein, Bella English, Roz Kabrhel, Janet Knott, Kevin Lowry, Barbara McMahon, Tom and Kathi Mullin, Doug and Sue Noyes, Manuel Ortiz, Sharon Rosenberg, Kate McMahon Upson, Joan Vennochi, Kate Walsh, Rainy Wilkins, and Lise Woodard. My children, Timothy, Patrick, and Katherine, deserve special thanks for providing a sense of perspective when I lost my own.

At Brandeis, I am indebted to Assistant Provost Rick Silberman, University Librarian John Unsworth, and General Counsel Steven S. Locke, who were instrumental in the temporary transfer of Mrs. Shriver's papers to Brandeis. Tom Putnam at the JFK Library is owed a special round of applause for the pivotal role he played in that operation.

This book would not exist but for the efforts of Colleen Mohyde, my estimable agent, and her grand assistant, Frances Kennedy, and for the spade work done by Margaret Feuer, Katie May, and Sarah Marnell. Priscilla Painton, a patient and insightful editor at Simon & Schuster, conceived this project and was thoughtfully assisted throughout by Megan Hogan, Ann Tate Pearce, Jonathan Evans, and Jessica Breen. I salute them all.

Words are inadequate to express my gratitude to Peter May, who accompanied me on every step of this journey, picking me up when I stumbled and setting me back on course. In this endeavor, as in all others, I could not have done it without him.

NOTES

BDG   *Boston Daily Globe*
 BG   *Boston Globe*
 BP   *Boston Post*
 CR   *Congressional Record*
CST   *Chicago Sun-Times*
CDN   *Chicago Daily News*
CDT   *Chicago Daily Tribune*
 CT   *Chicago Tribune*
 DN   *Daily News*
INS   *International News Service*
LAT   *Los Angeles Times*
NYP   *New York Post*
NYT   *New York Times*
SEP   *Saturday Evening Post*
 UP   *United Press*
 WP   *Washington Post*
 WS   *Washington Star*
WTH   *Washington Times-Herald*

LIBRARIES AND ARCHIVES

AHC   American Heritage Center, University of Wyoming, Laramie
BHS   Bentley Historical Society, University of Michigan, Ann Arbor
CHM   Chicago History Museum, Chicago
GRFPL   Gerald R. Ford Presidential Library, Ann Arbor, MI
HI   Hoover Institution Archives, Stanford University, Palo Alto, CA
HHPL   Herbert Hoover Presidential Library, West Branch, IA
JFKPL   John F. Kennedy Presidential Library, Boston
KFA   Kennedy Foundation Archives, Washington, DC
LBJPL   Lyndon Baines Johnson Presidential Library, Austin, TX
LC   Library of Congress, Manuscript Division, Washington, DC
MCA   Manhattanville College Archives, Purchase, NY
NAUS   National Archives of the United States, College Park, MD
RSA   Roehampton School Archives, London, England
SUA   Stanford University Archives, Palo Alto, CA
WJCPL   William Jefferson Clinton Presidential Library, Little Rock, AR
SL   Schlesinger Library, Radcliffe Institute, Harvard University,
          Cambridge, MA

COLLECTIONS

AMBP   Anne McGlone Burke Papers, CHM, Chicago
EBP   Eleanor Bumgardner Papers, BHS, University of Michigan, Ann
          Arbor, MI

EMKOHP Edward M. Kennedy Oral History Project, Miller Center, University of Virginia, Charlottesville, VA
CBP Clay Blair Papers, AHC, University of Wyoming, Laramie, WY
EKSPP Eunice Kennedy Shriver Personal Papers, Special Olympics, Washington, DC
HHP Herbert Hoover Papers, HHPL, West Branch, IA
DHP David Horowitz Papers, HI, Stanford University, Palo Alto, CA
JFKP John Fitzgerald Kennedy Papers, JFKPL, Boston
JLP James Landis Papers, LC, Washington, DC
JPKP Joseph Patrick Kennedy Papers, JFKPL, Boston
JVBP James V. Bennett Papers, JFKPL, Boston
MFP Myer Feldman Papers, JFKPL, Boston
MESP Mary Elizabeth Switzer Papers, SL, Radcliffe Institute, Cambridge, MA
MVWP Miriam Van Waters Papers, SL, Radcliffe Institute, Cambridge, MA
PGP Patricia Gold Papers, SL, Radcliffe Institute, Cambridge, MA
REFKP Rose Elizabeth Fitzgerald Kennedy Papers, JFKPL, Boston
RSSP Robert Sargent Shriver Papers, JFKPL, Boston

INTRODUCTION

xv *A correction in the* New York Times: Correction, NYT, August 29, 2009.

xvi *"Dear Daddy, I know you are very busy"*: Edward Shorter, *The Kennedy Family and the Story of Mental Retardation*, 60.

xvi *"In how many families"*: RFK, in *The Fruitful Bough*, JFKPL.

xvi *"He Left One Son"*: *Daily News*, November 21, 1969.

xvi *"To us, they were marvelous creatures"*: REFK, *Times to Remember*, 122.

xviii *She sent that check for $60*: EKS to REFK and JPK, March 8, 1945, box 8, KFA.

xxi *"courage and toughness in a male world"*: Barbara Kevles, "The Kennedy Who Could Be President (If She Weren't a Woman)," *Ladies' Home Journal*, March 1976.

xxi *"an intellectual mechanic"*: Arthur J. Dyck, interview with the author.

xxi *"If that girl had been born with balls"*: Peter Collier and David Horowitz, *The Kennedys: An American Drama*, 159.

xxi *"Needless to say, after so many years"*: Transcript of EKS speech, November 16, 2007, JFKPL.

xxii *"the first of the tragedies"*: REFK, *Times to Remember*, 287.

xxii *It was "all so unnecessary"*: EKS "Hope for Retarded Children," *SEP*, September 22, 1962.

xxiv *"When she told me"*: Frank Gifford, interview with the author.

PROLOGUE

1 *singling out instead*: JFK, Remarks on signing Mental Retardation Facilities and Community Mental Health Centers Construction Act, October 31, 1963, JFKPL.

2 *"This bill will expand our knowledge"*: Ibid.

2 *The memory still stung*: Elizabeth M. Boggs, oral history interview, July 17, 1968, JFKPL.

3 *the 5.4 million children and adults*: Fact Sheet on Mental Retardation and the National Association for Retarded Children, EKSPP; Memorandum for Honorable Myer Feldman from Wilbur J. Cohen, June 15, 1962. MFP, box 13, JFKPL.

3 *Eunice secured from Jack a commitment*: EKS, oral history interview, May 7, 1968, JFKPL.

4 *"It was said, in an earlier age"*: JFK, Remarks on signing Mental Retardation Facilities and Community Health Centers Construction Act, October 31, 1963, JFKPL.

ONE: The Middle Child

7 *Rose Fitzgerald Kennedy went to a dance*: "Ex-Mayor John F. a Grandpa Again: Mr. Fitzgerald's Daughter Mother of a Girl," *BDG*, July 11, 1921.

7 *the Hotel Pemberton: Then & Now: Hull and Nantasket Beach*, Committee for the Preservation of Hull's History, Charleston, SC: Arcadia, 2001.

7 *The fashionable hotel*: Alexander von Hoffman, John F. Kennedy's birthplace; a Presidential Home in History and Memory, National Park Service, US Department of the Interior, August 2004, 43–46.

8 *"Nothing I'd rather do"*: JPK to Chris Dunphy, June 21, 1921, JPKP, JFKPL.

8 *"The idea was"*: REFK to RC, January 24, 1972, REFK Papers, box 12, JFKPL.

8 *Labor pains had roused her*: "Ex-Mayor John F. a Grandpa Again," *BDG*, July 11, 1921.

8 *Eunice Fitzgerald had contracted*: "Youngest Daughter of Ex-Mayor Dead," *BDG*, September 26, 1923.

8 *"Unfortunately when Eunice was born"*: REFK to RC, Jan. 24, 1972, REFK Papers, box 12, JFKPL.

10 *"It was all a completely new"*: REFK, diaries, REFK Papers, box 5, JFKPL.

10 *Eunice was worryingly thin*: REFK, diaries, February 14, 1923, REFK Papers, box 1, JFKPL.

11 *"those jottings foretold"*: REFK, *Times to Remember*, 91.

11 *"I don't think she was quite the same"*: EKS to RC, February 26, 1972, REFK Papers, box 10, JFKPL.

11 *"Took care of children"*: REFK, diaries, January 7, 1923, REFK Papers, box 5, JFKPL.

11 *"that church isn't just something for Sundays"*: REFK, *Times to Remember*, 83.

11 *"rather pale and of a nervous"*: Doris Kearns Goodwin, *The Fitzgeralds and the Kennedys*, 363.

12 *"Joe Sr. left on 5 o'clock"*: REFK, diaries, REFK Papers, box 5, JFKPL.

12 *"Eddie Moore became his closest friend"*: REFK, *Times to Remember*, 89.

12 Boston *"is no place to bring up Irish Catholic children"*: Joe McCarthy, *The Remarkable Kennedys*, 42.

13 *"Physically she was very healthy"*: REFK to RC, January 7, 1972, REFK Papers, box 10, JFKPL.

13 Rose *"was puzzled by what all this could mean"*: Ibid.

14 *"I don't think that probably on the outside"*: REFK to RC, January 14, 1972, REFK Papers, box 10, JFKPL.

15 *"quite discouraged with the penmanship"*: JPK to EKS, February 11, 1936, REFK Papers, box 13, JFKPL.

15 *"I always thought"*: REFK, diary notes, REFK Papers, box 13, JFKPL.

15 *"When psychologists recommended"*: EKS, "Hope for Retarded Children," 71–75.

15 *"Much as I had begun to realize"*: REFK, diary notes, REFKP, box 13, JFKPL.

15 she demonstrated *"excellent social poise"*: David Nasaw, *The Patriarch: The Remarkable Life and Turbulent Times of Joseph P. Kennedy*, 153.

16 Their father *"was easily upset"*: REFK, *Times to Remember*, 152.

16 *Rosemary's loneliness is palpable*: RK to EKS, April 1, 1931, JPK Papers, box 1, JFKPL.

16 She was, Eunice remembered, *"quite stern"*: EKS to RC, February 26, 1972, REFK, box 10, JFKPL.

17 *"There was a downstairs bathroom in Bronxville"*: Ibid.

17 *"We had a lot of apples"*: Ibid.

18 *Eunice's gastrointestinal ailments*: Hank Searls, *The Lost Prince: Young Joe, the Forgotten Kennedy*, 59.

18 *"I am getting along fine in school"*: EKS, undated letter to her parents, REFK Papers, box 13, JFKPL.

19 *"I can remember thinking"*: EKS to RC, February 26, 1972, REFK Papers, box 10, JFKPL.

19 *Eunice's memory that Rose*: Ibid.

19 *"Dear Mother, I am sorry that you are away"*: EKS to REFK, February 13, 1929, REFK Papers, box 13, JFKPL.

19 *"Dear Mother, I miss you a[n] awful lot"*: EKS to REFK, March 2, 1932, REFK Papers, box 13, JFKPL.

19 *"Mrs. Kennedy didn't say"*: Laurence Leamer, *The Kennedy Women*, 153.

19 *When her father was home*: EKS to RC, February 26, 1972, REFK Papers, box 10, JFKPL.

19 *"It's solitary confinement"* REFK to RC, January 7, 1972, REFK Papers, box 10, JFKPL.

20 *Like her mother, her father "was gone a lot"*: Ibid.

20 *"was more concerned with the boys' future:"* Ibid.

21 *"[A]fter all, when girls grow up"*: REFK, *Times to Remember*, 115.

21 *Bob had sold four of his rabbits*: EKS to REFK, REFK Papers, box 12, JFKPL.

22 *"We don't want any losers"*: REFK, *Times to Remember*, 143.

22 *"As a child, she was not outstanding"*: REFK diary notes, REFK Papers, box 12, JFKPL.

22 *Eunice remembered that her mother*: REFK diary notes on children, REFK Papers, box 10, JFKPL.

23 *"I will admit now"*: EKS, eulogy for RK, January 10, 2005, box 9, KFA.

23 *"Pat had a special empathy"*: REFK, *Times to Remember*, 125.

23 *"If anyone in the family"*: Luella Hennessey-Donovan, oral history interview, September 25, 1991, JFKPL.

24 *"I have been hearing"*: EKS to REFK and JPK, January 14, 1938, REFK Papers, box 13, JFKPL.

24 *"Of all the surprising things"*: EKS to REFK, January 29, 1938, REFK Papers, box 13, JFKPL.

24 *So accustomed*: EKS to REFK and JPK, January 14, 1938, REFK Papers, box 13, JFKPL.

24 *When the school term ended*: "Two Kennedy Girls Sail," *NYT*, April 21, 1938.

TWO: London

25 *It fell to Joseph P. Kennedy and six-year-old Teddy*: photo caption, *NYT*, May 8, 1938.

26 *Smitten with all the photogenic Kennedy children*: Collier and Horowitz, *The Kennedys*, 83.

26 *Joe had just announced*: "Kennedy Presentation Edict Leaves Boston Debs Unmoved," *BG*, April 12, 1938.

26 *Kick certainly did that*: Lynne McTaggart, *Kathleen Kennedy*, 25.

26 *Edward Cavendish*: Will Swift, *The Kennedys Amidst the Gathering Storm*, 75.

26 *"Of course everybody loved her"*: Ibid., 38.

27 *the spirited Kick "did not have an intellectual bone"*: Ibid.

27 *Eunice did*: Paige Huidekoper Wilson, interview with the author.

28 *"I really like Noroton"*: EKS to JPK and REFK, undated, REFK Papers, box 13, JFKPL.

28 *"She was quite pretty"*: REFK, *Times to Remember*, 167.

28 *"too tight in the seat"*: REFK to EKS, February 14, 1957, JPK Papers, box 35, JFKPL.

28 *"the way some people wear"*: REFK to EKS, May 2, 1973, REFK Papers, box 55, JFKPL.

28 *She sent newsy letters from Noroton*: EKS to REFK, February 7, 1938; EKS to REFK and JPK, undated, REFK Papers, box 13, JFKPL.

28 *She wrote to her father*: EKS to JPK, November 7, 1937, REFK Papers, box 13, JFKPL.

29 *Mother Violet walked her rabbits*: *School Journal*, 1927–1948, RSA.

29 *Each day began with the Rising Bell*: Description of daily routine at Roehampton, April O'Leary, *Living Tradition: The Chronicle of a School*; Antonia White, *Frost in May*.

31 *"lavished far more attention"*: O'Leary, *Living Tradition*, 186.

31 *"In September 1938 the school"*: *Family Chronicle*, September 1938, RSA.

31 *the most popular girl*: Anne Elizabeth, "Chatter," New Bedford (MA) *Standard Times*, June 11, 1939.

32 *"No such thing"*: Sister Dorothy Bell, interview with the author.

32 *Equally suspect*: Hazel Hunkins Hallinan, "Nine Young U.S. Ambassadors," *Parents*, September 1939.

32 *"like birds of paradise"*: Collier and Horowitz, *The Kennedys*, 65.

32 *In Dorothy Bell's memory*: Dorothy Bell, interview with the author.

32 *Her brother Jack wrote*: JFK to EKS, undated letter, REFK Papers, box 13, JFKPL.

33 *More than two dozen nuns*: "28 Nuns Are Rescued by Kennedy," *INS*, July 21, 1938.

33 *It was to Kennedy*: *Roehampton Association Report*, Autumn 1938, RSA.

34 *Joe had leased a villa*: Cari Beauchamp, "It Happened at the Hotel du Cap," *Vanity Fair*, February 13, 2009.

34 *An only child*: Maria Riva, *Marlene Dietrich*, 469.

35 *"so we should be full of it"*: EKS to JPK, September 4, 1938, REFK Papers, box 13, JFKPL.

35 *"Joe has found no girl"*: EKS to JPK, December 28, 1938, JPK Papers, box 2, JFKPL.

35 *No outing impressed*: EKS, unpublished essay on the coronation of Pope Pius XII, EKS Personal Papers.

36 *"all the girls thought"*: EKS, 1939 diary, EKS Personal Papers.

36 *"I hated those parties"*: Leamer, *The Kennedy Women*, 278.

36   *"Would it be funny"*: This and all other 1939 diary entries in this chapter: EKS, 1939 diary, EKS Personal Papers.

THREE: From the Sacred Heart to Stanford University

42   *At capacity, the* Washington: "Washington Lands 1,746 from Europe," *NYT*, September 19, 1939.

42   *"they felt safe"*: EKS, 1939 diary, EKS Personal Papers.

43   *"Everyone we have met"*: REFK, *Times to Remember*, 256.

43   *"great fun"*: Ibid.

43   *The dinner*: menu from *Washington*, EKS Personal Papers.

43   *"Some refused"*: EKS, 1939 diary, EKS Personal Papers.

44   *"It can't be eighteen months"*: KK to JPK, September 18, 1939, JPK Papers, box 2, JFKPL.

45   *"Destiny first made us"*: Turner Catledge, "FDR Address, a Solemn Message," *NYT*, September 22, 1939.

45   *"When my mother"*: Goodwin, *The Fitzgeralds and the Kennedys*, 594.

45   *"although we all miss you"*: EKS to JPK, November 5, 1939, REFK Papers, box 13, JFKPL.

46   *"her difficulty"*: EKS to JPK, November 20, 1939, JPK Papers, box 2, JFKPL.

46   *"She was diagnosed"*: Hennessey-Donovan, oral history interview, September 25, 1991, JFKPL.

46   *"Everyone at College"*: REFK to JPK, undated letter, JPK Papers, box 2, JFKPL.

46   *She had been elected*: EKS to JPK, November 20, 1939, JPK Papers, box 2, JFKPL.

46   *"Mother heard a rumor"*: Ibid.

46   *"As for myself"*: EKS to JPK, undated letter, REFK Papers, box 13, JFKPL.

47   *Mother Dammann was not deterred*: Grace Dammann, "Principles Versus Prejudices," Class Day Talk, May 31, 1938, Social Action Collection, MCA.

47   *The Barat Settlement*: "Barat Settlement to Observe Anniversary," *Catholic News*, May 25, 1940.

48   *"It means something"*: Mother Mary Patterson to REFK, March 15, 1940, REFK Papers, box 13, JFKPL.

48   *When not intervening with the nuns*: REFK to JPK, March 28, 1940, JPK Papers, box 2, JFKPL.

48   *she won a doubles championship*: "Sonia Wise Wins Tennis Title at Manhattanville," *Gazette and Daily*, York, PA, June 8, 1940.

48   *"The chief topic of conversation"*: REFK, *Times to Remember*, 265.

49 *"We all nearly collapsed, and Eunice"*: PKL to JPK, June 26, 1940, REFK Papers, box 13, JFKPL.

49 She *"had begun to get sort of emotional"*: EKS to RC, REFK Papers, box 10, JFKPL.

50 *"Manifestly, there were other factors"*: REFK, *Times to Remember*, 286.

50 *Jack had also won a more competitive race*: EKS to JPK, August 6, 1940, REFK Papers, box 13, JFKPL; "Kennedys Excel at Sailing," *NYT*, September 4, 1940.

50 *Students at the Convent*: Dorothy Bell, interview with the author; O'Leary, *Living Tradition*, 96.

51 *"In my years of service"*: JPK, radio address, October 29, 1940, ed. Amanda Smith, *Hostage to Fortune: The Letters of Joseph P. Kennedy*, 482–89.

51 *"Democracy is finished"*: Louis Lyons, "Kennedy Says Democracy All Done in Britain, Maybe Here," *BG*, November 9, 1940.

51 *"I really have much more"*: EKS to REFK, undated letter, box 8, KFA.

52 *"Please tell Johnny"*: Ibid.

52 *"He was quite enthusiastic"*: EKS to Clay Blair Jr., recorded interview, CBP, AHC, UW.

52 *"We sent her out there"*: REFK, recorded interview, February 1, 1968, HHPL.

53 *"There was a little question"*: Ibid.

53 *"bought a new set"*: EKS, diary entry, EKS Personal Papers.

54 *"more people killed"*: Ibid.

54 *"She was so skeletal"*: Ibid.

54 *In the "war diary"*: EKS, war diary, undated entry, EKS Personal Papers.

55 *"People all foreigners"*: Ibid.

55 *"Quite a catch"*: Ibid.

55 *Cousin Eve*: Cousin Eve, "Society Writer on a Cruise to South America," *CDT*, May 25, 1941.

55 *"Father also told the interesting fact"*: REFK, diaries 1935–1941, REFK Papers, box 5, JFKPL.

55 *For all of her travels*: Ibid.

55 *When the* Brazil *anchored*: EKS, undated diary entry, on *Brazil* stationary, EKS Personal Papers.

56 *"plenty mad, and I don't blame her"*: Ibid.

57 *"Many nights the school would call"*: Goodwin, *The Fitzgeralds and the Kennedys*, 640.

57 *Herbert Hoover had inquired*: HH to JPK, November 12, 1941, HHP, HHPL.

57 *"She is a wonderful girl"*: HH to Dr. J. P. Mitchell, November 15, 1941, HHP, HHPL.

57   *The procedure involved drilling*: Waldemar Kaempffert, "Turning the Mind Inside Out," *SEP*, May 24, 1941; "Neurosurgical Treatment of Certain Abnormal Mental States: Panel Discussion at Cleveland Session," *JAMA*, August 16, 1941.

58   *Joe assured Joe Jr., Jack, and Kick*: Nasaw, *The Patriarch*, 536.

58   *Eunice said she had no idea*: Leamer, *The Kennedy Women*, 323.

58   *Rose told St. Coletta*: REFK to Sister Sheila, March 29, 1971, REFK Papers, box 57, JFKPL.

59   *In a lighthearted round robin letter*: REFK to her children, December 5, 1941, REFK Papers, box 55, JFKPL.

59   *"smooth as glass"*: EKS to JPK and REFK, January 5, 1942, REFK Papers, box 55, JFKPL.

59   *"Mrs. Poole has taken me sightseeing"*: Ibid.

59   *She moved into Lagunita Court*: Ibid.

60   *As different as Stanford looked*: SUA, Special Collection, Founding Documents, box 24.

60   *A new academic program*: Ibid.

60   *Her mother urged her to give up gum*: REFK to EKS, January 29, 1942, box 8, KFA.

61   *"We received a letter from the doctor"*: JPK to EKS, February 28, 1942, box 8, KFA.

61   *Before she even registered for classes*: EKS to REFK, undated letters, box 8, KFA.

61   *"I am not recommending"*: REFK to KK, February 5, 1942, box 7, KFA.

61   *But rush she did*: REFK to her children, January 20, 1942, JPKP, box 2, JFKPL.

61   *Her letters home*: EKS to REFK, undated letters, REFK Papers, box 55, JFKPL, and box 8, KFA.

62   *Thirty years later*: EKS to Clay Blair Jr., recorded interview, CBP, AHC, UW.

63   *By August 1944*: SUA, Special Collections, box 24.

63   *"These soldiers"*: Nick Bourne, UPI report, October 20, 1943.

63   *Rose came west*: Graham Stuart to REFK, June 19, 1942, REFK Papers, box 125, JFKPL.

63   *"She is probably the envy"*: REFK to JPK, June 15, 1942, JPK Papers, box 2, JFKPL.

63   *"Eunice even said"*: REFK to JPK, June 24, 1942, JPK Papers, box 2, JFKPL.

64   *"Swimming, boating, and"*: "Work for Victory," editorial, *Stanford Daily*, Palo Alto, CA, August 13, 1942.

64   *"Jack gave me a point of view"*: REFK to EKS, September 29, 1942, box 42, KFA.

64   *Rose came to visit again*: REFK to her children, November 3, 1942, JPK Papers, box 2, JFKPL.

65   *"I am very happy"*: REFK to her children, October 6, 1943, REFK Papers, box 55, JFKPL.

65   *"I think the Kennedys"*: EKS to REFK, January 27, 1944, box 8, KFA.

65   *Then came word*: "Ann Brokaw Dies in Auto Crash," *NYT*, January 12, 1944.

FOUR: Dollar-a-Year Girl

66   *"What a crowding and jostling"*: Sylvia Jakes Morris, *The Price of Fame*, 79.

66   *"I thought I had become"*: Ibid.

67   *"It really is funny"*: McTaggart, *Kathleen Kennedy*, 138.

67   *"Everyone pointed to our family"*: REFK, diary entry, REFK Papers, box 3, JFKPL.

68   *"The power of silence is great"*: JPKJR to JPK, cable, May 7, 1944, JPK Papers, box 3, JFKPL.

68   *"With your faith"*: McTaggart, *Kathleen Kennedy*, 160.

68   *"Don't let anybody say"*: KK to Lady Astor, undated letter, box 7, KFA.

68   *"Mother, Jack, and that religious old soul"*: Ibid.

69   *"[A]s sister Eunice from the depth"*: Collier and Horowitz, *The Kennedys*, 135.

69   *"She was perplexed"*: EKS to Father Bertram Conway, July 10, 1944, box 8, KFA.

69   *"Mother looked up"*: EMK, *True Compass*, 85.

69   *The youngest son*: Ibid.

70   *"we were organized"*: Joan Blair and Clay Blair Jr., *The Search for JFK*, 392.

70   *"So ends the story"*: KK, diary entry, September 20, 1944, Collier and Horowitz, *The Kennedys*, 170.

71   *"I just checked"*: EKS to JPK, October 9, 1944, box 8, KFA.

71   *Eunice attended both, wearing*: EKS to REFK and JPK, January 21, 1945, box 8, KFA.

71   *"We have an incompetent"*: JPK to KK, January 8, 1945, box 13, KFA.

72   *She was offered a salary*: EKS to REFK and JPK, January 11, 1945, box 8, KFA.

72   *In what her father described*: JPK to KK, March 16, 1945, box 13, KFA.

72   *"Uncle Sam took twelve dollars"*: EKS to REFK and JPK, March 8, 1945, box 8, KFA.

72   *Joe had made certain that money*: Nasaw, *The Patriarch*, 131.

73 *"This whole family is quite disturbed"*: REFK to EKS, March 5, 1942, box 8, KFA.

73 *Eunice first exhibited*: EKS to REFK and JPK, undated, JPK Papers, box 1, JFKPL.

73 *"I am the assistant to a Mr. McCahon"*: EKS to JPK, undated letter, box 8, KFA.

73 *Mother Tenney recommended*: Mother Tenney to EKS, January 18, 1945, EKS Personal Papers.

74 *"the term 'German prisoners of war' includes"*: Memorandum of Conversation, Lieutenant Harris and Miss Kennedy, August 22, 1945, box 8, KFA.

75 *"Must get back & answer some mad woman"*: EKS to REFK, April 13, 1945, box 8, KFA.

75 *Typical was an exchange*: EKS (for E. Tomlin Bailey) to Virginia Lee Wilson, box 8, KFA.

76 *"Please tell Eunice"*: KK to the family, April 3, 1945, EKS Personal Papers.

76 *even as newspapers*: Austine Cassini, "The Charming People," *WTH*, September 24, 1945.

76 *"I lunched with Richard's sister"*: KK to EKS, March 24, 1945, box 8, KFA.

76 *"Darling Eunice"*: Richard Wood to EKS, February 23, 1945, box 13, KFA.

76 *"He gave the great news"*: KK to EKS, undated letter, box 13, KFA.

76 *"We were all having"*: EKS to Clay Blair Jr., recorded interview, CBP, AHC, UW.

76 *"a rather lowly functionary"*: Ibid.

77 *"soliciting his views"*: EKS to JPK, undated letter, box 8, KFA.

77 *"What with working in the State Dept."*: EKS to REFK, undated letter, box 8, KFA.

77 *"you spelled Joseph 'Joesph'"*: JPK to EKS, February 16, 1945, box 8, KFA.

77 *"Is he not in part responsible"*: EKS to JPK, undated letter, box 8, KFA.

77 *"Now to Grew"*: JPK to EKS, February 16, 1945, box 8, KFA.

78 *Kick had met him in January*: KK to the family, January 27, 1945, EKS Personal Papers.

78 *"There is no place"*: Lynne Olson, *Citizens of London*, 5.

79 *"I am rather busy at the moment"*: EKS to JPK, May 25, 1945, box 8, KFA.

79 *"I guess I shall stay on"*: EKS to JPK, September 15, 1945, box 8, KFA.

80 *"dull and repetitious"*: Sister Mary Cleophas to EKS, September 14, 1945, EKS Personal Papers.

80 *Mother Tenney recommended*: M. B. Tenney to EKS, February 12, 1945, EKS Personal Papers.

81 *"to see how Jack's speech went"*: EKS to JPK, September 15, 1945, box 8, KFA.

82   *"It wasn't like he was headed"*: EKS to Clay Blair Jr., recorded interview, CBP, AHC, UW.

83   *"I used to go around and ring doorbells"*: Ibid.

83   *"I can still see the two of them"*: Goodwin, *The Fitzgeralds and the Kennedys*, 707.

84   Eunice *"was saying"*: Mary McNeely, oral history interview, May 5, 1964, JFKPL.

84   *"The Irish are social"*: Joe DeGuglielmo, oral history interview, May 4, 1964, JFKPL.

84   *"I was dead wrong"*: John Droney, oral history interview, November 30, 1964, JFKPL.

85   *"I don't think"*: EKS to Clay Blair Jr., recorded interview, CBP, AHC, UW.

FIVE: Juvenile Delinquency

90   *"You never knew"*: William Sutton to Clay Blair Jr., recorded interview, CBP, AHC, UW.

90   *"a small and very"*: Joseph Alsop, oral history interview, June 16, 1964, JFKPL.

90   *"I was lucky"*: Eleanor Roberts, "Women in Government," *WP*, July 3, 1948.

91   McInerny *"went to Mr. Kennedy"*: James V. Bennett, oral history interview, REFK, November 11, 1974, JFKPL.

91   *"Tim told me of your call"*: Tom Clark to JPK, December 24, 1946, EKS Personal Papers.

91   *"She would be in close contact"*: Ibid.

91   *"energetic and ambitious"*: John White, *WTH*, February 26, 1947.

91   *"Eunice Kennedy"*: Al Hailey, "Eunice Kennedy Not Interested in Pay," *WP*, February 4, 1947.

92   *"in the fundamentals of common decency"*: James Gilbert, *A Cycle of Outrage*, 28.

92   *"There are extremely interesting"*: editorial, *BP*, February 17, 1946.

92   *"If every community in America"*: Tom Clark to National Conference on Prevention and Control of Juvenile Delinquency, November 20, 1946, Washington, DC, EKS Personal Papers.

93   Eunice *told a gathering*: David Sentner, "51% of Criminals in U.S. Under 21," *New York Journal-American*, April 17, 1947.

93   *"Shortages of personnel"*: EKS to Tom Clark, March 4, 1947, Records of the Children's Bureau, central files 1945–1948, box 145, NAUS.

93   Clark's *"plan for scholarship aid"*: EKS to JPK, undated letter, box 8, KFA.

94   *"Lt. Murphy talked about need"*: EKS, notes on juvenile delinquency, EKS Personal Papers.

94   *"would be glad to defray"*: JPK to EKS, January 21, 1947, box 8, KFA.

95   *"Never had I met a woman so"*: Scott Stossel, *Sarge*, 86.

95   *"only to find you picking"*: RSS to EKS, undated letter, EKS Personal Papers.

95   *"to do away with many"*: JPKJR to JPK, April 23, 1934, in Smith, *Hostage to Fortune*, 131.

95   (*"Arrived safely"*): EKS to JPK, Western Union telegram, September 28, 1946, box 8, KFA.

96   *"the most impressive thing"*: Thomas Maier, *The Kennedys: America's Emerald Kings*, 142.

96   *"I could go up there"*: KK to EKS, undated letter, box 13, KFA.

96   *"a terrific walker"*: Ibid.

96   *"a good chance"*: Ibid.

97   *"Kick's house is really very cute"*: EKS to REFK and JPK, October 1, 1946, box 8, KFA.

97   *"I have seen Peter Fitz"*: KK to EKS, December 22, 1946, EKS Personal Papers.

97   *Kick would ask Eunice to tamp down rumors*: KK to EKS, October 19, 1947, EKS Personal Papers.

98   *"He asks a lot about her"*: Maier, *The Kennedys*, 142.

98   *At a small party*: McTaggart, *Kathleen Kennedy*, 214.

98   *In a letter home from England*: EKS to REFK and JPK, October 1, 1946, box 8, KFA.

98   *"Please marry Sargent"*: KK to EKS, October 19, 1947, EKS Personal Papers.

99   *"I am sorry the pep is slow"*: Dr. Sara Jordan to EKS, January 3, 1946, EKS Personal Papers.

99   *"I hope that on your projected trip"*: Dr. Emil Novak to EKS, September 13, 1946, EKS Personal Papers.

99   *"[A]nd since you seem to be so upset"*: Dr. John W. Norcross to EKS, January 21, 1949, EKS Personal Papers.

100   *"Sarge was in love with Eunice"*: Robert A. Liston, *Sargent Shriver: A Candid Portrait*, 55.

100   *"She was highly"*: Mary Pitcairn to Clay Blair Jr., recorded interview, CBP, AHC, UW.

100   *"Of all the kids"*: George Smathers to Clay Blair Jr., recorded interview, CBP, AHC, UW.

100   *Eunice went with them*: Richard Nixon recounted this story to Bobby Shriver, who shared it in an interview with the author.

101   *"We want you to be happy children"*: Collier and Horowitz, *The Kennedys*, 160.

101   *"They had nothing"*: John P. Plum, "Action to End Receiving Home 'Squalor' Asked," *WTH*, March 28, 1947.

101   *"The unhappy squalor these children"*: Ibid.

102 *"Eunice was really more interested"*: George Smathers to Clay Blair Jr., recorded interview, CBP, AHC, UW.

102 *"It's fair to say"*: EKS to Clay Blair Jr., recorded interview, CBP, AHC, UW.

102 *"He sort of drifted along"*: Ibid.

102 *She, on the other hand*: "Eunice Kennedy Plans Busy Speaking Tour," *INS* report, January 22, 1947.

103 *"The government of the United States"*: EKS to Tom Clark, March 4, 1947, Records of the Children's Bureau, central files 1945–1948, box 145, NAUS.

104 *"the interest you are taking"*: EKS to Katharine F. Lenroot, February 12, 1947, Records of the Children's Bureau, central files 1945–1948, box 145, NAUS.

104 *"It is difficult to make such suggestions"*: Katharine F. Lenroot to EKS, September 19, 1947, Records of the Children's Bureau, central files 1945–1948, box 145, NAUS.

105 *"I am sure that Alonzo"*: Henry to EKS, February 23, 1947, EKS Personal Papers.

105 *"harder to keep in touch with"*: EKS to REFK, undated letter, box 8, KFA.

105 *"Jack has just been chosen"*: EKS to JPK, May 7, 1949, box 8, KFA.

105 *"Spending the amount of time I did"*: Elizabeth Coxe Spalding to Clay Blair Jr., recorded interview, CBP, AHC, UW.

106 *"One night I was visiting Eunice"*: Blair and Blair, *The Search for JFK*, 593–94.

106 *"confusing for Jack"*: Blair and Blair, *The Search for JFK*, 593–94.

106 *"A lovely-looking blond from West Palm Beach"*: Blair and Blair, *The Search for JFK*, 588.

107 *"They are all blocked"*: Elizabeth Coxe Spalding to Clay Blair Jr., recorded interview, CBP, AHC, UW.

107 *"Mary Pitcairn is very interested in men"*: EKS, undated diary entry, EKS Personal Papers.

107 *"Secret of Kick's success"*: Ibid.

107 *"Saying: You're the kind of girl"*: Ibid.

107 *"Joe McCarthy came to dinner"*: Ibid.

108 *an unidentified guest "says McCarthy"*: Ibid.

109 *It was Eunice who took the call*: Goodwin, *The Fitzgeralds and the Kennedys*, 739.

SIX: Women in Prison

110 *"I wish that today"*: RSS to EKS, undated letter, EKS Personal Papers.

111 *"Lloyd Bowers asked for you"*: RSS to EKS, undated letter, EKS Personal Papers.

111 *Dorothy Kilgallen could not*: Dorothy Kilgallen, syndicated Voice of Broadway column, August 9, 1948.

111 *"Saw a good bit of Hugh"*: EKS to JPK, undated letter, EKS Personal Papers.

111 *"quite busy with a French foreign lover"*: EKS to JPK, undated letter, EKS Personal Papers.

113 *"She had written"*: EKS to Miriam Van Waters, November 21, 1947, MVWP, SL.

114 *"it would be impossible"*: Nasaw, *The Patriarch*, 628.

114 *Eunice "talked over the idea"*: REFK to Sister Sheila, March 29, 1971, REFK Papers, box 57, JFKPL.

114 *"I can't understand"*: RSS to EKS, undated letter, EKS Personal Papers.

115 *"I think it's a fine book"*: Ibid.

115 *"latch onto a cool"*: RSS to EKS, undated letter, EKS Personal Papers.

115 *"This is a boring letter"*: Hugh Fraser to EKS, December 5, 1948, EKS Personal Papers.

115 *"I wonder how much"*: Hugh Fraser to EKS, April 30, 1949, EKS Personal Papers.

115 *three scribbled jottings*: EKS, handwritten notes on envelopes, November 7, 1948, February 20, 1949, April 26, 1949, EKS Personal Papers.

115 *"I am still waiting"*: Hugh Fraser to EKS, April 30, 1949, EKS Personal Papers.

116 *"He was so crazy about her"*: ESK, interview with the author.

116 *"That's pretty accurate"*: Ibid.

116 *"a colored girl from a good family"*: Helen Hironimus to EKS, June 10, 1949, EKS Personal Papers.

116 *"One of them I got work"*: EKS to Clay Blair Jr., recorded interview, CBP, AHC, UW.

117 *"They very rarely let someone"*: EKS to JPK, February 1, 1950, box 8, KFA.

117 *"was just the cover story"*: ESK, interview with the author.

117 *"Ever since the beginning"*: James Landis to EKS, January 19, 1949, JLP, LC.

118 *"rather a simple, direct"*: EKS, undated diary entry, EKS Personal Papers.

118 *to thank the warden*: EKS to JPK, undated letter, box 8, KFA.

118 *"Dearest Daddy"*: EKS to JPK, January 21, 1950, EKS Personal Papers.

119 *"Most of the girls"*: EKS, Alderson notebooks, JLP, LC.

119 *"The sponsor program"*: Julia Gorman Porter to James V. Bennett, August 22, 1950, Bureau of Prisons, Record Group 129, box 123, NAUS.

120 *"need people to get"*: EKS, Alderson notebooks, JLP, LC.

120 *"lots of sex among the girls"*: Ibid.

120 *"high-pitched voices"*: Ibid.

120 *Eunice appealed to Bennett*: Ibid.

120   *"a cute girl"*: Ibid.

120   *"all dressed up"*: Ibid.

121   *In every face*: Ibid.

121   *"If this child had been guided"*: Ibid.

121   *"The group looks bewildered"*: Ibid.

121   *"Jim Bennett asked what I was going to do"*: Ibid.

122   *"will do anything"*: Ibid.

122   *helping to find her a job*: EKS to Monsignor James Lynch, September 19, 1951, box 5, KFA.

122   *with a gift of monogramed stationary*: Bride's gift registry, EKS Personal Papers.

123   *"She was a remarkable secretary"*: ESK, interview with the author.

123   *"Will a special clearance be necessary?"*: Catherine Dickinson to EKS, September 24, 1963, EKS Personal Papers.

123   *"I used to say that I am the only guy"*: Leamer, *The Kennedy Women*, 416.

123   *"your happiness"*: EKS speech to Alderson inmates, February 21, 1950, EKS Personal Papers.

123   *"Perhaps you don't know"*: Ibid.

124   *"It is the woman who will finally pay"*: Ibid.

124   *"You are free and I am free"*: Ibid.

124   *"running around like animals"*: Ibid.

125   *"You always felt she had"*: ESK, interview with the author.

125   *"any suggestions of ideas"*: EKS to James Landis, undated letter, JLP, LC.

125   *Perhaps she felt preempted*: Norma Lee Browning, "Prison Without Bars," *CDT*, June 11 and June 18, 1950.

125   *"She got a commitment"*: EKS to Nina Kinsella, June 12, 1950, box 8, KFA.

125   *a thief entered the suite*: "Kennedy Gems Stolen," *NYT*, April 30, 1950; "Steal Gems of Ex-Envoy's Kin in Hotel," *CDT*, April 30, 1950.

125   *"She pretended she was asleep"*: ESK, interview with the author.

SEVEN: Chicago

127   *"Welcome to Chicago!!!"*: RSS note to EKS, EKS Personal Papers.

127   *Jean, who took a job*: RSS to JPK, July 9, 1951, EKS Personal Papers.

129   *By 1950, the nuns had been*: For a history of the Sisters of the Good Shepherd in Chicago, see Roger J. Coughlin and Cathryn A. Riplinger, *The Story of Charitable Care in the Archdiocese of Chicago, 1844–1959*; Suellen Hoy, *Good Hearts: Catholic Sisters in Chicago's Past*.

129   *Al Capone regularly dropped off*: *Caritas Christi Urget Nos: A History of the Offices, Agencies, and Institutions of the Archdiocese of Chicago*, vol. 2, 896.

129 *"I'd go to juvenile court"*: EKS to Clay Blair Jr., recorded interview, CBP, AHC, UW.

129 *a summary she and Sarge wrote of her time in Chicago*: RSS to James A. Fayne, November 16, 1959, box 8, KFA.

130 *He dated a young widow*: Stossel, *Sarge*, 112.

131 *Eunice, too, went on dates*: "'Pacific' First-Nighters Show in Themselves," *CDT*, November 15, 1950.

131 *a cousin she recruited to volunteer*: Leamer, *The Kennedy Women*, 418.

131 *In February 1951*: RSS to Maurice Fisher, November 9, 1951, EKS Personal Papers.

131 *"I asked her if the boys"*: EKS interview with Queen Frederica, box 11, KFA.

131 *"There are two types of girls"*: Ibid.

131 *If the queen succeeded*: Ibid.

132 *"Eunice's face had the look"*: JKS, unpublished essay, EKS Personal Papers.

132 *"Despite the discomfiture"*: Ibid.

132 *No sooner had the sisters*: "Auxiliary Will Give Party for Girls in Good Shepherd Home," *CDT*, December 17, 1951.

133 *"Eunice appeared at a luncheon"*: JPK to EMK, June 25, 1952, JPK Papers, box 4, JFKPL.

133 *In fact, Eunice had marched*: Mary S. Colbert, oral history interview, May 5, 1954, JFKPL.

133 *"She wore a big"*: Ruth M. Batson, oral history interview, January 24, 1979, JFKPL.

134 *the Kennedy siblings*: REFK to RFK and ESK, July 13, 1950, Smith, *Hostage to Fortune*, 643–44.

134 *"Up here, this anti-Communism"*: Stossel, *Sarge*, 109.

134 *"There was a great rhubarb"*: Charles Bartlett, oral history interview, January 6, 1965, JFKPL.

134 *"the Adlai Stevenson–Eunice Kennedy"*: Bob Farrell, "New York at Night," *Brooklyn Eagle*, August 11, 1952.

135 *"Adlai Stevenson's romance"*: Dorothy Kilgallen, *New-Herald*, December 27, 1952.

135 *"We sat through Mass"*: Stossel, *Sarge*, 113.

135 *"Am Furious"*: RSS to REFK and JPK, Western Union telegram, February 8, 1953, REFK Papers, box 55, JFKPL.

135 *It is a story that*: the Reverend Bryan Hehir, interview with the author.

135 *"They are all dead now"*: the Reverend Theodore Hesburgh, interview with the author.

136 *"I was not that personally close"*: Ibid.

136 *"frank and honest exchange"*: Ibid.

136 *"He was the best, the very best"*: Stossel, *Sarge*, 113.

136 *"I don't know what made me"*: Ibid., 114.

136 *"She loved her children too much"*: Mary Cunningham Agee, interview with the author.

136 *"Sarge was one of the very, very few"*: Stossel, *Sarge*, 114.

137 *The wedding of Eunice Mary Kennedy*: William Fulton, "Eunice Kennedy Becomes Bride of Chicagoan," *CDT*, May 24, 1953.

137 *a silver ashtray inscribed "from one of those who lost"*: Bobby Shriver, interview with the author.

137 *"I am grateful"*: EKS to Monsignor James Lynch, September 19, 1951, box 5, KFA.

138 *"He reports that he quipped"*: Winzola McLendon, "This Kennedy Had Extraordinary Wedding Guests," *WP*, February 18, 1965.

138 *"What a wonderful opportunity"*: Erich Brandeis, Looking at Life column, June 13, 1953, EKS Personal Papers.

138 *"The honeymooners are"*: PKL to REFK and JPK, June 4, 1953, REFK Papers, box 55, JFKPL.

138 *"rather cold"*: REFK to PKL, June 19, 1953, REFK Papers, box 55, JFKPL.

138 *"terrifically amusing"*: Ibid.

138 *"where Ted was"*: Ibid.

138 *"I had a roommate"*: Timothy Shriver, "My Father, My Roommate," *WP*, January 25, 2011.

138 *"Sargent, you snore"*: Ibid.

138 *despite press reports*: "Nephew for Sen. Kennedy," AP report, *Newport Daily News*, April 29, 1954.

139 *Eunice introduced Monsignor Cooke*: Coughlin and Riplinger, *Story of Charitable Care in the Archdiocese of Chicago*, 218.

139 *"We of the Kennedy Foundation"*: John Evans, "School Gets Kennedy Gift of $1,250,000," *CDT*, February 21, 1952.

140 *"I think of [a] family and of their home"*: Archbishop Richard Cushing, sermon delivered at dedication of St. Coletta chapel, June 30, 1953, EKS Personal Papers.

141 *"I don't want to do that"*: EKS, undated diary entries, EKS Personal Papers.

141 *In August 1958 she visited*: EKS to REFK and JPK, August 23, 1958, REFK Papers, box 12, JFKPL.

141 *his with the Chicago Board of Education*: "Robert S. Shriver, 39, Heads School Board," *CDT*, October 29, 1955.

141 *The rebuff brought on*: RSS to JPK, undated letter, EKS Personal Papers.

143 *No less prominent*: Steven Noll and James W. Trent, eds., *Mental Retardation in America: A Historical Reader*, 325.

143 *1 percent to 3 percent of all babies born*: Fact Sheet on Mental Retardation and the National Association for Retarded Children, EKSPP; Memorandum for Honorable Myer Feldman from Wilbur J. Cohen, June 15, 1962. MFP, box 13, JFKPL.

144 *"There was an overpowering smell of urine"*: EKS, "Hope for Retarded Children," 71–78.

144 *"It was not popular or fashionable"*: EKS speech to Annual Crusade Dinner of the Greater Boston Association for Retarded Children, November 22, 1959, HHP, HHPL.

145 *"He was a beautiful-looking little boy"*: Margaret Tedone, interview with the author.

145 *"I had never seen anything so awful"*: Ibid.

146 *"did not know how an idea became a law"*: Ibid.

146 *"If going in was bad"*: Ibid.

146 *the occasional trespassing chicken*: RSS to JPK, undated letter, box 2, KFA.

147 *"It was a wonderful playroom on a rainy day"*: Dorothy Schrot, interview with the author.

147 *"whacked us around"*: Bobby Shriver, interview with the author.

147 *"she sat right down in the sandbox"*: Dorothy Schrot, interview with the author.

147 *"I didn't approach her"*: Ibid.

148 *Once, when the damp grass*: Ibid.

148 *"She'd fall asleep and wake up crying"*: Ibid.

148 *"Eunice was never preoccupied"*: Catherine "Deeda" Blair, interview with the author.

148 *"go up and down the elevator"*: REFK to EKS, May 19, 1959, JPK Papers, box 36, JFKPL.

148 *"We would go to the movies"*: Catherine "Deeda" Blair, interview with the author.

149 *"I remember them being there"*: Maria Shriver, interview with the author.

149 *"Many nights I'd be sitting there"*: Stossel, *Sarge*, 118.

149 *Charles Bartlett, the journalist*: Kevles, "The Kennedy Who Could Be President."

149 *"I never knew anyone else"*: Catherine "Deeda" Blair, interview with the author.

149 *"I know that many people"*: "Kennedy Sister Reaps Dividends from Investments of Her Talents," *AC*, May 23, 1962.

150 *Bill Blair remembered*: William McCormack Blair Jr., interview with the author.

150 *"We'd all have the same material"*: the Reverend John Cavanaugh, oral history interview, March 27, 1966, JFKPL.

150 *"Eunice is still improving"*: RSS to JPK, undated letter, EKS Personal Papers.

150 *Bobby and Maria were sent to Cape Cod*: Helen Fleming, "Meet Chicago's 2 Hostesses," *CDN* undated, EKS Personal Papers.

151 *She enrolled in a twice-weekly*: EKS lecture notes, EKS Personal Papers.

151 *she sent a flurry of letters to Ted Sorensen*: EKS to Ted Sorensen, February 20, April 16, and May 6, 1957, EKS Personal Papers.

152 *"This is a copy of a speech"*: EKS to Ted Sorensen, February 21, 1957, EKS Personal Papers.

152 *Stevenson could not win*: EKS speech, "Adlai E. Stevenson," October 19, 1956, EKS Personal Papers.

153 *"Mental retardation research has no status"*: EKS speech to Annual Crusade Dinner of the Greater Boston Association for Retarded Children, November 22, 1959, HHP, HHPL.

154 *The first proving ground*: "Million Donated to Mass. Hospital by Kennedy Fund," *CDT*, September 13, 1959.

154 *"I have seen sights that will haunt"*: EKS, "The Sun Has Burst Through," *Parade*, February 2, 1964.

154 *"Illinois is still for you"*: EKS to JFK, January 9, 1959, EKS Personal Papers.

EIGHT: Consultant to the President

156 *"The solution of Rosemary's problem"*: JPK to Sister Anastasia, May 29, 1958, JPK Papers, JFKPL.

156 *"the crisis of the campaign"*: JPK to Enrico Galeazzi, March 9, 1960, JPK Papers, box 222, JFKPL.

156 *"are all over the state"*: Kenneth P. O'Donnell and David F. Powers with Joe McCarthy, *Johnny, We Hardly Knew Ye*, 157–59.

156 *"It means that we've got to go"*: Ibid.

156 *"Jack's sister, Rosemary"*: "Kennedys All in It Together," *New York Mirror*, July 14, 1960.

156 *Rosemary's circumstances*: Boggs, oral history interview, July 17, 1968, JFKPL.

157 *"I used to think it was something to hide"*: "Pride of the Clan," *Time*, July 10, 1960.

157 *"Rosemary is in a nursing home"*: Nan Robertson, *NYT*, July 1960.

157 *"The story had just come out"*: John Seigenthaler, oral history interview, July 22, 1964, JFKPL.

157 *"Eunie knows more about"*: Ibid.

158 *once annoying aides*: Elizabeth (Liz) Carpenter, oral history interview, December 3, 1968, internet transcript copy, LBJPL.

158 *"The Kennedy Foundation was worried"*: EKS, oral history interview, May 7, 1968, JFKPL.

158 *"a screwball comedy"*: Thurston Clarke, *Ask Not: The Inauguration of John F. Kennedy and the Speech That Changed America*, 39–40.

158 *Eunice spent a week at St. Elizabeth's*: EKS, oral history interview, May 7, 1968, JFKPL.

159 *"She and Jack were physiologically alike"*: RSS to Clay Blair Jr., recorded interview, CBP, AHC, UW.

159 *a supper party for twenty-four*: "Stars to Attend Exodus Opening," *CDT*, December 11, 1960.

159 *Parents of children*: US Department of Health, Education, and Welfare, Mental Retardation Programs and Services, Office of Program Analysis, June 1957, MFP, box 4, JFKPL.

160 *"some resentment"*: Boggs, oral history interview, July 17, 1968, JFKPL.

161 *"This is the first year I have asked"*: Elizabeth M. Boggs, Federal Legislation Affecting the Mentally Retarded 1955–1967: A Historical Overview. *Mental Retardation* 3 (1971): 103–27.

161 *Nobel Prize–winning author*: Pearl S. Buck, *The Child Who Never Grew*.

161 *Hollywood stars Roy Rogers*: Dale Evans-Rogers, *Angel Unaware*.

161 *"massive buildings"*: Noll and Trent, *Mental Retardation in America*, 389.

161 *eight one-story dormitories housed 256 children*: Elizabeth F. Shores, "The Arkansas Children's Colony at Conway: A Springboard for Federal Policy on Special Education," *Arkansas Historical Quarterly* 57, no. 4 (Winter 1998): 408–34.

162 *new doctoral program*: Boggs, Federal Legislation Affecting the Mentally Retarded, *Mental Retardation* 3 (1971): 103–27.

162 *"Just lie down and get well"*: EKS, oral history interview, May 7, 1968, JFKPL.

162 *"The foundation can't go on trying"*: Ibid.

162 *"get hold of Mike Feldman"*: Ibid.

163 *Despite spraining an ankle*: "Uses Cane to Get Around," AP Wirephoto caption, January 17, 1961.

163 *"To Eunice, whose work in Wisconsin"*: EKS to David Horowitz, December 1, 1981, DHP, box 1–2, the Center for the Study of Popular Culture Records, HI, SU.

163 *"We'll make Bobby attorney general"*: Harris Wofford, *Of Kennedys & Kings*, 92.

164 *"snakes, rats, mice, and bugs"*: RSS Papers, box 290, JFKPL.

164 *"Timberlawn was a magical place"*: Bobby Shriver, interview with the author.

164 *"I loved the ritual of the game"*: Timothy Shriver, *Fully Alive: Discovering What Matters Most*, 11–12.

165 *"She was more of a sister"*: Dorothy Tubridy, interview with the author.

165 *"It took me three days"*: EKS, oral history interview, May 7, 1968, JFKPL.

165 *a working dinner at Timberlawn*: Neil A. Drayton, New Item for All Employees, March 7, 1962, EBP, BHS, UM.

165 *"was the size of a small ham"*: Ibid.

165 *Household records*: RSSP, box 290, JFKPL.

166 *"It sounds harmless"*: REFK to RFK, April 29, 1963, REFK Papers, box 58, JFKPL.

166 *Friends knew to slip their checkbooks*: Carole Dell, interview with the author.

166 *Eunice and Sarge wheeling out*: Frank Mankiewicz, interview with the author.

166 *"The result, I fear"*: Frank Mankiewicz to EKS, December 18, 1961, EKS Personal Papers.

166 *the food was usually dreadful*: Frank Mankiewicz, interview with the author.

167 *One chef chased Eunice*: Michael Gardner, *King of Sprinkler Lane*, 79.

167 *"In those days, it was always black tie"*: Catherine "Deeda" Blair, interview with the author.

167 *"What a fun, mad party"*: RSSP, box 293, JFKPL.

167 *"there were no guests injured"*: Ibid.

167 *"No Matter How You Twist It"*: Ibid.

167 *the entertainment usually provided*: Ibid.

168 *"She assembled a very impressive group"*: Dr. Robert E. Cooke, interview with author.

168 *Cooke first floated*: Robert E. Cooke, oral history interview, March 29, 1968, JFKPL.

168 *"many expectant mothers get less"*: EKS, "Hope for Retarded Children," 71–75.

168 *"Dr. Shannon, in no uncertain terms"*: Robert E. Cooke, "The Origin of the National Institute of Child Health and Human Development," *Pediatrics* 92, no. 6 (December 1993): 868.

169 *That lung condition*: Dr. Lawrence K. Altman, *"A Kennedy Baby's Life and Death,"* *NYT*, July 29, 2013.

169 *it would also claim the life*: Ibid.

170 *"When I reported to Mrs. Shriver"*: Cooke, "Origin of the National Institute of Child Health and Human Development," 868.

170 *Shannon's opposition*: Ibid.

170 *"The manner in which our nation"*: JFK, Statement by the President on the Need for a National Program to Combat Mental Retardation, October 11, 1961, JFKPL.

171 *"We were action oriented"*: EKS, oral history interview, May 7, 1968, JFKPL.

171 *"I think most of us produce"*: Leonard Mayo, oral history interview, April 30, 1968, JFKPL.

171 *"had not reckoned with the fact"*: Dr. Edward Davens, oral history interview, March 29, 1968, JFKPL.

171 *"There was great pressure"*: Judge David L. Bazelon, oral history interview, March 5, 1969, JFKPL.

171 *Eunice was "like a spark plug"*: Ibid.

171 *"Eunice is not the easiest"*: Edwin R. Bayley, oral history interview, December 19, 1968, JFKPL.

171 *Eunice "envisioned interviews with every one"*: Ibid.

172 *"The big problem was"*: Dr. Patrick J. Doyle, oral history interview, March 4, 1968, JFKPL.

172 *"Sometimes you had the feeling"*: Ibid.

172 *"A lot of deans of medical schools"*: Ibid.

172 *"this was a hobby"*: Dr. Bertram S. Brown, oral history interview, January 29, 1969, JFKPL.

172 *"John F. Kennedy felt"*: Myer (Mike) Feldman, oral history interview, September 21, 1968, JFKPL.

172 *The president "wasn't intimately familiar"*: Ibid.

173 *"There was just one platitude"*: Cooke, oral history interview, March 29, 1968, JFKPL.

173 *Eunice and Mayo met with Hoover*: EKS to HH, November 21, 1961, HHP, HHPL.

173 *"If I had been around in 1928"*: Ibid.

173 *Eunice arranged for Jack to greet*: Abbie Rowe, White House Photographs, November 14, 1961, JFKPL; EKS speech to the National Association for Mental Health, March 5, 1962, EBP, BHS, UM.

174 *"that your father may be restored"*: Leonard Mayo to EKS, December 19, 1961, EKS Personal Papers.

174 *"had several jobs"*: Boggs, oral history interview, February 17, 1969, JFKPL.

174 *"Don't find fault"*: EKS, undated diary entry, EKS Personal Papers.

175 *"If we had to do it over"*: EKS, oral history interview, May 7, 1968, JFKPL.

175 *The president agreed that more candor*: Ted Sorensen, *Kennedy*, 320.

175 *the ghostwriter did not know*: David Gelman, interview with the author.

175 *he found Eunice to be "imperious and demanding"*: Ibid.

176 *"I was to fly back immediately"*: Coates Redmon, *Come As You Are: The Peace Corps Story*, 62; "Shrivers in Visit," *Bridgeport Post*, July 16, 1962.

176 *"She wanted to sound like her brother"*: David Gelman, interview with the author.

176 *"gazing out to the sea"*: Redmon, *Come As You Are*, 69.

176 *"Eunice ran it like a campaign"*: David Gelman, *USA Today*, November 7, 1993.

177 *Eunice gave Gelman a Sulka silk tie*: Eric Gelman, interview with the author.

177 *"Mrs. Shriver had a very strong"*: Doyle, oral history interview, March 4, 1968, JFKPL.

178 *"I don't want you to feel pressured"*: Mayo, oral history interview, April 30, 1968, JFKPL.

178 *"when one knows instantly"*: Ibid.

178 *The final report contained more than*: A Proposed Program for National Action to Combat Mental Retardation, Report of the President's Panel on Mental Retardation, October 16, 1962, JFKP, JFKPL.

178 *"All of us were struck"*: Davens, oral history interview, March 29, 1969, JFKPL.

178 *"discussed the recommendations"*: Ibid.

178 *Eunice used the Kennedy Foundation's first*: Myer Feldman, Memorandum re Joseph P. Kennedy Jr. Foundation Awards, December 4, 1962, MFP, box 13, JFKPL.

179 *Would the attorney general find out*: EKS to RFK, August 20, 1962, EKS Personal Papers.

179 *Could he secure an immigration visa*: Sue Johnson from the Joseph P. Kennedy Jr. Foundation to Angie Novello, Office of the US Attorney General, July 30, 1964, EKS Personal Papers.

179 *Would he make a dinner speech*: RFK, address to Dinner of Champions, October 17, 1961, EKS Personal Papers.

179 *In a message to Congress*: Special Message on Mental Illness and Mental Retardation, February 5, 1963, JFKP, JFKPL.

180 *"with evangelical zeal"*: Anthony Lewis, "Shriver Moves into the Front Rank," *NYT*, March 15, 1964.

180 *"Dr. Schmidt, your work"*: David J. Fischer, Foreign Affairs Oral History Project, Association for Diplomatic Studies and Training.

181 *"can be put quite plainly"*: Gunnar Dybwad to EKS, June 20, 1963, MFP, box 13, JFKPL.

181 *"deserve the credit for most of it"*: Doyle, oral history interview, March 4, 1968, JFKPL.

181 *She kept Jack abreast*: David B. Ray Jr., oral history interview, March 5, 1968, JFKPL.

181 *"the combination of energy"*: McGeorge Bundy, oral history interview, March 1964, JFKPL.

181 *"She's one of the best lobbyists"*: News clipping, October 24, 1963, News Bureau, EKSP Personal Papers.

181 *"I was inspired this morning"*: LBJ to EKS, October 24, 1963, EKS Personal Papers.

182 *she was having lunch*: William Manchester, *The Death of a President*, 255–56.

182 *He worried how Eunice would react*: Joseph T. English, interview with the author.

182 *"but nothing can overcome Eunice"*: Stossel, *Sarge*, 298.

182 *On their knees in Sarge's office*: Joseph T. English, interview with the author.

182 *Ted would return the pills to English*: Ibid.

182 *"Right medicine, Doc, wrong girl"*: Ibid.

NINE: From Camp Shriver to Special Olympics

186 *a "palace guard now without a palace"*: Stossel, *Sarge*, 523.

187 *"It's a terrific compliment"*: Michael Gillette, *Launching the War on Poverty: An Oral History*, 33.

188 *"Eunice pestering Jack"*: Jacqueline Kennedy Onassis, interviews with Arthur M. Schlesinger Jr., 117.

188 *"a little bit of a denigration"*: ESK, interview with the author.

188 *"That's how I met Robert Kennedy"*: Frank Mankiewicz, interview with the author.

189 *"I think my speech"*: EKS to JFK, June 5, 1962, EKS Personal Papers; "Kennedy Sister Urges Peace Corps at Home," *LAT*, June 3, 1962.

189 *"To receive a degree"*: EKS, speech at Santa Clara University, June 2, 1962, EKS Personal Papers.

189 *"The foundation still lacks"*: EKS to RSS, August 18, 1962, RSS Papers, JFKPL.

190 *Carol Channing*: Carol Channing to EKS, February 23, 1964, EKS Personal Papers; Dan Rostenkowski to RSS, February 25, 1964, EKS Personal Papers.

190 *"The fact that you made it"*: EKS to Mary Switzer, February 27, 1964, MESP, box 643, SL.

190 *Eunice was readmitted to the hospital*: "Mrs. Shriver Ill," AP, August 21, 1964.

190 *a "deep personal commitment"*: Anthony Lewis, "Shriver Moves into the Front Rank," *NYT*, March 15, 1964.

190 *"I regard Sargent Shriver"*: Anthony Lewis, "White House Hints Shriver Could Fill 2nd Place on Ticket," *NYT*, January 8, 1964.

191   *"Just as I went into politics"*: McCarthy, *Remarkable Kennedys*, 89.

191   *"I never got the feeling"*: Frank Mankiewicz, interview with the author.

191   *Nicholas Katzenbach*: Nicholas Katzenbach, oral history interview, November 29, 2005, EMKOHP, MC, UVA.

192   *"We will need men"*: EKS, RFK Senatorial Campaign 1964—Speeches by EKS, EKS Personal Papers.

192   *"After the assassination"*: Doyle, oral history interview, March 4, 1968, JFKPL.

193   *"Mrs. Shriver called"*: Shorter, *Kennedy Family and Mental Retardation*, 150.

193   *"didn't want to have anybody"*: Stafford Warren, oral history interview, June 7, 1966, JFKPL.

193   *"Let me ask you, Frank"*: Frank Mankiewicz, interview with the author.

194   *"the most forward-looking"*: Rhode Island congressman John E. Fogarty, oral history interview, April 14, 1965, JFKPL.

194   *Eunice wrote to LBJ*: EKS to LBJ, December 12, 1967, EKS Personal Papers.

194   *"an interpretation that"*: William D. Casey memo to Ervin Duggan, December 16, 1967, White House central files, LBJPL.

195   *"What child would not love"*: Timothy Shriver, interview with the author.

195   *Some were local teenagers*: Erin Donaghue, "Neighbors Mourn Passing of Local Icon," *The Gazette*, August 12, 2009.

196   *"In retrospect, I think some of it"*: Bobby Shriver, interview with the author.

196   *Some of the inmates*: Leon Dash, "Convicts, Retarded Succeed Together," *WP*, June 30, 1971.

196   *"I'll be back on the street one day"*: Ibid.

196   *counselors who came from "all strata of society"*: Ibid.

196   *"They'd beat me up"*: Anthony Shriver, interview with the author.

196   *"It's okay, you can cry"*: Mark Shriver, *A Good Man*, 46.

197   *"We had no idea what it would be like"*: EKS, "Hope for Retarded Children," 71–75.

197   *"What was amazing about her"*: Kathleen Kennedy Townsend, interview with the author.

197   *In 1967 she made inquiries*: John Theban, executive director of Family and Child Services of Washington, DC, to EKS, December 21, 1967, EKS Personal Papers.

197   *A typical day at Camp Shriver*: EBP, box 7, BHS, UM.

197   *In 1962 three-year-old Tim Shriver*: Ibid.

198   *"I believe the children should be called 'exceptional'"*: Unidentified Camp Shriver counselor, EKS notes, June 18, 1962, EBP, box 7, BHS, UM.

198 *"To see him not just sitting"*: Shirley Bulka to EKS, July 1, 1970, EKS Personal Papers.

199 *Eunice often brought professional athletes*: "Brown, Giardello Make Big Hit with Youngsters," *WP*, June 18, 1965. Samuel Stafford, "Joey's a Pal to His Son," *Washington Daily News*, June 18, 1965.

199 *On a single day in 1965*: Mary Lou Norton to EKS, July 14, 2006, EKS Personal Papers.

199 *"There was no division"*: Timothy Shriver, interview with the author.

200 *When Eunice visited their Children's Center*: Bettye Caldwell, interview with the author.

201 *"It is a very respectable attack"*: EKS, "An Answer to the Attacks on Motherhood," *McCall's*, June 1965.

202 *"my mother didn't raise children"*: Kathleen Kennedy Townsend to David Horowitz, February 15, 1980, DHP, box 1–2, the Center for the Study of Popular Culture Records, HI, SU.

202 *"Eunice Shriver would probably have made"*: Robert F. Kennedy Jr. to David Horowitz, November 7, 1979, DHP, Box 1–2, the Center for the Study of Popular Culture Records, HI, SU.

202 *"Whoever she was"*: Polly Devlin, "Eunice Kennedy Shriver: The Spark," *Vogue*, March 1968, EKSPP.

202 *"most mothers are happier"*: EKS, "At Home with Mrs. R. Sargent Shriver Jr.," *NYP*, October 27, 1963.

203 *"I watched him listen"*: Timothy Shriver, "My Father, My Roommate," *WP*, January 25, 2011.

203 *Before heading to the office*: Mark Shriver, *A Good Man*, 64.

203 *Bettye Caldwell thought that Eunice*: Bettye Caldwell, interview with the author.

203 *At the urging of Esther Peterson*: "Some Recommendations of the President's Commission on the Status of Women," October 11, 1963, MFP, box 7, JFKPL.

204 *"She was the most competitive"*: ESK, interview with the author.

204 *"It was the same meal every Tuesday"*: Ibid.

204 *"They did not have any secretary"*: Sarah Anderson to EKS, July 23, 1967, EKS.

205 *"I'm a huge fan of my mother's"*: Maria Shriver to Meg Grant, "Finding the Joy," *AARP the Magazine*, December 2013–January 2014.

205 *"If something came on the TV about that"*: Anthony Shriver, interview with the author.

205 *"In our family, we grew up"*: Ibid.

205 *"Mrs. Shriver, are you sure"*: Gardner, *King of Sprinkler Lane*, 83.

206 *"Of course it will, Mike"*: Ibid.

206 *"Once upon a time"*: Bobby Shriver, undated story, EKS Personal Papers.

206 *"Bobby hid the tools"*: REFK to EKS, May 11, 1966, REFK Papers, box 58, JFKPL.

207 *"There is a change with teenagers"*: EKS, notes on bringing up children, EKS Personal Papers.

208 *As early as 1958*: James N. Oliver, "The Effect of Physical Conditioning and Activities on the Mental Characteristics of Educationally Subnormal Boys," *British Journal of Educational Psychology*, 28 (1958): 155–65.

208 *"I had never even seen a retarded child"*: AMB, interview with author.

209 *"The next thing I knew"*: Ibid.

209 *"I remember I didn't have my glasses on"*: Ibid.

209 *She had proposed*: Elizabeth Shelton, "Special Sports League Suggested," *WP*, November 3, 1966.

209 *In the revised eleven-page proposal for a "National Olympics for the Retarded"*: AMBP, CHM.

210 *The money "came with strings"*: AMB, interview with the author.

210 *"It is our hope that the Chicago Special Olympics"*: EKS, transcript of remarks, March 29, 1960, press conference in Chicago, AMBP, CHM.

211 *"The Chicago Special Olympics prove"*: EKS, transcript of remarks, 1968 World Games, July 20, 1968, Eunice Kennedy Shriver: One Woman's Vision, accessed on October 6, 2017, www.eunicekennedyshriver.org /articles/article/60.

211 *"I wish to announce a national Special Olympic"*: EKS, transcript of remarks, 1968 World Games, www.eunicekennedyshriver.org/articles /article/72.

211 *"I decided out there"*: Continuation of notes *re* recreation program, January 1981, KFA.

211 *"She didn't think about people's feelings"*: AMB, interview with the author; Phil Hersh, "Burke's First Field Day Put Special Olympics into Play," *CT*, July 20, 1993.

212 *"with a young president"*: Hubert Humphrey, *The Education of a Public Man: My Life and Politics*, 185.

212 *Justice Burke eventually came*: EKS to AMB, January 29, 1968; Richard J. Daley to AMB, April 2, 1968; EKS to AMB, July 23, 1968; AMBP, CHM.

212 *had their contents inserted*: "Congressman Andrew Jacobs Jr. of Indiana, Real Founder of Special Olympics Happy with Selection of Shriver," *Congressional Record*, March 24, 1995, Extension of Remarks, E683.

212 *"Here were people"*: Ana Bueno, *Special Olympics: The First 25 Years*, 11–12.

212 *"You know, Eunice, the world will never be the same"*: Jack McCallum, "Small Steps, Great Strides," *Sports Illustrated*, December 8, 2008.

TEN: An American in Paris

214 *"LBJ was tickled"*: Joseph A. Califano Jr., *The Triumph & Tragedy of Lyndon Johnson: The White House Years*, 267.

214 *"We are going to Paris"*: Stossel, *Sarge*, 492.

214 *"It was Jean and Pat who called"*: William McCormack Blair Jr., interview with the author.

214 *"He's smart. He's imaginative"*: ESK, interview with the author.

215 *"That's an iffy question"*: "Senate Group Backs Shriver," AP, April 19, 1968.

215 Bobby *"deferred to her on family matters"*: Frank Mankiewicz, interview with the author.

215 *Jack and Bobby were*: Louise Hutchinson, "RFK Different from Jack, Eunice Says," *CT*, May 19, 1968.

216 *residents "living in filth and dirt"*: "Excerpts from Statement by Kennedy," *NYT*, September 10, 1965.

216 *"Older people say"*: Hutchinson, "RFK Different from Jack".

216 *"I used to think"*: REFK to Harry Reasoner of CBS News, "Rose Kennedy at 76," November 18, 1967.

217 *"She talked about Mary"*: the Reverend Richard Fragomeni, interview with the author.

217 *"How do you think the Blessed Mother"*: the Reverend Donald MacMillan, interview with author.

217 *the thirty-four depictions of the Madonna*: Mary Cunningham Agee, interview with the author.

217 *"When women were not given much space"*: the Reverend Bryan Hehir, interview with the author.

218 *a "maternal feminist"*: Maria Shriver, eulogy for her mother, August 14, 2009, St. Francis Xavier Church, Hyannis Port, MA.

218 *she and Sarge invited a group*: Alfred R. Jonsen, *The Birth of Bioethics*, 290–91.

218 *Estimates of the number*: Linda Greenhouse and Reva B. Siegel, *Before Roe v. Wade*, 23.

218 *a template to revise criminal statutes*: Ibid., 4.

218 *Mankiewicz said abortion*: Frank Mankiewicz, interview with the author.

218 *abortion as "morally problematic"*: Richard A. McCormick, *Notes on Moral Theology*, 474.

219 *to protest publication*: EKS, letter to Foulton Oursler, *Reader's Digest*, July 25, 1951, EKS Personal Papers.

219 *the editors should commission*: Ibid.

219 *"If couples want to limit"*: EKS, "An Answer to the Attacks on Motherhood," *McCall's*, March 1965.

219   *"With drug stores full of contraceptive"*: Ibid.

220   *"She would say, 'You mark my words'"*: ESK, interview with the author.

220   *"If you talk to some poor overworked mothers"*: Ibid.

220   *Pope John XXIII had established*: Peter Steinfels, "The Life and Death of a Leading Lay Catholic," *NYT*, December 21, 2005.

222   *The* New York Times *praised*: editorial: "Do It Yourself Abortion?" *NYT*, September 9, 1967.

222   *a "smokescreen" by religious leaders*: Eve Edstrom and Carol Honsa, "Abortion Conference Termed Stacked," *WP*, September 9, 1967.

222   *"amounted to an erudite panel of dogs"*: Ibid.

222   *"to all mothers to be or in being"*: Eunice Shriver, dedication, in Robert Cooke et al., *The Terrible Choice*.

223   *Pearl Buck, the Nobel Prize–winning author*: Pearl Buck, foreword, in Cooke et al., *The Terrible Choice*, ix–xi.

223   *"My Bobby lies over the ocean"*: Stossel, *Sarge*, 494.

223   *"what Mr. Shriver is doing"*: Mary Strasburg, "Eunice Shriver Breezes in from the Campaign Trail," *WP*, April 19, 1968.

223   *"I mean these criticisms"*: REFK to EKS, October 31, 1968, REFK Papers, box 58, JFKPL.

224   *"She would say, 'My mother came'"*: Catherine "Deeda" Blair, interview with the author.

224   *"they are supposed to be worn"*: REFK to EKS, February 26, 1968, REFK Papers, box 58, JFKPL.

224   *"we have made a deal"*: RSS to REFK, March 12, 1968, REFK Papers, box 58, JFKPL.

225   *"We were in Indianapolis"*: ESK, interview with the author.

225   *"Why aren't there any Negro members"*: Strasburg, "Eunice Shriver Breezes In."

225   *"For those of you who are black"*: Evan Thomas, *Robert Kennedy: His Life*, 366.

226   *"Now it's on to Chicago, and let's win there"*: Ibid., 391.

226   *"We sat in the house"*: Stossel, *Sarge*, 504.

227   *Aides to Bobby shoved Sarge aside*: Thomas, *Robert Kennedy*, 365.

227   *"She was happy for her family"*: ESK, interview with the author.

227   *"He grew out slowly"*: EKS, essay on Robert F. Kennedy, box 5, KFA.

227   *"As she crisscrossed the Atlantic"*: Shriver, *A Good Man*, 159.

228   *"I was just shattered"*: Scott M. Reid, "Rafer Johnson Helped Something Special Grow from Tragedy," *San Gabriel Valley Tribune* (CA), July 24, 2015.

228   *"I was the original number one skeptic"*: Stossel, *Sarge*, 506.

228   *Eunice opened her home to children*: Maxine Cheshire, "Shrivers Stir Gossip in Paris," *WP*, September 27, 1968.

228 *home now was the ambassador's residence*: Eugenia Sheppard, "Shrivers' Paris Home Humming," *Detroit News*, February 16, 1969; "The Liveliest Ambassador," *Time*, November 1968.

229 *There was some "private seething"*: Betty Beale, *WS*, June 2, 1968.

229 *She had brought her own equipment*: clipping in EKS Personal Papers, Jan Terry, "Eunice Packs Suitcase of Surprises," *WP*, May 14, 1968.

230 *Ellen Varmus worked for two years*: Ellen Varmus, interview with the author.

231 *Donald and Carole Dell were at one dinner*: Carole Dell, interview with the author.

231 *Twenty-four-year-old David Mixner*: David Mixner, interview with the author; blog post on death of Sargent Shriver, www.davidmixner .com/2011/01/page/4.

232 *"We've had concerts by Yehudi Menuhin"*: RSS to JPK, May 1969, REFK Papers, box 58, JFKPL.

232 *"They gave me a wonderful time"*: Kathleen Kennedy Townsend, interview with the author.

232 *"What made Eunice special"*: Ibid.

233 *"They are for the most part"*: REFK, letter to EKS, October 29, 1968, REFK Papers, box 59, JFKPL.

234 *"That was perfectly all right with me"*: EKS, "Eunice Talking," *WS*, May 1, 1970.

234 *"I just remember my mother"*: Stossel, *Sarge*, 547.

234 *"marveled at Mrs. Shriver's media savvy"*: Gardner, *King of Sprinkler Lane*, 91.

234 *When John A. Volpe*: John A. Volpe to EKS, June 20, 1969, box 5, KFA.

235 *Eunice had talked Ted out of his plan*: J. Randy Taraborrelli, *After Camelot*, 101.

236 *"I don't believe he is without faults"*: RFK in *Fruitful Bough*, JFKPL.

236 *Pat told her children*: Christopher Kennedy Lawford, *Symptoms of Withdrawal*, 5.

236 *Jean told hers*: Jean Kennedy Smith, *The Nine of Us*, 79.

ELEVEN: Maternal Feminism

237 *The family dogs Lassie and Shamrock*: "Rockville Gets New Neighbors," *WP*, March 27, 1970.

237 *The Shrivers made an easy transition*: EKS to Barbara Walters, May 18, 1970, EKS.

238 *In May there was less frivolity*: Myra MacPherson, "Happy Has-Beens Attend an Opening," *WP*, May 5, 1970.

238 *The Shrivers joined*: B. D. Colen, "Memorial Service Held for Kent Four," *WP*, May 9, 1970.

238 *"Now is a good time"*: REFK to EKS, June 12, 1971, REFK Papers, box 58, JFKPL.

238 *"I would appreciate it"*: REFK to RSS, June 1, 1973, REFK Papers, box 55, JFKPL.

238 *"Be careful of the inscriptions"*: REFK to EKS, November 25, 1974, REFK Papers, box 58, JFKPL.

238 *"I think if when they destroy"*: REFK to EKS, May 7, 1973, REFK Papers, box 58, JFKPL.

238 *Rose calmed herself*: "Reception for Shriver Draws Large Crowd," *WP*, April 11, 1970.

239 *"It will be very good"*: William Chapman, "Shriver Takes Over as Chief of Democratic Campaign Unit," *WP*, June 25, 1970.

239 *Eunice, who had urged Sarge to make the run*: Maxine Cheshire, "Well, Anyway, They'll Have a Nice Place to Eat Supper: VIP," *WP*, June 7, 1970.

239 *Eunice bet Novak $5*: Michael Novak, interview with the author.

239 *With her men's trousers, her Cuban cigars*: Maria Shriver, eulogy for her mother.

240 *"I'd call to complain"*: Ibid.

240 *Novak found Eunice*: Novak, interview with the author.

240 *"Why can't you do it like my father"*: Harris Wofford, interview with the author.

241 *Forty percent of respondents*: Greenhouse and Siegel, *Before Roe v. Wade*, 208.

241 *Hawaii became the first state*: Ibid.

241 *Governor Nelson Rockefeller*: Bill Kovach, "Rockefeller, Signing Abortion Bill, Credits Women's Groups," *NYT*, April 12, 1970.

242 *"I do not say that the fetus"*: EKS to Bobby Shriver, April 17, 1970, EKS Personal Papers.

242 *She put her money*: Peggy Hannon to EKS, November 7, 1972, EKS Personal Papers.

242 *"Twelve hundred people attended"*: Colman McCarthy, "Can Science and Ethics Meet? The Kennedy Symposium," *WP*, October 13, 1971.

242 *The centerpiece of the conference*: Stuart Auerbach, "Doctors Ponder Ethics of Letting Mongoloid Die," "On the Decision to Allow a Mongoloid Infant to Die," Letters to the Editor, *WP*, October 23, 1971.

243 *"That night, after dinner"*: Press release, Kennedy Foundation, October 20, 1971, EKS Personal Papers.

243 *"Now, too late, that surgeon"*: EKS, speech, EKS Personal Papers.

243 *In 1968 Joseph Francis Fletcher*: Joseph Francis Fletcher, "The Right to Die," *Atlantic Monthly*, April 1968, 59–64.

243 *It was not until 1984*: "'Baby Doe' Rules Proposed," *NYT*, December 8, 1984.

243 *"Even after the first stirrings"*: Stanley S. Herr, *Legal Laws and Landmarks of the 20th Century*, the Century Recognition Project, the National Historic Preservation Trust on Mental Retardation.

244 *That New York City doctors performed*: David Harris, Donna O'Hare, Jean Pakter, Frieda G. Nelson, "Legal Abortion 1970–1971—The New York City Experience," *American Journal of Public Health* 63, no. 5, (May 1973): 409–18.

244 *the Kennedy Foundation donated $1.35 million*: Stuart Auerbach, "GU to Study Medicine's Life and Death Decisions," *WP*, October 2, 1971.

244 *"She's very impatient"*: Harris Wofford, interview with the author.

244 *Arthur J. Dyck, who held a joint faculty*: Arthur J. Dyck, interview with the author.

245 *"Eunice has taken over"*: REFK, diaries, REFK Papers, box 12, JFKPL.

245 *"Of course, I would like"*: REFK to EKS, January 8, 1975, REFK Papers, box 58, JFKPL.

245 *"I remember thinking"*: Bobby Shriver, interview with the author.

246 *"She was very impaired"*: Anthony Shriver, interview with the author.

246 *"There was a culture of silence"*: Ibid.

246 *"She was progressing"*: REFK to the Reverend Robert Kroll, May 1, 1972, REFK Papers, JFKPL.

247 *"Wanted or unwanted"*: EMK to Mrs. Edward J. Barshak, August 3, 1971, PGP, SL.

247 *Public attitudes were changing*: Tom W. Smith and Jaesok Son, "Trends in Public Attitudes Toward Abortion," National Opinion Research Center, May 2013.

247 *Sarge was not George McGovern's first*: Frank Mankiewicz, interview with the author.

247 *"Don't Quit"*: EKS and RSS to Thomas Eagleton, Western Union telegram, EKS Personal Papers.

247 *"acid, amnesty, and abortion"*: Timothy Noah, "Acid, Amnesty, and Abortion: The Unlikely Source of a Legendary Smear," *New Republic*, October 22, 2012.

248 *"She had really wanted Sarge to do well"*: Colman McCarthy, interview with the author.

248 *"In these days of commercialism"*: Opening ceremony remarks, August 14, 1972, Los Angeles, EKS Personal Papers.

249 *"homecoming of sorts"*: Ellen Varmus, interview with the author.

249 *Eunice was on the beach*: Lucille Larkin, interview with the author; Louise Sweeney, "Eunice Shriver at Jet Speed," *Christian Science Monitor*, December 15, 1975, www.csmonitor.com/USA/Souchn/2009/0811/p02s14=ussc.html.

249 *"She did what she wanted to do"*: Ibid.

249 *Bob Schieffer, who covered the campaign*: Bob Schieffer, interview with the author.

249 *Gary Hart, McGovern's campaign manager*: Gary Hart, Stossel, *Sarge*, 603.

249 *Some places were more welcoming than others*: Sharon Dickman, "Mrs. Shriver Snubbed at Bull Roast," *BES*, October 9, 1972.

250 *"She felt we could do nothing without strong families"*: Barbara Mikulski, interview with the author.

250 *"some of the staff were crazy"*: Anthony Shriver, interview with the author.

250 *Lucille Larkin remembered going to Timberlawn*: Lucille Larkin, interview with the author.

251 *"Most of what we did"*: Anthony Shriver, interview with the author.

251 *As his older brother Bobby had learned*: "Kennedy, Shriver Sons Face Marijuana Charge," *WP*; August 6, 1970; Bill Kovach, "Robert Kennedy Jr. and Cousin, Shriver Son, in Marijuana Case," *NYT*, August 6, 1970.

251 *For Bobby Shriver, the hijinks ended*: Mark Shriver, *A Good Man*, 101.

251 *Christopher Kennedy Lawford, Pat's oldest*: Lawford, *Symptoms of Withdrawal*, 131.

251 *the experience scared him*: Bobby Shriver to David Horowitz, February 10, 1980, DHP, box 1–2, Center for the Study of Popular Culture Records, HI, SU.

251 *"the story of my father saving my life"*: Mark Shriver, *A Good Man*, 102.

252 *"She didn't care"*: Lucille Larkin, interview with the author.

252 *"There are thousands"*: Bettye Caldwell to EKS, October 26, 1972, RSS Papers, box 201, JFKPL.

252 *"laughing like hell about stuff"*: Lucille Larkin, interview with the author.

252 *"Where's Eunice?"*: Ibid.

252 *Sarge "was totally devoted to her"*: Maria Shriver, eulogy for her mother.

252 *She loved him no less*: Carole Dell, interview with the author.

253 *a program of character education*: Lawrence Kohlberg, "Education, Moral Development, and Faith," *Journal of Moral Education* 4, no. 1 (1974).

253 *a network of Life Support Centers*: Maris Vinovskis, *An "Epidemic" of Adolescent Pregnancy? Some Historical and Policy Considerations*, 33, 34, 54–70.

253 *the National Institutes of Health was contemplating*: Victor Cohn, "Live-Fetus Research Debated," *WP*, April 10, 1973.

254 *two hundred Catholic schoolgirls from the Stone Ridge School*: Victor Cohn, "NIH Vows Not to Fund Fetus Work," *WP*, April 13, 1973.

254   *"If there is a more unspeakable crime"*: Ibid.

254   *"The fetus is being studied in these situations"*: EKS, "The Ethics of Experimenting on Human Fetuses," *WP*, April 21, 1973.

254   *"If I shared your philosophical position"*: Joshua Lederberg to EKS, April 16, 1973, EKS Personal Papers.

254   *"The commission will focus the most creative minds"*: Jonsen, *Birth of Bioethics*, 99.

256   *"I came to the conclusion"*: Kevles, "The Kennedy Who Could Be President."

256   *"Mrs. Shriver Backs Kennedy"*: "Mrs. Shriver Backs Kennedy in Pregnant Teen-Ager Plan," *NYT*, November 5, 1975.

256   *"Ford appeared in black tie"*: Tom Shales, "It Was a Really Live Show," *WP*, March 10, 1975.

256   *"she did not want to ask for government money"*: Jay Emmett, interview with the author.

257   *the 1975* Funny Lady *premiere*: Recounted by ESK in an interview with the author; Timothy Shriver, *Fully Alive*, 102.

257   *Walters does not remember*: Barbara Walters, interview with the author.

257   *"I, an anarchist"*: Dorothy Day, *The Duty of Delight: The Diaries of Dorothy Day*, 586.

258   *Sarge was the ninth Democrat to enter the*: Warren Weaver, "Shriver Enters '76 Presidential Race," *NYT*, September 21, 1975.

258   *"But if my sister Eunice should decide to run"*: Kevles, "The Kennedy Who Could Be President."

258   *"You didn't even mention"*: Stossel, *Sarge*, 639.

258   *His phone rang regularly*: Laurence Tribe, interview with the author.

259   *Eunice "was firm in her convictions"*: Ibid.

259   *"Wherever she goes"*: Christopher Lydon, "Eunice Kennedy Shriver, Campaigner," *NYT*, January 30, 1976.

259   *Eunice was uncharacteristically quiet*: Mickey Kantor and Harris Wofford, interviews with the author.

259   *"She is reading my books"*: Day: *Duty of Delight*, 594.

260   *She had nicknamed him Donut Arms*: Joseph A. Califano Jr., interview with the author.

260   *Estimates of the number*: Greenhouse and Siegel, *Before Roe v. Wade*, 205.

260   *US Supreme Court ruled on June 20, 1977*: Lesley Oelsner, "Court Rules States May Deny Medicaid for Some Abortions," *NYT*, June 21, 1977.

261   *"are many things in life that are not fair"*: President Jimmy Carter, news conference, July 12, 1977, excerpts, *WP*, July 13, 1977.

261   *"Life is unfair"*: President John F. Kennedy, news conference, March 21, 1962, YouTube, www.youtube.com/watch?v=8TaJKPG_YHI.

261 *"In terms of the equity argument"*: Joseph Califano Jr., *Governing America: An Insider's Report from the White House and the Cabinet*, 70–71.

261 *"It is unfortunate"*: Ibid.

261 *"In July, unknown to the public"*: Ibid.

261 *"We've got to face the rape and incest argument"*: Ibid.

262 *"When I heard about his proposal"*: Ibid., 74.

262 *"only 92 Medicaid abortions were funded"*: Ibid., 85.

262 *"Joseph, when we get over this"*: Ibid.

262 *Ellen Goodman, a syndicated columnist*: Ellen Goodman, "At Large: Teenagers and Sexuality" *BG*, June 14, 1977.

263 *In a rebuttal*: EKS, "The Absence of Loving," *BG*, July 7, 1977.

263 *Eunice was "so well connected"*: Califano, *Governing America*, 71.

263 *"Dr. Stuart Shapiro"*: Stuart Shapiro, oral history interview, MC, EMKI, May 15, 2009.

264 *"I certainly have not worked on this bill"*: Califano, *Governing America*, 73.

264 *She drove, ignoring speed limits*: Tom Songster, interview with the author.

264 *"She was the grand dame"*: Orrin Hatch, interview with the author.

265 *"Due in large measure"*: Califano, *Governing America*, 71.

265 *Ted's office felt compelled*: "Names and Faces," *BG*, June 1, 1978.

265 *"Once in a while, one deserves to pause"*: Thomas Watson Jr. to EKS, undated, EKS Personal Papers.

TWELVE: Protecting the Present, Seeding the Future

266 *"Bright orange surveyor's tape"*: Robin Reisig, "Chopping Up Timberlawn," *WP*, August 25, 1979.

267 *"I don't think I've"*: EKS, remarks at twenty-fifth wedding anniversary party, May 27, 1978, EKS Personal Papers.

267 *The Shrivers' new home*: Kenneth Bredemeier, "Shrivers Buy NW Mansion of Rockefeller for $750,000," *WP*, July 20, 1979.

267 *When Eunice rushed up*: Dan H. Fenn Jr., oral history interview, MC, EMKOHP, November 4, 2004.

267 *It had been a long wait*: EKS to EMK, Western Union telegram, March 12, 1962, EKS Personal Papers.

267 *He had gotten off to a rocky*: YouTube, www.youtube.com/watch?v=b6qLFAnBIFg. EMK to Roger Mudd, CBS News Special Report, November 4, 1979.

268 *When Eunice was unable*: Stuart Shapiro, oral history interview, MC, EMKOHP, May 15, 2009.

268 *"Character is enormously important"*: Steven V. Roberts, "Ted Kennedy: Haunted by the Past," *NYT*, February 3, 1980.

268 *"He's had a hard time"*: Ibid.

268 *She chided the* Chicago Tribune: EKS, "The Joan Kennedy Book and Ethics," *CT*, November 5, 1985.

269 *"Who in our family"*: Patrick Kennedy, interview with the author.

269 *She excoriated the* Washington Post: EKS, "My Mother Might Well Be a Saint," *WP*, October 28, 1980.

269 *She wrote a similar letter to the* New York Times: EKS, "A Grotesque Portrait of Our Parents," *NYT*, December 3, 1992.

269 *"It's a strange thing"*: JPK to John W. McCormack, August 8, 1951, in Smith, *Hostage to Fortune*, 656–57.

269 *"You do that to be safe"*: Maria Shriver, interview with the author.

270 *"Where else but in gothic fiction"*: Clare Boothe Luce, quoted in Ralph G. Martin, *Seeds of Destruction: Joe Kennedy and His Sons*, xviii.

270 *"Eunice had the Kennedy ambition"*: Lawford, *Symptoms of Withdrawal*, 263.

270 *"Would she have agreed with her nephew"*: Patrick Kennedy, interview with the author.

271 *"When she goes out"*: News clipping, AP, July 22, 1990, EKS Personal Papers.

271 *"She fought to exclude letters"*: Anonymous source.

271 *Joe Kennedy believed*: Smith, *Hostage to Fortune*, xvii.

271 *The project was an invasion of privacy*: EKS to Amanda Smith Hood, February 16, 2001, February 26, 2002, and March 18, 2003; Amanda Smith Hood to EMK, March 19, 2001. Anonymous source.

272 *Amanda declared herself "mystified and bewildered"*: Amanda Smith Hood to EKS, February 11, 2002. Anonymous source.

272 *"I saw a lot of Teddy's bad behavior"*: Anthony Shriver, interview with the author.

273 *"She was a great advocate"*: Claudia Ingram Weicker, interview with the author.

273 *Stanley B. Jones*: Stanley B. Jones, oral history interview, MC, EMKOHP, March 9, 2007.

274 *"I knew she was a strong Roman Catholic"*: Gillian Healy, interview with the author.

275 *"I asked her in the interview"*: Lisa Derx, interview with the author.

276 *"Mrs. Shriver talked to the director"*: Renee Dease, interview with the author.

276 *Connie Garner saw beneath*: Connie Garner, interview with the author.

276 *Ethel Kennedy remembers*: Ethel Kennedy, interview with the author.

276 *"She was a working addict"*: Bobby Shriver, interview with the author.

276 *There was, in Maria Shriver's view*: Maria Shriver, interview with the author.

276 *Garner, a rare woman*: Connie Garner, interview with the author.

277 *Eunice told Lisa Derx*: Lisa Derx, interview with the author.

277 *"Eunice has no compassion"*: Barbara Gibson and Ted Schwartz, *Rose Kennedy and Her Family*, 55.

277 *"I got to see Mrs. Shriver"*: William Alford, interview with the author.

278 *Dot Tubridy, Eunice's longtime friend*: Dorothy Tubridy, interview with the author.

278 *A beach destination*: Mark Shriver, interview with the author.

278 *"Get on to yourself!"*: Maria Shriver and Bobby Shriver, interviews with the author.

279 *"She was not warm and fuzzy"*: Bobby Shriver, interview with the author.

279 *Bobby recalled the shiver of fear*: Bobby Shriver, interview with the author.

279 *Sue Swenson learned that*: Sue Swenson, interview with the author.

280 *"I can get along with anyone"*: Ela Work, interview with the author.

280 *One assistant exploited*: Al Kamen, "Shriver's Ex-Secretary Sentenced," *WP*, February 8, 1984.

281 *In Mary Cunningham Agee*: Mary Cunningham Agee, interview with the author.

281 *"I am not carrying a placard"*: Ibid.

282 *"I do not believe"*: Joan D. Chittister, *Bill Moyers Journal*, November 12, 2004, PBS online, transcription, www.pbs.org/moyers/journal/archives /chittister_new_flash.html.

282 *"When suffering comes into your life"*: Mary Cunningham Agee, interview with the author.

282 *"We prayed the rosary"*: Timothy Shriver, *Fully Alive*, 17.

283 *Even as her siblings celebrated*: The agenda for the Kennedy Foundation trustees meeting, April 9, 1984, includes alternative uses of assets, including for "restoration of historic Cape Cod house," KFA.

283 *Eunice resisted*: EKS to RSS et al., September 22, 1983, KFA.

284 *"Do not use Mr. Kennedy's money"*: REFK, undated memo, REFK Papers, box 59, JFKPL.

284 *"I am sure you can all afford"*: REFK, letter to her children, January 9, 1969, box 59, JFKPL.

284 *"With reference to Eunice"*: REFK to JKS, February 11, 1972, REFK Papers, box 59, JFKPL.

285 *"I love all my children"*: REFK, personal files, REFK Papers, box 126, JFKPL.

285 *"Mother felt that so many"*: EKS to PKL, June 16, 1971, REFK Papers, box 86, JFKPL.

285 *The foundation gave the college $100,000*: Ibid.

286 *"If one believes in charity and family"*: Trustees memo, January 25, 1948, KFA.

286 *Marty Krauss, a professor at Brandeis University*: Marty Krauss, interview with the author.

286 *Kathleen affiliated with*: Kathleen Kennedy Townsend, interview with the author.

286 *Victoria Reggie Kennedy remembered*: Victoria Reggie Kennedy, interview with the author.

287 *Reaching Up joined*: Cathy Rainone, "JFK Jr.: The CUNY Connection," CUNY, last modified September 16, 2011, www1.cuny.edu/mu /forum/2011/09/16/jfk-jr-the-cuny-connection.

287 *Mark designed what he called the Choice Program*: Mark Shriver, *A Good Man*, 111.

287 *"I really admired her efforts"*: Marty Krauss, interview with the author.

287 *Kathleen Kennedy Townsend later applied the lessons*: Kathleen Kennedy Townsend, interview with the author.

288 *Tim was the second of the Shriver siblings*: "Maria Owings Shriver Wed to Arnold Schwarzenegger," *NYT*, April 27, 1986; "Personalities," *WP*, June 2, 1986.

288 *Her mother, a master*: Jacqueline Trescott, "Turning Out for 'Twins,'" *WP*, December 6, 1988.

289 *"Eunice and I would go door-to-door"*: Carole Dell, interview with the author.

289 *She asked only*: The text of the *New York Times* ad can be viewed at www .firstthings.com/article/1992/11/005-a-new-american-compact-caring -about-women-caring-for-the-unborn.

289 *"No sooner did I agree"*: Mark Shriver, interview with the author.

289 *The Shrivers had recruited*: Desda Moss, "Disabled's Champion Steps Back," *USA Today*, April 11, 1990.

289 *In 1991 Eunice nearly lost her own life*: Eric Brace, *WP*, January 21, 1991.

289 *a license to cut benefits for*: Robert Pear, "After a Review, 95,000 Children Will Lose Disability Benefits"; editorial, "Mercy for Disabled Children," *NYT*, September 13, 1997.

289 *She was in the Roosevelt Room*: Elena Kagan, "Additional Materials— Folder 4," Clinton Digital Library, accessed May 25, 2017, https://clinton .presidentiallibraries.us/items/show/23220.

290 *"If Eunice Shriver was at your door"*: Senator Thomas Harkin, interview with the author.

290 *In a letter to the* Washington Post: EKS, "Disability Fraud," *WP*, January 12, 1998.

290 *"Get that nice man on the phone"*: Steven Eidelman, interview with the author.

291 *Eunice almost didn't select her*: Sue Swenson, interview with the author.

291 *"We made a template"*: Sharon Lewis, interview with the author.

292   *"Oh, we heard from Eunice"*: Senator Christopher Dodd, interview with the author.

292   *"Mrs. Shriver really saw access"*: Sharon Lewis, interview with the author.

292   *"Connecticut governor Lowell Weicker"*: Timothy Shriver, *Fully Alive*, 148.

293   *forming Unified Sports in 1988*: Ibid., 177.

293   *"Why don't you move to Washington"*: Ibid., 158.

293   *"The last thing on my list"*: Ibid.

EPILOGUE

294   *Thousands of twinkling lights*: Philip Rucker, "Annual Best Buddies Ball Rolls to a Glitzy Finale," *WP*, October 20, 2008.

295   *Washington Fine Properties*: "A Bargain at $8 Million," *Washingtonian* on-line, last modified January 1, 2010, www.washingtonian.com/2010/01/01/a-bargain-at-8-million-2.

295   *"I would gladly scrap"*: Stossel, *Sarge*, 680.

296   *The Reverend Richard Fragomeni*: the Reverend Richard Fragomeni, interview with the author.

296   *She survived another car crash*: Jack Harper, video, WCVB-TV, July 6, 2001.

296   *"Keep working"*: Sue Swenson, interview with the author.

297   *Eunice still credited her brother*: EKS, oral history interview, May 7, 1968, JFKPL.

297   *"I knew that this work had to be Jack's"*: Timothy Shriver, *Fully Alive*, 70.

297   *"In a strange way"*: Transcript of remarks, Kennedy Forum, November 16, 2007, JFKPL.

298   *"When I was a little girl"*: Laetare acceptance speech at Notre Dame, May 15, 1988, EKS Personal Papers.

298   *She haunted bookshops*: Maria Shriver, eulogy for her mother, August 14, 2009.

298   *"She was a woman who didn't choose"*: Ibid.

299   *"The only reason I put it"*: Carole Dell, interview with the author.

300   *"She said, 'Is Teddy being helpful?'"*: Senator Sam Brownback, US Senate floor speech, *Congressional Record*, September 8, 2009.

300   *Upstairs in her bedroom*: Lowell Weicker, interview with the author.

300   *their funerals a final, fitting contrast*: Bryan Marquard, "Eunice Kennedy Shriver, 88; Member of Kennedy Clan, Founder of Special Olympics," *BG*, August 11, 2009; "Schedule of Events for Kennedy Memorials," *NYT*, August 29, 2009.

300   *several Special Olympics athletes*: Timothy Shriver, interview with the author.

BIBLIOGRAPHY

Aloisi, James A., Jr. *Magic in the Air*. Boston: Ashburton Hill, 2007.

Armstrong, Richard. *Out to Change the World*. New York: Crossroad Publishing, 1984.

Baldrige, Letitia. *A Lady, First*. New York: Viking, 2001.

Berkowitz, Edward D. *Mr. Social Security: The Life of Wilbur J. Cohen*. Lawrence: University of Kansas Press, 1995.

Beschloss, Michael. *Taking Charge: The Johnson White House Tapes, 1963–1964*. New York: Simon & Schuster, 1997.

———. ed. *Jacqueline Kennedy: Historic Conversations on Life with John F. Kennedy*. New York: Hyperion, 2011.

Blair, Joan, and Clay Blair Jr. *The Search for JFK*. New York: Berkley, 1976.

Bradford, Sarah. *America's Queen*. New York: Penguin, 2000.

Bradlee, Ben. *A Good Life*. New York: Simon & Schuster, 1995.

———. *Conversations with Kennedy*. New York: W. W. Norton, 1975.

Branch, Taylor. *America in the King Years*. 3 vols. New York: Simon & Schuster, 1988–2006.

Brogan, Hugh. *Kennedy: Profile in Power*. Harlow, UK: Longman, 1996.

Buck, Pearl S. *The Child Who Never Grew*. New York: John Day, 1950.

———. *The Kennedy Women*. New York: Cowles, 1970.

Bueno, Ana. *Special Olympics: The First 25 Years*. San Francisco: Foghorn, 1994.

Burns, James MacGregor. *John Kennedy: A Political Profile*. New York: Avon, 1960.

Califano, Joseph, Jr. *Governing America: An Insider's Report from the White House and the Cabinet*. New York: Simon & Schuster, 1981.

———. *Inside: A Public and Private Life*. New York: Public Affairs, 2004.

———. *The Triumph & Tragedy of Lyndon Johnson: The White House Years*. New York: Touchstone, 2015.

Cameron, Gail. *Rose: A Biography of Rose Fitzgerald Kennedy*. New York: Putnam, 1971.

Canellos, Peter, et al. *The Last Lion: The Fall and Rise of Ted Kennedy*. New York: Simon & Schuster, 2009.

Carey, Allison. *On the Margins of Citizenship*. Philadelphia: Temple University Press, 2009.

Carr, William H. A. *Those Fabulous Kennedy Women*. New York: Wisdom House, 1961.

Clarke, Thurston. *Ask Not: The Inauguration of John F. Kennedy and the Speech That Changed America*. New York: Henry Holt, 2004.

———. *The Last Campaign: Robert F. Kennedy and 82 Days That Inspired America*. New York: Henry Holt, 2008.

Clinch, Nancy Gager. *The Kennedy Neurosis*. New York: Grosset & Dunlap, 1973.

Clymer, Adam. *Edward M. Kennedy: A Biography*. New York: William Morrow, 1999.

Cohen, Adam. *Imbeciles*. New York: Penguin, 2016.

Collier, Peter, and David Horowitz. *The Kennedys: An American Drama*. New York: Summit, 1984.

Conkin, Paul. *Peabody College*. Nashville: Vanderbilt University Press, 2002.

Cooke, Robert, et al. *The Terrible Choice: The Abortion Dilemma*. New York: Bantam, 1968.

Coughlin, Roger J., and Cathryn A. Riplinger. *The Story of Charitable Care in the Archdiocese of Chicago, 1844–1959*. Chicago; Catholic Charities, 1981.

Cunningham, Mary. *Powerplay: What Really Happened at Bendix*. New York: Simon & Schuster, 1984.

———. *Compassion in Action*. St. Helena, CA: Nurturing Network, 2006.

Cutler, John Henry. *Honey Fitz*. New York: Bobbs-Merrill, 1962.

Dallas, Rita, and Jeanira Ratcliffe. *The Kennedy Case*. New York: Putnam, 1973.

Dallek, Robert. *An Unfinished Life: John F. Kennedy, 1917–1963*. Boston: Houghton Mifflin, 2003.

———. *Camelot's Court: Inside the Kennedy White House*. New York: HarperCollins, 2013.

Damore, Leo. *The Cape Cod Years of John Fitzgerald Kennedy*. New York: Four Walls Eight Windows, 1993.

Day, Dorothy. *All the Way to Heaven*, New York: Image, 2010.

————. *The Duty of Delight: The Diaries of Dorothy Day*. New York: Image, 2008.

————. *Loaves and Fishes*. Maryknoll, NY: Orbis Books, 1997.

De Margerie, Caroline. *American Lady*. New York: Viking, 2012.

Deutsch, Albert. *Our Rejected Children*. Boston: Little, Brown, 1950.

Dinn, Sheila. *Hearts of Gold*. Woodbridge, CT: Blackbirch Press, 1996.

Downey, Kirstin. *The Woman Behind the New Deal*. New York: Anchor, 2009.

Dyja, Thomas. *The Third Coast*. New York: Penguin, 2013.

El-Hai, Jack. *The Lobotomist*. Hoboken, NJ: Wiley & Sons, 2005.

Farrell, John A. *Tip O'Neill*. Boston: Little, Brown, 2001.

Fay, Paul B., Jr. *The Pleasure of His Company*. New York: Popular Library, 1966.

Flynn, Elizabeth Gurley. *My Life as a Political Prisoner*. New York: International, 1963.

Ford, Liam T. A. *Soldier Field: A Stadium and Its City*. Chicago: University of Chicago Press, 2009.

Gager, Nancy. *Kennedy Wives, Kennedy Women*. New York: Dell, 1976.

Gardner, Gerald, ed. *The Shining Moments*. New York: Pocket, 1964.

Gardner, Michael. *King of Sprinkler Lane*. Lulu, 2014.

Garrow, David. *Liberty and Sexuality*. New York: Macmillan, 1994.

Gibson, Barbara. *Life with Rose Kennedy*. New York: Warner Books, 1986.

Gibson, Barbara, and Ted Schwarz. *Rose Kennedy and Her Family*. New York: Birch Lane, 1995.

Gilbert, James. *A Cycle of Outrage*. New York: Oxford University Press, 1986.

Gilbert, Nancy. *The Special Olympics*. Mankato, MN: Creative Education, 1990.

Gillette, Michael. *Launching the War on Poverty: An Oral History*. Oxford: Oxford University Press, 2010.

Goodwin, Doris Kearns. *The Fitzgeralds and the Kennedys*. New York: Simon & Schuster, 1987.

————. *No Ordinary Time*. New York: Simon & Schuster, 1994.

Gorney, Cynthia. *Articles of Faith*. New York: Simon & Schuster, 1998.

Graham, James W. *Victura: The Kennedys, A Sailboat, and the Sea*. Lebanon, NH: ForeEdge, 2014.

Greenhouse, Linda, and Reva B. Siegel. *Before Roe v. Wade*. New York: Kaplan, 2010.

Hamilton, Nigel. *JFK: Reckless Youth*. New York: Random House, 1992.

Harris, Mary. *I Knew Them in Prison*. New York: Viking, 1936.

Hersh, Burton. *Edward Kennedy: An Intimate Biography*. Berkeley, CA: Counterpoint, 2010.

Hess, Stephen. *America's Political Dynasties*. New Brunswick, NJ: Transaction, 1997.

Hinton, Elizabeth. *From the War on Poverty to the War on Crime*. Cambridge, MA: Harvard University Press, 2016.

Hoy, Suellen, *Good Hearts*. Urbana: University of Illinois Press, 2006.

Humphrey, Hubert. *The Education of a Public Man: My Life and Politics*. Minneapolis: University of Minnesota Press, 1991.

Hunt, Amber, and David Batcher. *The Kennedy Wives*. Guilford, CT: Lyons, 2015.

Jonsen, Albert R. *The Birth of Bioethics*. New York: Oxford University Press, 1998.

Kennedy, Caroline. *Rose Kennedy's Family Album*. New York: Grand Central, 2013.

Kennedy, Edward M. *The Fruitful Bough: A Tribute to Joseph P. Kennedy*. Halliday Lithograph, 1965. Printed for private distribution.

———. *True Compass*. New York: Twelve Books, 2009.

Kennedy, Rose Fitzgerald. *Times to Remember*. Garden City, NY: Doubleday, 1974.

Kessler, Ronald. *The Sins of the Father*. New York: Warner, 1996.

Keve, Paul. *Prisons and the American Conscience*. Carbondale, IL: University of Southern Illinois Press, 1991.

Knupfer, Anne Meis. *Reform and Resistance*. New York: Routledge, 2001.

Koehler-Pentacoff, Elizabeth. *The Missing Kennedy*. Baltimore: Bancroft, 2015.

Koskoff, David E. *Joseph P. Kennedy: A Life and Times*. Englewood Cliffs, NJ: Prentice-Hall, 1974.

Lambert, Angela. *1939: The Last Season of Peace*, New York: Weidenfeld & Nicolson, 1989.

Larson, Kate Clifford. *Rosemary*. Boston: Houghton Mifflin Harcourt, 2015.

Lawford, Christopher Kennedy. *Symptoms of Withdrawal*, New York: Harper, 2005.

Leamer, Laurence. *The Kennedy Women*. New York: Ballantine, 1994.

———. *The Kennedy Men*. New York: William Morrow, 2001.

Leaming, Barbara. *Kick Kennedy*. New York: St. Martin's, 2016.

Lemann, Nicholas. *The Promised Land*. New York: Vintage, 1992.

Lincoln, Evelyn. *My Twelve Years with John F. Kennedy*. New York: David McKay, 1965.

Lucas, Richard. *Axis Sally*. Havertown, PA: Casemate, 2010.

Maier, Thomas. *The Kennedys: America's Emerald Kings*. New York: Basic Books, 2003.

Manchester, William. *The Death of a President*. New York: Harper & Row, 1967.

Martin, Ralph G. *Seeds of Destruction: Joe Kennedy and His Sons*. New York: G. P. Putnam's Sons, 1995.

Matthews, Chris. *Jack Kennedy, Elusive Hero*. New York: Simon & Schuster, 2011.

McCarthy, Joe. *The Remarkable Kennedys*. New York: Popular Library, 1960.

McCarthy, Mary. *Memories of a Catholic Childhood*. Orlando, FL: Harcourt, 1957.

McCormick, Richard A. *Notes on Moral Theology*. Larham, MD: University Press of America/Rownan and Littlefield, 1984.

McTaggart, Lynne. *Kathleen Kennedy*. Garden City, NY: Doubleday, 1983.

Meisler, Stanley. *When the World Calls*. Boston: Beacon, 2011.

Mitford, Deborah, Duchess of Devonshire. *Wait For Me!* New York: Farrar, Straus and Giroux, 2010.

Morris, Sylvia Jukes. *The Price of Fame*. New York: Random House, 2014.

Moskowitz, Miriam. *Phantom Spies, Phantom Justice*. Seattle: Justice Institute, 2010.

Nasaw, David. *The Patriarch: The Remarkable Life and Turbulent Times of Joseph P. Kennedy*. New York: Penguin, 2012.

Newfield, Jack. *RFK: A Memoir*. New York: Dutton, 1969.

Noll, Steven, and James W. Trent, eds. *Mental Retardation in America: A Historical Reader*. New York: New York University Press, 2004.

O'Connor, Thomas H. *The Boston Irish*. Boston: Northeastern University Press, 1995.

————. *Boston Catholics*. Boston: Northeastern University Press, 1998.

O'Donnell, Kenneth P., David F. Powers, and Joe McCarthy. *Johnny, We Hardly Knew Ye*. Boston: Little, Brown, 1972.

O'Leary, April. *Living Tradition: The Chronicle of a School*. London: Woldingham School, 1992.

Olson, Lynne. *Citizens of London*. New York: Random House, 2010.

Oppenheimer, Jerry. *The Other Mrs. Kennedy*. New York: St. Martin's, 1994.

Perry, Barbara. *Rose Kennedy*. New York: W. W. Norton, 2013.

Pitts, David. *Jack and Lem*. New York: Da Capo, 2007.

Rainie, Harrison, and John Quinn. *Growing Up Kennedy*. New York: Berkley, 1983.

Reiser, Stanley Joel, Arthur J. Dyck, and William J. Curran. *Ethics in Medicine*. Cambridge, MA: MIT Press, 1977.

Redmon, Coates. *Come As You Are*. New York: Harcourt, Brace, Jovanovich, 1986.

Risen, James, and Judy Thomas. *Wrath of Angels*. New York: Basic Books, 1998.

Riva, Maria. *Marlene Dietrich*. New York: Ballantine, 1992.

Roberts, John, ed. *Escaping Prison Myths*. Washington, DC: American University Press, 1994.

Rogers, Dale Evans. *Angel Unaware*. Ada, MI: Revell, 2004.

Rosenberg, Heidi Matiyow. *Federal Policy Toward Delinquent Youth: Legislative and Programmatic Milestones from Kennedy to Ford, 1960–1976*. Dissertation. Ann Arbor: University of Michigan, 2008.

Roth, William. *The Assault on Social Policy*. New York: Columbia University Press, 2014.

Scheerenberger, R. C. *A History of Mental Retardation: A Quarter Century of Progress*. Baltimore: Paul H. Brookes, 1987.

Schlesinger, Arthur. *Robert Kennedy and His Times*. New York: Houghton Mifflin, 1978.

———. *The Letters of Arthur Schlesinger Jr*. New York: Random House, 2013.

Schorr, Lisbeth, and Daniel Schorr. *Within Our Reach*. New York: Anchor, 1988.

Schroth, Raymond A. *Bob Drinan*. New York: Fordham University Press, 2011.

Searls, Hank. *The Lost Prince: Young Joe, the Forgotten Kennedy*. New York: Ballantine, 1969.

Shapiro, Joseph. *No Pity*. New York: Three Rivers Press, 1993.

Sheed, Wilfrid. *Clare Boothe Luce*. New York: Dutton, 1982.

Shorter, Edward. *The Kennedy Family and the Story of Mental Retardation*. Philadelphia: Temple University Press, 2000.

Shriver, Mark. *A Good Man*. New York: Henry Holt, 2012.

Shriver, Timothy. *Fully Alive: Discovering What Matters Most*. New York: Sarah Crichton Books, 2014.

Smith, Amanda, ed. *Hostage to Fortune: The Letters of Joseph P. Kennedy*. New York: Viking, 2001.

Smith, Jean Kennedy. *The Nine of Us*. New York: HarperCollins, 2016.

Smith, Sally Bedell. *Grace and Power*. New York: Random House, 2004.

Sorensen, Ted. *Kennedy*. New York: Harper Perennial, 1965.

Spoto, Donald. *Jacqueline Bouvier Kennedy Onassis*. New York: St. Martin's, 2000.

Steel, Ronald. *Walter Lippmann and the American Century*. Boston: Little, Brown, 1980.

Stossel, Scott. *Sarge*. New York: Smithsonian, 2011.

Stuart, Janet Erskine. *The Education of Catholic Girls*. London: Longmans, Green, 1911.

Swanson, Gloria. *Swanson on Swanson*. New York: Random House, 1980.

Swift, Will. *The Kennedys Amidst the Gathering Storm*. New York: HarperCollins, 2008.

Rawls, John. *A Theory of Justice*. Cambridge, MA: Harvard University Press, 1971.

Taraborrelli, J. Randy. *Jackie, Ethel, Joan: Women of Camelot*. New York: Warner Books, 2000.

————. *After Camelot.* New York: Grand Central Publishing, 2012.

Terkel, Studs. *American Dreams: Lost and Found.* New York: New Press, 1980.

Thomas, Evan. *Robert Kennedy: His Life.* New York: Simon & Schuster, 2000.

Torrey, E. Fuller. *American Psychosis.* Oxford: Oxford University Press, 2014.

Trent, James W., Jr. *Inventing the Feeble Mind: A History of Intellectual Disability in the United States.* Berkeley: University of California Press, 1995.

Tye, Larry. *Bobby Kennedy: The Making of a Liberal Icon.* New York: Random House, 2016.

Vinonskis, Maris. *An "Epidemic" of Adolescent Pregnancy? Some Historical and Policy Considerations.* New York: Oxford University Press, 1987.

White, Antonia. *Frost in May.* London: Virago Modern Classics, 1933.

White, Theodore H. *The Making of the President 1960.* New York: Harper Perennial, 1961.

————. *The Making of the President 1964.* New York: Harper Perennial, 1965,

————. *The Making of the President 1972.* New York: Harper Perennial, 1972.

————. *In Search of History.* New York: Harper & Row, 1978.

Widmer, Ted. *Listening In: The Secret White House Recordings of John F. Kennedy.* New York: Hyperion, 2012.

Williams, Daniel K. *Defenders of the Unborn: The Pro-Life Movement Before Roe v. Wade.* New York: Oxford University Press, 2016.

Wofford, Harris. *Of Kennedys & Kings.* Pittsburgh: University of Pittsburgh Press, 1980.

Youcha, Geraldine. *Minding the Children.* Cambridge, MA: Da Capo, 2005.

INDEX

ABOUT THE AUTHOR

Eileen McNamara spent nearly thirty years as a journalist at *The Boston Globe*, where she won a Pulitzer Prize for Commentary and was among the first to raise the alarm about clergy sexual abuse. She is now Director of the Journalism Program at Brandeis University.